This
Business
of

COMMUNICATING

This
Business
of
COMMUNICATING

FOURTH EDITION

ROY M. BERKO
Towson State University

ANDREW D. WOLVIN
University of Maryland

RAY CURTIS
Lorain County Community College

WCB Wm. C. Brown Publishers

Book Team

Editor *Stan Stoga*
Developmental Editor *Jane F. Lambert*
Production Editor *Julie Kennedy*

 Wm. C. Brown Publishers

President *G. Franklin Lewis*
Vice President, Publisher *Thomas E. Doran*
Vice President, Operations and Production *Beverly Kolz*
National Sales Manager *Virginia S. Moffat*
Advertising Manager *Ann M. Knepper*
Marketing Manager *Kathleen Nietzke*
Production Editorial Manager *Julie A. Kennedy*
Publishing Services Manager *Karen J. Slaght*
Manager of Visuals and Design *Faye M. Schilling*

Cover design by Didona Design Associates

Library of Congress Catalog Card Number: 89–61638

ISBN 0–697–03048–2

Printed in the United States of America by Wm. C. Brown Publishers,
2460 Kerper Boulevard, Dubuque, IA 52001

10 9 8 7 6 5 4 3 2

CONTENTS

Preface xvii
New features xix

SECTION I—THE ACT OF COMMUNICATING 1

Chapter 1—THE COMMUNICATIVE PROCESS 2

The Process of Communicating 4
Sending and Receiving 4
    ATTENDING 5
    INTERPRETING 5
    PERCEPTIONS 5
The Language System 7
Nonverbal Communication 7
Models of Communication 8
Linear Model 8
Interactional Model 10
Transactional Model 11

Chapter 2—INTRAPERSONAL COMMUNICATION 15

Self-Concept 17
Communication Anxiety 19
The Effect of Communication Anxiety 19
Overcoming Communication Anxiety 20
    SYSTEMATIC DESENSITIZATION 20
    COGNITIVE MODIFICATION 21
    SKILLS TRAINING 21
    SELF-HELP 21
Work-related Communication Anxiety 21
Reaching Conclusions 21
Distortion 22
Perception 23
    SELECTION 23
    ORGANIZATION 24
    INTERPRETATION 24

Stereotypes 25
Experience 25
Stress 26
Stress and Business 26
Stages of Stress 28
Reacting to Stress 28
Dealing with Stress 28
Controlling Stress 29

Chapter 3—LISTENING 34

Listening Environment 37
Listening Process 38
Motivation 38
Receiving the Stimulus 38
Attending 38
PERCEPTION 39
INTEREST 39
Interpreting 39
Responding 39
STORAGE 39
FEEDBACK 39
Levels of Listening 40
Discriminative Listening Level 40
Comprehensive Listening Level 40
Therapeutic Listening Level 40
NON-DIRECTIVE THERAPEUTIC LISTENING 40
DIRECTIVE THERAPEUTIC LISTENING 41
Critical Listening Level 41
Appreciative Listening Level 41
Listening Problems 42
The Biology of Listening 42
Negative Self-concept 42
Meaning Within the Listener 43
Not Understanding How to Listen 44
Poor Listening Conditioning 44
Improving Your Listening 45

Chapter 4—VERBAL LANGUAGE 51

Language Defined 53
Dialects 54
Standard American English 55
Nonstandard Dialects 55

Principles of Language Meaning 56
Problems in Communicating 57
    Assumption 57
    Clarity 57
    Concreteness 58
    Fact Versus Inference 59
        DISTINGUISHING FACTS AND INFERENCE 59
Written and Spoken Language 60
    Phony Fancies 60
    Nounery 61
    Passive Voice 61
    Wasted Words 62
Female-Male Language and Communication 62
    The Sexism of Standard American English 62
    Male and Female Language and Language Usage 63

Chapter 5—NONVERBAL COMMUNICATION 69

Sources of Nonverbal Communication 72
Importance of Nonverbal Communication 72
Verbal-Nonverbal Relationships 73
    Substitute 73
    Complement 73
    Regulate 73
    Conflict 74
Clusters and Congruency 74
    Kinesics 74
        MOVEMENT 75
        EMBLEM CLASSIFICATIONS 75
        EYE BEHAVIOR 76
        FACIAL EXPRESSION 76
        TOUCH 78
        READING KINESICS 78
    Vocal Cues 79
        PARALANGUAGE 79
        HESITATIONS, PAUSES, LAUGHTER 79
    Proxemics 80
        PERSONAL SPACE 80
        PRIVACY SPACE 81
        SPACIAL ARRANGEMENTS 81
    Physical Characteristics 83
    Artifacts 83
    Aesthetics 85
        MUSIC 85

LIGHTING 86
COLOR 86
Chronemics 87
Cultural Effects 88
Greetings 89
Conversing and Other Interactions 89
Gestures 90
Time 90
Meetings 91
Improving Nonverbal Communication 91

Chapter 6—INTERPERSONAL COMMUNICATION:
A BUSINESS FOCUS 97

Effective Interpersonal Communication 99
Interference 100
Environmental Interference 100
Physiological Interference 101
Semantic Interference 101
Syntactic Interference 102
Organizational Interference 103
Psychological Interference 104
Social Interference 104
Self-disclosure 105
Interpersonal Relationships in the Organization 106
Interpersonal Skills in the Business Environment 107
Telephone Use 107
TECHNIQUES USED WHEN RECEIVING MESSAGES 108
TECHNIQUES USED WHEN PLACING CALLS 109
Management-Employee Relationships 109
CRITICIZING 110
HANDLING GRIEVANCES 111
DEALING WITH DIFFICULT PERSONALITIES 112
DIRECTING 113
GIVING DIRECTIONS 114
JOB TRAINING 115
Conflict and Conflict Resolution 116
Conflict in the Work Environment 116
Conflict Resolution 117
OPTIONS FOR CONFLICT RESOLUTION 117
STYLES OF CONFLICT RESOLUTION 118
ASSERTIVENESS 121
The Changing Role of Interpersonal Communication in
Business 124

SECTION II—BUSINESS COMMUNICATION 129

Chapter 7—COMMUNICATION IN THE ORGANIZATION 130

Ways in Which Businesses Communicate 134
Communication Within Departments 134
Communication Between Departments 135
Communication Outside the Company 135
Proprietary and Confidential Communication 136
Informal Channels 136
The Business Grapevine 136
The Role of Corporate Communication 138
SPEAKING ACTIVITIES 139
ISSUES MANAGEMENT 139
COMMUNICATION SKILLS 140
Communication Department 140
Organizational Commitment 142
Organizational Structure, Climate, and Culture 142
Communication as a Function 145
Recruiting 145
Hiring 145
Training 145
Job Maintenance 146
Job Performance 146
Performance Appraisal 147
Obstacles to Effective Corporate Communication 147
Lack of a Communication Policy 147
Ineffective Communication Networks 148
Inability to Change 148
The Authoritarian Attitude of Management 148
Too Many Levels of Management 149
Insufficient Communication Training 149
The Nature of Corporate Change 149
Lack of Innovation 149

Chapter 8—COMMUNICATORS IN ORGANIZATIONS 155

The Work Force and Organizational Change 157
Theories of Worker Motivation 159
Scientific Management Model 160
Human Relations Model 160
Early Motivation Theories 160
IMMATURITY-MATURITY THEORY 160
HIERARCHY OF NEEDS THEORY 161

THEORY X   161
THEORY Y   161
MOTIVATION-HYGIENE THEORY   162
Contemporary Motivation Theories   163
ERG THEORY   163
ACQUIRED-NEEDS THEORY   163
EQUITY THEORY   164
EXPECTANCY THEORY   164
GOAL-SETTING THEORY   165
REINFORCEMENT THEORY   165
Theories of Manager Behavior   165
Types of Managerial Behavior   165
Analyzing Managerial Behavior   167
SYSTEMS MANAGEMENT   167
MANAGERIAL GRID   167
Communication as a Management Function   168
Planning   168
THE TOP-DOWN PROCESS   169
THE BOTTOM-UP PROCESS   169
THEORY Z   170
QUALITY OF WORK LIFE AND QUALITY CIRCLE MOVEMENT   171
Organizing   173
Leading   174
Evaluating   174
Communication as an Employee Function   174

Chapter 9—ETHICS AND BUSINESS 179

The Ethical Dilemma   181
Ethics and Business   182
Ethics Defined   183
Business Ethics Defined   184
Ethics in Business   185
Capitalism and Ethics   185
Changes in Ethical Practices   185
Corporate Responsibility   185
Using Ethics   187
Ethics in Business Communication   189

Chapter 10—DECISION-MAKING IN BUSINESS 192

The Importance of Decision-making   194
Making the Decision   195
Defining the Problem   195

Decision-making Techniques 196
    The Inductive Process of Decision-making 196
        IDENTIFYING THE PROBLEM 197
        BRAINSTORMING 197
        TESTING THE SOLUTION 197
        SELECTING THE SOLUTION 197
        EVALUATING THE RESULTS 198
    Practical Decision-making Process 198
        DECISION-MAKING SITUATION 198
        DECISION-MAKING PROCEDURE 199
Crisis Decision-making 204

SECTION III—BUSINESS COMMUNICATION SKILLS 209

Chapter 11—INTERVIEWING AS A BUSINESS FUNCTION 210

Types of Interviews and How to Prepare for Them 212
    The Informative Interview 212
        INFORMATIVE INTERVIEW OUTLINE 213
    The Problem-solving Interview 214
        PROBLEM-SOLVING INTERVIEW OUTLINE 214
    The Persuasive Interview 214
    The Employment Interview 215
        REGULATIONS GOVERNING EMPLOYMENT INTERVIEWS 215
        GETTING READY FOR THE INTERVIEW 217
        PARTICIPATING IN THE EMPLOYMENT INTERVIEW 220
        ROLE OF THE EMPLOYMENT INTERVIEWER 221
    The Performance Appraisal 222
        METHODS OF APPRAISAL 222
        EFFECTIVE APPRAISAL INTERVIEWS 223
        PERFORMANCE APPRAISAL OUTLINE 225
    The Counseling Interview 226
        COUNSELING INTERVIEW OUTLINE 226
    The Reprimand Interview 227
        REPRIMAND INTERVIEW OUTLINE 227
    The Stress or Interrogation Interview 228
        STRESS INTERVIEW OUTLINE 228
    The Press Conference 229
    The Talk Show 230
Structuring the Interview 230
    The Opening 230
    Purpose Statement 231

The Body of an Interview 232
    TYPES OF QUESTIONS 232
    FORMAT 232
The Closing 233
Communication Responsibilities in the Interview 233
    Interviewee Responsibilities 234
    Interviewer Responsibilities 234

Chapter 12—GROUP COMMUNICATION IN THE BUSINESS SETTING 239

The Nature of Communication in Small Groups 241
    Setting a Purpose 241
    Group Structure 243
    Cohesion 243
Private Discussions 243
    Informal Discussions 243
    Round Table Discussions 244
    Brainstorming Sessions 244
    Planning Meetings 244
    Buzz Sessions 244
        THE 1–3–6 DECISION-MAKING TECHNIQUE 245
    Quality Circles 246
    Self-managing Work Teams 248
    Teleconferences 248
        TYPES OF TELECONFERENCE 249
        USES OF TELECONFERENCE 250
        TELECONFERENCE PROBLEMS 250
        PARTICIPATING IN A TELECONFERENCE 250
    Focus Group 251
Public Discussions 251
    Panel Discussions 251
    Symposium 252
    Forum 252
Conferences 252
Group Maintenance and Task Functions 253
    Getting Started 253
    Leader and Leadership 254
        LEADER STYLE 255
        LEADER ROLES 256
        LEADERSHIP ROLES 257
    Procedures 258
        AGENDA 258
        RULES OF OPERATION 259
        CRITERIA 261

Participants 261
   PARTICIPATION ACTIVITIES 262
   FOLLOWERSHIP 262
   RISKY SHIFT AND GROUP POLARIZATION 263
   GROUPTHINK 263
Communication Networks 263
Time and Place 263

Chapter 13—PLANNING THE PUBLIC SPEECH PRESENTATION 270

Parameters of Speaking 272
  The Participants 273
  The Setting 275
   PLACE 275
   TIME 276
   EMOTIONAL CLIMATE 276
  The Purpose and Purpose Statement 278
Sources of Information 279
  Self-knowledge 279
  Research Information 279
   PRINT AND RECORDED SOURCES 279
   INTERVIEWS 281
  Research Note-taking 281

Chapter 14—PREPARING THE PUBLIC SPEECH OR PRESENTATION 285

The Introduction 287
  Attention Getter 287
   TYPES OF ATTENTION-GETTERS 287
  Exposition 290
Statement of Central Idea 290
The Body 291
  Types of Issue Arrangements 291
   CHRONOLOGICAL ORDER 291
   SPATIAL ORDER 292
   TOPICAL ORDER 292
   CAUSAL ARRANGEMENT 293
   COMPARISON, CONTRAST, AND COMPARISON-CONTRAST ARRANGEMENTS 293
   PROBLEM-SOLUTION ARRANGEMENT 294
  Transitions 295
  Forms of Support 295

Illustrations 295
    SPECIFIC INSTANCES 296
    CLARIFIERS 296
    STATISTICS 296
    ANALOGIES 296
    TESTIMONY 297
    SUPPLEMENTARY AIDS 299
The Conclusion 303
  Summary 303
  Clincher 304
    Types of Clinchers 304
Putting the Speech Together 305
  Working Outline 306
  The Speech-planner Model 308
  Wording the Manuscript Speech 308
Preparing Your Speech Notes 310

Chapter 15—PRESENTING THE PUBLIC SPEECH OR PRESENTATION 315

Modes of Presentation 317
  Impromptu Presentation 317
    PREPARING THE IMPROMPTU PRESENTATION 317
  Extemporaneous Presentation 318
  Manuscript Presentation 318
  Memorized Presentation 319
The Physical Elements of a Speech 319
Vocal Delivery 321
  Some Hints Regarding Vocal Delivery 322
Media Appearances 322
Speech Anxiety (Speechophobia) 323
  Practice and Devices 324
  Skill Deficit 325
  Systematic Desensitization 325
  Negative Cognitive Appraisal 326
A Final Word on Presenting the Speech 326

Chapter 16—INFORMATIVE SPEAKING 329

Purposes of Informative Speaking 331
  Description 332
  Giving Direction 332
Characteristics of Informative Speeches 332
  Adaptation to Audience 332

Supporting Details 333
Level of Interest 333
Structure 333
Audio-Visual Materials 334
Types of Informative Speeches 334
Information Speech 334
Informative Briefing 334
Technical Report 335
Professional Paper 336
Informative Speech Format 336

Chapter 17—PERSUASIVE SPEAKING 340

Goals of Persuasive Speaking 342
Conviction 342
Actuation 342
Achieving Persuasion 342
Audience Adaptation 342
Good Intentions 343
Decision-making Analysis 343
    FIELD-RELATED STANDARDS 343
    GROUP STANDARDS 343
    INDIVIDUAL STANDARDS 343
Attitudes 344
Persuasive Strategies 344
Speaker Credibility 344
Psychological Appeals 345
Resistance to Change 347
Building the Arguments 348
    DEDUCTIVE ARGUMENTS 348
    INDUCTIVE ARGUMENTS 349
    PERSUASIVE STRUCTURE 349
Types of Persuasive Speeches 350
The Sales Talk 350
The Motivational Speech 354
Testimony 354
Persuasive Speech Format 355

Chapter 18—SPEAKING FOR SPECIAL OCCASIONS 361

Question-and-Answer Sessions 362
Special Occasion Speeches 363
Speech of Introduction 363
Speech of Welcome 365

Speech of Presentation 366
Speech of Acceptance 367
After-Dinner Speech 369
Appearing on Television 370
   Television Interviews 371
      LEARNING ABOUT THE TELEVISION INTERVIEW 371
      KNOW WHAT YOU WANT TO SAY 372
      KNOW AND EXERCISE YOUR RIGHTS 372
      INTERACT 373
      MAINTAIN CONTROL 373
Effective Public Communication Media Presentations 374
   Television Cameras 374
   Time Limits 375
   Teleprompters 375
   Studio Personnel 375
   Speaking to the Camera 375
   Microphones 375
   Visual Aids 376
   Physical Presentation Techniques 376

Index 379

PREFACE

On January 28, 1986, the space shuttle *Challenger* and its crew of seven lifted off from Kennedy Space Center only to explode 90 seconds later in mid-air. This tragedy led President Reagan to appoint a commission to review and recommend changes in the management of the National Aeronautics and Space Administration, for it was clear that the communication and the decision-making processes of this organization were seriously flawed. The resulting recommendations of the Rogers Commission stressed the critical need for NASA to develop plans and policies for implementing effective management communication at all levels.[1]

The critical need for effective communication is evident in all organizations. For those of you who are planning to enter the business world, two major issues confront you. Are communicative skills really needed in business? If so, what particular communication skills are needed by the person entering or engaged in the field of business? In a survey of executives of California companies, 66 percent noted that their communication skills played a major role in their advancement, and 94 percent claimed that they made extensive use of communication skills in their present position.[2] Numerous other studies indicate that there is an ever-growing need in business and industry to communicate information in an organized and coherent manner for a wide variety of purposes.[3] Organization have come to recognize that incalculable losses can result from the time wasted by executives in ineffective attempts to communicate. The need was probably best expressed by Edward Rohrback, the president of Hopes Windows, when he said, "The key word is communication . . . all our problems are common communication problems."[4]

If you accept the concept that communication skills are needed in business, you may ask, "Which ones?" Studies reveal the need for listening, idea shaping, decision-making, problem-solving, leadership, advising, instructing, exchanging information, giving orders, meeting management, interpersonal competency, use of audio and visual aids, working in groups, speaking before small groups, speaking with subordinates, relaying information, and persuasion. The University of Chicago's Industrial Relations Center summarized these needs in the objective of their Building Effective Communication workshop: "To explore basic elements of the communication process, getting at meaning, barriers to the open mind, asking with understanding, listening for understanding, planning and developing communication."[5]

This is the age of subject matter relevancy. In order for instruction to be understood and meaningful, it must be a microcosm of the real world. Education must answer the present student battle cry, "How can I use and apply this?" In the field of business, this means giving you something that can help you obtain a position, keep your job, or be advanced in your field.

It is the purpose of this book to help the reader understand theories of communication in order to gain insights and skills for operating effectively in the world of business. We have attempted to speak directly to you, the reader, in language that is interesting and understandable. Many real and imaginary examples have been used throughout the chapters in order to show how and why the ideas expressed are applicable to business and industry.

NEW FEATURES

This, the fourth edition of *This Business of Communicating,* incorporates the latest developments in management theory with the latest developments in communication theory to provide a comprehensive view of the principles and skills necessary for effective functioning in an organization.

This edition includes major changes from the third edition. Chapters on language and business ethics have been added. Restructuring of the material has resulted in separate chapters in informative, persuasive, and special occasion public speaking, including information on media presentations. A new emphasis has been placed on perceptions, conflict resolution and stress decision-making, and stress in the work-place. Most importantly, the materials have been restructured into a three-part arrangement: communication concepts, business communication theory, business communication skills. We have maintained the book's flexible structure so that chapters can be used in any order.

We hope that you will be able to employ the ideas in this book immediately in your everyday life, using them to enhance your present or future position in the business world.

We wish to thank the following reviewers for their useful suggestions concerning this edition of *This Business of Communicating:*

Robert Kemp, Laney College;
Mark Morman, Tyler Junior College;
Shirlee Levin, Charles County Community College;
Karen Roloff, Loyola University.

NOTES

1. *Actions to Implement the Recommendations of the Presidential Commission on the Space Shuttle Challenger Accident* (Washington: National Aeronautics and Space Administration, 14 July 1986), 3.
2. James C. Barnett, "The Communication Needs of Business Executives," *Journal of Business Communication* 8(1971):8.
3. A complete review of this literature is provided in Vincent S. DiSalvo, Dave Dunning, and Benjamin K. Homan, "An Identification of Communication Skills, Problems and Issues for the Business and Professional Communication Course" (Paper presented at the Central States Speech Association Convention, Milwaukee, 1982).
4. Hobart Rowen, "Labor-Management Effort is a Success," *Plain Dealer,* 4 May 1975, section 2, p. 9.
5. Bulletin announcing a special course entitled, "Building Effective Communication," the University of Chicago's Industrial Relations Center.

I ∎

THE
ACT OF
COMMUNICATING

1

□

The Communicative Process

OVERVIEW   Communication is a process by which information is passed from one source to another through our sensory channels. We communicate symbolically and nonverbally.

KEY WORDS
communication
source
effective communication
receiver
sending/receiving
sensory channels
attend
interpreting
decoding
perceptions

expectations
categorizing
responding
indefiniteness
semantics
symbolic view of language
nonverbal communication
linear model of communication
interactional model of communication
transactional model of communication

Communication deals with the processing of information. Effective communication is based on the degree of relationship between those taking part in the communicative act. The communicative act results from the utilization of the human senses as channels.

You have just read three sentences about the communicative act. Your understanding, or lack of understanding, of what you have just read can be explained by analyzing what has just taken place. The authors, the senders of the message (the **source**) have attempted to convey an idea to you through the written-reading-visual channel. We have written the first paragraph in General American English because we felt that a person reading this book, the receivers of the message (the **receiver**) would most probably have an understanding of that language. We have attempted to select words the average reader of a college textbook would be able to understand. We have attempted to use the grammar structure that would make the sentences follow a pattern the reader is used to—noun, verb, object. If the authors have been successful, you now have some understanding of three aspects of the communicative act: it is a process; it is dependent upon a relationship; and it is transmitted via one or more of the sensory channels. If you do understand, if you gain the intent of the communicative message, we have carried out **effective communication.**

THE PROCESS OF COMMUNICATING

■ The process of communication occurs in a split-second sequence. We receive the stimulus (information) that has been sent, examine it, interpret it, and respond to it in some way.

Sending and Receiving

□ We perform the **sending** and **receiving** of information through our **sensory channels**—seeing, hearing, touching, smelling, and tasting. One of the most common ways of sending messages between individuals is for one person to orally present the information and for the other person to hear it. A corporate president speaking to a meeting of the stockholders would be an example of the speaking-listening channel. Communication also may occur by touching. Placing your hand on someone's shoulder to get attention would be an example of tactile (touch) channeling. We also can send messages through smell. Perfumes and shaving lotions are intended to send a message about the user to the person who receives the scent, thus using the olfactory (smell) channel. In some instances more than one channel is used. A salesperson who is talking to a client also may be using pictures to clarify the points being made. In this instance the salesperson (the source) and the prospective buyer (the receiver) have analyzed the situation and have decided that there would be a better relationship between the parties if more than one channel of communication were used.

Attending

Once we receive a stimulus through our senses, we **attend** or focus on a specific stimulus, thus excluding all other stimuli. Attention occurs through the short-term memory system, which psychologists suggest has a duration of 2 to 25 seconds.[1] Thus, our attention to any one stimulus is very short at best. This attention span may very well be affected further by such factors as television viewing habits. An individual who has grown accustomed to the television format probably "tunes out" for a commercial break every 7 to 10 minutes, as most commercial television programming is scheduled in 7 to 10 minute segments.

Interpreting

Once received and examined, the stimulus is sent to the brain for **interpreting** in order to assign some type of meaning to it. It is this stage of the processing sequence that constitutes **decoding**—translating the message to one's own set of experiences in order to make the message meaningful. Each person has his/her own interpretation of the phrase *good salary,* for example. Someone just entering the business world will have one interpretation as to what is a good salary, while an executive with twenty-five years of experience will have a different amount in mind. Our perceptions, expectations, and categorizations affect our interpretations.

Perceptions

Our **perceptions** play an important role in interpreting. We screen the information through what might be described as a perceptual "filter." All of an individual's background, experiences, beliefs, attitudes, and knowledge make up this filtering system and determine how we react to the information. Persons who are called to testify as witnesses to a robbery frequently have very different interpretations of the same scene. Each person has screened what he observed through his own perceptual filter—and these perceptions can lead to very discrepant accounts of the same situation.

Expectations   Our perceptions are affected by our **expectations.** Essentially, we see and hear what we want to see and hear or what we expect to see and hear. A classic psychological study[2] illustrates the concept. In the 1930s the researcher constructed a speech that contained equal amounts of pro- and con-New Deal political arguments. When the speech was presented to audiences, those listeners who were in favor of President Roosevelt's New Deal program perceived the speech as totally pro-New Deal, while those people who were against the New Deal perceived the speech as support for their anti-New Deal stand.

To further illustrate the effect of expectations, select four people. Tell them that they will be shown a word for a fraction of a second and that each is to write down the word seen. Tell the first person that the word will have something to do with taste; the second that the word will represent a spread placed on bread; the third that the word indicates a closure on clothing; and the fourth that the word has something to do with baseball. Now give this design to each of the four persons.

```
┌────────────────────────────────┐
│                                │
│          ɾ ʊ ʈ ʈ c ɾ           │
│                                │
└────────────────────────────────┘
```

When the answers are collected it frequently is found that the first person has seen the word *bitter;* the second person *butter;* the third person *button;* and the fourth person *batter* or *hitter*. Each of the viewers has seen what he/she expected to see.[3]

Read the following sentence aloud:

The cow jumped over
over the noon.

Go back and look at the sentence again. Did you, in your original reading, say the word *over* twice? Did you say *noon* or *moon?* We often tend to see what we expect to see. Since your are familiar with the sentence "The cow jumped over the moon," you are very likely to have seen and read it as you know it is supposed to be, rather than the way it really is.

Categorizing Some researchers in linguistics suggest that all individuals have a basic set of categories in the brain to which all verbal and nonverbal stimuli are assigned through the process of **categorizing**.[4] These categories are developed as we go through the stages of learning a language through imitation of parents and others around us in early life.

Most language scholars, however, argue that each person will have a different category system stemming from his/her own experiences in language development.[5] Thus, there would be no specific number of categories within the brain. This would explain why different people have different responses in a word-association exercise. Reactions to the word *business,* for instance, might range from *corporation* to *actions on stage during a play.*

Responding We respond to communication input within ourselves, as well as to others, on both verbal and nonverbal levels. After we have interpreted the information, we accept, reject, or withhold final judgment—in some way we are satisfied. At this point we are **responding** internally. Then, based on the processing of information, we give the sender an oral response and/or a nonverbal reaction. These responses have a profound effect on the communication process.

Indefiniteness The effect of human communication is a process which continues indefinitely. Communication is considered to be dynamic rather than static in the sense that it is difficult, if not impossible, to suggest when a communication message truly begins and ends; thus, communication contains the element of **indefiniteness.** Something you say to someone today may have a profound effect on that person immediately or many years later. Consequently we have come to view human communication very much as a perpetual process which has the potential for lasting influence.

THE LANGUAGE SYSTEM

■

An individual's language system may be well established by the age of four or five.[6] The development of the system at such an early age enables one to use the language system symbolically. Experts in the study of **semantics** (the relationship of people to their language) emphasize that this symbolic function of language guides how we use the language as communicators.

This **symbolic view of language** suggests that we don't use words as objects in and of themselves. Rather, we use words to represent the objects and ideas about which we are communicating. Thus, the word *desk* is not the piece of furniture itself. Instead, *desk* is a word that English speakers have agreed, over the course of time, to use to represent the piece of furniture when describing the object, *desk*.

This view of words as representers leads semanticists to the conclusion that "words don't mean, people do." It is not the word itself that gives us meaning. It is the interpretation of any word that gives it meaning. How we use a word in context will specify that interpretation more clearly, but no two people can ever have exact meanings for any word. We always have some sort of conscious or subconscious emotional response to words.

To clarify this concept, consider the word *dog*. What did you picture when you read the word? Some people picture their dog; others a dog they had recently seen; still others may have become fearful as they thought about a negative experience they have had with a dog. If you like dogs, your response may have been different from a person who dislikes or is allergic to household pets.

In using and receiving verbal language, therefore, we must be aware of the symbolic nature of words. We must remember that meanings are in people and not in words, and that it is our interpretation of and response to the word that gives it meaning. And we also must be aware that communication is not only verbal but also nonverbal.

NONVERBAL COMMUNICATION

■

Knowingly or unknowingly, people communicate on several different levels at the same time. They usually are aware only of the verbal dialogue and do not realize that they also respond to nonverbal messages. All of us communicate with one another through **nonverbal communication,** which is all message sending beyond the verbal symbols. Though we have no dictionary and do not precisely understand the rules, there are some factors about nonverbal communication which have been revealed by research. It is estimated that in a communicative situation less than 35 percent of the social meaning of a message is carried verbally, while more than 65 percent is conveyed nonverbally.[7] Another estimate is that "more than two-thirds of oral communication is actually nonverbal or communication dominated by visual cues."[8] This suggests that the effect of the nonverbal language on communication is highly significant.

The continuous functioning of our nonverbal language illustrates that one cannot *not* communicate . We are constantly sending messages to other persons. Often we send these messages without being aware of it. We fidget, stare, look away, sit up straight, slouch, smile, or shrug our shoulders. From the time we get up and throughout the

We use words to represent ideas and objects. They are not the idea or object in and of themselves. (© Sprucer Gaut/Taurus Photos)

day, we are communicating attitudes and responses to all those other persons with whom we come in contact.

MODELS OF COMMUNICATION

The process of communication can be seen as an ongoing, dynamic process in which both verbal and nonverbal elements function to aid or interfere with effective communication.

In order to further understand the communicative process, models can be used to demonstrate the various component parts and the differences in patterns. Though there are many ways of describing the act of communicating, we have selected three models that represent the process: the linear model, the interactional model, and the transactional model.[9] It should be noted that a model is an attempt to graphically illustrate a process and is not the process itself.

Linear Model

We hear managers and workers say:

"But I sent him a memo on it."
her how to do that yesterday."
"I'm sure I sent that order through."
"We called Mr. Jones last week."
"We haven't had any complaints."
"No one's talked to me about it."

FIGURE 1.1 A Linear
Model of Communication
(One Direction
Communication)

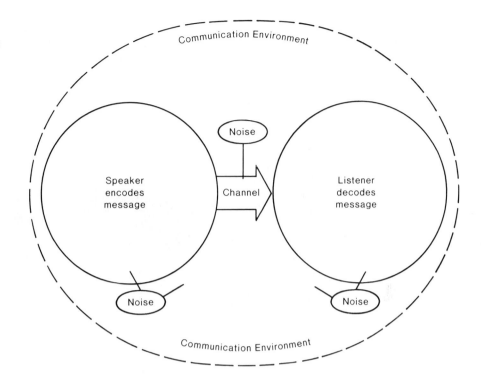

Such comments reflect a one-way view of the communication process, a view which can be represented by the **linear model of communication** (figure 1.1). People sometimes believe that if they say (or write) something, that this sending of a message is all there is to communicating. It is unfortunate if a manager, for example, assumes that issuing an order or directive is all that is necessary to assure that the order is carried out.

This linear view of communication ignores the important role of the listener in responding to (and consequently affecting) the sender and the message in order to provide feedback. This feedback can enable the sender to check to see if an order is understood, a policy accepted, a message clear, or a channel open.

Effective communicators recognize that there may be some instances when one-way communication is necessary, but must be aware of the difficulty of not receiving feedback and thus being able to adapt the message. When memos are sent, letters written, speeches presented with no question-and-answer session to follow, the sender must carefully analyze the audience and try to avoid creating communication problems. Words must be carefully analyzed to make sure they can be clearly understood. Ideas must be presented in such a way that they will be received with the intended meaning.

Effective communicators attempt to interact with each other as they deal with information and, whenever possible, open channels for feedback. With this in mind, let us examine the interactional model.

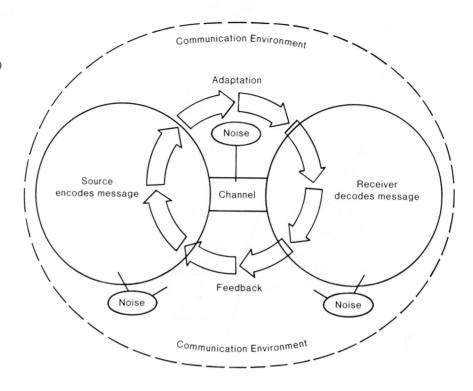

FIGURE 1.2 An Interactional Model of Communication (Two Direction Communication)

Communication Environment

Adaptation

Noise

Source encodes message

Channel

Receiver decodes message

Noise

Feedback

Noise

Communication Environment

Interactional Model

☐ "Will you please hand me the paper?" "No, not that paper, that one, the yellow sheet." "Thank you very much." Analyzing this communication shows that the source or speaker has sent a message verbally to the receiver or listener. The listener picks up a sheet of paper and starts to hand it to the speaker. The speaker, recognizing that the instructions were not clear because of the feedback (the wrong sheet of paper), alters the message by adapting or altering the oral message and supplementing it with a non-verbal message. This is an example of two-directional communication as represented by the **interactional model of communication** (figure 1.2).

A speech is followed by a question-and-answer session in which the listeners ask questions of the speaker in order to make sure that the information received is the information sent. A trainee in a workshop asks a question of the instructor and receives a clarifying answer. A manager instructing a new employee on how to operate a piece of equipment watches the new employee carry through the instructions and then adjusts the explanations to further clarify if errors are made. All of the preceding illustrate an interactional view of communication.

In the interactional model of communication a source must be aware of the possibility of difficulties in the communicative interaction and search out or respond to the feedback being given. Sometimes this requires asking questions of the receiver. At

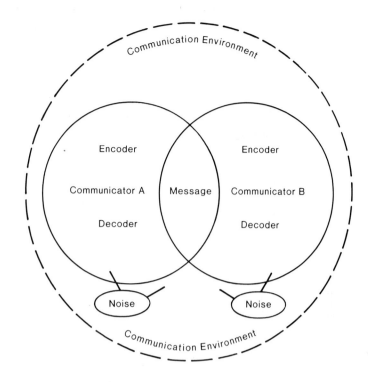

FIGURE 1.3 A
Transactional Model of
Communication
(Multidirectional
Communication)

other times, it means watching carefully for nonverbal feedback. When it becomes apparent that the receiver has had difficulty decoding the message, the source should make an effort to adapt the message he/she has sent by changing the words, altering the vocal tone, or giving a clarifying example.

Transactional Model

☐ While the interactional approach to communication has been the basis for much of the contemporary theory and research on human communication, a more recent view of the communication process offers a more detailed explanation of this complex human function. The **transactional model of communication** (figure 1.3), instead of looking at the two communicators as a specific sender and a receiver interacting with each other, views communication as the process of two communicators transacting message information simultaneously.

In the transactional model, the two communicators assume both roles—sender and receiver—at the same time. For example, as one communicator explains a new accounting process, the other person decodes the explanation and encodes feedback to tell that he/she does (or does not) understand the method. The person explaining the process, then, is decoding this feedback while encoding (and adapting) the accounting explanation. An observer would note that as the explainer indicates an idea with words and gestures, the other person, with a nod of the head and an "uh huh," indicates understanding. Note the simultaneous sending and receiving. Most of your daily communication follows this model.

SUMMARY

In this chapter we have examined the communicative process. The major ideas were:

Communication is a process by which information is passed from one source to another.

Effective communication is based on the development of a relationship between those taking part in the communicative act.

The communicative act results from the utilization of the human senses as channels.

In the process of communication we receive, examine, interpret, and respond to the stimulus.

We communicate symbolically.

We communicate on several different levels at the same time.

Communication is a process which continues indefinitely.

We communicate with one another nonverbally as well as with words.

Three models that can be used to explain communication are linear, interactional, and transactional.

Feedback is the message sent to the source to reflect how the original message was perceived.

Adaptation is the adjustment the original source makes based on the feedback given by the receiver.

THINGS TO DO

1. Write down one phrase or expression that is unique to your family or group of friends. These should be expressions that have meaning only for a select group and are not commonly used in the society as a whole. They may be ethnic expressions, in-group references, etc. Read the expression in class and let others try to figure out what it means, then reveal the source and meaning. From this activity the class should discuss the statement "Individuals, according to their backgrounds and experiences, have unique elements in their communication that may be understood only by those with common experiences and backgrounds."[10]

2. Each person in the class is to ask fifteen people what the word *hog* means. Do a class tally on the first definition given by each of the people asked. Discuss the theory in the book, "We must remember that meanings are in people and not in words."

3. "Each person is unique as a communicator because of his/her environmental influences." Explain this statement by using yourself as an example.

4. Five students will be selected by the instructor. They are to form a circle with their chairs in the middle of the classroom. The instructor will whisper the same topic in the ear of each student. The students are to carry on a "con-

versation" about that topic without using any spoken or written language. After about three minutes the instructor will indicate that the participants are to continue the discussion, using the same topic and now making sounds, but still not using words. In about two minutes they will be permitted to use words for the continuation of the conversation. Continue the interaction for another three minutes. After the completion of the three stages, the members of the group are to carry on a discussion of what it felt like and what happened during each of the stages. Members of the class may contribute by commenting on what they observed during the session.

5. Block off an hour of time when you expect to be participating in a great deal of communication. Carefully observe the channels used during that period of time. Make a list of how many channels were used, how they were used, and if you felt that the communication was successful. Report back to the class on your experience.

6. Carry out the experiment in the section of this chapter on perception concerning the *bitter, batter, button, butter* word with a group of your friends. Report back to the class on the results. What assumptions can we make about perceptions based on this project?

7. Set aside one-half hour in which you will not communicate orally. Select a time when a great deal of oral communication would normally be taking place. YOU MAY NOT SPEAK! Report back to the class on what happened, how you felt, and what difficulties you feel might confront someone who is not capable of speaking.

8. Observe (listen and watch) several people engaged in a conversation. Analyze what is taking place. Using the models described in this chapter, diagram the conversation. If it is possible, do the same thing in a platform speaking situation.

NOTES

1. N. Moray, "Broadbent's Filter Theory: Postulate H and the Problem of Switching Time," *Quarterly Journal of Experimental Psychology* 12 (1960):214.

2. Allen L. Edwards, "Rationalization in Recognition as a Result of Political Frame of Reference," *Journal of Abnormal and Social Psychology* 46 (1941):224–35.

3. *Effective Communication on the Job,* rev. ed. (New York: American Management Association, 1963), 76.

4. Roger Brown, *Words and Things* (New York: Macmillan, 1958).

5. For a discussion of language categories as they relate to communication, see Carl Weaver, *Human Listening* (Indianapolis: Bobbs-Merrill, 1972), 42–59.

6. Roy Berko, Andrew Wolvin, and Darlyn Wolvin, *Communicating: A Social and Career Focus* (Boston: Houghton Mifflin, 1985), 57.

7. Ray Birdwhistell, *Kinesics and Context* (New York: Ballantine Books, 1972).

8. John Koha, "Body Signs," *Cleveland Plain Dealer,* 15 December 1976, 8F.

9. The models presented are based on the views of communication agreed upon by the participants of the Eastern States Beginning Course Conference, University of Mary-

land, November, 1974. These were presented to the Speech Communication Association as the standard view of basic speech communications.

10. Roy Berko, Andrew Wolvin, and Darlyn Wolvin, *Handbook of Instructional Options, Communicating: A Social and Career Focus* (Boston: Houghton Mifflin, 1977), 59–60.

2

□

Intrapersonal Communication

OVERVIEW   The processing of internal messages, communication within the self, is intrapersonal communication. A person's intrapersonal communication is affected by his or her self-concept. Intrapersonal communication is used to make decisions and reach conclusions. A negative self-concept can contribute to a person being communicatively anxious. Stress is the result of intrapersonal tension and anxiety.

KEY WORDS

intrapersonal communication
self-concept
spiritual self
material self
social self
bodily self
communication anxiety
systematic desensitization
cognitive modification

skills training
self-help
distortion
perception
stereotypes
rationalization
experience
stress

You are sitting at your desk; you have a problem to solve. Or you are driving down the road planning the speech you are going to make. Or you have just been given a proposal for a new production method and you are mulling it over. What do these situations have in common? In each case you are processing information. Whether the source was the spoken word, a letter, or an inspiration from someplace within you, you are intrapersonally communicating. **Intrapersonal communication** is the name given to the processing of internal messages, or communication within the self.[1]

Before we can contact another person, we must first get in touch with ourselves. We must decide what to say, how to say it, what we believe, and what our reactions are. In order to understand intrapersonal communication, let us examine the role of self-concept, how we reach conclusions, and the process of listening.

SELF-CONCEPT

■

"**Self-concept** represents your psychological self—all the experiences, beliefs, attitudes, and values that make up the self; it includes how you perceive the world, how the world perceives you, and how you perceive yourself."[2] In other words, if you wrote a description of yourself from the standpoint of how you perceive yourself, how others perceive you, and how you think others perceive you, you would have a self-concept essay on "you."

It can be safely assumed that most people have never really tried to write that essay. Even if they did, they would probably have a great deal of difficulty. "The self-concept is not a snapshot of oneself that one carries in his or her head. Rather, it is something like a poor television picture, something moving but also involving its ghost images."[3]

Since the self-concept is the starting point of all your intrapersonal communication, let us assume that you wrote the essay of "you." Of what importance is it? If the essay was basically positive, then you would be working in an area of positive self-concept. If this were the case you would have confidence in the way you did things, carry positive attitudes into the decision-making process, and have confidence in your ability to reach conclusions. A manager who has a positive self-concept projects an image of assurance and appears to be in command of information and situations. Others perceive this in a favorable way and often react positively to a person with assurance, assuming that person to be in control and aware of what he/she is doing.

People evaluate themselves based on their physical attributes, emotional attributes, mental attributes, and relationships with others. The more positively an individual regards these attributes, the more probable it is that that individual will not have to fight off personal negative feelings that block meaningful actions. A person who projects self-confidence, assurance, and personal magnetism is one who enjoys a positive self-concept.

Since we tend to act consistently with the feelings we have about ourselves, people who have a negative self-concept may well start seeing themselves as failures and consequently act the part. If you go into something expecting to do poorly, you are likely to do poorly. This constitutes what is termed the self-fulfilling prophecy. The salesperson who approaches a customer with a "you are not going to buy this" attitude is not likely to get the sale. If you do not accept yourself, probably no one else will accept you either.

A person's self-concept influences the way that person deals with others. An individual with a positive self-image is likely to have a good sense of humor, be optimistic, deal with people in a direct and simple manner, not feel he/she has to prove anything, and is relaxed in the company of others. On the other hand, those who don't like themselves very much are likely to feel pressure to make others like them, and, thus, try too hard to be popular. Or they may panic when small mistakes are made, thus alienating others or giving others the feeling that they lack emotional control. The results of such actions, in a business setting, could result in the loss of sales, reluctance of superiors to offer advancements, and conflicts with fellow employees and upper management personnel. Indeed, this "difficult employee" is receiving more attention today in management study.

In actuality, the self is not one thing. Four components of self can be identified. The **spiritual self** relates to the way we think and feel. Your belief system and your attitudes are representative of this part of the self. The **material self** consists of our actual possessions: clothing, jewelry, car, etc. The **social self** is our relationship with others. It concerns how we manage those relationships and how we feel about our kinships with others. The **bodily self** is how we look, our physical height, weight, facial appearance, etc.

The more positively you perceive your spiritual, material, social, and physical self, the more likely it is you will have a positive self-concept.

Sometimes people feel they must change or alter any or all of the "selves" they possess. Thus, they may take courses, go to therapists, or take special training to alter their spiritual or social selves. They may go to image consultants for assistance in the

Our social self dictates how we manage our relationships with others and how we feel about our kinships with others. (H. Armstrong Roberts)

selection of clothing. They may turn to special training to learn social skills, to become more assertive, or to overcome shyness. Some resort to physical exercise, dieting, or surgery to change their physical features. Whatever the effort, if the end result is a more positive self-image, then the person will probably be able to function in a more positive manner.

The self-concept has a significant impact on our perceptions of ourselves as communicators. Persons who have positive self-concepts about their communication abilities usually are effective in communication situations, evidencing minimal communication apprehension and demonstrating self-assurance. A person who has a negative self-concept as a communicator, however, often communicates this lack of confidence.

A person's self-concept may result in attitudes which affect the way he or she communicates, or fails to communicate. Consequently, a person's negative self-concept may result in communication anxiety.

COMMUNICATION ANXIETY

■ **Communication anxiety** (also referred to as shyness or communication apprehension) is this nation's number one psychological problem, as it affects about 80 percent of Americans. It is the anxiety related to an individual's real or anticipated fear of communicating with others. Communication anxiety causes people to believe they have more to lose than to gain from communication. Anxious people fear rejection and criticism. What they often fail to realize is that the fear is a label they have placed on themselves—a label which may become a self-fulfilling prophecy. They expect to have difficulty in communicating, so they do.

Some people are situationally shy rather than generally apprehensive. The situationally shy person is only affected by the circumstances of specific situations. Such a person may only be afraid of public speaking, of reacting in a group, or in one-to-one interactions.

The Effect of Communication Anxiety

□ What is the effect of communication anxiety? Communication anxiety can make it difficult to meet new people. A person fearful of interacting will attempt to avoid coming in contact with people. This makes it necessary to avoid situations where the person will be expected to share with others (social gatherings or careers such as sales or personnel work).

Communication apprehension can prevent people from speaking up for what they believe. Anxious people may fail to defend themselves and thus be used by other people. In a business environment this could result in not getting pay raises, being given the least desirable assignments, and not defending oneself when wrongly accused of something.

Since anxious people may not share much of themselves with others, they may be regarded as something other than what they really are. It is not unusual for shy people to be perceived as snobbish, distant, or uncaring. These are outcomes of observing the person who does not participate in oral interactions.

Anxious persons sometimes become so preoccupied with their own reactions that they fail to be effective in their jobs. If they are so concerned about avoiding communicative situations, they may fail to carry out certain assignments. They may concentrate on how things will personally affect them, rather than on what the job requires.

Because of the lack of social contacts anxious people may find themselves depressed or lonely. They may display such physical signs as blushing, stuttering, handwringing, or physical illness. These are especially present when they feel they must orally participate. Some communicatively anxious persons even turn to drugs or alcohol to attempt to cover up for their insecurity.

It must be remembered that these descriptions of anxiety pertain only to those who are severely anxious. Not every communicatively anxious person withdraws. Some have learned to cope with their anxiety and put their needs ahead of their fears. In some societies, it is even an accepted practice to be apprehensive. The Japanese have high communication apprehension but find this no major problem as it is the "right" form of action for their society.[4] This, unfortunately for shy persons, is not the case in the United States. In the business world, "sometimes a career can be stopped cold by shyness."[5]

Overcoming Communication Anxiety

☐   If you perceive yourself to be communicatively anxious, at this point you might be saying, "What can I do about it?"

First, you must be aware that shyness isn't what you are, it is how you act. You can change! A shy person must learn to stop putting himself/herself down. Accept what you are and build on your strengths.

Accept compliments as well as criticism.

Stop worrying about being liked by everyone. Being liked by EVERYBODY is a near impossibility!

Most important of all, communicatively anxious people must learn to deal with problems in a constructive way. They must learn to set specific, reachable goals. Then they have to examine the behavior that surrounds reaching that goal. Next, they must develop and rehearse strategies for achieving the goals. This usually involves acting first and feeling later.[6]

How does one learn these attitudes and skills? Communication experts have identified four ways in which a person may change if he or she really wants to do so.

Systematic Desensitization

Systematic desensitization is a process by which one learns to relax. It usually centers on deep muscle relaxation which reduces anxiety. This relaxation can be achieved by listening to tape recordings especially developed for the purpose, or learning self-hypnosis.[7]

Cognitive Modification

Cognitive modification teaches a person to modify the negative self-talk in which anxious people usually participate. It is fairly common for anxious people to make statements like, "I can't talk to people like that," or "The last time I tried to ask a question I felt foolish," or "If I ask the boss for a raise she'll say no, so why bother?" There are courses that teach cognitive modification at many colleges and universities. Some psychological services also offer this training.

Skills Training

Some people need **skills training,** coaching in goal-setting, rehearsal, practice, and self-monitoring, in order to feel comfortable enough to actively participate in communicative events. By learning the structure of speeches, the skills needed to keep a conversation going, or how groups operate, a person who wants to participate may be able to do so. Without these skills, all the good intentions in the world may result in frustration and rejection due to the lack of knowledge of how to participate. This type of help is available through courses offered in educational institutions and is provided by many businesses that know their employees will benefit from such training.

Self-Help

Some people prefer to **self-help.** Through becoming aware they have a problem, reading some of the self-help books available and putting the authors' advice into practice, some people can make the necessary changes in their attitudes and skills.[8] There are also audio-cassettes which can be helpful.[9]

Work-related Communication Anxiety

☐ Communication anxiety is not only a problem for the individuals themselves, but it may have an effect on their job-related activities, thus affecting the organizations for which they work. Not only the employees, but also supervisors must be aware of the anxiety phenomenon and realize that individuals in their work units may be having difficulties because of it. Once identified, the supervisor should have the resources available to make recommendations for treatment if the person desires help. The recommendation for some type of action should be part of the performance appraisal process.

REACHING CONCLUSIONS

■ Since we process ideas internally as we receive them, much of what we really process is affected by our attitude toward self as much as by the real world around us. In addition to our self-concepts, and whether we are apprehensive about communicating, we are influenced by various factors regarding the intrapersonal activity of reaching conclusions.

FIGURE 2.1 Factors that affect the process of reaching conclusions.

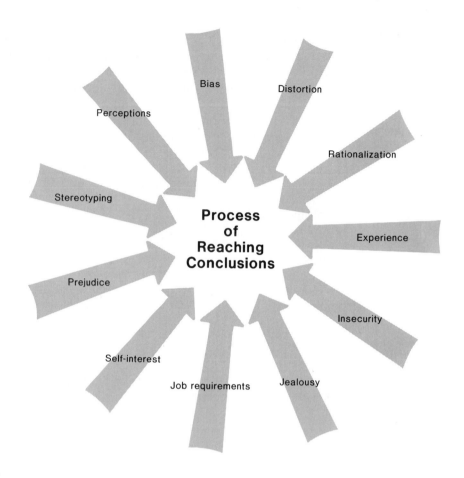

Individuals draw conclusions from the information they receive. Since reaching conclusions isn't always done on a purely rational basis, there are many factors that can and do get in the way (figure 2.1). Factors that can negatively affect reaching conclusions are distortion (self-interest, jealousy, insecurity, and position or job requirements), perceptions, stereotypes (biases and prejudices), confusing fact and inference, and experiences. Recognition and acceptance of these influences on our objectivity are necessary because they permit us to utilize various operational approaches that will allow us to reach practical, and hopefully effective, conclusions.

Distortion

☐ Objectivity may be influenced by **distortion,** the twisting of ideas. One's interpretations of facts can be distorted by many influences. Such factors as self-interest, jealousy, prejudice, insecurity, and position are all possible distorters. For example, job requirements can and do influence the way in which we perceive various problems and opportunities.

Picture yourself in the following situation. You are the sales manager of a large corporation. In order to reduce the bad debts of the company, the credit manager proposes that companies which have not paid for their past orders may not be sold any merchandise until the outstanding debts are settled. As a sales manager, you oppose this because it would restrict sales. You make your opposition to the proposed policy known even though you are aware that it is not in the best interest of your company to continue to have large outstanding debts. Your position in sales, and the importance of continuing to make those sales, distorts your view. On the other hand, as credit manager, you would probably oppose any proposal that would increase indebtedness in order to increase sales. Again, your position is likely to distort the view of changes in company policy.

Would your idea of a practical and reasonable solution to the United Mine Workers of America's coal strike differ if you were a member of the UMWA? Or a nonunion worker whose livelihood was being threatened by violence? Or a member of the UMWA's bargaining council? Or a coal mine owner? Or a consumer whose electricity was about to be turned off because there was no coal to generate electricity? It is all too easy to develop a kind of tunnel vision so that other options are lost in our perceptions.

Perception

☐

Why can two people participate in the same event and perceive it so differently? This happens because people structure their own reality. Our focus, the information we have or which we observe, is always limited since it is only part of the whole that we are experiencing. Two people watching the same accident will not both take in everything that happened. Thus, two people's perceptions of the same episode are often dissimilar. Using selective attention and inattention, we tend to observe things only from our perspective. The reason we see things differently is based on our perceptions.

"**Perception** is the process of becoming aware of objects and events from the senses."[9] Perceptions, rather than being an accurate record of events, are really no more than hypotheses which we use to make predictions. In taking action you must be aware that you are acting on your perceptions and not necessarily on all the information available. This, of course, leaves enormous room for error.

The perception process occurs in three stages—selection, organization, and interpretation.

Selection

When something occurs, you first select the data to which you are going pay attention. This selection may be on a conscious or unconscious level. There is a broad array of possible bits of information for you to grasp. There are varying factors which may catch or center your attention. These selection factors include: who is presenting the material, how it is being presented, its physical size, shape, or color, the surroundings, and whether it is written or on television. If you like the person who is speaking or writing, or agree with his or her ideas, you are likely to buy into the idea. If a razzle-dazzle presentation attracts your attention, you might watch what you might not normally observe. Whatever the reason, you select certain things to pay attention to, and you disregard others.

Organization

After you collect and select the information from the environment, you arrrange the data in some sort of order or classification. You might group the data by the order in which events occurred, such as perceiving that an accident happened by relating the first, second, and third incidents that lead up to the crash of the cars. Or you might classify things by their kind, such as *dogs, cats,* or *people,* for example.

Interpretation

After you select and organize, the third step in the act of perception is interpretation. Interpretation plays a very important role in every communicative act. In interpreting, you use past experiences, the biases and prejudices you hold, as well as assumptions, expectations, knowledge, and personal motives. For example, if you have had a bad experience with a particular brand of copy machine, and then walk into the supply room and see that the new copy machine is the same brand, you might quickly come to the conclusion that the new machine won't be any good either. Or if a person you really like is involved in a disagreement, you might come to the conclusion that he or she is right without listening to the evidence. Or what would be your reaction if you took your car to be serviced, and "*Mrs.* Goodwrench" was going to be the mechanic to work on your vehicle? Would your biases, either positive or negative preconceived opinions, play a role in your perception?

Some common tendencies appear to influence perceptions. These include:

1. *The influence of first impressions.* Upon seeing or hearing someone for the first time most people come to some quick decisions about that individual. It is often very difficult to alter first impressions.
2. *Assuming that everyone is like you.* Almost all of us fall into the trap of thinking that all people act or should act as we do. Therefore, your perceptions may overlook the fact that people from different cultures and environments rarely act or speak as we do.
3. *Accepting the positive and assuming the negative.* Many of us were taught to search for the negative aspects of situations. This may cause you to overlook positive aspects. This tendency to accept the negative is based on culturalization in which we accept the good as the normal and try to find the bad in order to correct it.

Perceptions hold an important place in the business environment. Research in managerial decision-making, for example, indicates that perceptions not only affect the choice of what to do, but the way in which choices are implemented as well.[10] In addition, the very nature of the business structure makes decision-making an important aspect of an organization. In business, when you are attempting to please supervisors in order to get promotions, to get customers to buy products, or work in harmony with your fellow employees, you may find yourself coming up against individuals whose morals, values, and beliefs are different from yours. These perceptive differences will affect their decision making and have a direct effect on you. You may find yourself in conflict with others because you have a different view of the world. You may find that, in order to maintain a relationship, you may have to put aside or alter your views, or decide to stick to your perceptions and pay the consequences.

Stereotypes
□

We sometimes develop stereotypes about such factors as people's sex, their race, the part of the country from which they come, or their educational background. We allow these **stereotypes,** biases, and prejudgments to influence the kinds of conclusions we reach. Further, we can be trapped by the process of **rationalization.** We rationalize when we provide plausible but sometimes untrue reasons for our conduct. We don't yet know all of the wonderful and intricate ways in which the mind processes ideas, so there may be considerable subconscious effects we are not even aware of that operate to influence us.

Experience
□

Experience is having lived through an event. You may wonder why experience was chosen as one of the "things that get in the way" of reaching meaningful conclusions. Relevant experience can be very valuable, but unfortunately that experience may be less and less useful. We are living in a world of constant and continuing change. Today's situations and opportunities are no longer the same as they were in the past, when things were less complicated and less technologically oriented. In fact, yesterday's solutions and approaches may be outmoded and obsolete for today's problems. If one continues to rely on previous experience that is not relevant to today's situations, problems, and opportunities it is likely that one's actions may prove less than effective.

The film *The Real Security*[11] asks, "Why is it that no silk company invented synthetics? Why is it that the canal builders did not invent the railroads? Why is it that the idea and concept of the telephone and the airplane were ridiculed and dismissed as folly?" Previous experience proved not to be a springboard for new ideas, but instead was an entrapment that resulted in resisting change and maintaining the old ways instead of adjusting to new sets of circumstances, opportunities, problems, and situations, all requiring new approaches. This does not mean that experiences are not important or relevant; however, care should be taken not to allow experience to blind us to the point of looking only into the past.

A good example of the changes in our experience is apparent in the popularity of computers today. Young children are becoming very sophisticated in the use of computers, so that they represent quite a different population of Americans than those who were raised without computers. The parents and teachers of these children probably have not had the same opportunities to utilize computer technology. The experience differences between these groups also creates perceptual difference.

STRESS

■

We live in a competitive society which operates by designating winners and losers. We are sometimes the victims of threats to our security, our retention of jobs, or our value system. We are surrounded by modern technology. The new-found freedoms—especially for women, children, and racial minorities—brings new responsibilities and for some, confusion and frustration. Many of our concepts of government, our beliefs, our needs, and our desires have changed. Competition, threats, and changes often create stress. **Stress** is a physical response to environmental demands which cause physical and emotional tension.

Stress, on one hand, is a very necessary and positive characteristic of human existence. Stress is the impetus for growth, change, and adaptation. In adjusting to the demands of our physical and symbolic environment, there are opportunities for personal and social creativity and discovery. On the other hand, mounting evidence suggests that chronic stress can have devastating physical and emotional consequences for us. Research suggests that "stress lowers our resistance to illness and can play a contributory role in diseases of the kidney; heart and blood vessels (including high blood pressure); migraine and tension headaches; gastrointestinal problems such as ulcers; asthma and allergies; respiratory disease; arthritis; and even cancer."[12]

What causes stress? Research indicates that stress is a biological response. The process centers on self-talk which causes hormones to secrete—which causes alarm; self-talk interprets the alarm as meaning "something" (usually, "I am afraid," or "I don't like what is going on,")—resulting in stress.

Another way of looking at this process is to understand that the biology stimulates the stress and the psychological, represented by intrapersonal self-talk, devises coping mechanisms in an attempt to protect the body. These coping mechanisms often are represented by such signaling devices as stuttering, a heightened pitch in the voice, increased volume, errors in grammar and pronunciation, fast-paced speaking, lapses in recall (resulting in pauses), vocal pauses such as "um," "uh," and "er," squinting, fingernail biting, grimacing, teeth-grinding, neck ache, rapid and pounding heartbeat, shaking or sweating.[13] Much of these are the result of the body tightening up to "protect itself."

"As humans, most of the stressors to which we adapt are symbolic rather than physical threats."[14] "The threat of rejection by a loved one, a heated argument with a colleague, the prospect of failure on an important task, the tension of a long wait, or the pressure of an approaching deadline for an uncompleted project can be potent stressors for humans. These symbolic threats are capable of triggering the same hormonal, muscular, and neural reactions that, for other animals, are associated with physical threats to their physical well-being."[15]

Stress and Business

□

According to the National Centers for Disease Control (CDC), stress, boredom and frustration at work are causing substantial health problems. In fact, a recent report indicates that "mental stress accounted for more than one in every ten occupational disease and injury claims."[16]

One factor contributing to work related stress is a poorly designed work station. (H. Armstrong Roberts)

There is increasing evidence that an unsatisfactory work environment may contribute to psychological disorders. One study indicates that stress at work usually stems from hard-driving or neurotic bosses, poorly designed work stations, the use of computer monitoring, job insecurity, and having a position with substantial responsibility but little actual power. CDC research indicates that "contributing to a worker's dissatisfaction with his (her) job are conditions such as work overload, lack of control over the job, nonsupportive bosses and colleagues, limited job opportunities, undefined tasks, rotating shifts, and operating at a machine-set pace."[17]

Stress is of such a concern in businesses that many organizations hire psychologists to work with their employees, offer stress-relief workshops, organize stress reducing recreation programs for employees, and allow time off, when necessary, to prevent employee burn-out due to overwork and pressure.

Stages of Stress

☐ When under stress the body usually reacts in three stages.

Stage 1: Alarm—the hormones are released which increase heartbeat and respiration, raise blood sugar levels, cause muscle tension, dilate pupils, and slows digestion.

Stage 2: Resistance—if the stress is overcome, the body repairs itself and the physical signs of stress disappear. If stress continues, the body remains alert and moves toward step three.

Stage 3: Exhaustion—the body is unable to handle the stress and succumbs to fatigue and stress-related diseases appear—headaches, heartbeat irregularities, constipation, or diarrhea. If stress is prolonged or severe, mental illness, ulcers, heart attack, or diabetes may result.[18]

Reacting to Stress

☐ If you are confronted by a stressful situation, you can *fight*—attack the person or thing causing the stress, take *flight*—retreat from the person or thing, or *stand fast*—do not give in or attack and stand your ground. These responses may be external physical reactions such as hitting or swearing (fight), or running away (flight), or they may be internal. Examples of internal reactions include suppressing the desire to take some external action, and physical reactions such as an increase in blood pressure or a slowing of the digestive process.

Remember, stress is not always bad for us. Stress can add excitement and vitality to our lives. What is negative is the way in which we handle the stress. If we internalize it and force ourselves to get ill, or if we are overly sensitive to every possible stressful situation, stress becomes counter-productive. Some people thrive on stress, finding that stress alerts them and makes them operate on a higher level.

Dealing with Stress

☐ When stress occurs, ask yourself these questions: "Do I have control, or is the control in the hands of someone else?" "Is this worth dealing with?" "Is this situation important to achieving my personal or professional goals?" "Is attempting to deal with the event more stressful than the event itself?" "Are the benefits greater than the energy I have to expend?"

A psychological approach to staying healthy centers on the Key of *C*:

Choice—try to choose between options, if possible. Think of new ways of approaching the problem, realize that often you and you alone control your choices.

Challenge—recognize that different people have different perceptions of situations; your perception and someone else's perception may not be the same. That does not make either of you right or wrong. It is not necessary for someone to have to win.

Commitment—in the final analysis there is only one person you have to please:

yourself. Keeping this in mind may keep you from being manipulated by others for their purposes.

There are some methods for handling business-related stress:[16]

1. Do one thing at a time. Focus on what you do. Do not look back or ahead while you are working.
2. Do the best you can and don't worry about the outcome.
3. Don't worry about things over which you have no control.
4. When a crisis occurs, face it. Take constructive action and organize a response. Be flexible.

Controlling Stress

☐

These are some things you can do to control stress:

Recognize your limitations. Yes, there are things you cannot do. There is nothing wrong with that. You also cannot please everyone.

Be honest as to why you stay in a stressful situation. Is that friendship really a sharing relationship? Can you find a job that will better serve your needs?

Fight for those things you value, but take flight from those that require more energy than they are worth. Is this issue important enough to expend the emotional and physical energy required?

Strive for what you, not society regards as worthwhile.

Rid yourself of the toxic people in your life. Not everyone deserves your respect and loyalty, they should earn it by being a positive rather than a negative factor in your life.

Set priorities for managing your time. What must be done and what would you like to do. They may not be the same.

Organize your time into three categories. First, tasks that must be achieved for personal or professional goals. Second, tasks that are important to other people, or those you just want to do. Third, tasks that are not important to your personal or professional goals and that you don't really want to do anyway.

Consider yourself first in your life as long as your actions are not harmful to others. Be friends with yourself, act and react based on your needs as you determine them, not on what others expect your needs to be. Pamper yourself if no one else does.

Consider changing your eating habits. Foods can encourage stress. Sugar, artificial colors, white bread, alcohol, and drugs can create chemical inbalances. Smoking, although thought to be relaxing, is actually stimulating.

Occasionally get away from it all.

For short-term relaxation, a clinical psychologist suggests you do one of these: a) Clench your fists tightly and count to ten. Release and let your whole body go completely limp. b) Take a deep breath and hold it while counting to ten. When you exhale, let it all out at once and let your body go completely loose and limp. c) Breathing normally, let go more and more as you let out each breath, while counting slowly from ten to zero, one number per breath. d) Imagine yourself basking in the warm sun on a beach or soaking in a hot tub until you can actually feel the warmth.[19]

You can systematize stress management by identifying:

- the cause of the tension or stress;
- how you would like it to be different;
- what you have tried that did not work;
- what is to be gained by keeping the situation in its current state;
- available alternatives;
- what you plan to do about it.

When all else fails, remember: don't sweat the small stuff. It is *all* small stuff. If you can't fight and you can't flee, . . . flow![20]

SUMMARY

In this chapter we have examined the communication which takes place within you—intrapersonal communication. The major concepts presented were:

Intrapersonal communication is the name given to the processing of internal messages, or communication within the self.

Self-concept represents your psychological self—all the experiences, beliefs, attitudes, and values that make up the self; it includes how you perceive the world, how the world perceives you, and how you perceive yourself.

The four components of self are: spiritual self, material self, social self, and the bodily self.

The more positively an individual regards his/her personal attributes, the more likely it is that that individual will not have to fight off negative feelings which block meaningful actions.

Communication anxiety causes people to believe that they have more to lose than to gain from communication.

Communication anxiety can be treated by systematic desensitization, cognitive modification, skills training, and self-help.

Individuals draw conclusions from the information they receive.

Factors that negatively affect reaching conclusions are distortion, perceptions, stereotypes, and experience.

Stress is the body's response to the demands made upon it which usually results in physical and emotional tension.

Stress can be dealt with through recognition and action.

THINGS TO DO

1. On a sheet of paper complete these statements. Write the first thing that comes into your mind:

I am . . .   I am a . . .
I would like to be . . .   I perceive myself as . . .
I believe others see me as . . .   I don't like to . . .
                              When I get angry I . . .

Read over your answers. Write a two-sentence summary that includes the ideas you have expressed. In their book *Monologue to Dialogue,* Brown and Keller indicate that we are what we are, based on our verb *to be.*[21] Discuss this statement as it applies to your two-sentence summary of self.

2. Using pictures, drawings, and magazine or newspaper clippings, make a mosaic (a composite made of overlaying artwork) illustrating the attitudes, beliefs, and values you have. Discuss your mosaic with the class from the standpoint of what effect this could have on you as a businessperson.

3. You were given a name at birth. You are to rename yourself. Do not use a traditional name (Marcia, Brad, Brooke, Eric): rename yourself by drawing a picture or writing several words that describe the *real* you. Place this new "name" on a three-by-five card. The class will be divided into dyads (two people). Each person is to ask his or her partner a series of questions about the drawing. Try to find out as much as you can about your partner. The dyads are now combined into groups of four. Each person is to introduce his or her partner to the other dyad. Following the introductions, answer the following questions, which will be used as the basis for a class discussion. How did it feel to have someone talk about you? Did the person say anything that made you feel sad or glad? What does the symbol you chose say about you as a person? What are the effects of labeling?

4. Perceptions Test. [22]

Answer each of these questions (T) true or (F) false.

    a. It is unlikely others will work to see things as I do to try to understand me. On the other hand, they will expect me to do so.

    b. People normally perceive their own behavior as being both consistent and logical.

    c. A high correlation exists between how accurately we perceive ourselves and our ability to perceive others accurately.

    d. People tend to see and hear only what is significant to them.

    e. The more secure and self-fulfilled a person is, the more effective he or she will be in correctly perceiving and accepting reality.

    f. It is unlikely other people will exert themselves to understand new ideas or to see both sides of a difference in opinion when they are personally involved in the disagreement.

After you have completed the test your instructor will give you the answers. Hold a class discussion concerning the answers.

5. Questionnaire.

Directions: This instrument[23] is composed of twenty-four statements concerning your feelings about communication with other people. Please indicate, in the space provided, the degree to which each statement applies to you by marking the number of whether you (1) Strongly Agree, (2) Agree, (3) Are Undecided, (4) Disagree, or (5) Strongly Disagree with each statement. There are no right or wrong answers. Many of the statements are similar to other statements. Do not be concerned about this. Work quickly—just record your first impression. After you have filled out this questionnaire your instructor will inform you of how to score it and the meaning of the score.

_____ 1. I dislike participating in group discussions.
_____ 2. Generally, I am comfortable while participating in group discussions.
_____ 3. I am tense and nervous while participating in group discussions.
_____ 4. I like to get involved in group discussions.
_____ 5. Engaging in a group discussion with new people makes me tense and nervous.
_____ 6. I am calm and relaxed while participating in group discussions.
_____ 7. Generally, I am nervous when I have to participate in a meeting.
_____ 8. Usually, I am calm and relaxed while participating in meetings.
_____ 9. I am very calm and relaxed when I am called upon to express an opinion at a meeting.
_____ 10. I am afraid to express myself at meetings.
_____ 11. Communicating at meetings usually makes me uncomfortable.
_____ 12. I am very relaxed when I answer questions at a meeting.
_____ 13. While participating in a conversation with a new acquaintance, I feel very nervous.
_____ 14. I have no fear of speaking up in conversations.
_____ 15. Ordinarily, I am very tense and nervous in conversations.
_____ 16. Ordinarily, I am very calm and relaxed in conversations.
_____ 17. While conversing with a new acquaintance, I feel very relaxed.
_____ 18. I'm afraid to speak up in conversations.
_____ 19. I have no fear of giving a speech.
_____ 20. Certain parts of my body feel very tense and rigid while giving a speech.
_____ 21. I feel relaxed while giving a speech.
_____ 22. My thoughts become confused and jumbled when I am giving a speech.
_____ 23. I face the prospect of giving a speech with confidence.
_____ 24. While giving a speech I get so nervous, I forget facts I really know.

NOTES

1. Richard Weaver, *Understanding Interpersonal Communication* (Glenview, IL.: Scott, Foresman and Company, 1978), 14, 39.
2. Roy Berko, Andrew Wolvin, and Darlyn Wolvin, *Communicating: A Social and Career Focus* (Boston: Houghton Mifflin, 1977), 128.
3. Charles Brown and Paul Keller, *Monologue to Dialogue,* 2nd ed. (Englewood Cliffs, NJ.: Prentice-Hall, 1979), 29.
4. "State Fright, Reticence, Communication Apprehension, Shyness and Social Anxiety: Competing or Compatible Constructs?" (Panel discussion, Speech Communication Association convention, November 3, 1985, Chicago, IL.).
5. Charles V. Main, "Helping Shrinking Violets Blossom," *American Way* (December 1982):50.
6. Ibid., 55.
7. Tapes include: "Deep Muscular Relaxation," by James McCroskey, West Virginia University, and "Speech Anxiety Reduction," by Joanna Pucel, St. Cloud State University.

8. Books include: Philip Zimbardo, *Shyness* (Reading, MA: Addison-Wesley Publishers, 1977); and Gerald M. Phillips, *Help For Shy People* (Englewood Cliffs, NJ: Prentice-Hall, 1981).

9. DeVito, Joseph, *The Communication Handbook: A Dictionary* (New York: Harper and Row, 1986), 224.

10. E. Frank Harrison, *The Managerial Decision-Making Process* (Boston: Houghton Mifflin, 1975), 168.

11. *The Real Security,* a film distributed by BNA Communications, 9401 Decoverly Hall Road, Rockville, MD 20850.

12. Brent Ruben, "Stress, Interpersonal Communication, and Assertiveness: Marshmallows, Machine-guns, and Target Shooters," (Paper presented at the Eastern Communication Association Convention, Pittsburgh, PA, 1981), 2.

13. Kennedy, Joyce Lain, "Here is How to Cope with Stress on the Job," *Cleveland Plain Dealer,* 14 August, 1988, 25.

14. Ruben, 2.

15. Ibid.

16. Kennedy.

17. Robert Byrd, "Job Stress Illness Up," *Washington Post,* October 3, 1986, F-2.

18. Beverly Byrum-Gaw, *It Depends* (Palo Alto, CA: Mayfield Publishing Company, 1981); Philip Zimbardo, *Shyness* (Reading MA: Addison-Wesley Publishers, 1977).

19. Dr. Alfred Barrios, clinical psychologist.

20. "Stress-Anxiety-Depression: C and T Unit Can Help with the Flow," *Profile,* Nord Community Health Center, Lorain, OH, volume 1, number 3, September 1984.

21. Brown and Keller, *Monologue to Dialogue,*

22. Dr. Walter John, Director of Training, Friendly Ice Cream Corporation.

23. PRCA, used with the permission of Dr. James McCroskey, West Virginia University.

3

☐

Listening

OVERVIEW
Listening is a critical skill that can be observed at all levels in an organization. The process of listening involves a sequence of interrelated stages. Depending on our purpose, we listen on various levels. Many people are not very effective listeners, but acquiring new listening techniques can help them to improve.

KEY WORDS

listening environment
listening
stimulus
auditory stimuli
visual stimuli
attention span
perceptual filter
storage
feedback
discriminative level

comprehensive level
therapeutic level
critical level
appreciative level
self-concept
buzz words
inciting words
inferential message
egospeak
paraphrasing

Effective listening has come to be recognized in American industry as one of the keys to improved productivity. "Listening was judged to be one of the super critical skills needed by people for organizational success."[1] Poor listening can be costly: "With more than 100 million workers in this country, a simple $10 mistake by each of them, as a result of poor listening, would add up to a cost of a billion dollars. And most people make numerous listening mistakes every week."[2]

Recognition of the significant role of listening in the organization is highly warranted. American workers spend a great deal of time as listeners. It has been determined that adults spend 42.1 percent of their communication time in listening, in contrast to 31.9 percent in speaking, 15 percent in reading and 11 percent in writing.[3] "Results from professional, technical, administrative and clerical people in a communications and research and development laboratory show that 50%–80% of the workday is spent in communicating . . . ," the majority of which was speaking and listening.[4]

The important role of listening can be seen at all levels in an organization. An individual must listen to the boss, fellow employees, peers, customers, suppliers, stockholders, community leaders, professional educational groups, labor unions and leaders, government officials, and communication media.[5]

Employees are encouraged to improve listening skills so that they can function effectively on the job. Indeed, listening is one of the most important communication behaviors an effective subordinate can have.[6] Likewise, managers are encouraged to attend to their listening skills: "an otherwise excellent manager may not be truly effective unless he [or she] is a good listener."[7] And the chairman of the Sperry Corporation illustrates the commitment to effective listening at the executive levels. He insisted that listening had to become part of Sperry's overall business philosophy, which included spending corporate funds on the "We Understand How Important It Is to Listen" advertising campaign.[8]

Eight areas of listening which affect productivity in an organization have been identified:

1. Sales people listening more carefully to customers and prospects.
2. Customer service representatives listening to customer complaints and problems.
3. Managers and supervisors listening to subordinate problems, suggestions, and solutions.
4. Groups listening for mutual understanding in order to coordinate their efforts.
5. Employees feeling they have value as individuals because they have listeners.
6. Listening to suggestions of all those involved in both producing and receiving goods or services in order to improve the quality.
7. Expanding the capacity of all persons in the organization to understand, assist, and work more effectively with others.
8. Improving the employment selection process and reducing costly turnovers through more careful listening.[9]

LISTENING ENVIRONMENT

The **listening environment,** where listening takes place as well as the atmosphere created, is an important aspect of listening in an organization. Managers must, "create an environment where listening is cherished—and opportunities for structured and unstructured listening are rife. Listening means managers listening to their people, of course. And it means teammates listening to each other."[10]

Building a listening environment in an organization can be a difficult task. Research shows that listening in the work environment is a complex activity. Factors causing listening difficulty include time pressures, interruptions, ongoing relationships, previous encounters, message sending, and perceptions.[11]

Perceptions of effective listening are important to the creation of a supportive climate in an organization and to overcoming some of the organizational problems associated with poor listening such as interpersonal conflict, low morale, and poor attitudes. One management consultant who specializes in developing listening programs for managers suggests that "individuals who listen to their fellow workers create a supportive organizational climate characterized by information-sharing and trust."[12]

An organization can provide a solid listening environment by: (1) providing a forum for listening; (2) creating a physical location for listening; (3) encouraging feedback and reinforcement; (4) providing listening training; (5) giving employees frequent opportunities for listening; (6) adopting the positive attitude that listening is valuable.[13] Some corporations are serious about developing a listening environment, particularly when it comes to listening to their customers. Apple Computer Corporation, Campbell Soup, Control Data, Ford Motor Company, and Stew Leonard's Supermarket are examples of corporations that have realized increases in productivity and quality after they developed strong and supportive listening environments.[14]

Individuals who listen to others help create a supportive environment in the organization. (H. Armstrong Roberts)

LISTENING PROCESS

■

Listening can be explained as an active process in which we attempt to grasp the facts and feelings of what we hear and see. The process of listening involves a sequence of interrelated stages which may occur simultaneously.

Motivation

☐

At the outset, the listener must have the motivation (desire) to listen. Since humans do not have a specific drive for effective listening, it is necessary to generate self-motivation to listen. Good listeners find it helpful to emphasize to themselves the importance of listening in a particular situation, to know what they are doing as listeners, and to establish their own objectives (as correlated to the speaker's purpose) for the listening experience.

Receiving the Stimulus

☐

The motivated listener then must receive the stimulus. The auditory reception of the **stimulus** (the message) is a detailed process. The listener receives not only **auditory stimuli** (vocal input) but also **visual stimuli**—the speaker's facial expression, posture, movement, and appearance. A prominent researcher estimates that as much as 93 percent of the total meaning of a message can result from the visual, nonverbal cues.[15] Sensitivity to nonverbal cues can enable the listener to understand and to interpret the speaker's intended meaning more precisely. If a supervisor, listening to a line-worker's suggestions, drums her fingers on the desk while she says "That's a very interesting idea," there is reason to believe that the nonverbal action may, in fact, be indicating something totally different from the verbal message.

Attending

☐

After the message has been received through auditory or visual channels, it must be attended to through the memory system by which we store information. In attending, the listener focuses on the auditory stimulus, the visual stimulus, or both, and concentrates on the message received in order to store it for later use.

While there is disagreement as to how the memory system—that part of the brain that receives and holds the information—biologically operates, it is agreed that it is affected by the attention span. The **attention span** (the length of time a person can or will pay attention) is quite limited. Part of this restriction may be caused by environmental factors. For example, "it's entirely possible that our capacity for sustained attention and deliberate thought is being altered by television viewing."[16] People raised in the television generation have come to expect a seven-to-ten minute program format with time out for a commercial break. This shortened attention span may affect our capacity to listen to speeches, to participate in conversations, and generally to function as listeners in all settings.

Perception

Attention to the message is affected by the listener's memory system and by the perceptual filter. The **perceptual filter** screens the stimulus so that one's predispositions alter the message received. The listener's background, experiences, roles, and mental and physical states influence perception, suggesting there is truth to the old adage, "We see and hear what we want to see and hear."

Interest

Another attention factor is our interest or our willingness to receive the message. You may not be interested in the message if the topic doesn't seem relevant to you, the presentation is boring, or it is lacking in humor. Studies suggest that "the louder, the more relevant, the more novel the stimuli, the more likely they are to be peceived by the listener."[17] To make a sale, a salesperson has to find out what will engage the listener with the message and then must maintain the customer's attention.

Interpreting
☐

Once the message has been received by the listener through the auditory, visual, and attention processors, the message must be interpreted by the listener. Interpretation involves fitting the verbal and nonverbal messages into the proper linguistic categories which have been stored in the brain, and then analyzing the messages for their meanings. This decoding system varies according to an individual's perceptual filters and the category system, so the orginal intent of a speaker's message may become distorted, misinterpreted, and changed as the listener's meaning is assigned. A salesperson may find that if she attempts to sell a copy machine to a person who is strongly in favor of "buying American," she will be unsuccessful if she even suggests that a Japanese product is better than one made locally. The intended purchaser may interpret the sales person as being "anti-American" and thus distort any message received after reaching this conclusion.

Responding
☐

After a message has been interpreted by the listener, he or she must respond to it by reacting in some way. This response may be in the form of storage or feedback.

Storage

The receiver may put the information in **storage** by placing the ideas into the memory for future recall. Though we are not exactly sure how the memory works, remembering is often aided by making a mental image of what has been received, tying the idea to something already remembered, letting a fact trigger memories of other facts, or mentally summarizing what is read.

Feedback

Such an internal response may also couple with an external response; the listener may send **feedback** (a form of response) to the speaker. This feedback might take the form of requests for further information or clarification ("Can you give me an example of that?"); positive support for the speaker's message ("That is a good idea."); disagreement with some part of the information ("I don't believe your statistics are right."); or, a therapeutic response which encourages the person to continue ("I'd like to hear more about that.").

LEVELS OF LISTENING

Clearly, listening is a complex process which involves concentration and retention of the message throughout the stages of the communication. The complex listening process occurs on various levels depending in large part on the speaker's intended purpose. Consequently, we listen for different reasons.

The reasons for listening describe the different levels of listening. Listeners function to discriminate, comprehend, provide a therapeutic response, critically evaluate, or appreciate a message.

Discriminative Listening Level

A person may listen at the **discriminative level** for the purpose of distinguishing sound (or visual) differences. An industrial worker or auto mechanic often has to listen discriminatively to the sound of his or her machinery to know if it is functioning properly. Persons trained as security officers quickly learn visual discrimination of suspicious individuals through nonverbal cues such as walk, stance, eye shifts, and gestures.

Comprehensive Listening Level

Much of the listening we do is at the **comprehensive level.** The listener's objective is to understand the material. This requires that you listen objectively to the entire message for understanding—not for evaluation of what is transmitted. A good comprehensive listener will discriminate to determine what is important to remember, what is needed to clarify, or what is irrelevant. Then, he/she will work for retention of the relevant information. Listening to briefings, conference reports, training instructions, or directions all entail clear, comprehensive listening in a business environment.

Therapeutic Listening Level

You may find yourself, as a coworker or even as a supervisor, sometimes listening at the **therapeutic level.** The therapeutic listener provides a sounding board for a person to talk a problem through to a solution. A good manager should try to understand an employee's problems by being a supportive therapeutic listener.

Non-directive Therapeutic Listening
In non-directive therapeutic listening the receiver suspends all judgment and does not evaluate what is being said. He/she allows the sender to reach his/her own solution.

A supervisor who must discuss an employee's series of errors, for example, may want to listen non-directively as the employee talks out the problems related to the job and suggests ways in which he or she can improve.

A key to non-directive therapeutic listening is listening with empathy: understanding where the other person is coming from by imagining yourself in the other person's place. A non-directive therapeutic listener must have faith that the person can solve his/her own problem and must also have the time available to seriously attend to the other person.

Directive Therapeutic Listening

Sometimes it is necessary for the therapeutic listener to become actively involved in the help-process. Some psychologists and counselors believe that once a person has recognized he/she has a problem, the individual may need help in finding and reaching a satisfying solution. In these cases, directive therapeutic listening takes place when the listener suggests solutions, alternate behaviors or ways in which to put a possible solution into action. Of course, all of this is dependent upon the person wanting to make behavior alterations or changes.

Directive therapeutic listening is most effectively done by persons, such as psychologists, counselors, and counselor-supervisors, specifically trained in intervention therapy. No matter how well intentioned, those not trained to aid individuals in working through a problem or toward reaching a workable course of action, can often do more harm than good when they attempt to be helpful. Many would-be counselors fail because they want to give advice when they are not equipped to do so.

Critical Listening Level

☐ The **critical level** of listening centers on understanding a message and then evaluating it. To determine whether to accept or reject a message, a listener needs to have standards of judgment in order to do a careful analysis of the strengths and weaknesses of a position or decision. These standards can come from an understanding of the persuasive process and the development of a persuasive proposition by reasoned arguments, psychological appeals, and the expertise of the speaker. The key to critical listening is to test any persuasive proposition by asking if the recommendation is reasonable and expected. These answers come about by analyzing the arguments, appeals, and motives of the speaker. Though it is difficult, setting aside preconceived ideas or biased attitudes can help you listen more objectively to the ideas being presented.

You may have to listen critically in order to evaluate a briefing that advocates a new policy or procedure, to weigh the relative merits of solutions proposed in a staff meeting, or to assess whether or not to purchase a particular new word processing system for the office.

Appreciative Listening Level

☐ A person may listen at the **appreciative level** to gain pleasure or a sensory impression from the material. Noontime concerts in the employee cafeteria, movies sponsored by the Human Resources Department, or after-dinner speeches are just some of the occasions where a person might listen appreciatively in a business setting.

Each person will have different appreciative responses, depending on his or her interests and experiences as they relate to the material.

LISTENING PROBLEMS

■ Many people are not very good listeners. It is estimated that we miss (do not effectively receive and process) approximately three-quarters of what we listen to.[18] Five primary causes for ineffective listening can be identified: biological reasons, negative self-concept, not understanding that meaning is within the listener, a lack of understanding of how to listen, and poor listening training.

The Biology of Listening

☐ We can listen and think three to four times faster than the average person can speak.[19] Recent studies indicate that with no great difficulty an individual can receive information at about 500 words per minute.[20] In rapid conversation, people speak about 200 to 250 words per minute, and the normal public speaker, newscaster, or lecturer speaks between 100 to 200 words per minute.[21]

Since speakers are presenting material at a much slower rate than the listener can receive and process, our minds have time to wander; to tune in and to tune out. In addition, our attention is not a continuous thing; it is often broken. Estimates are that we can only attend to one source of stimuli for only a few seconds, and twenty seconds at the most.[22]

The listener is further affected by his or her physical or psychological state at the the time of the listening event. It is apparent that how you feel physically, for example, can affect your listening proficiency. If you have a headache, it will be much more difficult to concentrate on the message. Likewise, the listener who is worried about some problem will find concentration to be that much more of a challenge.

These biological and psychological factors can result in daydreaming, letting other stimuli attract our attention, turning off the listening process, and sometimes being distracted enough not to tune back in.

Negative Self-Concept

☐ **Self-concept,** the way we perceive our self, can have an effect on our listening. A positive or negative self-concept undoubtedly influences an individual's listening habits. We tend to be reminded, throughout life, of our poor listening skills. We are seldom reinforced for positive listening behaviors. As a result, people probably are conditioned, at an early age, to view themselves as poor listeners. We hear messages from parents, teachers, friends, such as "your're not listening to me"; "be quiet and listen"; and "why don't you ever listen to me?" Such messages reinforce our belief that we're not very effective at listening. If you assume that this is true, you can quickly gain the attitude that you really can't listen very well and, therefore, don't need to expend the effort to correct bad habits or improve your listening skills. Persons at all levels of management in organizations have come to perceive themselves as poor listeners—often because no one ever suggested that they might be otherwise.

In addition, persons who do not perceive themselves positively may be so concerned about what they are doing wrong, or worry that others may not like them, or of doing or saying the wrong thing, that they are side-tracked from attending to the message being sent.

Meaning Within the Listener

☐

Understanding the intended meaning in a message requires an understanding of the meaning of the verbal and nonverbal symbols being sent. Sometimes the listener must deal with **buzz words:** words that may interfere with your ability to listen if you are not familiar with them. Each organization and field of specialization (such as accounting or public relations) has its own internal jargon—terminology—for specific functions, and it is necessary to learn how to use these words in the proper context. Further, the listener's processing of the intended meaning can be affected by symbols serving as emotional triggers (**inciting words**) that sound an internal alarm and evoke an emotional response from the listeners. "Pink slip" has come to be associated with "being let go" or "fired," so listeners might be "set off" with the use of such a phrase. And the listener might find it useful to sort out the factual information presented in a message as distinguished from the **inferential message** which is assumed and not necessarily based on fact. The employee who reports on "pink slips" might be reporting inferences rather than facts, creating all sorts of needless emotional turmoil.

The basis for any effective communication is the development of a relationship between the sender and the receiver. A communication barrier is very likely to arise if the sender does not realize the receiver is incapable of receiving the message being sent or if the receiver does not give the sender feedback to indicate that the message has not been received. The sender must constantly be aware of to whom he or she is speaking, the nature of topic, and where the communication is taking place. Then the sender must try to figure out if the terms being used, in the context in which they are being used, will carry the intended meaning of the message to the receiver. The receiver, on the other hand, must assume the responsibility for giving feedback, verbally or nonverbally, to the sender if the listener does not understand the way the message is being sent or the language used.

Since our backgrounds and experiences are different, it must be understood that meaning is found within the communicators themselves and not in the words or gestures being sent. In order to be effective, the message must be decoded as closely as possible to the meaning of the original encoded message.

If, as the receiver, you do not understand the message, and do nothing about it, you are displaying poor listening skills. More important, you may get fired, lose a promotion, or spend hours doing incorrect work.

Not Understanding How to Listen

☐

Many of us have not been taught principles of listening. When we entered school, the teachers knew we could not read, so they taught us. We could not write, so they proceeded to work on that skill. We were capable of hearing, so the unfortunate assumption was also made that we could effectively listen. Because of this, many individuals never really learned how to listen. Few schools offer direct instruction in listening. The International Listening Association, however, is providing the impetus for creating greater academic interest in the subject. The two-year advertising campaign by the Sperry Corporation, "We Understand How Important It Is To Listen," generated considerable corporate interest in training employees, managers, and executives in listening behavior. We often are not even aware that we are not listening effectively because we may not know what effective listening is all about.

Poor Listening Conditioning

☐

Some of us are conditioned not to listen—not at all or only on a specific cue. If you were never put in a position of having to respond to what you listened to, you may have formed the attitude that it is unimportant to listen. If you were told to do something, but the request was not followed up, or you assumed that nothing would be done if you didn't follow the directions, then you might have formed the attitude that effective listening is irrelevant. After enough of these experiences, we conclude that it is senseless to listen.

Have you ever been engaged in communication with someone, but the person did not seem interested in whether you were really processing the information? Or, how attentive are you when you find that others are only speaking to "hear themselves talk"? Enough of these experiences may result in an attitude of "Why bother to listen?" or "Why listen if nothing will come of it?"

How many times have you heard, "I'm only going to tell you this twice," or "I'm going to give you the directions and then repeat them"? Both of the phrases say, "Don't listen the first time." How about "This is the last time I'm going to say this"? That statement means "Now is the time to listen; those times before when I gave the directions were really not important." These experiences encourage us to avoid paying much attention to the message sent.

Organizations have come to recognize the consequences of poor listening training (and the resulting lack of understanding on the part of people as to how to listen effectively). Corporate and governmental organizations have developed in-house training programs for improving the listening skills of employees, managers, and executives. A survey of the status of listening training programs in the Fortune 500 corporations indicated that training directors perceived the lack of training and information about listening—and the lack of feedback on listening skills—to be a major problem area in their organizations.[23] Based on this study, and corporate self-perceived needs, many organizations have instituted listening improvement programs.

IMPROVING YOUR LISTENING

■

Can anything be done to improve a person's listening abilities? Yes! First we must recognize that listening is hard work, and that it takes effort. We should also understand that we must listen beyond the bottom line. Just listening for the general trend may not be enough in many instances.

Following are some characteristics of effective listening. Mastering them and putting them into effect should improve your listening skills.[24]

A good listener is prepared to listen. You cannot hear a turned-off radio or television—how do you expect to hear a turned-off speaker? Turning the speaker on is the first step to listening. Be mentally and physically ready to participate in the communication. And set an objective, a purpose for your listening. Make a conscious effort to listen!

A good listener is aware that listening is a two-sided experience. We often listen only to what we think the message is, rather than taking into consideration who is sending it, the conditions under which the message is being sent, and the purpose behind the message.

A good listener allows the entire message to be received. How often have you interrupted when you thought you had the general idea of the message, only to find out that it was not what the speaker intended? Have you filled out applications without listening to the directions and found that you actually did not do the right thing? Listen to the whole—part may not be enough.

A good listener suppresses what he/she wants to say until it is his/her turn to speak. Persons who interrupt conversations suffer from what is called egospeak. **Egospeak** is the "art of boosting your own ego, by speaking only about what you want to talk about, and not giving a hoot in hell about what the other person is speaking about."[25] If you attempt to communicate with an egospeaker, you quickly learn that the person really is not interested in what you are saying. Comments you make are met with "That's OK, but what happened to me was. . . ." or "You think that's something, well I. . . ."

Are you an egospeaker? If so, you really are not listening; you are only waiting for the other person to pause so that you may jump in.

A good listener is conscious of inciting words. There are words that "set us off," carrying explosive meanings, and make us react without giving the speaker a chance to be heard. We often have to keep our control and listen to the message so as not to lose the context of the idea because of inciting words. If someone, for example, uses an obscenity, do you turn off the entire message? Do words like "made in Japan," "corporate takeover," "utility company," or "credit risk" carry implied meanings that cause you to stop receiving or to make immediate assumptions?

A good listener controls distractions. Is the person seated next to you talking? Can you hear the speaker? No? Do you do anything about it? If not, you are asking for listening problems.

Sometimes it is necessary to close windows, move closer to the speaker, or ask someone to keep quiet. If you cannot receive the message because of a distraction you could adjust, but do not, then you are encouraging poor listening.

A good listener anticipates the subject and the speaker. Listen and try to think ahead. The biological studies we referred to earlier in the chapter indicated that you have a lot of extra time when you are listening. Keep your mind alert and active—anticipate what is coming. A well-organized speaker will give you clues. Listen for phrases such as, "the next major idea is . . ." or "there are five steps to the process"; each of these tells you how to listen.

One of the joys of reading a murder mystery is to try to figure out what's coming next. Listening to a speaker can offer the same kind of exercise for sharpening concentration skills.

A good listener creates a need to listen to important things. Are you going to have to make a report to other employees based on this presentation? Must you know the information the sales manager is presenting? The speaker is boring! So what? You must know the material, so you are going to have to force yourself to break the boring-barrier and listen. Take notes—force yourself to listen—do not allow yourself to turn off. An analogy to a car might clarify this concept. We, like the car, cannot do all of our activities in the same gear. Sometimes we have to shift gears, that is, shift our listening attention. If you find it necessary to really listen to someone, shifting into a posture with your feet on the floor, while looking directly at the person, will allow you to concentrate your attention on that person and key in on his/her verbal as well as nonverbal symbols and actions.

Sometimes we have to shift into reverse and go back over material. This might mean you have to ask a question about material you didn't grasp or understand.

A good listener often paraphrases what has been said. By repeating, to either yourself or the other person, what the sender has just said, you are making sure that you understand it as well as allowing the other person to correct your feedback. This practice forces you to listen intently as you know you will have to feed the message back to the source. It also makes the source feel that he/she is important to you as you are really listening to what he/she is saying, and thus may create a better relationship between you.

A good listener monitors the way he/she listens. Did you catch yourself slumping down in the chair? Are you aware that you are counting the holes in the acoustical tile of the ceiling? Do you know that you have not listened to anything the speaker has been saying? If not, you are not monitoring your listening. Be aware; keep alert. Monitoring your own listening behavior may be difficult and distracting at first. But you should find that you can increase your sensitivity to your own listening responses and therefore improve your listening skills.

A good listener realizes the need to develop a method of remembering.[26] Do you often think that you are really listening, but just can't remember what has been said? There are ways to improve your comprehension.

Taking notes, for example, forces you to paraphrase. **Paraphrasing** causes you to rethink the material as you write it. This is especially true if you put it into your own words rather than writing down exactly what the speaker has said. If you can't write down what was said, you probably don't understand it or remember it.

Another device is to associate what is being said to something with which you are already familiar. Make a mental image. If the computer installer is teaching you to operate some new equipment and uses the word "dumping," you might visualize the material being thrown into a can for later retrieval. This word picture might later trigger your memory of the procedure you were taught.

Still another device is to tie the new fact to something already remembered. For example, if you are trying to remember that the twenty-first Amendment ended Prohibition, remember that the traditional drinking age is twenty-one, and tie the two together.

A good listener works to improve his/her listening behavior. Individuals who work at listening, taking the time and trouble to systematically identify their listening problems and then consciously strive to overcome those problems, are on their way to improved skills as listeners. Awareness of listening behavior is really the first step, an awareness you have achieved through reading this chapter on listening. But don't stop here. Now work individually and with your coworkers, your classmates, or your family members to become more efficient, more responsive, and more sensitive as a listener by putting into effect some of the skills to which you have been exposed.

Listening is vital in the world of business and organizations. Good listening abilities and habits are often the basis for promotions, sales, and the respect of your superiors and your peers. A good communicator is both a good speaker *and* a good listener.[27]

SUMMARY

In this chapter you have been introduced to the complex communication process of listening. Since a person spends so much time as a listener, it is important to work to develop skills to listen effectively.

Listening plays an important role in the functioning of any business or governmental organization.

Listening involves the motivation to listen, reception of the message, interpretation of the meaning, and response.

We listen for discrimination, comprehension, in order to provide therapeutic response, critical judgment, or for appreciation.

A good listener is prepared to listen, is aware that listening is a two-sided experience, allows the whole message to be received, suppresses what he/she wants to say until it is his/her turn to say it, is conscious of inciting words, is aware that posture may affect listening, is aware of the need to control distractions, anticipates the subject and the speaker, creates a need to listen to important things, paraphrases, monitors the way he/she listens, and works to improve his/her listening.

THINGS TO DO

1. Select a period of one-half hour in which you will be involved in a situation that will require you to be an active listener (a business meeting, a class, a lecture, or a series of telephone conversations). Monitor your listening patterns. Keep a log of your patterns. Do you egospeak? Are you daydreaming? Are you being distracted but do nothing about it? The class will have a discussion based on each student's experiences.

2. Your instructor will play the tape *Listening Is Good Business* by Ralph G. Nichols[28] or show the film *The Power of Listening*.[29] Use this as the basis for a discussion on the importance of listening in business.
3. Your class instructor or a guest speaker will present a lecture about a business communication topic. Take notes on the lecture. Following the presentation, members of the class will share their lecture notes. What were the major points made? Did you all agree on them? Did you take too few or too many notes? What is the relationship of note taking to listening?
4. Make a list of words that incite you. Share them with the class. Discuss what makes a word evoke strong reaction.
5. Observe the listening pattern of a group (your family at dinner, people in your office, or members of your class in a scholastic or social setting) for a period of one-half hour. What patterns did you notice? What advice could you give them, based on your reading of this chapter, to improve their listening patterns?
6. A. Read the statements below. Indicate whether you thoroughly agree, agree, disagree, or thoroughly disagree with each.

   1) Corporations have a major responsibility to their investors to make as much profit as they can no matter what they have to do to make those profits.
   2) Employees should be hired for life into an organization as is done by many Japanese companies.
   3) Unions have outlived their usefulness as a viable force in the American labor movement.
   4) Automobile manufacturers should be made liable for financial payment to all individuals injured in any accident caused by a malfunctioning auto which is under warranty.
   5) Businesses that have government contracts should be required by law to have female executives in direct numerical proportion to the number of women in the society.

   B. Your class will be divided into groups of five to seven students. Each group is to discuss the topics so that all members of the group either thoroughly agree, agree, disagree, or thoroughly disagree with each statement. You may alter the wording to help you reach a conclusion. As you discuss, before you give your point of view you *must* paraphrase what the person before you said. The group is to yell "foul" each time a person speaks without paraphrasing.
   C. After completing part B, discuss the advantages of paraphrasing as a process in group action and in effective listening.

NOTES

1. Vincent S. DiSalvo, "Listening Needs in the Work Force" (Paper presented at the International Listening Association Summer Conference, July 1984), 2.
2. "Secrets of Being a Better Listener," *U.S. News and World Report* (26 May 1980): 65.

3. Paul T. Rankin, "Listening Ability: Its Importance, Measurement and Development," *Chicago Schools Journal* 12 (1930):177–179.
4. E. T. Klemmer and F. W. Snyder, "Measurement of Time Spent Communicating," *Journal of Communication* 22 (June 1972):142–179. Other research supports Rankin's conclusions about the prominence of listening. See, for example, J. Donald Weinrauch and John R. Swanda, Jr., "Examining the Significance of Listening: An Exploratory Study of Contemporary Management," *Journal of Business Communication* 13 (February 1975):25–32; and Elyse K. Werner, "A Study of Communication Time" (M. A. thesis, University of Maryland, 1975).
5. Ernest Parker Mills, *Listening: Key to Communication* (New York: Petrocelli Books, 1974), 5. See also John L. DiGaetani, "The Business of Listening," *Business Horizons* (October 1980):40–46.
6. Cal W. Downs and Charles Conrad, "Effective Subordinancy," *Journal of Business Communication* 19 (Spring 1982):27–38.
7. Sherman K. Okum, "How to Be a Better Listener," *Nation's Business* (August 1975):59.
8. Susan Mundale, "Why More CEOs Are Mandating Listening and Writing Training," *Training/HRB* (October 1980):37.
9. Frank Cancelliere, "Listening: Key to Productivity," *Connections* (November 1983):43.
10. Tom Peters, *Thriving on Chaos* (New York: Alfred A. Knopf, 1988), 305.
11. Marilyn H. Lewis and N. L. Reinsch, Jr., "Listening in Organizational Environments," *Journal of Business Communication* 25 (Summer 1988): 63.
12. Judi Brownell, "Perceptions of Listening Behavior: A Management Study," (unpublished study, Cornell University, 1988), 28–29.
13. Peters, 306–307.
14. Ibid.
15. Albert Mehrabian, *Silent Messages* (Belmont, CA: Wadsworth, 1971), 43.
16. Dorothy Singer and Jerome Singer, "Is Human Imagination Going Down the Tube?", *Chronicle of Higher Education* (29 April 1979): 65.
17. Larry Barker, *Listening Behavior* (Englewood Cliffs, NJ: Prentice-Hall, 1971), p. 31.
18. Ralph G. Nichols and Leonard A. Stevens, *Are You Listening?* (New York: McGraw-Hill, 1957), 107.
19. *The Power of Listening*, a film, CRM McGraw-Hill Films, LaGrange, IL 60525.
20. *The Power of Listening*. Also see Weaver, *Understanding Interpersonal Communication*, 99.
21. Charles T. Brown and Paul W. Keller, *Monologue to Dialogue* (Englewood Cliffs, NJ: Prentice/Hall, 1979): 63–64. See also Norbert Wiener, *Cybernetics* (Cambridge, MA: MIT Press, 1961), and *The Human Use of Human Beings* (New York: Doubleday and Company, 1954).
22. Brown and Keller, *Monologue to Dialogue,* 63–64. See also Wiener, *Cybernetics,* and *The Human Use of Human Beings*.
23. Gary T. Hunt and Louis P. Cusella, "The Status of Listening Training Programs in Selected Fortune 500 Organizations: A Preliminary Report. (Paper presented at the International Listening Association Conference, Denver, 1981). See also Gary T. Hunt and Louis P. Cusella, "Listening Needs in Organizations: An Exploratory Study" (Paper presented at the Eastern Communication Association Convention, 1983).
24. *The Power of Listening,* and Weaver, *Understanding Interpersonal Communication,* pp. 112–115; also Roy Berko, Andrew Wolvin, and Darlyn Wolvin, *Communicating: A Social and Career Focus,* 4th ed. (Boston: Houghton Mifflin, 1989), Chapter 4.

25. Edward Addeo and Robert Burger, *Egospeak* (New York: Bantam Books, 1974), xiv.
26. Jay Samuels, University of Minnesota, as quoted from "Memory Drawer Needs Only Order, Prof Says," *Cleveland Plain Dealer,* January 1985, 2B.
27. Vincent DiSalvo, D. C. Larsen, and R. Seiler, "Communication Skills Needed by Persons in Business Organizations," *Communication Education* 25 (November 1976):270–275.
28. Ralph Nichols, *Listening Is Good Business* (St. Paul, Minnesota: Telstar Productions), Audio tape.
29. *The Power of Listening.*

4

Verbal Language

OVERVIEW   Language is central to your ability to communicate and is based on a system of symbols and rules. Standard American English is the dialect of English which most Americans speak. The major language problems that result in misunderstandings are making assumptions, failing to be clear and concrete, using inference when fact is called for, and failing to understand. Both written and spoken language is meant to accomplish the same goals but the styles of written language and oral language are not the same.

KEY WORDS
language
syntax
semantics
dialect
Standard American English
linguistic racism
intra-dialect alienation
assumption
clarity
concreteness
denotation

connotation
fact
factual statement
inference
inferential statement
phony fancies
nounery
passive voice
wasted words
sexist language
pro-social language

The world as you know it today would not be possible without the presence of language. You use language to express yourself and to elicit responses from other people. Language is a social tool through which you interact with others.[1] Language is central to your communication.

Besides your own use of language, the sophistication of a society is often dependent on the sophistication of the language spoken in that society. Because language is the way in which we think as well as communicate, the more complex the language, the more likely it is that the participants in that society can accurately describe, explain, and develop concepts, and invent new ideas.

When you speak, you usually intend to communicate to your listener. Often, instead of understanding, conflict and confusion result because of the use of language. This is not the fault of the language; language is imprecise since what is meant by the sender may not be what is understood by the receiver. In communication there are no mistakes, only outcomes. If, for example, you use the word "powerful" to describe a new idea that a co-worker has proposed, that person might take the word to mean "it's a good idea." A bystander might assume that you indicated the idea is too strong and, therefore, not good. A third receiver might assume that you were being sarcastic and were putting the idea down, rejecting it. Which of the receivers is correct? Only you know what you really meant. The others are interpreting based on their use of the language, or making assumptions about your use of the terms based on past experiences with you and the language you use.

LANGUAGE DEFINED

■

Language is the structure system of symbols that catalog the objects, events, and relations in the world. Most languages use **syntax** (grammar rules) and **semantics** (words) to set up a structure which helps to make sense of what is said and heard or written and read.[2]

Since language is symbolic and rule based, the study of language involves the study of meanings—the meanings of speech sounds used as arbitrary symbols and agreed upon markings that divide the symbols into groups. The arbitrary symbols in English are the 26 letters of the alphabet. These are combined to create words. For example, the letters *b u s i n e s s* have been grouped together to represent an organization that carries on a form of activity that supplies commodities or services. Any combination of letters could have been assigned to represent that meaning; however, those eight letters were selected.

The markings that have been agreed upon to divide the symbols into groups are called punctuation. Thus, a sentence, a unit of speech consisting of a meaningful arrangement of words, may be indicated by the use of a period at the end of the group of words. For example, there is a period at the end of the sentence, "The business is a success since it made a profit last year." Other marking symbols in our language include the comma, question mark, colon, and semi-colon. Each has a specific purpose in helping the reader understand the language presented in written form. Though not as readily apparent, you also punctuate as you speak. As you speak, you stop and breathe

People use language in different ways depending on their background and experiences. (© Laimute E. Druskis)

at the end of sentences, raise your voice at the end of questions, and pause briefly to set off ideas in a series. These actions are verbal punctuation marks.

Since your level of thinking is greatly dependent on your language competence, the more developed your language skills are, the more advanced you will be in processing information. Since speech is habitual, automatic, and ingrained, the major factors influencing language learning are your physical ability to do so, and the influences that surrounded you. Individuals born with normally functioning senses (such as the eyes, ears, and mouth) and cortex (the section of the brain where communication is processed) learn language in a fairly standard way. As a child you were spoken to or overheard others speaking. Eventually, you absorbed the symbols of your society and started to use the language. How proficient you have become is based on a combination of your biological instruments, the amount and quality of the language that surrounded and continues to surround you, and your ability to practice the language.

DIALECTS
■

A **dialect** is a social or regional variation of a language. Over long periods of time, dialects may develop into separate language. For instance, French, Italian, and Spanish were original dialects of Latin.[3]

There are hundreds of dialects in use in America. Each of the dialects is an equally viable, linguistically sophisticated mode with the potential for expressiveness. The only difference among the dialects lies in the situation in which each is most appropriately used.[4]

Standard American English

☐ "**Standard American English** (SAE) is the dialect of English which most Americans speak."[5] Some individuals believe that SAE is the only correct language and that it should be the only language spoken in the United States.

Why is Standard American English the dialect of choice? Through linguistic analysis we can ascertain the norm or standard of usage in any given language community. "A dialect is regarded as standard when it has acquired such prestige that its use is considered essential to professional performance for social and economic advancement. . . . Nonstandard dialects are viewed as lacking this prestige."[6] It should be understood that in this context the term nonstandard is not equated with substandard but simply means "different from the standard."

Linguists agree that three basic reasons explain why a society should have a single dialect.[7]

1. A standard dialect serves the social function of binding people together and creates a common bond for interaction and identification for society members.
2. Individuals having influence and responsibility will be able to communicate clearly to those whom they influence. Since Standard American English is the medium used in communicative environments such as business, industry, and government, this is the form both the employer and employee is expected to use in order to communicate with others.
3. There must be a common means of technique and learning. A language mismatch causes misunderstanding and learning problems.

Nonstandard Dialects

☐ Many nonstandard dialects stem from imported servile classes such as indentured laborers from Hawaii or slaves from Africa. In other instances dialects are a means of expression with a familiar foreign language framework. For instance, Spanglish (a blending of Spanish and English) and Jewish (a blending of Yiddish—a European, Germanic-based dialect—and English) are foreign language deviations. Dialects also arise when a learner in a subcultural group is isolated from users of the standard dialect. Such an example in the United States would be the Appalachian dialect which evolved because individuals living in the mountainous areas of West Virginia had sporadic contact with mainstream Americans. In addition, dialects may be regional, reflecting speech patterns developed in a geographic area, such as Brooklyneese or Bostonian.[8]

All language systems are perfectly adequate for communication by the members of the group using the dialect. We learn the dialect we have been exposed to and use the dialect common to those with whom we identify. Therefore, it is easily understood why many African Americans speak Black English, or why Hispanics speak Spanglish.

Problems may emerge when the speaker attempts to interact with members of other groups. "Often the use of a dialect causes linguistic racism. **Linguistic racism** is characterized by a negative stereotypical response to users of nonstandard dialects. It is based on the assumption that such persons are inherently inferior to users of the standard form."[9]

Research shows that there are social and professional disadvantages of speaking some dialects. "The speaker must come to grips with a dilemma: if he/she is to succeed in this society, he/she must cultivate the complementary use of Standard American English in situations in which it is to his/her advantage to do so."[10] But, the non-standard speaker must also be aware that **intra-dialect alienation** may occur when the minority member chooses to reject a "native" dialect in favor of the standard dialect. Such a person is often described as "putting on airs," and can become a victim of alienation from the native community.[11]

PRINCIPLES OF LANGUAGE MEANING

The basic principles which describe language and its meanings include:

1. *Meanings are found in people, not in the symbols of a message.* Words have no meaning in and of themselves; they only take on meaning as individuals assign meaning to the combination of letters. Therefore, two people from different backgrounds may decode a symbol in different ways.

2. *Meanings are learned.* Meanings are a function of personal experience. As we learn our language, imitating how those around us use the language, we also learn the meaning of symbols. For example, what is a pencil? You probably would describe a pencil as a cylinder of wood or plastic encasing a piece of graphite which is used for writing. How do you know that? In all likelihood, someone either held up the object and said, "This is a pencil," or, someone asked you to hand them the pencil and then described it if you didn't understand the request. Someone, somehow, shared the meaning of the word with you and you acquired the knowledge of that symbolic meaning.

3. *We learn words and acquire their meanings by perceiving new words in relation to other words, objects, or perceptions for which we already have meanings.* In other words, we build meaning upon meaning. If, for example, you didn't know what a cylinder or graphite was, the description of the pencil would have little meaning.

4. *People can have similar meanings for words only if they have had similar experiences, or can anticipate similar experiences.* As two people communicate, they will only understand each other if they can agree on the meaning of the terms being used. If I speak only French and you speak only German, no matter how hard we try, easy and efficient communication will be impossible. Let's assume that the word "poke" means a light jab to you. If I'm a southerner, poke probably means a brown paper bag. Therefore, you are going to have difficulty understanding my irritation when you hit me after I've said, "Give me a poke," and I'm going to be surprised by your actions.

5. *To give people a meaning, or to change their meanings, you must pair the meanings with identifications for which they already have an understanding.* Basically, if you want someone to understand you, then you must use language they understand or clarify by using definitions or examples which are part of their background.

PROFLEMS IN COMMUNICATING

The major language problems that result in misunderstandings in communicative messages are making assumptions, not being clear, failing to be concrete, using inference for fact, and not understanding the differences between written and oral language.

Assumption

Some people think assumptively. The **assumption** is that when they tell a listener something, they have given the message to the receiver, and that it has been received and understood. This is not always true. The receiver must receive and decode the message, and then translate what has been sent into the intent of the sender.

There are flaws in assumptive reasoning on the part of the sender since the receiver may be incapable of or unwilling to gain the intent of the message. First, the receiver may not be listening effectively. The listener may be daydreaming or not paying attention. Second, the listener may not want to receive the message. For example, if there is a negative relationship between the sender and receiver, the receiver may not want to listen to what the sender has to say. Third, biases may stop the receiver from decoding the implied meaning of the message. For example, if the sender is discussing the positive effects of changing the equal opportunity hiring practices of a business and the receiver has strong racial or ethnic biases, the message will probably not receive a fair hearing. Another reason for the lack of sender-receiver clarity is the very nature of language. Different people perceive messages in various ways depending on their backgrounds. For example, if an accountant is attempting to explain certain aspects of the financial status of the company to a new employee who has little accounting training or experience, the employee may not understand the technical terms used.

Clarity

Clarity, making something clear and understandable, is a necessity of effective communication. To ensure clarity, the sender should be certain that the receiver will be able to grasp the intent of the information. In order to comprehend it is important that the language used is not beyond the receiver's understanding. In addition, it is necessary to add details and use examples.

In adding details the sender should include all information necessary for comprehension. For example, notice how in this series of statements the addition of details makes each statement clearer than the preceding one:

> George bought his own business.
> Yesterday, George bought his own business.
> Yesterday, George bought his own insurance company.
> Yesterday, George bought his own Nationwide Insurance Agency.
> Yesterday, George bought his own Nationwide Insurance Agency in Baltimore, Maryland.

For clarity, it is necessary to use understandable terms rather than abstract ones. Experts often forget that others are not knowledgeable in that activity's terminology.

Doctors and lawyers may confound us with terms that are meaningless from the layperson's viewpoint. Accountants may use "number talk" that is beyond the average person. Computer experts have taken "computer talk" and incorporated it into our language in ways that confuse many people. Unless you are familiar with computers you may be unable to decode such terms as *graphic-user interface, reboot,* and *shareware,* which are supposed to be *user friendly.*

Businesses have become aware of the need to encourage clients to understand their messages. For example, since 1987 Ford Motor customers are finding a new document in the glove boxes of their new Ford, Lincoln and Mercury cars—a plain English version of the company's Warranty Information Booklet. Designed to be easy to use and to understand, the booklet was designated by Ford as part of its campaign to rewrite the company's documents in plain English. The company's booklet used to say, "CLAIMS PROCEDURE—To obtain service under the Emissions Performance Warranty, take the vehicle to a Ford Motor Company dealer as soon as possible after it fails an I/M test along with the documentation showing the vehicle failed an EPA-approved emissions test." The present booklet states, "How do you get service under the Emissions Performance Warranty? To get service under this warranty, take your car to a Ford Motor Company dealer as soon as possible after it has failed an EPA-approved test. Be sure to bring along the document that shows your car failed the test."[12]

Some people, businesses, and government agencies confound rather than clarify by using terms that seem to mean one thing when, in fact, they may be understood to mean something else. Or, they use terms that are so unclear that there is no way to understand. For example, in describing a possible dangerous meltdown at nuclear plant, a company referred to it as an "unscheduled event." A lawyer, in order to avoid biasing the jury, referred to his client's mistress as his "long-time companion." A government workers' pay raise was announced as a "salary adjustment" in order to soften the public's negative reaction. A shovel is worth about $9.95, but a "displacement instrument," at least according to the Pentagon, is worth $85.00. A funeral director still performs the same duties, even if the person's identification image has been changed by the use of the title "grief therapist." The point is clear—clarity is the result of using clear, understandable language.

Concreteness

☐

Concreteness means being specific rather than abstract; being real rather than artificial. Concrete language attempts to describe specific experiences and behaviors. In order to develop concreteness, one needs to add details to a general statement. For example, rather than making the general statement "Sarah did well on the job last year," use a statement which is more concrete such as, "Sarah did well on the job last year which can be shown by her sales increase and the award she received for having the highest number of customer courtesy reports." Instead of the general statement, "I had a good time at the banquet," a concrete statement would be "I had a good time at the banquet since most of my friends were there, the food was delicious, and the keynote speaker talked about my favorite subject—salesmanship!"

In developing concreteness, awareness should be paid to the difference between concrete and abstract terms commonly referred to as *denotations* and *connotations*. **Denotation** is "referential meaning; the objective or descriptive meaning of a word."[13] Business examples of denotative terms, words that have a concrete dictionary definitions, include: computer, file folder, debit, and advertisement. **Connotation** is "the feeling or emotional aspects of a word's meaning, generally viewed as consisting of the subjectivity and evaluation (for example, the good-bad, strong-weak, fast-slow dimension); the associations of a term."[14] Examples of connotative words used in business include: integrity, valuable, and efficient. These words all need clarifications and examples to understand the user's intent.

Fact Versus Inference

☐

A **fact** is that which has been proven, usually through scientific investigation, or has been deemed true because of long-term acceptance. Examples of factual statements are "Two parts of hydrogen and one part of oxygen, when combined, result in water," and "George Bush was inaugurated as the 41st President of the United States in January, 1989." A **factual statement** is "a statement made after observation that is limited to what has been observed."[15]

Inference is the passing from one judgment to another, or from a belief or cognition to a judgment. An example of an inference is, "Since pollution causes public health hazards, any business that is convicted of any type of polluting should be closed down." The speaker bases the final statement on a leap of belief based on the original statement.

An **inferential statement** is "a statement that can be made by anyone, is not limited to the observed, and can be made at any time and about any time (past, present, or future)."[16] An inferential statement was made in *Time* magazine's 1989 inauguration issue when the writer stated, "George Bush is more sensitive and caring than Ronald Reagan, more of a hands-on administrator, and a more accessible leader."[17] There is no fact presented, just inference.

Unfortunately, in communication, some people use factual and inferential statements interchangeably. If this is done intentionally, it is, of course, unethical. On the other hand, sometimes it is done naively, with no intention to confuse or underhandedly convince the receiver. Listeners must always be aware of the possibility of inference being passed along as fact.

Ethical and responsible speakers who are aware of the difference between fact and inference will introduce inferential statements with identifying phases such as, "I believe," or "I think," or "It seems to me."

Distinguishing Facts and Inference

Understanding the difference between factual and inferential statements can help you to acknowledge when you or someone else is using one or the other. Understand that one type of statement is not necessarily better than the other. "We need both types of statements; both are useful, both are important. The problem arises when we treat one type of statement as if it were the other. Specifically, the problem arises when we treat an inferential statement as if it were a factual statement."[18] Table 4.1 illustrates the differences between factual and inferential statements.

TABLE 4.1 □   Differences Between Factual and Inferential Statements[19]

Factual Statements	Inferential Statements
1. may be made only after observation	1. may be made at any time
2. are limited to what has been observed	2. go beyond what has been observed
3. may be made only by the observer	3. may be made by anyone
4. may only be about the past or the present	4. may be about any time—past, present, or future
5. approach certainty	5. involve varying degrees of probability
6. are subject to verifiable standards	6. are not subject to verifiable standards

WRITTEN AND SPOKEN LANGUAGE

■

"For many people in the world today, language still exists only in its spoken form. Writing is a way of representing something that could be spoken. Writing is therefore a secondary way of representing language; it is not an alternative way. Written forms cannot exist apart from the spoken forms on which they are based; spoken forms can exist whether or not they are written. This is not intended to deny the usefulness of writing. It is simply intended to emphasize the proper relationship between speaking and writing."[20]

Written and spoken languages are meant to accomplish the same goals—to develop ideas, inform, and persuade. However, the styles of written language and spoken language are not the same because one is meant to be read and the other to be heard. These differences are found in both the semantics and the syntax.

Spoken language is aimed at immediate understanding. The listener must be able to grasp ideas as they are presented. The receiver has no opportunity, as he or she may have when reading, to go back and re-examine the material.

Research shows that spoken language uses significantly more personal references, more personal pronouns of the first-person and second-person singular and plural, shorter thought units, more word repetition, more monosyllabic words, and more familiar words.[21]

In order to use language clearly you must be aware that your word choice will affect your listener. Being aware of and avoiding phony fancies, nounery, passive voice, and wasted words[22] will improve your speaking and language usage.

Phony Fancies

□

Phony fancies are fuzzy words or expressions used to sound important, impressive, or knowledgeable—often when you're feeling none of the three! They're phony because they masquerade as communication. In fact, instead of transmitting meaning, they obscure it.

Examples of phony fancies and some clear and simple alternatives are:

Phony Fancy	Clear Alternatives
for the purpose of finding	to find
in reference to	about
pertaining to	about
prior to	before
due to the fact that	because
in the event that	if
in the majority of instances	usually

Nounery

☐

Nouns are used to describe an event or a process, explain how to do something, ask for something to be done, or put forth a concept or theory. **Nounery** is the overuse of nouns. Often we use noun clusters, expressions of two words or more that consist entirely of nouns, but could be expressed in one word. Businesses use these phrases often to hide real meaning or to sound knowledgeable. Examples of noun clusters are employment termination (firing), cost impact consideration systems (price), and profit margin reduction (loss).

Another form of nounery is turning verbs into nouns. Examples of noun-to-verb nounery are: he exhibits a tendency to (he tends), allow me to express my appreciation (I appreciate), and let us take into consideration (let's consider).

Nounery can also be created by turning nouns into verbs. Examples are: to automatize (automation), to prioritize (priority), and to result in (result).

In order to replace nounery, use verbs as much as possible. Verbs are active, living words that tell the listener what happened, not what resulted. And, if you find yourself using verbs ending with *ize,* or two nouns grouped together, be aware that you are not using clear and simple English.

Passive Voice

☐

A common fault in using vocabulary when speaking is to employ the passive voice. In life, people or events cause things to happen. **Passive voice** avoids using the specific names of the person or people who brought about the action. The passive voice is a hedge. It is usually used when the speaker wants to avoid taking responsibility or to pass the buck.

Examples of passive voice and the problems it causes include:

It is recommended that a fan pump be installed on No. 9 machine. Who is making the recommendation? Who is to take the action?
Last week a memo was sent out to all members of this department. Who sent the memo? It is much clearer to say, *Last week I sent you a memo.*

There is an obvious clarity and responsibility difference between *We came to the conclusion that* and *I believe that.*

Avoid the passive voice by using active verbs that tell what you or others have done in specific terms and specific identifications.

Wasted Words

☐   **Wasted words** are those terms used in communication that do not meet the listener's needs. They don't clarify, explain, interest, or intrigue. They add nothing to the listener's pleasure or understanding. In fact, they usually get in the way of clarity.

Examples of wasted words and how to replace them include:

Wasted Words	Replacement
each and every man and woman	everyone
few in number	few
and so as a result of	and so
never at any time	few
advanced planning	planning
first priority	priority
end product	product
he was assertive by nature	he was assertive
the point is that we are already overstaffed	we are overstaffed
we have a problem with this media thing	we have a problem with the media

Avoiding wasted words, the extra words, often forces you to say what you mean much more clearly.

FEMALE-MALE LANGUAGE AND COMMUNICATION

■   The last decade has seen a change in the American business. More and more women have been entering the work-force at levels equal to or exceeding those of men. Before the increase in the number of women executives, male language patterns dominated the upper echelons of most organizations. Yes, women were present, but often in secretarial or low-level administrative jobs. The influx of women has prompted the investigation of an important aspect of business interaction—communication and language.

An analysis of female-male language has several facets. First is the question of whether or not Standard American English is, in fact, sexist. Other apsects are how males and females use language and how usage affects the business and organization participant.

The Sexism of Standard American English

☐   "Psychologists believe that roles are patterns of expectation by the self and others about appropriate behavior of an individual in a given social setting. Those roles are learned by means of our symbolic interactions, through which we also acquire the norms of culture and society. They are defined in the language of the society and once we acquire them, we believe in them."[23]

If language reinforces the concept that there are certain male roles, and other females roles, and if you think of people only in terms of he and him, then you assume certain things about yourself and others. If the assumption is that males are dominant and females are subordinate because the pronoun he is used to refer to all people—including all leaders and influential people, then males learn to play their dominant role and females submissive roles. If the assumption is that all repairmen, mailmen, and truck drivers are male, and that nurses and secretaries are female, then a child quickly learns both prescribed and proscribed roles.

English, for many years, was clearly a **sexist language.** It ignored women by referring to all individuals as *him,* it defined women by specific roles, and it put women in categories that differed from those attainable by males.

"The masculine-gender pronouns that eighteenth century grammarians used when they set up the rules of grammar did not reflect a belief that masculine pronouns could refer to both sexes. They reflected the cultural reality that males dominated society."[24] The word **sexism** was coined in the 1970s with the growth of a Women's Liberation Movement which had as its purpose the achieving of equal rights for women. An important part of this movement was the desire to change language by recognizing the equality of women. The attempt was not always met with agreement and admiration. In 1972, *Time* magazine termed the attempt to remove sexist references from the language "Ms-guided."[25] Proponents of non-sexist terms were booed and asssured that they couldn't legislate language change. In spite of the negativism, "In the past decade there has been a mini-reformation of the language that has surpassed the expectations even of many feminists."[26] By the mid-1970s neuter terms such as *firefighter (fireman)*, *camera operator (cameraman)*, and *humanity (mankind)* started to replace sex-specific terms. These terms still may not be the language of the majority, but they have become common where once they seemed awkward. Interestingly enough, though it is hard to prove that it is the result of the movement, there has been an increase in the number of females fighting fires, serving as police officers, and repairing telephone lines.

Major linguistic sources have acknowledged the sexism of our language and have taken actions to change it. *The Associated Press Stylebook,* the guide used by many newspapers, now offers such warnings as, "copy should not express surprise that an attractive woman can be professionally accomplished, as in: 'Mary Smith doesn't look the part but she's an authority on. . . .'"[27] And the *Dictionary of Occupational Titles* was revised in 1977 to delete potentially discriminatory job titles.

"The current movement for language change has been in process for nearly two decades. There is some consensus about acceptable changes, but no full agreement among people outside of the academic world about the effects of 'he/man' language and women's self-esteem and on men's perceptions of women."[28] It is generally accepted, however, that language can affect learning, career development, and personal well-being.

Male and Female Language and Language Usage

Do men and women use language differently? The answer, according to numerous communication researchers, is a resounding yes. "Many casualties in the war between the

According to many researchers, men and women use language differently. (Zefa/H. Armstrong Roberts)

sexes results from a failure to realize that men and women actually speak different languages."[29]

Research concerning language styles shows that *men* are likely to:[30]

use more obscene expressions and expletives
use more commanding language
use dominant language
include content that deals primarily with tasks
use competitive and sports-oriented language
use language which treats people as part of a team or a system
make direct assumptions more often than ask questions
use words like *can* and *will* rather than indirect forms such as *might*
use terms that refer to self more than to the listener
focus on goals, plans, or accomplishments rather than anxiety, doubts, or personal
    limitations
use nonstandard speech for emphasis
use words that confront the listener if necessary

Women are likely to:

be more grammatically correct

use more **prosocial language** ("language that displays behavior that benefits others rather than the person performing the behaviors and may even involve personal risk or loss"[31]

use more submissive language

turn statements into questions or make them indirect statements

use tentative phrases such as *I guess* or *Don't you think?*

emphasize feelings and relationships

focus on identity and relating more than on the physical and technical features of task achievement

react with respect for, or deference to, the listener

allow options other than their own

use indirect verb forms such as *might* or *would* more than *can* or *will*

make few bald assertions

qualify statements with adjectives or adverbs such as *very, kind of, possibly,* or *really*

use standard speech and rarely use nonstandard or taboo words

An examination of a specific instance should help to show the differences between the way males and females tend to use language.

Situation: A recommendation is to be made by one organization to another company. The course of action is being discussed.

A woman might say, "Don't you think it would be better to send them the report first?" It would not be unusual for a male to follow her statement by stating, "Yes, it would be better to send the report first." Others at the meeting would come away, therefore, with the impression that it was the man's idea because the woman never really directed the action.

If the first speaker was a man, he would probably say, "It would be better to send that report first."[32]

This example, of course, is dependent upon the people involved and their following the norms as revealed by the research. It will be interesting to see if future research shows (due to the competitive nature of business and industry, the increase in the number of women in the board room, and the evolving role of women) a change in the traditional language roles of the sexes.

Language is a fundamental part of communication, and is therefore an important part of business. Business people must be aware that in order to be effective in their careers, they must use language effectively. Employee promotions are often based on their communication skills. Sales and service result from communication. Studies show that as much as 92 percent of a chief executive's time is spent in communication and 60 percent of first-line managers time is spent communicating.[33] Without the ability to select and use language effectively, much of the time spent in business communication will be wasted.

SUMMARY

In this chapter we have examined verbal language. The major concepts discussed were:

The world as we know it today would not be possible without the presence of language.

In communication there are no mistakes—only outcomes.

Language is the structure system of symbols that catalog the objects, events, and relations in the world.

Languages consist of syntax and semantics since they are symbolic and rule-based.

A person's level of thinking is greatly dependent on his or her language competence.

A dialect is a social or regional variation of a language.

Standard American English is the dialect which most Americans speak.

All language systems are perfectly adequate for communication by the members of the group using the dialect.

Linguistic racism is characterized by a negative stereotypic response to users of nonstandard dialects.

Meanings are found in people, not in the symbols of a message.

Meanings are learned.

We learn words and acquire meanings for them by perceiving a new word in relation to words, objects, or perceptions for which we already have meanings.

People can have similar meanings for words only to the extent that they have had similar experiences, or can anticipate similar experiences.

To give words a meaning, or to change their meanings for others, you must pair the meanings with identifications for which the receivers already have an understanding.

Assumptions, clarity, concreteness, fact, and inference are important concepts in language effectiveness.

Both written and spoken language are meant to accomplish the same goals, however the styles of written language and spoken language are not the same.

Standard American English is a sexist language.

Males and females use language in different ways.

THINGS TO DO

1. Find an article, advertisement, or employment announcement which is sexist. Rewrite the piece to eliminate the sexism.
2. Adjust these phrases and sentences so they are gender-free:
   a. mankind
   b. the common man
   c. The average student is worried about his grades.
   d. mailman
   e. As a teacher, he is faced daily with the problem of paperwork.
   f. Each student will do better if he has a voice in the decision.
   g. authoress
   h. male nurse
   i. The class interviewed Chief Justice Burger and Mrs. O'Connor, the woman Supreme Court justice.

j. Both Bill Smith, a straight-A sophomore, and Kathy Ryan, a pert junior, won writing awards.

k. This is a man-sized job.

3. Write each of the following sentences using the concept of clarity presented in this chapter. (You may make up additional information to achieve your goal.)

   a. Barbara did a good job on that financial report.

   b. Business is great.

   c. My college's business curriculum covers my future needs.

   d. The instructor is interesting.

4. Do you feel that individuals in this country who speak dialects have disadvantages in the business world?

5. Do you agree with the following statement? Be prepared to defend your answer. All language systems are perfectly adequate for communication by the members of the group using the dialect.

6. A recent newspaper article was entitled, "Now Men are Riled in Backlash Over Sexist Language." The contention expressed by this and other sources is that the issue of sexist language is not relevant and there is nothing wrong with American English as it has been used for hundreds of years. Do you agree with this contention?

7. Give an example of linguistic racism you have experienced or know about.

8. Do you believe, from observation or personal experience, that intra-dialect alienation exists? If so, what are the ramifications of intra-dialectic alienation?

9. Be prepared to give a personal example illustrating each of these concepts:

   a. Meanings are found in people, not in the symbols of a message.

   b. Meanings are learned.

10. Give a personal example which illustrates that you were affected by assumption, clarity, concreteness, and confusion of fact and inference.

11. Identify whether each of the following statements is fact or inference:

   a. My secretary is lazy.

   b. My boss is the most wonderful person in the world.

   c. My supervisor is always trying to see if she can catch me not working.

   d. You weren't working late at the office last night, I called and there was no answer.

   e. You weren't working late at the office last night, I called and your secretary said you had left a half-hour before. She said you told her you were going out to dinner.

   f. My boss is rich; he lives in an expensive condo.

   g. Your secretary is subordinate. She doesn't contribute any ideas during staff meetings.

   h. We tested the secretary and she can type 79 words per minute.

   i. The union officers are out for themselves.

   j. Ms. Jones isn't interested in my ideas, she never takes notes when I am speaking.

k. The company's financial report indicates that they made a profit last year.
l. People don't like me because I'm a foreigner.
m. The consultant's report recommends we use "Word Perfect" as our company's word processing program.

NOTES

1. Blaine Goss, *Processing Communication* (Belmont: Wadsworth, 1982), 55.
2. Joseph DeVito, *The Communication Handbook: A Dictionary* (New York: Harper and Row, 1986), 176.
3. Ibid., 94–95.
4. Delorese Tomlinson, "Bi-Dialectism: Solution for American Minority Members," *The Speech Teacher* 24 (September 1975):234.
5. Ibid., 232.
6. Charles Harpole, "Eric Report: Nonstandard Speech," *The Speech Teacher* 24 (September 1975):226.
7. Tomlinson, 234.
8. Ibid., 232.
9. Ibid., 232.
10. Ibid., 233.
11. Ibid., 235.
12. Lee Gray, "Ford Offers a Readable Warranty Booklet," *Simply Stated . . . In Business* 18 (March 1987).
13. DeVito, 93.
14. Ibid., 76.
15. Ibid., 113.
16. Ibid., 155.
17. "A New Breeze is Blowing," *Time* (30 Jan. 1989): 18.
18. DeVito, 113.
19. Ibid., 113.
20. B. L. Pearson, *Introduction to Linguistic Concepts* (New York: Alfred Knopf, 1977).
21. Lois Einhorn, "Oral and Written Style: An Examination of Differences," *Southern Speech Communication Journal* 43 (Spring 1973): 306.
22. Cheryl Reimold, *How to Write a Million Dollar Memo* (New York: Dell, 1984), 31.
23. Roy Berko, Andrew Wolvin, Darlyn Wolvin, *Communication: A Social and Career Focus,* 4th edition (Boston: Houghton Mifflin, 1989), 169.
24. Carolyn Bocella Bagin, "Are All Men Equal? The Generic Dilemma," *Simply Stated* 62 (January 1986): 1.
25. Mary Schnuch, "This Ms-Guided Language Succeeds," *Atlanta Constitution* 9 (Aug. 1983): 3B.
26. Ibid.
27. Dr. Jerie McArthur, as quoted in "Garble Gap: Men, Women Just Don't Talk the Same Language," *Cleveland Plain Dealer,* March 31, 1984, B-1.
28. Barbara Bate, *Communication and the Sexes* (New York: Harper and Row, 1988), 102.
29. Dr. Lillian Glass as quoted in "Garble Gap: Men, Women Just Don't Talk the Same Language," *Cleveland Plain Dealer,* 31 March 1984, B-1.
30. Bate, 95.
31. DeVito, 240.
32. McArthur, B-4.
33. "Career Readiness: Perceptions of Business Communication" (Faculty Development Improvement Grant, Youngstown State University): 1.

5

Nonverbal
Communication

OVERVIEW Knowingly or unknowingly, people communicate on several different levels at the same time. These levels are verbal and nonverbal. Nonverbal communication is all message sending and receiving not manifested by words, spoken or written. Our nonverbal patterns come from hereditary and environmental influences. The nonverbal channels are kinesics, vocal cues, proxemics, physical characteristics, artifacts, aesthetics, and chronemics. Every culture has its own body language.

KEY WORDS

verbal communication
nonverbal communication
Neurolinguistic Programming
cybernetics
substituting relationship
complementing relationship
regulating relationship
conflicting relationship
clusters
congruency
nonverbal channels
kinesics
emblems
illustrators
affect displays
regulators
touch

vocal cues
paralanguage
proxemics
intimate zone of space
personal zone of space
social zone of space
public zone of space
privacy space
physical characteristics
artifacts
aesthetics
Behavioral Kinesiology (BK)
chronemics
hyperkinetic
hypokinetic
action chain

In the field of business we are constantly communicating both verbally and nonverbally.

Knowingly or unknowingly, people communicate on several different levels at the same time. Most of us, however, are usually only aware of the verbal dialogue and don't realize that we are responding to both verbal and nonverbal messages. In the field of business we are constantly communicating both verbally and nonverbally.

Verbal communication consists of the words we use, while **nonverbal communication** is all message sending and receiving not manifested by words, spoken or written.

Even though you may not be totally aware of your nonverbal message sending and receiving, nonverbal communication does exist. In contrast to verbal dialogue, however, we do not have a dictionary for totally understanding the rules. We now know that "All of us communicate with one another nonverbally, as well as with words. . . . We gesture with eyebrows or a hand, meet someone else's eyes and look away, shift position in a chair."[1]

One expert in the field hypothesized that "more than two-thirds of oral communication is actually nonverbal or communication dominated by the visual clues."[2] There even has been a formula developed to explain the impact of a message: "Total impact of a message = 7 percent verbal + 38 percent vocal + 55 percent facial."[3] Still the experts suggest that, statistically, 35 percent of the social meaning of a message is carried verbally, while more than 65 percent is conveyed nonverbally.[4]

Why, then, are many people unaware of the impact of nonverbal communication? "Most people are unaccustomed to paying attention to their bodies when speaking, and they will frequently send out a huge array of neutral or flatly contradictory signals."[5] In addition, much nonverbal communication is below our level of actual awareness, both as senders and receivers. For example, how aware are you of what your hands are doing while you speak, or the position of your body, or the way you are walking? Do you really pay attention to the exact pitch or volume of your voice, or where your eyes are looking? We may be very selective about the words we speak, but just "do what we are doing" with our bodies without even thinking about it. Yet, "each person is just as responsible for his/her nonverbal actions as for the word used."[6] In fact, if the evidence is right, "Body signs—visual communication—can reveal more about what you are thinking than what you are actually saying—or oral communication."[7]

Actions speak louder than words, and nowhere is this more evident than in the way nonverbal communication can make or break a negotiation or business transaction. It's generally recognized that people who know how to read and use body language are more effective than those who do not.[8]

SOURCES OF NONVERBAL COMMUNICATION

Neurolinguistic Programming is an "attempt to codify and synthesize the insights of linguistics, body language, and **cybernetics** (the study of communication systems)."[9] From the results of neurolinguistic studies it can be concluded that we gain our nonverbal communication patterns from hereditary and environmental influences.

Hereditarily, we find ourselves responding to and communicating in various situations with such physical responses as eye blinks, facial flushes, and body tightening. A pebble hits the window as you are driving; you duck. A loud sound is heard; you may tighten up your body. Your boss says something that irritates or embarrasses you; your face may flush. These are all examples of inherited neurological reactions. Your body performs certain impulsive acts in order to convey messages to you.

People learn body language "the same way they learn spoken language—by observing and imitating people around them as they're growing up."[10] An individual's ethnic background, social class, lifestyle all affect communication, both verbally and nonverbally.

Regional, class, and ethnic patterns of body behavior are learned in childhood and persist throughout life.[11] All people, therefore, do not learn the same body language clues. Just as with verbal communication, there may be differences in interpretation of nonverbal language due to differences in background. These differences can lead to communicative problems in coding and decoding messages.

IMPORTANCE OF NONVERBAL COMMUNICATION

Very few of us ever realize how much we depend on nonverbal clues in our everyday life as well as in our business contacts. "Nonverbal communication signals to members of our own group what kind of person we are, how we feel about others, how we'll fit into and work with a group, whether we're assured or anxious, the degree to which we feel comfortable with the standards of our own culture, as well as deeply significant feelings about the self, including the state of our own psyche."[12] We are what we communicate. What we communicate nonverbally, since much of it is below our level of awareness, often signals our real self, what we really think and feel, and what we do or don't want from others.

In the world of business we are responsible for persuading, instructing, and working with others. These functions are accomplished through understanding and effectively using the best possible means of verbal and nonverbal communication.

We also find that it does not take us long to decide to accept or reject a person and what he or she says. Much plus or minus reaction is based on such nonverbal influencers as clothing, physical appearance, gesture patterns, use of space, facial expressions, and vocal animation. Since within the business environment such factors as being hired, retaining a job, fulfilling your job description, and achieving promotions are the result of communication skills, learning to effectively read and use nonverbal as well as verbal signs is of great importance to the prospective or present business practitioner.

VERBAL-NONVERBAL RELATIONSHIPS

■

There is a relationship between verbal and nonverbal communication.[13] Nonverbal communication can substitute for, complement, regulate, and conflict with verbal communication.

Substitute

☐

Nonverbal language can take the place of verbal messages, and thus create a **substituting relationship.** You can nod agreement or disagreement, point to an individual and gesture for that person to leave, or show disgust with facial and body expressions, while sending no verbal message.

Complement

☐

Nonverbal and verbal messages may serve in a **complementing relationship.** As you give someone verbal directions, you can accompany each verbal signal with a gesture. You say, "Stand up," as your hand moves upward, and continue with "Go out the door and turn to the right," as you point toward the door and gesture to the right.

Regulate

☐

Nonverbal communication can also indicate some control over the verbal, thus creating a **regulating relationship.** As you say, "Don't come any closer," you hold your arm out and your hand up to stop the intruder.

Conflict

☐

One of the most important relationships between verbal and nonverbal language occurs when there is a **conflicting relationship** between the two. There are times when what a person says with his/her body makes a lie out of what he/she is saying.[14]

When there is conflict between verbal and nonverbal behavior, the nonverbal is probably the most accurate. We have, through the socializing process, been taught to manipulate words. Fortunately, or unfortunately, since the nonverbal gestures and behaviors tend to be closer to our real emotional level of feelings, we often have difficulty controlling them. It is difficult to stop your face from flushing when you are embarrassed, or your voice from quivering when you are nervous or increasing in pitch as you become angry. You may say, "I'm interested," but tapping your fingers and looking away from the speaker are often signs of the real message.

In attempting to assign meaning to nonverbal signs, it should be remembered, as with verbal symbols, that the meaning is in the communicator and not in the sign itself. We must also be aware that an individual sign may be meaningless and that the source of the sign must be considered. Thus, looking at clusters and for congruency becomes an important aspect of nonverbal communication.

CLUSTERS AND CONGRUENCY

■

In reading a person's nonverbal communication, it is imperative that a person be aware of clusters and congruency. **Clusters** are groups of gestures. When an individual becomes angry, for example, the arms tighten across the chest, the body becomes stiff, the jaw sets, and the eyes narrow. Each of these gestures in and of itself may be meaningless; however, as they cluster together they have significance. In addition, it is imperative that we be aware of a person's past patterns; then we may recognize when there has been a change in the individual. It is through **congruency** (consistency of past patterns to present actions) that we can tell the boss is having a bad day or that something is bothering our fellow worker. By taking into consideration the way an individual has acted in the past and comparing it to present patterns, we can attempt to read his or her nonverbal communication.

Not only must we be aware of clusters and congruency, but consideration should also be given to cultural differences that affect interpretations.

As with other types of communication, nonverbal messages are carried via channels. These **nonverbal channels** take the principal forms of kinesics (body language), vocal cues (paralanguage, pause, laughter), proxemics (space), physical characteristics (physical attractiveness, body shape, size, skin color), artifacts (clothes, makeup, eyeglasses, jewelry), aesthetics (music, light, color), and chronemics (time).

Kinesics

☐

Kinesics refers to the physical action used by a communicator. We express attitudes and emotions by the way we stand or sit. For example, a participant in a business conference who slouches in a chair may be communicating boredom or disinterest.

Movement

We communicate physically through movement, eye behavior, and facial expression. While talking you move your hands, your feet, or your head. Observe yourself and others during a conversation, a business meeting, or while speaking on the phone. You will probably note that you are gesturing or using your hands (pointing, waving, playing with a pen), or moving your feet or legs. It is interesting to note that "even people born blind move their hands when they talk, although they've never seen anyone do it."[15] When people listen they nod their heads, nod vigorously if they agree, smile when they are pleased, look skeptical by raising an eyebrow or pulling down the corners of the mouth when they have reservations about what is said. They shift positions or look at their watches if they want to end the conversation.[16] It is not at all uncommon for individuals to imitate the behavior of those who are in charge. Employees may unconsciously fall into step when walking with an employer or superior, cross their legs if the boss does, or synchronize cigarette puffing with a supervisor.[17]

Emblem Classifications

Four nonverbal emblem classifications have been defined by researchers: emblems, illustrators, affect displays, and regulators.[18]

Emblems   **Emblems** are gestures that have a direct verbal translation or dictionary definition within a specific societal group. For example, extending the pointing finger upward means one. That same gesture, placed so that the finger touches the lips, means shh or be quiet. A horizontal nod of the head means yes, while a vertical nod of the head means no. On the floor of the New York Stock Exchange an entire series of emblems are used to identify transactions, directions, costs, and purchases.

Illustrators   **Illustrators** are gestures that accompany speech and help enhance the words being spoken. Gestures are used to point, show spatial relationships, or draw an imaginary path. Examples of illustrators include saying, "The washer was about the size of a quarter," and while the statement is being made the speaker forms a circle with her thumb and forefinger enclosing a circle about the size of a quarter.

Affect Displays   **Affect displays** are facial configurations that show emotions such as happiness or sadness. Pouting, winking, or raising or lowering the eyelids and eyebrows are examples of affect displays. Intensity of facial color when someone is embarrassed or uncomfortable is yet another example of an affect display. We often read a person's moods by watching affect displays.

Regulators   **Regulators** are nonverbal acts that maintain and control the back-and-forth nature of speaking and listening between individuals. Regulators include head nods, body shifts, and eye movements. These actions encourage and discourage speakers to continue or stop interacting. In addition, regulators can encourage or discourage individuals from getting closer based on such factors as a person backing away as you come near, or his crossing his arms or turning his body sideways. Seating positions may indicate that you are open for conversation if you shift into an alert position with your eyes directed at the speaker, or show boredom if you slump in the chair. Finger tapping, foot bouncing, and staring off into space are other examples of regulators.

Eye Behavior

"One of the most potent elements in body language is eye behavior. Americans are careful about how and when they meet one another's eyes. In our normal conversation, each eye contact lasts only about a second before one or both individuals look away. When two Americans look searchingly into each other's eyes, emotions are heightened and the relationship tipped toward greater intimacy."[19] Since the eye is an extension of the brain, it reacts as no other part of the body. It has been ascertained that the pupil of the eye is a very good indicator of how people respond to various situations. When a person is interested in something, the pupils will tend to dilate (get larger); if the response is a negative one, they will tend to contract (get smaller). Since people can't control the response of their eyes, the theory purports that it is possible to detect a person who is or is not lying through a sophisticated use of this theory, entitled pupilometrics.[20]

Eye behavior depends on the culture of an individual. Every group has its own patterns. Latin Americans and Arabs, for example, tend to have longer looking times than Americans, while Asians and Northern Europeans have shorter ones.[21] Most Americans find a normal eye glance of 3 to 10 seconds comfortable. An overlong look— a stare—may signal affection, hostility, disrespect, a threat, or an insult.

A recent publication suggests that a person's eye contact in business or other situations can be improved by following four basic rules:

1. "To establish a closer relationship with a business or social acquaintance, hold his or her gaze as long as possible as you meet, say hello, and pass.
2. To end a business or social conversation, stop looking at the other person, especially if you are the dominant one in the relationship.
3. If you want to create a warm business or social relationship with a person of the opposite sex, but are not interested sexually, limit the amount of time you look into that person's eyes while listening or talking.
4. To express doubt in what another person says, raise your eyebrows, look directly into the other person's eyes, then lower your lashes as you look away."[22]

All of this, of course, is dependent on your being able to assimilate these actions into your daily patterns so that they become a natural part of your communicative repertoire. Furthermore, they can only be used with any assurance if the other person is from the same cultural background.

Facial Expression

Some nonverbal communication specialists feel that the face is the most natural channel of nonverbal expression.[23] It is felt that since we subconsciously express our inner feelings through involuntary facial movements, our face, along with vocal tone, may well be the key to understanding the emotional content of a message.

Some facial expressions appear to be universal. A smile means happiness. World-

Often power and confidence are shown by the way in which a person uses his face and body.

wide facial expressions are similar for the emotions of anger, fear, surprise, contempt, and sadness.

Why, if the face is so expressive, do we often fail to pick up the clues? A major problem arises because most of the time people do not watch each other's faces. Often, we are so concerned with the words, or with what we are saying, that we fail to notice what others are doing.

Often power and confidence are shown by the way in which a person uses his/her face and body. During his term of office, President Reagan's first Secretary of State, Alexander Haig, was considered by many to be "one of the most impressive and over-powering people in the government, and the reason is not so much for what he says, but for how he says it. Look at how he testifies before Congress. He uses eye contact . . . sits very upright and slightly forward in his chair. His shoulders are square and he turns toward every individual he responds to. His face is mobile and he uses gestures constantly. He is responsive and active."[24]

Touch

Touch is a form of intimate behavior which includes holding and caressing. Many of your touching patterns are based on your background. Touching comes naturally to many people, yet it is difficult for some people to either give or allow themselves to be hugged. If you came from an environment where people hugged each other freely, touched each other while speaking, and frequently put arms around each other, then you probably give and receive touches easily. If your family's rule was "hands off," then odds are that you feel uncomfortable touching or being touched.

Of all the senses, only touch has the power to communicate depth, form, texture, and warmth. Although it is the simplest and most direct way of relating, studies show that even the most casual touch can have profound emotional effects.[25]

We are aware that the right touch can make a big difference in business situations. A simple pat on the back or shoulder can show approval, give reassurance, or emphasize a point. Touch can help diffuse tense work situations by conveying more understanding than words can accomplish.

Used incorrectly, however, touch can be perceived as an invasion of privacy, a sexual come-on, or a reminder of superiority. There are some who feel that touching has sexual overtones and is part of power plays.

To touch or not to touch becomes a delicate situation in business. In general, the word in the workplace is: "Don't touch," for the potential for misunderstanding is just too great. "Any contact in a business office that suggests personal, romantic, or even friendly involvement shouldn't be indulged in."[26]

In reality, some touching is inevitable in every workplace. At times of happiness, such as when someone gets a promotion, there may be a natural tendency to touch. However, in this age of sexual harassment law suits and sensitivity to power and control, it is wise to moderate tendencies you might have to touch others while at work.

Caution is especially important in jobs where the business protocol is conservative and formal. While hugging and kissing is acceptable in artistic and show business environments, major corporate offices are not usually the place for informality.

Reading Kinesics

If movement, eye behavior, facial expression, and vocal cues are such an important part of communication, why do many of us miss the messages being sent by others? You miss the message being sent because:[27]

1. You don't look. We often are so concerned with what we have to say, or in listening to the words of others, that we simply don't pay much attention to what others are doing.
2. It takes training to read the signs. With little or no understanding of the channels and basic meanings of nonverbal signs, you may find yourself simply not understanding the message a person is sending.
3. Different people feel emotions differently and for varying amounts of time. Since each of us have different environments and heredity, we may respond differently to the same stimuli. Some people are quick to show emotion; others build to the display of feelings slowly. We tend to read others' actions based

on our personal experiences and reactions. Once we realize that looking for congruency is important, we often are better able to key in on the meanings of others.

4. People try to hide certain emotions or change them. Have you ever found yourself in the situation where you didn't want someone else to know how you really felt? Sometimes we want to mask our emotions from others so they can't tell what we feel. If the other person is not really alert to our actions, he/she may miss the slight cues we give.

5. We simply don't care. Our world is very complex. Many of us are so self-centered that we don't really pay much attention to what others are doing or saying. Unless we feel that it will affect us, we may not make the effort to really try to communicate fully.

6. It is complicated. Since it takes time, effort, concentration, knowledge, and understanding to break the communication code, you may just not be able to combine all of these in order to really figure out what is being sent. In addition, since there are no clear definitions for many of our kinesic signs, the receiver may simply be unable to read them.

Vocal Cues

☐

Vocal cues encompass paralanguage, hesitations, pauses, laughter, and the way these affect our verbal signs as well as what they represent in and of themselves.

Paralanguage

Paralanguage refers to all the vocal sounds except the word itself. The vocal quality communicates nonverbally to the listening ear. You can hear vocal stridency, harshness, and even vocal tension. The quality of the voices provides clues as to the emotional state of the speaker. These perceptions of feelings can affect the flow of communication. An employee who has a tense vocal quality, for instance, may be perceived as a worker under pressure who is having difficulty handling the work load.

Hesitations, Pauses, Laughter

Hesitations, pauses, and laughter also affect a message. People who are unsure of themselves may stammer, stop, or frequently pause within a sentence. They also may use non-words and meaningless phrases to fill in these voids. Such words and phrases as *you know,* and *and stuff like that,* are typical of nonmeaningful vocalized pauses that indicate a lack of idea development. They are almost always accompanied by body shifts, facial flushes, breaking of eye contact, and looking at the floor or ceiling.

Laughter can show enjoyment. On the other hand, "inappropriate laughter can indicate anxiety or awkwardness of the situation."[28] A person who is uncomfortable often tries to cover up for this. Some people find themselves giggling at the wrong times and when the situation is not really funny. Much like a flushed face, laughter often indicates uneasiness.

Proxemics

☐

A third important nonverbal channel is that of **proxemics:** the dimensions of space and environment and how we use them. Each of us has an invisible bubble of space around us which contracts and expands based on our cultural background, emotional state, and the activity we are performing. In addition, such dimensions as demographic features (sex and race); relations between people; the interaction setting; the topic or subject matter under discussion; physical impairments of the communicators; and heat and humidity affect our perceptions of our space.

Personal Space

Everyone has an invisible bubble of personal space that contracts and expands. In our society we use four main zones.[29]

Intimate Zone—direct physical contact to a distance of eighteen inches. We allow those with whom we are in love, hold close friendships, or certain family members to get that close to us. We may allow them to touch us—the highest level of personal intimacy. A spouse or lover may be allowed to enter our personal space. On the other hand, a boss who leans over your shoulder while you are trying to write a report, or puts a hand on your shoulder while talking to you, will probably cause you to feel uncomfortable and make you pull away. The boss has invaded your intimate space while not being on intimate terms with you and has made you uncomfortable.

Personal Zone—Most Americans feel comfortable with about three feet of space around them when they are with individuals whom they know, but with whom they do not have intimate relationships. Officially, the zone is 1½ to four feet. This is the distance that we use when talking to others. Persons getting closer than that will usually cause us to pull back unless our relationship with them is intimate. If this doesn't work you will probably attempt to place some barrier between you and the invader, such as a chair or a desk. You might cross your arms in front of you or, if you are holding an attaché case, notebook or purse, put that in front of your body to shield yourself. If you find yourself backing away from someone, or feel uncomfortable, you might do a quick reading to see if the person is too close. If so, you might alert them to the fact that they are invading your territory. In a business setting, invasion of territory often takes place in an unconscious effort to get close to and share ideas and information with the other person. Some individuals do not realize that this causes others to be very uncomfortable.

Social Zone—4 to 12 feet. This space is reserved for strangers or those with whom you don't have an intimate or personal relationship. This is the area employed during business transactions or exchanges, for example, with a sales clerk.

Public Zone—more than 12 feet. When we give speeches or present reports we are surrounded by our public zone. We keep distances from those with whom we have no relationship at all. As we develop a relationship we allow the person to get closer to us.

We can often tell if our relationship with a person has changed by how close we allow him or her to get to us. If a fellow employee moves into our personal space and we do not feel uncomfortable, that individual may have gained the stature of personal relationship. If we allow someone to touch us, or get very close to us, it may indicate that we have developed an intimate relationship with that person. On the other hand, if we no longer want to hold hands with or allow a person to touch us who has been allowed to invade our intimate zone in the past, it may indicate that our feelings for that person have changed—either based on a short-term action (having an argument, being insulted by what was said), or on long-term relationships (divorce, being fired).

When a person is angry or under stress, his/her bubble may expand causing the need for more space. Notice how, if you are at work and you have to get some job done in a short period of time, you don't want anyone near you. If a fellow employee irritates you, you might move away quickly, get out of his/her territory, or demand that the person leave your work area. Our need for more room increases as we feel boxed-in, emotionally or physically.

As with the interpretations of other nonverbal cues, Americans must recognize that these dimensions of space are very characteristic of space in the United States. Business persons conducting business in other countries often report on totally different uses of space by the people with whom they come in contact.

Privacy Space

Not only do we have personal space needs, but we have **privacy space** needs. If people are denied privacy, they feel deprived of something that is very basic to them. "A person's privacy is a sense of himself, and any business that doesn't recognize the need for employees to have that identity is making a mistake that can cost millions in lost productivity."[30] "People who don't feel that they have any say in their space are reduced to child-like status. Productivity fails. It bothers workers. Whether they're conscious of it or not, they need a space where they can establish their separateness."[31]

It is ironic that in most business settings special efforts are made to insure privacy space for those in management positions; however, very often little effort is made on behalf of the workers to protect their privacy. In the office the workers usually have little say about where they sit, with whom they sit, or with whom they must converse. In many cases no provision is even made for a personal space as small as a desk drawer or a locker.

If you do have a specified space, giving it some definition of individuality is important to establish a feeling of privacy. Personalizing the space with photos, postcards, prints, or plants says that the space is yours.

Spacial Arrangements

It is important to realize that such factors as how the furniture is arranged can affect efficiency and operation for an office or meeting. Using a rectangular table, for instance, with the group leader at the head of the table will usually lead to a much more formal atmosphere and less interaction between people than if they are seated around a circular table.

Secretarial desks that are placed facing each other (figure 5.1) will lead to much more interaction between the secretaries than would happen if they were side-by-side (figure 5.2), because the individuals will find it easier to talk to each other head-on

FIGURE 5.1

FIGURE 5.2

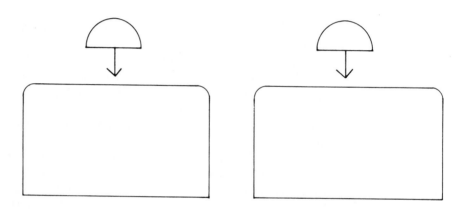

FIGURE 5.3

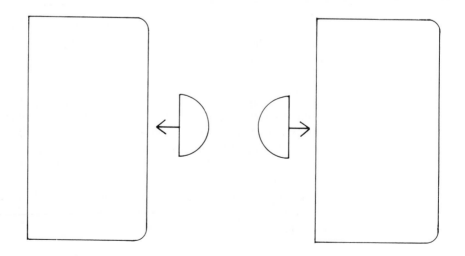

than if they have to turn toward each other each time they wish to converse. Placing the secretaries with their backs to each other (figure 5.3) will lead to even less communication. In this case there is a spacial distance between them that will necessitate their shouting, or turning completely around, in order to converse.

In laying out an office, the furniture arrangement should be considered. In addition, placement of plants, lamps, and large decorative objects can result in encouraging or discouraging interactions. If they block the views of employees from each other, they will discourage interaction. If they do not block, then interaction is encouraged.

Physical Characteristics

☐

Physical characteristics, such as physique, general attractiveness, body and breath odors, height, weight, and hair and skin color, communicate information about an individual. Whether we like it or not, or are aware of it or not, such factors as outer beauty and physical attractiveness play an influential role in determining responses for a broad range of our communicative encounters.[32]

A study of University of Pittsburgh graduates revealed that men 6 feet 2 inches tall or taller received starting salaries 12.4 percent higher than equally qualified men who stood 6 feet or less.[33] Although short women may be positively looked upon as being "petite," they are not immune from prejudice in the job market. "Those women 5 feet 3 or less earn measurably less than their taller female classmates."[34] "Personnel managers, given equally qualified applicants, tend to hire the taller ones first."[35]

The conclusion that must be reached from the studies concerning physical characteristics and their effects on hiring and salary is that " . . . unfortunately, people are hired by image. This means that people are hired because of looks rather than ability."[36] If this is in fact true, what can individuals do to counteract the prejudice?[37] "1. Precede face-to-face meetings with a variety of introductory techniques, such as telephone calls, letters, and having a mutual acquaintance talk about you to the other person. All of this should help form a first impression which is not based on how you look. If a strong enough impression is formed, how you look matters little. 2. When introductory techniques cannot be used, work to create a good impression."[38] Such factors as proper selection of clothing, being well prepared, and being well qualified help.

Artifacts

☐

Artifacts, the clothing that a person wears, makeup, eyeglasses, and beauty aids all carry messages. A person's character is revealed by the clothes worn and the way they choose them. Clothing is an extension of personality. People judge others to a great extent by their clothing. People are more likely to be honest and straightforward with someone who is well dressed. People who are dressed in low-status clothing are likely to be perceived as participating in out-of-line conduct and inconsiderate behavior.[39] Examples of this were clearly evident in the seventies when individuals who wore blue jeans and had long hair and unkempt appearances were labeled "hippies," a negative connotation.

When you step into a room, even though no one in the room knows you or has seen you before, the others will make many decisions about you based solely on your appearance. Think about your own experiences. What was your first impression of your instructor? If you have gone for a job interview, how did you perceive the person interviewing you? How many of these conclusions were based on the clothing worn?

"The way you dress—the image you present—can contribute to success or failure in business."[40] John Molloy, a famous "wardrobe engineer," has made a career of telling business executives (male and female) how to dress. He keys in on which colors to choose, styles to select, and image to present. Molloy's premise is that if you want to be the president of the corporation, then you must dress like the president of the corporation.[41]

Industry considers clothing so important that 65 to 75 percent of the companies in the United States have a dress code in order to insure that the "corporate image" be kept intact.[42] It's important to study the industry you're in, its image and the image of the company you're working for[43] in making selections of clothing.

Many times new employees feel that they can change the image of the company which has hired them. Many attempts have been made, but few have worked. Businesses and industry tend to be very conservative and slow to change. "What's acceptable in business will not be influenced from the bottom."[44]

What is acceptable attire in the business world? At present, the man who wants to package himself for success in a business career should stick to traditional clothing. "In general, men should wear suits (black or navy), simple, tasteful jewelry, white shirts with straight collars, wing-tipped black or dark brown laced shoes, over-the-calf socks (preferably black), ties must touch the belt buckle, shirt sleeves should remain buttoned."[45]

The recommended women's business uniform consists of a skirted suit and blouse. In most cases the suit should be dark and the blouse should contrast with the skirt and jacket. The blouse should be simply cut, with no frills or lace. The wardrobe consultants advise that a woman at any level who wants to move up should not wear a sweater to work. She should not wear a vest for business, particularly one that accents the contours of the body. Shoes should be plain pumps, in a dark color, with closed toe and heel. The heel should be about an inch and a half. Best colors for shoes are blue, black, deep brown, and gray. Research shows that the hair style is one area where a businesswoman has some leeway. Hair should be medium in length, no longer than shoulder length, should lie neatly without constant attention, and not be excessively curly or wavy. Jewelry (except very cheap pieces) is acceptable but the less worn the better.[46]

Whether you like it or not, want to follow the pattern or not, you must realize that your success or failure may well be based on the clothing you wear. As one working woman put it, "I sort of hoped my master of business administration degree would be enough. Now they tell me I have to wear a uniform."[47] And, wear it she does; not to do so could cost her her job.

A prime example of the importance of clothing and physical appearance is the famous case of Christine Craft, who was removed as co-anchor of the news on KMBC-TV, Kansas City, Missouri. Craft said her KMBC bosses told her research showed that too many viewers perceived her as "too old, too unattractive, and not deferential to men."[48] Attention was directed toward her makeup and clothing. They even hired a fashion consultant to pick out the clothes Craft was to wear on TV. "The wardrobes of newscasters can make people believe they are trustworthy or crafty. Whether they care. Look at the way IBM dresses."[49]

Other artifacts that can communicate about us are cosmetics, badges, tattoos, and jewelry. Based on such factors as lipstick, eye shadow, eye liner and makeup, we can reach conclusions about an individual. In general, the business environment demands subtle use of cosmetics. As with makeup, conservative jewelry which does not hinder the work process is recommended. Large earrings can interfere with telephoning. Cufflinks that get caught on instruments, bracelets that make noise and get in the way, rings that snag fabrics are negative artifact factors. Wearing sun glasses with dark lenses or the popular tinted lens glasses effectively cuts off visual contact and may cause frustration on the part of the follow workers who can't see your eyes, and, therefore, have difficulty reading your moods and eye shifts.

Though the exact role of clothing and other artifacts is still unknown, we do know that they communicate about us and influence others' responses to us.

Aesthetics

□

Such **aesthetics** factors as music, light, and color have an effect on us. Our moods are altered by soft and slow music and the beat of the music, the brightness or dullness of the lighting, and intensity or calmness of colors.

Behavioral Kinesiology (BK) is a scientific field which indicates that every major muscle of the body relates to an organ. All the organs in our body are affected by a larger proportion of the music and other aesthetics which we are exposed to daily.[50] In testing over 20,000 records, researchers have discovered that rock music has a subliminal "stopped" quality that causes the listener subconsciously to come to a halt at the end of each measure. This has a weakening effect on the body. This is only one of the many conclusions which reveals that businesses must select carefully the music, the lighting, and the colors they select for the office and retail environment.

Music

While walking through a supermarket, you subconsciously pace yourself in time to the music being played. During the day the music has a slow, wandering sound, while near closing time the beat speeds up and you march right out of the store. Office environments can also be altered by the type of music played.

The inclusion of music in the work environment has received endorsement by unions as well as general researchers: "Music is a friend of labor for it lightens the task by refreshing the nerves and spirit of workers."[51] Music can serve as an environmental aid because it has the ability to soothe emotions and give a physical and psychological life to employees.[52] "The use of background music assists people to cope with routine tasks, helps to keep them alert in the job and wary of safety hazards, and reduces fatigue."[53]

Specifically, the findings regarding music are:

1. Performance was significantly better when music was used as a background rather than motor noise or silence.

2. Visual tasks were performed better when radio broadcasts were piped into work areas than when people worked in silence.
3. There was an 18 percent improvement in mental tasks and a 17 percent improvement in assembly tasks when music was used in the background.
4. Music has a significant effect on muscular activity which increases or diminishes according to the music being played.
5. Music reduces the number of errors in routine office work up to as much as 37 percent.
6. In a routine office work situation productivity increased 8 percent and late attendance dropped by 36 percent after the introduction of a planned background music program.

Lighting

When entering a room, we are all affected by the amount of light in that environment. Bright lights stimulate, low-level light soothes, colored lights create moods within us, and constantly changing lights (such as at discos and other places of entertainment) create psychological excitement. In businesses, careful study should be done of lighting, both natural and synthetic (lighting fixtures and lamps). Designers and architects are fond of using skylights and extensive windows in public buildings and offices. Natural lighting is recognized as a valuable part of the work environment.

One of the most important environmental factors is natural light.[54] If an employee works in a natural environment or has access to a natural environment, then he or she is stimulated and feels better. Anything that gives employees an emotional lift, such as natural light, is important in a business.

Special consideration should be given to task lighting in business environments. It has been found that rather than having all areas of an office with identical illumination, only work areas requiring high light quality are so illuminated. Other areas should be lit according to their needs.[55]

Proper light can bring about greater productivity, better work quality, reduced fatigue and eye strain, and increased morale.

It is now recommended by business experts that staff members who spend most of their time in the office should be given prime views with natural light. In turn, supervisors and managers who spend less time in their offices should be given side offices without views and windows.[56] This, of course, breaks down the traditional concept in American business of the power associated with the number and size of windows in an office; but, it probably is in the best interest of the organization to rethink such traditional views based on the research concerning the effects of lighting in the workplace.

Color

Do you feel differently when you sit in a room that is predominantly red than you do in a room that is light blue? Is there really meaning to the phrases *red hot, he's feeling blue,* and *I'm in a black mood?* Researchers in the field of color psychology definitely feel that colors do make moods.

Color is a significant element in personality and influences us.[57] There are some basic principles about colors that have been discovered: colors have symbolic meaning, and colors selected for business environments have an effect on the workers.

Symbolic Meaning of Color   The colors that surround us bring about feelings within us; they carry specific messages. The colors of red and orange are associated with excitement, stimulation and aggression; blue and green are associated with calm, security and peace; black, brown, and gray suggest melancholy, sadness, depression; while yellow can stimulate cheer, gaiety, and fun; and purple is associated with dignity, royalty, and sadness.[58] Pleasant hues have been rank ordered by preference: blue, green, purple, red, and yellow.[59] The most arousing color is red, followed by orange, yellow, violet, blue, and green.[60] Blue, yellow, yellow-green, and orange are considered beautiful colors; while white, black, and brown are considered ugly.[61]

Knowing this, what are the implications? Children tested in beautifully colored rooms scored higher on tests than children in ugly colored rooms.[62] This can be carried over into the work environment by assuming that individuals in beautifully colored environments will tend to do better work than those in ugly environments. Knowing that red makes one nervous, while blue is calming,[63] suggests that offices and other work stations should not be predominantly red. In addition, "since green is most frequently associated with sickness and nausea, fewer rooms should be so painted."[64] Also, "a time interval spent before a warm color is perceived as shorter than that spent before a cool color," leads to the conclusion that if they are surrounded by warm colors, time will pass more quickly for employees. Knowing that large size often frightens some people, painting large pieces of machinery the same as the background colors of the environment will make the machinery appear less obvious and therefore less threatening.

Effect on Workers   Office colors must be chosen carefully for walls, floor coverings, draperies, and furniture, as these are the surroundings in which workers find themselves. If that surrounding brings about stress, less productive time use will result than if the individual is comfortable in the work area. Walls, ceilings, and reflective surfaces should be light, soft colors; floors and carpets may be darker. Moods are created by the colors chosen. Blue, green, or violet are associated with serenity or coolness and can help to create a calm, relaxed mood. Warm colors such as red, orange, or yellow can suggest cheerful and friendly atmospheres, if that is what is desired.[65]

Large work areas can be made to look smaller when the area is broken up with different colors. This allows workers to feel an identity with their own environment, thus ensuring security and a sense of personal space.

Chronemics

☐

Chronemics, the use of time, is an important communicator. It must be remembered that actual clock time varies among individuals, as does their biological clock time. Some people are **hyperkinetic**—they can't sit still, their bodies are always in action, they operate on fast time. Others are **hypokinetic**—they take forever, their bodies operate slowly, they operate on slow time.

In the United States to be "on time" usually means five minutes early to five minutes late. That is, in most situations. When going to a doctor or dentist's office, we are expected to be "on time"; however, we expect the medical practitioner to be late. In other areas, this time pattern does not hold true. In Switzerland, as the saying goes, you can set your watch by the trains. The Swiss demand and expect exact promptness. In Japan, to be on time usually means to be early to show respect for your host. In Mexico and many South American countries, the word "mañana" (tomorrow) quickly becomes the best description of time. The people in these areas tend to be rather lax, by our standards, in their promptness.

The theory of action chains may explain why people of different cultures, and racial and ethnic backgrounds have difficulty dealing with each other's use of time. "An **action chain** is a behavioral sequence with two or more participating organisms, in which there are standard steps for reaching a goal. If you leave out one of the steps, the chain is broken, and you have to start all over again."[66] If we draw an analogy of this theory to time use, different perceptions of time use could well break the chain of operation. This is, of course, very important in the business environment. If a personnel manager expects a person to arrive on time (by American time standards), and the individual arrives late, then the possibility of the flow of steps leading to hiring may be broken. Or, if a businessperson from Mexico (using the "mañana" time theory) arrives late for an appointment with a Japanese businessperson, the flow of events may also be halted. American business people have to learn, when dealing, for example, with Middle Easterners, that the area is a slow action chain culture. "In the Middle East, if you aren't willing to take the time to sit down and have coffee with people, you have a problem. You must learn to wait and not be too eager to talk business."[67]

CULTURAL EFFECTS

Every culture has its own body language, and children absorb its nuances along with spoken language as they grow up. Because of cultural differences, a person's sex, ethnic background, social class, and personal style all influence body language." The person who is truly bilingual (speaks more than one language fluently) is also bilingual in body language."[68]

Whenever there is a great cultural distance between two people, problems are bound to arise from the differences in behavior and expectations. People of Northern European heritage—English, Scandinavians, Germans, Swiss—tend to avoid personal contact and need more space around themselves. They also tend to show less outward emotion. Those whose heritage is Italian, French, Spanish, Russian, Latin American, or Middle Eastern tend to like close personal contact and to show much more outward emotion.[69]

Normative American behavior is the basis for our sending and decoding of nonverbal messages, while others use different perceptions. For example, adult male North Americans feel comfortable with a distance of arms' length to about four feet apart for private conversation. South Americans like to stand much closer. The American and the Arab are even less compatible in their space habits, as the Arabs thrive on close contact.[70] Americans basically look another person in the eye when they are speaking, occasionally glancing away. "A good Puerto Rican girl invariably lowers her eyes as a sign of respect and obedience when she is being questioned by someone in authority."[71] This could lead a native American to interpret a Puerto Rican female's answering of interview questions as dishonest because she is not looking him in the eye.

Knowledge of cultural differences in nonverbal communication is an extremely important factor for businesspersons. A recent experience of representatives of a U.S. steel company who were negotiating with a group of Chinese government representatives for a trade agreement illustrates the problem of cross-cultural misreadings. All through the discussions the Chinese kept smiling and nodding their heads, seemingly in agreement with everything the U.S. company's negotiators were saying. But after the talks were ended, the Chinese, instead of cheerfully signing the agreement, said, "Now we seem to be in real trouble on several points." What the Americans learned later was that the Chinese, in smiling and nodding, really meant, "We hear you" or "We understand what you are saying," and not, "We agree with you."[72]

Specific nonverbal behaviors can have a direct effect on business relationships between Americans and individuals from other cultures.[73] A knowledge of these may save some embarrassing moments and loss of business.

Greetings

☐   When being introduced and in parting, it is commonplace for Americans to shake hands. Though this is also the pattern in Europe, hand-shaking is not the custom worldwide. In parts of South America a slight bow is a common courteous gesture of greeting. An Oriental who has to leave a gathering will usually bow before departing, communicating his apology. In some Mediterranean, Middle Eastern, and South American countries, males embrace as a common form of greeting.

Conversing and Other Interactions

☐   An educated Englishman will tend to lift the chin slightly when conversing. To an American business person, this may be perceived as snobbery. In the United States it might indeed be snobbery, while for the English this shows pose and a polite gesture. In conversation with Arabs, raising the eyebrows indicates a negative reaction, not surprise as in America.

British and Arabic businesspeople practice rigorous eye contact as they speak. This is so intense, on the part of the Arabs, that it may make their American counterpart uncomfortable. Arabs pay a great deal of attention to eye movements, as they feel the eyes are the mirrors of the soul. Sometimes, U.S. businesspeople are surprised to go to a formal meeting and carry on negotiations with an Arab wearing dark glasses. This practice may be fairly common, because the Arab may not want you to be aware of what his eyes are doing or that he is studying you.

Most Americans feel comfortable with about three feet of space around them as they talk to others. We allow those with whom we are intimate to invade this territory. In dealing with Arabs and South Americans, you may find that they don't feel comfortable unless they are facing you directly and are extremely close. In fact, you may feel their breath upon you. If you move away, they may conclude you are unfriendly or don't like them.

As you interact with businesspeople from other cultures, you will also find that they often have bodily smells which are offensive to you. American use of deodorants and colognes is not a world standard. Ignoring what your nose says is "wrong" may be a very important part of whether or not the sale is made.

Gestures
☐

Americans sometimes perceive strong emotional displays, especially vigorous gesturing, as too emotional, immature, or vulgar. However, many Southern Europeans, Middle Easterners, and South Americans use frequent and energetic gestures. In business dealings with people from those areas, the absence of strong gestures might be considered suspect, as it shows an abnormal pattern of movement.

Time
☐

One of the most frequently misinterpreted nonverbal signs is the use of time. Serious misunderstandings can result unless the individuals are aware of their differences of perception. Such differences may extend to show how preparation is done, when engagements such as meetings are to begin and end, and the period of time negotiations should take.

Americans are trained to be efficient. We take pride in efficiency. This suggests that one properly prepares in advance for a meeting, a speech, or a business contact. We have a special relationship with time—we spend it, waste it, save it, or divide it. Our tendency is to prepare for business conferences, interviews, and meetings. This is the efficient thing to do. But, if we expect this of individuals from other cultures, we may be disappointed. Moreover, we may become angry because others do not show us "respect." If some Asians (not the Chinese or Japanese) and Arabs seem unprepared for the session we have scheduled with them, this should not be considered disrespectful. Those in other cultures are just not guardians of time and, therefore, they will operate in an action chain which does not include prior preparation.

The Arab action chain toward business centers on getting to know a person, interacting with him or her, meeting again after the social interaction, and then dealing with business matters. Driven by the clock, Americans want to meet, settle the issue, and complete the deal.

Americans and others in the Western world generally regard the clock with respect. An appointment is set and tardiness is a serious breach of respect. This is not the pattern, for example, in much of Mexico, South America, or the Caribbean. Americans dealing in some countries quickly learn to ask if the scheduled meeting is to be "American time" or "local" time.

Once a deal is struck, most American businesspeople assume that the agreed upon dates and times will be adhered to for delivery or fulfilling the obligation. Arabs and South Americans tend to be procrastinators. If exact production and manufacturing schedules are dependent upon dealings with these people, then problems might result.

Meetings

☐ Americans tend to have major business meetings in an office. The typical business executive keeps the desk between him or her and the other person. This would offend many Latin Americans who feel uncomfortable with the fence between the participants.

Seating positions at a table hold great importance for many Asians. Since Asians may feel that whoever sits at the head of the table is in charge, they will feel uncomfortable, or may refuse to sit at a rectangular or square table. A circular table is much preferred.

Americans tend to be very casual regarding dealing with opened doors. If you are negotiating with a German, you would be wise to close the door. An open door or entering without asking permission is the height of rudeness. On the other hand, Arabs are unlikely to feel comfortable in a private, enclosed office. They are used to dealing in open areas, often with observers present. American business people are often upset by media coverage at "private" conferences, while Arabs often accept the media as part of the acceptable audience.

Obviously, it is impossible for you to be expected to know the cultural patterns of all countries. It would be wise, however, if you are assigned to foreign accounts, whether in that country or with immigrants to the United States who still adhere to their cultural patterns, to find out about the basic greeting, time, space, and meeting patterns.

IMPROVING NONVERBAL COMMUNICATION

■ Knowing about nonverbal communication immediately prepares an individual to be a better sender and receiver of messages. By starting to pay attention to what you and others are doing, you become a more effective communicator. It is imperative that you learn to listen with your eyes as well as with your ears to messages sent and received.

There are some theories in regard to specific ways in which individuals can improve their nonverbal sending and receiving.[74]

1. Some specialists think that women have a more difficult time assimilating business leadership roles because corporate values and behavior patterns have traditionally been male. Recommendations for women entering the corporate ladder are to adopt an open, straight-forward style that coincides with both male and female behavior traits. "Women should not attempt to ape men. The most successful women know how to maintain their professionalism without losing their femininity. They do this by allowing themselves to be warmer and more responsive than most men, while at the same time keeping their distance, not smiling too much, and not tilting their heads or using 'fashion model' gestures."[75]

2. Pay attention to first impressions. For example, be aware of whether you are evaluating a person on the basis of physical appearance or artifacts. Also be aware that others are judging you on the first impression you give.

3. Maintain eye contact. Use the eye patterns to which your society adheres, remembering that those from other cultures may not be using the same code.

4. Make your words and nonverbal signals consistent. Most people aren't very good actors and have trouble faking their nonverbal signs when it does not agree with the verbal.

5. Don't violate people's sense of personal space. Evaluate whether your relationship with another person is intimate, personal, social, or public. Moving too close and inappropriate touching could lead to negative perceptions. If the person you are talking to pulls away, or starts backing up, you may be too close. Also, be aware that individuals from different cultures use space in different ways and what may be negative to you may be positive to them.

6. Pay attention to your tone of voice. Your paralanguage can be a personal clue to what your real feelings are and what you really mean. You also should listen to how other people are sending messages, as well as the words they are speaking.

7. Examine your posture and walk. Since walk and posture convey messages of your attitude, interest, and attentiveness, monitor your body use. You may be giving negative cues when you really aren't bored or feeling negative about a speaker's proposal.

8. Be aware of how inanimate objects affect communication. Do you find yourself looking at your wristwatch during a conversation? You might be subconsciously telling yourself that you want to leave. Is there a desk between you and a prospective buyer? It is probably creating a barrier to personal involvement. Are the chairs in a position that leads to open conversation if that is desired? All of these are inanimate objects that can affect your communication with others.

9. Be aware of the way you dress. Like it or not, much of your impression, and therefore your effectiveness as a business communicator, depends upon the image you create. Your clothing is an important part of that image. Much time and effort has been spent in analyzing clothing and how it affects your self-image as well as others' perceptions of you. Are you sending the image you want to convey? Are you aware of the way others' nonverbal behavior affects you in your relationships?

SUMMARY

In this chapter we have examined nonverbal communication. The major concepts presented were:

People communicate with verbal and nonverbal messages.

Nonverbal communication is all message sending and receiving not manifested by words, spoken or written.

People are often unaware of nonverbal communication.

Body signs can reveal more about what you are thinking than what you are actually saying.

Our nonverbal patterns come from hereditary as well as environmental influences.

Our nonverbal messages reveal a great deal about us.

There is a relationship between verbal and nonverbal communication. Nonverbal may substitute for, complement, regulate, or conflict with the verbal.

It is imperative that a person, in reading another's nonverbal communication, be aware of clusters and congruency.

Emblem classifications include emblems, illustrators, affect displays, and regulators.

The nonverbal channels are kinesics, vocal cues, proxemics, physical characteristics, artifacts, aesthetics, and chronemics.

The four personal space zones are intimate, personal, social, and public.

Every culture has its own body language.

People can improve their nonverbal sending and receiving.

THINGS TO DO

1. Topics for discussion:
   a. "Every culture has its own body language." Indicate some cultural pattern that you, a friend, or someone you have observed has that is unique to your culture (e.g., time use, hand use, vocal excitement or control).
   b. Name a situation in which you have been involved which was affected by your clothing, grooming, or physical appearance.
   c. Why do you feel most people are not aware of the nonverbal messages they send and receive?
   d. "People learn body language the same way they learn spoken language—by observing and imitating people around them as they're growing up." If this is true, you should be able to identify several nonverbal mannerisms you have that are like those of people you came in contact with during early childhood. Identify two of them and be prepared to share them with your classmates.
   e. Do you feel that John Molloy's observations on dressing for success are valid? React to his clothing requirements for men and women.
   f. What effect do specific colors have on you? Be prepared to give specific examples.
   g. Have you experienced any personal difficulties because of action chains? If so, be prepared to share your experience(s).
2. A theory called biorhythms indicates that our bodies go through various cycles and are controlled, to an extent, by these cycles. Investigate the theory. Plot your biorhythms for a week and see how well the predictions and the actions parallel.
3. Interview someone in the field of business, preferably someone who is responsible for hiring, evaluating, or supervision. Find out what effect clothing and physical appearance have on the organization's practices. (OR) Interview a businessperson who deals with physical factors of an organization (construction, decoration, office assignment, and workspace use). Find out what problems arise due to these environmental factors.
4. Daily, each of us uses the tools of verbal-nonverbal relationships (substituting, complementing, regulating, and conflicting between). Identify two specific situations where you have used these tools. Be prepared to discuss these with your classmates.
5. Select one of the nonverbal channels or subtopics of the channel discussed in

the chapter. Be prepared to discuss the channel as it relates to some aspect of business and industry. Use specific examples other than those mentioned in the book to develop your idea.

6. Carry on a conversation with someone while both of you are standing. Without making it apparent, continue to move in on the person as you speak. What does he or she do? Try this activity with a first-generation Mideasterner (Arab or Israeli) or an Oriental. Do they react the same way? Discuss your results as they pertain to the section on space invasion in the text.

7. Members of the class are to dress in their best clothes and go shopping in several stores. They should then go shopping in similar stores while dressed in old grubby clothing. Were they treated the same? The class should discuss the experiment in relationship to the comments made in the book regarding the effect of artifacts.

8. You will be divided into dyads (groups of two). Engage in a conversation with one other person, changing positions as described here. Spend two minutes in each position: (1) opposite the other and within three feet; (2) opposite each other but with chairs placed at an angle; and (3) side by side. Note how these variations alter your feelings, interaction, and productivity.[76] Discuss your reactions.

NOTES

1. Flora Davis, "How to Read Body Language," *Readers Digest* (December 1969):127–130, as condensed from *Glamour* (September 1969).
2. John Leo Koshar, "Body Signs," *Cleveland Plain Dealer,* 15 December 1976, 8F; based on the work of Arnold G. Abrams.
3. Davis, "Body Language," 128.
4. Ray Birdwhistell, *Kinesics and Context* (New York: Ballantine Books, 1972).
5. Michael R. Meyer, "You: The Body Politic," *Washington Post,* 27 April 1981, B3; reporting on studies of Norm Jorgensen (communication consultant), James Gray (image consultant), and Nancy Henley (body politics lecturer).
6. "How Everyone Talks with His Mouth Shut," *Elyria Chronicle-Telegram,* 11 May 1975, A-8.
7. Koshar, "Body Signs."
8. Meyer, "You: The Body Politic."
9. Daniel Goleman, "People Who Read People," *Psychology Today* (July 1979):69.
10. Edward and Mildred Hall, "The Sounds of Silence," *Playboy* (June 1971):204.
11. Davis, "Body Language," 127.
12. Hall and Hall, "The Sounds of Silence," 206.
13. Ibid., 140.
14. Davis, "Body Language," 129.
15. Norbert Freedman, director, Clinical Behavioral Unit at Downstate Medical Center, Brooklyn, as reported to Ruth Winter.
16. Hall and Hall, "The Sounds of Silence," 139.
17. "How Everyone Talks with His Mouth Shut," A8.
18. Mark L. Knapp, *Nonverbal Communication in Human Interaction,* 2nd ed. (New York: Holt, Rinehart and Winston, 1979), 13–17.
19. Davis, "Body Language," 128.

20. Edward T. Hall interviewed by Kenneth Friedman, "Learning the Arabs' Silent Languages," *Psychology Today* (August 1979):45–54.
21. Julius Fast, "Excuse Me, But Your Eyes Are Talking," *Family Health:* 23–25.
22. Ibid., 25.
23. Knapp, *Nonverbal Communication in Human Interaction.*
24. Meyer, "You: The Body Politic," B3.
25. Don Oldenburg, "The Touchy Topic of Hugging," *Washington Post,* 11 February 1985, B-5.
26. Ibid.
27. Based on the concepts presented in Gerald Volgenaur, "Face Offers Clues to Moods," *Elyria Chronicle-Telegram,* 6 February 1977, B-5.
28. "How Everyone Talks with His Mouth Shut," A8.
29. Edward T. Hall, *The Silent Language* (New York: Premier Books, 1959).
30. For an expanded discussion of space see Edward T. Hall, *The Silent Language* (New York: Premier Books, 1959).
31. Mary Tobin, "Each His Own Space: A Wise Firm Policy," *Elyria Chronicle-Telegram,* 17 January 1982, E-1; based on the work of C. Frederic John.
32. Ibid.
33. Janice Munson, "Clothes Make the Job," *Cleveland Plain Dealer,* 27 February 1978, 2B.
34. Jackie Roedler, "Want More Success? Get a Pair of Elevator Shoes," *Elyria Chronicle-Telegram,* 7 January 1972, 3.
35. Carol Karmer, "Bigot's Last Refuge—Putting Down Short Men," *Elyria Chronicle-Telegram,* 31 March 1975, 3; based on a study of Saul Feldman.
36. Roedler, "Want More Success?" 3.
37. Lawrence Rosenfeld, "Beauty and Business," *New Mexico Business Journal* (April 1979):23–26.
38. Ibid., 26.
39. John E. Gison, "What Your Clothes Say About You," *Success Unlimited* (April 1980):33–34.
40. Munson, "Clothes Make the Job," 2B.
41. John Molloy, *Dress for Success* (New York: Warner Books, 1978).
42. Munson, "Clothes Make the Job," 2B.
43. Ibid.
44. Ibid.
45. James T. Yenckel, "Fashion, The Executive Suite," *Washington Post,* 28 February 1980, D5; based on the book by William Thourlby, *You Are What You Wear.*
46. John T. Molloy, *The Woman's Dress for Success Book* (Chicago: Follett, 1977).
47. James T. Yenckel, "Fashion, The Executive Suite," D5.
48. Howard Rosenberg, "Cosmetics of TV News," *Cleveland Plain Dealer,* 18 April 1982, 8D and 10D.
49. Ibid.
50. Patricia McCormick, "Rock Music Can Weaken Muscles," *Elyria Chronicle-Telegram,* 12 January 1979, Sunday Magazine; 15.
51. A. J. Scott, "Music in the Workplace," *Personnel Journal* (July 1980):598 rpt from *Work and People* (Autumn/Winter 1978), Department of Productivity, Melbourne, Victoria, Australia.
52. David J. Hyslop, "Physical Environment in the Office," *The Changing Office Environment* (v: National Business Education Association, 1980).

53. Scott, "Music in the Workplace," 599.
54. "Work Environment: Its Design and Implications," *Personnel Journal* (January 1981).
55. *The Changing Office Environment,* 125.
56. "Work Environment: Its Design and Implications."
57. Hall and Hall, "The Sounds of Silence," 12.
58. Deborah T. Sharpe, *The Psychology of Color and Design* (Chicago: Nelson-Hall, 1974).
59. Albert Mehrabian, *Public Places and Private Spaces* (New York: Basic Books, 1976).
60. Ibid.
61. Ibid.
62. Mark Knapp, 96, as taken from H. Wong and W. Brown, "Effects Upon Mental Works as Measured by Yerkes' Multiple Choice Method," *Journal of Comparative Psychology* 3 (1923):319–331.
63. *The Psychology of Color and Design,* 85.
64. Ibid., 134.
65. *The Changing Office Environment,* 127.
66. Edward T. Hall as interviewed by Kenneth Friedman.
67. Ibid.
68. Davis, "Body Language," 127.
69. Hall and Hall, "The Sounds of Silence," 140.
70. Davis, "Body Language," 130.
71. Julius Fast, 24.
72. John Koha, "Body Signs," *Cleveland Plain Dealer,* 15 December 1976, 8F.
73. Based on Larry Samovar, Richard Porter, eds., *Intercultural Communication: A Reader,* 4th ed. (Belmont, CA: Wadsworth, 1985), Edward Hall, *The Hidden Dimension* (Garden City, NY: Doubleday and Company, 1966); and Loretta Malandro and Larry Barker, eds., *Nonverbal Communication* (Reading, MA: Addison-Wesley, 1983).
74. Meyer, "You: The Body Politic," B3.
75. Ibid.
76. Based on an activity contained in Charles Brown and Paul Keller, *Monologue to Dialogue* (Englewood Cliffs, NJ: Prentice-Hall, 1979), 238.

6

☐

Interpersonal
Communication:
A Business Focus

OVERVIEW   A great deal of our time is spent talking with people on an interpersonal, one-to-one basis. To be effective, this communication should be purposeful. Interpersonal communication is multichanneled (verbal and nonverbal). Often interference causes problems when we send and receive messages. Interpersonal communication is at the heart of many business dealings—self-disclosure, telephone use, management-employee relationships, directing, job training, conflict and conflict management, and employee assertion. The changing world is causing re-evaluation of interpersonal communications within the business world with an eye toward altering them to better fulfill the needs of both employee and employer.

KEY WORDS   interpersonal communication   conflict
                relationship   hidden agenda
                multichanneled   conflict resolution
                interference   peacemaking
                environmental interference   win-lose
                physiological interference   lose-lose
                semantic interference   win-win
                gobbledygook   avoidance
                syntactic interference   accommodation
                organizational interference   smoothing-over
                psychological interference   compromise
                social interference   competition
                self-disclosure   integration
                need-satisfaction   nonassertive
                homophily   aggressive
                heterophily   assertive
                One-Minute Manager Theory   victimized
                direct intervention   simple assertive statement
                indirect coping   empathic statement/response
                reactive coping   confronting response
                directing   DESC Scripting

W e spend most of our time talking with people on an interpersonal level—individually (one to one) or in small groups.[1] This **interpersonal communication** between people involves the exchange of messages and the development of a relationship based on the effect of those messages.

As we attempt to exchange ideas with other people, we have a purpose in mind. Our purpose may be an attempt to aid them in understanding some idea or concept, to gain new information, to change their point of view, to get them to understand why we feel as we do, or to influence them to take some type of action. The success of our interpersonal communication determines whether or not we are successful in achieving our end goal. As we communicate with the individual(s), our mutual feelings about and towards each other—our **relationship**—has an effect. Our communication is affected by such aspects of relationships as whether we like or dislike, or are in a power or control position over the other individual (parent, boss, teacher, supervisor) or in a subordinate position (child, student, employee). In many instances, the hierarchy of power in interpersonal relationships may determine not only the message but also the effect of the message. Experts tend to agree that most problems in communication occur in the relationship dimension rather than in the content dimension—in the way we feel about or toward each other rather than in what is said.[2]

As we exchange ideas, we normally do so by the use of symbols (words) which represent letter combinations that a particular society has agreed represent certain ideas; and by the use of images, the ideas or concrete objects that the symbols represent. Another factor affecting our communicating is values (" . . . a basic feeling about what is important, what counts").[3]

During any interpersonal transaction, the communication is **multichanneled.** We use both verbal and nonverbal channels in message sending and receiving. It is important to remember to be sensitive to these channels so as not to miss much of the content and purpose of a message.

Let us examine interpersonal communication by looking at what effective interpersonal communication is and how to attempt to intercept and eliminate transactional breakdowns. In addition, we will examine specific interpersonal skills that are needed in the business environment.

EFFECTIVE INTERPERSONAL COMMUNICATION

■

For the development of interpersonal communicative competency, four components must be present: (1) being aware of how and why barriers occur in communication; (2) selecting the most appropriate communication acts from a repertoire of communication acts; (3) implementing these communication choices effectively through verbal and nonverbal means; and (4) evaluating these communication attempts according to the elements of appropriateness and effectiveness.[4]

It is useful to examine the causes of communication barriers and explore a repertoire of communicative suggestions that can be implemented to develop a more effective interpersonal interaction.

INTERFERENCE

■

Interference[5] is defined as a factor or factors that cause barriers to effective communication, thus eliminating the successful transfer of information between the communicators. Let us say you are attempting to take a supply order from a client over the telephone and there is static over the phone line. You may find yourself unable to hear the order clearly, so you may not be able to receive the message as sent. Or you receive a letter from a Japanese businessperson requesting information about a service that your company offers. The letter is in Japanese and you do not read or understand that language. Or you have had an argument with your boss, and one of the people with whom you work comes into your office to ask a question. She is speaking to you, but you are so preoccupied with the disagreement you have just had that you do not pay attention. All of these barriers to interpersonal communication have been caused by interference.

Interference may enter the communicative interaction or transaction at any phase of the sending-receiving process. In any of the models of communication there may be interference when the source cannot encode the message because he/she does not have the language fluency to encode the message. Or the source may be able to encode the message, but may not be able to send it out over the channel because of the inability to speak or the inability to write (if the message is to be sent over the writing-reading channel). The source may send the encoded message out over the channel, but it may not be received because the receiver cannot hear or read, or there may be so much noise in the room that he/she just can't gain the symbols. Or, though the receiver gets the message, he/she may not be able to encode it because of the abstraction of the symbols used or the use of unfamiliar jargon, abbreviations, or terms in which the message is coded.

There are seven types of interference: (1) environmental, (2) physiological, (3) semantic, (4) syntactic, (5) organizational, (6) psychological, and (7) social.

Environmental Interference

☐

In some situations the sender's message does not get to the receiver because of interference in the communicative environment. If you are sitting in a small-group discussion and the person seated next to you is speaking loudly to a neighbor, you may not hear the speaker's comments. The air conditioning fan is over your desk in the office and the noise is loud enough to be distracting when someone is talking to you. These are both examples of environmental interference entering into the oral communicative environment.

When interference invades the communicative environment (**environmental interference**), both the source and the receiver have to be aware of the possibility of a breakdown and work toward removing the interference. Either asking the person talking to please be silent, since you cannot receive the message, or moving to another chair would cure the talking neighbor problem. Either asking for a replacement of the air conditioning fan or moving your desk should stop the physical noise in the office example.

Physiological Interference

☐ **Physiological interference** can take place when the source has difficulty sending a message or the receiver cannot gain the message. A person who has severe laryngitis may not be able to produce any sounds and thus be unable to speak loudly enough or clearly enough to send a message. A person with a stutter may not be able to send a message containing certain letter-sound combinations or may be too upset by an oral communication situation to want to speak. A deaf person will have trouble hearing a spoken idea.

A written note rather than trying to speak may be necessary for the person with laryngitis. The stutterer may also find written notes helpful. Since some stutterers operate very effectively if they are not speaking directly to another person, a good substitute for oral messages may be a pre-recorded message. Facing someone who you know is deaf and who lip-reads may insure the necessary relationship to open the channels of communication. Knowing that you may have to listen intently to someone who has a speech impairment may allow you to receive a message that you might have otherwise missed. Awareness of the possibility of physiological noise may alert both parties to a possible need for making adjustments.

Semantic Interference

☐ We have all been faced with situations where we simply could not understand what someone was trying to explain to us either because we did not understand the words being used or because they incited strong emotions within us. These are **semantic interference.**

Experts in a field—accountants, computer analysts, economists, doctors, machinists—sometimes forget that those who are not experts in that field may not know the vocabulary they are using. If they do not take this factor into consideration, then there is little chance that a meaningful relationship will develop; thus, little if any effective communication will take place.

As sources of messages we often assume that because we know what a word means, everyone else will know the word. In addition, we assume that because a word means something to us, it will mean exactly the same thing to someone else. Neither of these assumptions is correct. *Pop* in the midwestern part of the United States is *soda* in the East. *Flashlight* in the United States is *torch* in England. *MBO* may be perfectly clear to a businessperson whose corporation is operating under the *Management By Objectives* procedure, but to a layperson it means absolutely nothing. The confusion caused by the use of letters rather than words to describe such things as organizations, activities, and machinery makes it impossible in some instances to understand a message.

To be effective communicators, both the source and the receiver should be conscious of semantic interference and try to make the message clear. The speaker should try to guess the receiving level of the listener and define terms that need clarification, using words instead of letters when dealing with the uninitiated.

If it is necessary to use unfamiliar terms, it is wise to offer some sort of explanation or definition, to use other synonyms, or even to provide some examples of what you intend to suggest in the use of the term. A manager explaining a new procedure to an employee, for example, needs to define any terms in the operation that might be unfamiliar.

A further suggestion in using language is to avoid "dehumanizing" through our symbols. We have a tendency to categorize and lump people together in impersonal groups or institutions. We hear talk of "the workers," "the executives," "the diplomats," "the secretaries," "the custodians," or "them" as if they were not really individual human beings.

Government agencies and corporations suffer from the development of "bureaucratese"—language loaded with technical or corporate jargon, acronyms, and euphemisms to communicate internal operations. The federal government has been under fire for several years to clear up government documents (especially tax forms) and communications so that the general public can understand the language more easily. The former *Washington Star* newspaper ran a daily column on **gobbledygook**—imprecise language that may intentionally or unintentionally confuse—with many excerpts from federal memos. A definition illustrates the problem. "The cognitive development of any individual organism is functionally dependent on that organism's substantive comprehension of the variables involved in the dynamic process of symbolic transmission we typically refer to as communication."[6] (Aren't you glad that that wasn't the definition we used earlier in this book to explain "effective communication"?)

We should also be aware that the emotional overtones of words influence interpretations. Some workers fear the influence of *automation,* for example, as an encroachment on their jobs and livelihood. Others have developed a fear of the *computer* as having too much personal information on people. And the term *retirement* has negative connotations for people in their sixties, especially as Congress debates the pros and cons of mandatory retirement.

Both the sender and the receiver have an obligation to ask for clarification of words and ideas not presented in a way that can be understood. Many a student has failed a class, many a new employee never learned to operate equipment, and many directions were never followed because either the sender did not use terms that could be understood or the receiver did not ask for definitions and clarifications. If communication is truly the development of a relationship, then there must be a sharing of the responsibility for making sure that the message is sent and received as intended.

Syntactic Interference

The words used (semantics) and the grammar structure (syntax) are the two components of any language. Even if the semantics are clear, there may be misunderstanding (**syntactic interference**) if the way in which the words are placed within the sentence leads to confusion. "Cut down the tree, not?" If you heard or read that sentence, what would it mean to you? Most people who were exposed to the sentence assumed that it meant, "Don't cut down the tree." If that was your understanding, you would not have performed properly. In Pennsylvania Dutch, the statement means, "Do you want me to cut down the tree?" Why the misunderstanding? Because there is a difference between Standard America English syntax and German syntax. Standard American English and Pennsylvania Dutch use many of the same words. However, Pennsylvania Dutch speakers and writers use the grammatical structure of the German language. The result? Confusion, if one does not understand Pennsylvania Dutch. Those whose first language is one other than Standard American English (e.g., Spanish, French, Black English) have to translate not only the words used, but the ways in which they are used. The grammar structure of noun-verb-object is not the pattern of all languages. We may therefore find ourselves trying to figure out meanings from the way in which the words are ordered. The following examples were taken from letters sent to insurance companies. Do you think the writers meant what the words say?

> You have changed my little boy to a little girl. Will this make a difference?
> In accordance with your instructions, I have given birth to twins in the enclosed envelope.
> I am glad to report that my husband, who is missing, is dead.

It is imperative that business people be aware of standard grammar rules. Many sales have been lost, prospective employes not hired, and misunderstandings developed because the quality of the grammar of a businessperson was considered to be below that expected of a well-educated person. An employer may quickly decide that you are not the type of person to represent the company if during your employment interview you make grammatical mistakes, speak with disagreements of tenses, and lack clarity of ideas.

Organizational Interference

In telling a story, little children often relate the first thing that happened, jump to the fifth, then to the third, repeat the first, then go on to the fourth. It leads to great confusion. Children, unfortunately, are not the only people who do this. **Organizational interference** takes place when there is no pattern to the ideas being discussed and the receiver gets confused. Ideas that lack sequence cannot be followed.

Some ideas lend themselves to being presented in a chronological order according to what came first; what has to be done first, then second, then third, etc.; or according to the dates when something happened. Other ideas require a spatial order that follows some geographical format. A topical arrangement, in which a general subject is broken down into parts, and causal arrangement, in which one tells what happened, what resulted or what the outcome was, and how it came to be, are still other methods of development.

We also can organize by detailing the differences between ideas, the similarities between matters, or both the differences and similarities (contrast, comparison, comparison and contrast). Yet another method of development is problem-solution. In this means of organizing ideas, the source structures the presentation by explaining the problem and then discussing the possible solutions, finally leading to the best possible plan of action for solving the problem.

All of the methods described have one basic purpose—to structure ideas in such a way that the receiver will understand the message of the source because there has been no organizational interference.

Psychological Interference

☐ We all find ourselves in some communicative situations when we simply cannot emotionally function effectively as sources or receivers, which causes **psychological interference.** An emotional upset caused by an accident on the way to work, someone saying something to you that is upsetting, the fear of possibly losing your job, trauma brought about by fear that you can't learn a new procedure—any of these can cause a person to be an ineffective interpersonal communicator. We often have to release our extreme emotions before we can receive the real message sent. Trying to discuss a matter or to reason with an extremely emotionally upset person can be an exercise in futility. After that person has released tensions, you might be able to more logically approach a matter. We must remember, however, that emotions cannot be completely eliminated from our communication.[7] All things being equal, emotion may be stronger than logic, and a rational person who attempts to use logic as the sole basis for all decisions should not assume that there is no emotion involved in the decision.

We are born with strong emotional drives, and we react on this level before the socially learned logic system comes into play. This is why we often say something when we get aggravated only to catch ourselves and realize that we should not have said it. Even then, however, emotion still plays a part in our thoughts and actions.

In dealing with short-term psychologically disoriented individuals, it may be better to delay or avoid the communication. In some cases, however, it might be wise to settle the disturbance before proceeding with the interactions, as little progress may be made until the individual has worked through the extreme emotional response.

Some individuals are psychologically upset to the degree that they can be classified as neurotic, psychotic, or paranoid. We cannot communicate with these individuals in the same way as with individuals who do not possess these strong tendencies. Disturbed persons often need special handling and special individuals to deal with them. In the business environment, counselors and/or psychologists are often available for troubled employees. If you are in a supervisory role, you have a responsibility to the organization to try to guide such a person toward the necessary help. Most of us simply are not trained to play psychologist no matter how good our intentions may be.

Social Interference

☐ Rules and regulations of society as a whole, or of a specific segment of society (family group, church members, business concerns, political groups), often have an effect on us in our capacity both as sources and as receivers. If certain words are regarded as unacceptable (obscenities, for example), then use of those words will result in a negative reaction and may cause the receiver to turn off the communication. Certain topics should not be discussed with certain people. Their reaction is negative if you approach them on such issues. The rules and regulations we carry around as our values and attitudes have a direct effect on our communication and can cause **social interference.** This may have a profound effect on business communication, as you must constantly be aware that the values of customers may not be the same as yours. Offending their social values may lose them as customers.

Eye contact is a case in point. Some African Americans and Orientals have been brought up with the attitude of not looking someone directly in the eye when speaking.[8] If you have been brought up with the idea that an individual who is speaking to you but does not look you directly in the eye is not truthful, you will make assumptions about the Black American or Oriental speaker that may not be valid. People with drawls, accents, or certain speech habits may be classified—according to your environmental influences—as illiterate, uncouth, or immoral. These preconceived attitudes may well get in the way of effective communication.

SELF-DISCLOSURE

The values we hold determine much of what we say and do in interpersonal communication. Our verbalizations and actions reflect our values and our values can be inferred from our verbalizations and actions. Sometimes we decide to reveal what we think or feel; at other times, we decide that the ideas, beliefs, and information may be too private for others to know.

Self-disclosure, one's communication of a private world to another, is truly an important part of behavior. Another person can only get to know you by what you reveal verbally or what the person perceives about you from your nonverbal behavior. In making the decision whether or not to reveal, a person must remember, "You can know me truly only if I let you, only if I want you to know me."[9]

We must be aware that self-disclosure involves a risk. Once someone knows something about you, that information can no longer be private. The conscious act of sharing yourself entails a decision as to whether or not you want others to get to know you. If you decide not to share yourself, then others may think you are shy, stuck-up, distant, or become suspicious of what you are hiding. On the other hand, if there is something you prefer not to share, then that is your privilege.

Information which you give on a job résumé, in an employment interview, to your boss, or to your fellow workers has been selected by you as a means of allowing people to know you better. It also has some implications for promotion and retention.

The hard-work ethic is based on the premise that the boss will promote the best employee, the one who is most successful in job performance. Unless employees personally communicate their achievements, the boss will never know about them. The rule of getting ahead is, "Communicate your contributions and accomplishments to your employer."[10] Many employees fail to follow this Eleventh Commandment and also fail to take steps forward in their careers.

Many of us have been taught not to "toot your own horn." In other words, do not brag about our accomplishments. Unfortunately, sometimes the system is so set up that if you do not let others know about your accomplishments, they will go unrecognized. You are your own best public relations director. You must determine what is in your best interest and work to achieve that. Usually, that means making sure that managers and superiors are aware of your accomplishments. This does not mean being a constant braggart; however, if promotions and advancements are based on accomplishments and your accomplishments go unrecognized, then the advancement will go to others. "People forget, at peril of their career advancement, that the decision not to communicate—keep their mouths shut and their noses to the grindstone—is a negative decision that opens the way to all kinds of misunderstandings. Hard work alone is not magic—the results of that effort have to be communicated if it is to advance your career."[11]

INTERPERSONAL RELATIONSHIPS IN THE ORGANIZATION

■ Individuals form relationships and maintain those relationships so long as the persons involved derive something from the experience. This is evident in the variety of relationships that develop within any organization—between employees, between bosses and workers, between management peers, etc. To be effective, however, the communicators must be able to meet each other's interpersonal needs and maintain a level of trust in the relationship.

Just like social relationships, interpersonal relationships within the organization for which you work may depend on **need-satisfaction**—the satisfaction of your and others' interpersonal and intrapersonal needs. In working with others, it may be wise for you to consider that most relationships are based on need-satisfaction. In other words, does the time and effort that I am spending pay off in some way to satisfy my needs? One theory of needs indicates that we desire to satisfy our physiological needs (food, shelter), and our psychological needs for safety (protection against bodily or emotional harm), love and belongingness (to be part of a societal group—family, friendships), self-esteem (respect for yourself), and self-actualization (total satisfaction in all areas).[12] Another prominent theory suggests that we have three basic need areas: affection (to be loved and be loved), inclusion (to be a significant contributor to a relationship), and control (to have command over one's environment or situation).[13]

Our response to others in relationships may be regarded in terms of the concepts of homophily and heterophily. The terms refer to the degree of similarity (**homophily**) or difference (**heterophily**) of individual attributes which may affect communication interactions.[14] Similarity or lack of similarity of interpersonal needs, status, occupations, backgrounds, education, etc., all can have an impact on the willingness and even the ability we have to communicate with other persons in interpersonal relationships. A manager who has a need to impress his superior, for instance, will be operating at that need level rather than being responsive to the needs of subordinates. A person who feels that you are a rival for a job, to satisfy a basic need, might respond to you in a different way than a non-competitor will. If you are in a power position, such as a manager or supervisor, you may find that those working below you on the organizational chart will not be willing to share personal information or permit a friendship to develop for fear the relationship will be used against them. On the other hand, some people may try to manipulate a relationship in order to ask for favors. The very nature of the hierarchical structure of the typical organization, which causes certain individuals to have control over the promotions, hirings, firings, and evaluations of others, makes for complicated patterns of interpersonal communication.

A communication situation constantly facing business people is using the telephone. (© Jim Bradshaw)

INTERPERSONAL SKILLS IN THE BUSINESS ENVIRONMENT

■ Interpersonal communication is at the heart of most business dealings. It is helpful to consider some of these activities, what they are, and how you might be better able to deal with them as businesspersons. We will examine telephone use, management-employee relationships, directing, job training, conflict and conflict management, and employee assertion.

Telephone Use

□ A communicative situation constantly facing business people is the telephone. Businesses use telephones to "keep in touch, solve problems, deal with emergencies, and to carry out many kinds of transactions."[15] Many individuals find that messages they have sent are not received, follow-ups are not made as requested, phone numbers are incorrectly taken and given, misunderstandings take place, and people get offended because of the manner in which the phone call is made or received. Here are some telephone techniques and suggested phrases that should make using the phone more communicatively productive.[16]

Techniques Used When Receiving Messages

Answer the phone promptly. Individuals become upset when they have to listen to numerous phone rings when they know the business is open and someone should be answering.

In answering calls answer with a standard message (e.g., "Collins Auto Parts, Mrs. Weiss speaking"). Avoid, "Hello." It conveys no actual information other than that the phone has been answered and then obligates the caller to ask for information that should have been included by the answer in the first place.

Acknowledge requests. Give a specific answer to questions or requests rather than saying. "Uh huh," "Nope," "What?" or "Yeah." Respond with, "I understand that you'd like to speak to Mr. Smith" or "I'll try to locate Mr. Jones; he's away from his desk at the moment."

When answering the phone, identify yourself. This allows the caller to know to whom he or she is talking, and is a point of reference. It also encourages the caller to copy your example and identify herself/himself.

Sound positive and interested. A negative attitude on the phone projects a negative image for the organization.

Take notes. Record pertinent information as it is given.

Repeat major ideas to make sure you have the correct information. Repeat numbers, spelling of names and places, and any material you are to convey to another or will need for follow-up or to return the call.

Hold or transfer calls promptly and properly. A customer or client who is cut off often becomes extremely distraught. This is even worse if the call is long distance. If you are transferring a call indicate what the caller will hear (music, a dial tone, or dead air) and how he/she will know that the call has been successfully transferred. If you know the phone system in the organization sometimes cuts off calls, give the caller the extension number to which he/she is going to be transferred, so that if there is a problem the caller will be able to easily contact the correct number.

Use a suitable closing remark. Indicate what the expected follow-up will be and that the call has come to an end (e.g., "Thank you for calling, Mr. Edwards, I will tell Mr. Jones to call you at 734–2600 by three o'clock this afternoon.").

Screen calls. Many organizations and individuals have regulations concerning who will speak to whom and under what conditions. Correct screening answers would be, "Yes, he is in. May I tell him who is calling?" or "Mrs. Diamond is in a meeting. May I have her return your call?"

If you are going to leave the phone, tell the caller specifically what is going to happen. For example, "I will have to leave my desk to get that file. It should take me about two minutes. I'll put you on hold or would you prefer that I call you back?"

Don't leave a caller on hold more than 60 seconds. The caller does not know where you have gone or what you are doing. Short periods of time seem like eternities when you are on hold.

Follow through. Take action immediately to insure that the message is carried out. Prompt responses and follow-ups for requested services bring positive reactions from customers.

Techniques When Placing Calls

Ask for repetition of the information. As the caller, if you think the person to whom you are speaking does not, or may not have the correct information, request that he/she repeat it. In order not to make it sound like you don't trust the person to whom you are speaking, put the burden on yourself by saying, "Just to be sure I gave you the right information, could you repeat the number I gave you?" Or say, "I'll be expecting Mrs. Swegard to be calling me back at 765–4519 by three this afternoon."

Use a rate that can be understood. When giving numbers and other information that is to be written down, make sure the rate is slow enough so that the receiver can transcribe the information.

Talk in terms the other person can understand. Avoid using jargon and initials unless the caller is familiar with them.

Don't assume that the receiver is a mind-reader. Give the specifics of why you are calling and what you want. If you wish to have the call returned, indicate that. If you are going to be in and out of the office, indicate specifically when you want the call returned.

Make a checklist of the exact ideas you want to convey. Don't rely on your memory—you might forget an important item or idea.

Have all information you need at your fingertips. If you need statistics or examples, your appointment calender, or forms to fill out—have them ready and available. It is not only discourteous, but shows a lack of preparation if you cause the potential customer to wait while you get these items.

Management-Employee Relationships

☐ "The manager who gets results is the effective communicator."[17] One aspect of effective management communication centers on clarity, or the lack of interference. The supervisor must be sure that the employee clearly understands what is to be done, how it is to be done, what to do if there are difficulties, and what the possible consequences are for not successfully carrying out the responsibility. It is often important for employees to clearly see how they will benefit from an activity. The lack of clarity may result in interference and thus lead to communicative barriers.

"Workers judge their supervisors by what they THINK his/her motives are."[18] The supervisor who is known to keep promises, report facts honestly, and listen sincerely does not have to fall back on threats, manipulation, and phony good-fellowship in order to achieve job success. He/she creates little or no psychological interference. Supervisors who are isolated from employees often are subject to suspicion. Communication becomes difficult when individuals are seldom seen or spoken to. Once a lack of trust is developed (psychological interference), it is often very difficult to achieve a positive relationship in which to foster open communication. It must be noted, however, that building trust with workers can be quite difficult in any organization. There is a tendency for workers to exercise caution in what they self-disclose to their bosses—an understandable reaction to the supervisor-subordinate roles in any bureaucracy. Many employees believe that if they told their supervisors what they really felt about the organization, they would have great difficulty with their bosses. They feel that if they want promotions, raises, etc., they had best not openly disagree with their supervisors.[19]

Management characteristics which lead to the establishment of effective interpersonal relationships between employees and the manager are: (1) praises subordinates; (2) understands a subordinate's job; (3) can be trusted; (4) is warm and friendly; (5) is honest; and (6) is a person with whom subordinates are free to disagree.[20]

Management personnel would be wise to remember that "what counts, in the final analysis, is not what people are told but what they accept."[21] It is much easier to accept an individual who is forthright and honest, even if you do not agree with that person, than one who is constantly open to suspected motives and who practices manipulative activities.

A communicative approach to management that has been extremely successful is called the One-Minute Manager theory. The **One-Minute Manager Theory** assumes that almost everybody wants to be working in a meaningful way. Employees want to know they are appreciated. If they feel appreciated they will knock themselves out for you.[22] At the same time, a manager has so many responsibilities that he/she must control the time allotted to any interactions.

According to the One-Minute Manager theory, the effective manager:

1. Establishes and explains goals thoroughly. The goals are briefly written out (no more than 250 words. . .) and agreed upon by boss and subordinate(s).
2. Practices one-minute praise:
   Tells people up front that he/she is going to let them know how they are doing.
   Praises people immediately.
   Tells them specifically what they did right.
   Tells them how good he/she feels about what they did right, and how it helps the organization and others who work there.
   Stops for a moment of silence to let them know how good he/she feels.
   Encourages them to do more of the same.
   Shakes hands or touches people in a way that makes it clear that he/she supports their success in the organization.
3. If necessary, takes an employee aside for a one-minute reprimand.[23]

Criticizing

One interpersonal task that often confronts managers is the necessity to criticize or reprimand employees. In criticizing, it is important to attempt to make your point without being accusatory, threatening, or judgmental—without hurting the other person's feeling or putting him/her down. The risk of offending another can be reduced by:

1. Not overlooking the person's good points.
2. Using "I" messages rather than "you" messages. An "I" statement would be "I feel hurt. What you are doing doesn't seem to be taking my needs or those of the organization into account." A "you" statement is, "You're acting unfairly and you're wrong. . . ." People are likely to get very defensive when they are given "you" statements.
3. Giving compliments as well as criticism. This will often soften the negative message.
4. Diffusing anger, if this is possible. Let the other person say what he/she has to say in his/her own defense. It may be necessary to continue the reprimand at a later time if the person is unable to listen constructively because of strong emotional feelings.[24]

Handling Grievances

Another type of interpersonal communication that takes place between supervisors and employees centers on grievances. There are many kinds of employee complaints. The easiest for the good supervisor to handle are those cases in which the employee has analyzed the problem, found the cause of the trouble, and presents a straightforward request for the supervisor's help in correcting it.[25] The supervisor then must determine whether the grievance is valid and if the proposed solution is in the best interest of the employee and the organization.

The supervisor will find that his or her tasks, regarding grievances, center on:

Diagnosing. In diagnosing, the manager determines what is wrong and defines the nature of the grievance or disturbance.

Adjusting. It is also the supervisor's task to adjust by bridging the gap between the employee's demands and the satisfactions which he/she gets.

Prevention. In prevention, the manager attempts to conduct the organization's business in harmony with the human demands of employees, and to assist the employees to adapt their demands to the conditions of the business. If this can be done, grievances can be minimized.

Any grievance can be understood by paying attention to:

a. the complaint itself or other expressions of the grievance. What is the person really complaining about?
b. the concrete conditions with which the employee is dissatisfied or upon which he/she projects dissatisfaction. Often general gripes, with no examples, are heard. It is impossible to deal with non-specific matters as there is nothing specifically that can be corrected.
c. the employee's demands on job security, fair pay, advancement, and social

recognition. Are there matters that you can deal with or are these part of negotiations or union agreements?

d. the employee's position in the company and his/her informal relations with the working group and supervisors. Is the person representing an isolated attitude or is the opinion representative of a significant group?

e. the employee's personal situation—individual and social. Some employees can be classified as difficult personalities. If so, the employee may have to be dealt with via non-traditional methods.[26]

Dealing With Difficult Personalities

Some people you will have to deal with have difficult personalities, who, through interpersonal means, cause stress for themselves and others. They tend to have the inability to accept feedback, corrective suggestions, or job evaluations, and they don't perceive themselves as being difficult.

There seem to be patterns by which difficult personalities operate:

Victimization. They feel that others are out to get them. They commonly use phrases like, "I am being victimized by . . . (the organization, you, those who I am working with)."

Non-accountability. They often disappear for periods of time, fail to submit records, or want to work independently although the job does not require working alone. A common statement may be, "I must be free to do my job."

Low degree of empathy. They will tolerate no criticism and demand to be told how good they are.[27]

There are basically three approaches which may be used to deal with difficult personalities—direct intervention, indirect coping, and reactive coping.

Direct Intervention In **direct intervention,** the manager actively attempts to change the person's pattern. This is done by collecting data on what the person has done, ascertaining how it affects the worker as well as others, meeting with the person, asking for his/her perceptions, presenting the complaint or observation, agreeing with the person on a course of action based on the company's and the person's need system, agreeing on an assessment date, and then following up. If the problem is solved, the issue is dropped. If not, a separating action (firing or reassignment) may be taken, or there is a recognition based on the necessity for further changes. The types of help usually suggested are retraining, counseling, change of job, or self-help.[28]

Indirect Coping In **indirect coping,** the manager arranges to work around the person. If the person is difficult to work with in a group then he/she is not assigned to group activities. If the person does not work well with another employee, then each is given responsibilities that eliminate any contact between the two.

The difficulty of this indirect approach is that it very seldom solves the problem; instead, the effort may serve to hide it. Because the problem is still present, it could, and usually does, resurface.

Reactive Coping   In **reactive coping,** the manager refuses to become involved with either the problem or the person. Instead, the leader allows the person to continue to operate in his/her own way and accepts the conflicts that result. This almost never solves the problem. This course of action is usually taken when the employee is so good at a specific task that more negative consequences would come from firing him/her or giving him/her another job, than from putting up with the stress created.

In dealing with difficult personalities, it must be remembered that many such people are extremely successful. They may get what they want because they are difficult, and no one wants to buck them. They may also be extremely talented but cannot work well with others.

Directing

Much of the interpersonal interaction in organizations centers on **directing,** the giving of orders, and the giving of directions. Whether on the supervisory or production levels, it is often necessary to explain new procedures, instruct employees in the operation of equipment, and clarify policies.

Order Giving   An important responsibility of individuals involved in management or supervisory roles is order giving. A recommended process for order giving is composed of seven distinct steps.[29] By following this process, organizational interference may be eliminated.

Step 1: *Planning.* It is absolutely essential that the order giver have a plan. Important considerations are: What action is needed to get certain results? What is the time available? What are the allowable costs? Who should carry out the order? What kind of order is best suited to getting the task done?

Step 2: *Preparing the order receiver.* Get the attention of the order receiver—call a meeting to inform the receiver that the directions or order will be given. When an order is given, it should be accompanied by a briefing session at which time the objective is pointed out and the method discussed. If prior information is going to be needed, hand it out before the actual presenting session.

Step 3: *Presenting the order.* The tone and manner in which the orders are expressed are often as important as the words chosen. Even words that are innocuous in themselves can arouse resentment by being used in an offensive way, thus creating psychological interference. The directions should be clear and precise—the fewer words the better, but take care to clarify any complicated ideas or unclear terms, or semantic interference may result. Make sure you follow a step-by-step procedure in order to avoid organizational interference.

Step 4: *Verification.* Watch for feedback or search it out. Make sure the receiver understands what is expected and how it is to be carried out.

Step 5: *Action.* The receiver should now know that is expected and then carry it out.

Step 6: *Follow-up.* Unfortunately, most supervisors stop at Step 5. This often proves fatal, as there is no way of knowing whether the action is being carried out effectively. Checkups and follow-ups are extremely important in any order-giving cycle because, even though the order receiver is doing the right thing, he/she may run into some unforeseen difficulty that interferes with carrying out the order, such as material failure or tool shortage.

Step 7: *Appraisal.* If everything goes as planned, then the sender has learned a valuable lesson that should be repeated. If not, then corrections must be made. "Almost always when an order has somehow gone wrong and the expected results have not been achieved, faulty order-giving is to blame."[30] If the follow-up proves that something is wrong, the order giver should ask these questions: Did I prepare the person? Did I present the right order? Did I verify a reaction? Did I follow up the order?

Giving Directions

One of the common communicative activities that businesspersons find themselves involved in is the process of **directing**—giving directions. Directions describe such things as how to do a task, how to get a desired end effect, how to achieve a goal, or how to geographically get someplace. Some general principles of effective direction giving include: be specific, include the necessary details, organize the ideas, use understandable terms, encourage feedback, break the task into parts, and follow up.

In giving directions make sure that you choose words that exactly indicate what should be done and how to do it. In explaining, for example, how a piece of machinery works, refer to the specific dials, knobs, or instruments which are important to know.

Make sure that you illustrate, either by doing the procedure, or giving all the steps in a logical order with exactly what should be done at each step. Phrases like, "you know," "stuff like that," and "push that whatchamacallit" are of little value. Indicate if something must be done with the right or left hand, the specific tool that must be available to carry out the operation, the exact names of chemicals or substances that must be combined and in what order. Don't just say, "type the letter." Indicate what margins you want, what spacing, if it should be on a letterhead, if you want to proof-read it before it is sent out, or any variations from the usual procedure that might be necessary. It is a good idea to write a list of the sequential order that should be followed, or provide a drawing of the machinery, or have a model of what the end product should look like.

Remember that someone new to the job, or who doesn't have your background and experience, may not be familiar with the terminology of the job, the names of the streets, the meanings of the initials and jargon that you commonly use to describe something. Define terms that you feel the person will not easily understand. The phrase "HRD plan" may be clear to you, but someone not familiar with the Human Resource Development methods of business will be lost. Use the words, indicate that it is usually referred to as "HRD," and briefly explain what it is, if you feel that this will help the person.

Some new employees, or communicatively apprehensive (shy) ones, may feel that they will be perceived as dense or will be punished for asking questions. Try to encourage the person to whom you are giving directions to ask. You also may aid them by asking them questions as you go along to make sure you are getting the feedback necessary to realize whether or not the direction-receiver is understanding the message.

Make sure that you don't overload the receiver. If there are many steps in a process, or if the directions are very complicated, it might be wise to break the explanation into parts or give the person a handout, such as a picture, or a list of the steps to follow.

Be certain that you follow up the order-giving, if at all possible. Have the person demonstrate how to operate the machine. Request that the person repeat your directions.

Much time and money is wasted yearly by having to repeat directions, retrain employees, and destroy improperly written memos, letters, and reports. Tempers become frayed and people become frustrated when they don't understand and can't fulfill their job needs. By being specific, giving the necessary details, organizing the ideas, using understandable terms, encouraging feedback, and following up, the odds of effective direction-giving increase. If employees don't understand, you will have to repeat the entire message over, so why not save time and do it right the first time?

Job Training

Many people in training positions (foremen, supervisors) claim that they do not have time to train their subordinates because they are too busy correcting mistakes. These mistakes might never have been made if the workers had been properly trained in the first place. The basis for proper training is a step-by-step procedure and the effective use of interpersonal skills.[31] Four steps in training are as follows.

Step 1: *Prepare the worker.* A worker who knows what is going to be done and why it is going to be done is more likely to be able to carry out the assignment. Knowledge of the importance, benefits, and rewards of doing the job aid an individual in having a positive attitude toward doing it.

Step 2: *Present the operation.* Organize the ideas in a step-by-step procedure that can be followed exactly by the learner (see the section on Organizational Interference earlier in this chapter). Be organized. Be sure you know the procedure and carry it out. Encourage questions. Avoid information overload. Do not give the receiver more information than can be handled in one session. It might be necessary to divide the training into several sessions if the process is complicated.

Step 3: *The learner performs the operation.* Stay with the learner until the operation has been performed to make sure that it can be done successfully. Compliment success. Ask what the learner is doing and why. Encourage questions about the operation. If the process is not being done correctly, evaluate whether the procedure, in the way in which you presented it, was the best explanation possible. If so, repeat the procedure; if not, adjust the message—define terms in order to control semantic interference, demonstrate what you had explained previously, or break the operation down into smaller units. It may even necessitate a different approach for just this one employee. Not all people learn the same way and alternate methods may be needed for certain people.

Step 4: *Follow-up.* Even after the person has learned the procedure things can go wrong. Keep an eye on the learner's progress and keep the channels open for communication.

CONFLICT AND CONFLICT RESOLUTION

A major interpersonal area of concern when people work together is that of conflict. **Conflict** is the emotional state you experience when the behavior of another person interferes with your behavior. Conflict usually centers on a struggle between incompatible interests, often resulting in psychological interference. Conflict can be a major cause of personal difficulty in the work environment.

Conflict in the Work Environment

Changes in procedures, working conditions, salary, rights and responsibilities, or philosophies of operation are possible sources of conflict in businesses and industries. The issues that arouse conflict may be real or perceived.

Research has identified six specific sources for conflict in the business environment:

The role of power. In a communicative situation, people who are powerful or powerless tend to act in certain ways. The powerful person may demand, control, or threaten. The powerless person may feel put upon, insecure, and unappreciated. A fight for emotional survival may be constantly waged between the powerful and the powerless.

The structure of the organization. Some organizational charts align people against each other. The modes of operation might encourage a fight for power and position because of the line of command where officer must compete against officer, supervisor against supervisor, and worker against worker, rather than working together in a cooperative structure. In addition, union and management may perceive each other as adversaries, resulting in a power struggle for control.

Fear (real or perceived). The ability to be rewarded or punished has many underlying potential conflict parameters. In some organizations the constant threat of disciplinary action, which may include temporary layoffs, demotion, or even firing, can create a conflict environment. Individuals who feel watched and not trusted, who are disciplined and never praised, often feel stressed and are apt to act in conflicting ways.

Personality differences. The work environment may place people together who have strong philosophical and ethical differences. These differences can be the seeds from which conflict grows.

Hidden agenda. Because of the need to satisfy certain job or personal requirements, some people act in a way that best serves their interests. A sales manager may oppose a new sales plan that eliminates salaries and puts all the salesmen on commissions. Even though the new plan may be in the best interest of the company, the sales manager may come up with many reasons for not putting the plan into action. The **hidden agenda,** the real motivating but unstated reason, may well be that he perceives a loss in personal revenue if the action is taken.

Change. Whenever change is proposed, a possibility for conflict arises. Attempting numerous changes increases the likelihood of resistance. This is especially true if the proposed changes alter the lifestyle of the individuals involved (e.g., job loss, decreased responsibility, changed working conditions, need to relocate). The acceptance of change takes time and depends on the individual's desire to change.

Conflict Resolution

☐

Conflict resolution is an attempt to reconcile differences in order to accept, reduce, or eliminate the conflict. Conflict resolution is based on an understanding of the basic principles of conflict. These include:

Conflict does not have to be hidden or disposed of. Reasonable people can disagree and don't have to be either right or wrong. Or they can recognize that, due to the nature of the conflict, the participants may be powerless to bring about change. Sometimes, the best way of dealing with conflict is to acknowledge that it exists and that, due to certain conditions or requirements, there is little or nothing that can be done about it. For example, a company has purchased a particular brand of computers, and several employees want to work with another brand. Since the employees have no control over the purchasing of equipment, the conflict over which system to use is for naught.

Often, *conflict can't be dealt with as an intellectual issue unless the individuals involved are really interested in solving the dilemma.* Logically explaining something to another person will do little good unless that person is open to active listening. Because of the very nature of the way in which most people perceive conflict, most arguing does not solve problems. People usually think that the way to deal with conflict is to change the other person. Rather than being directed at the resolution of some specified issue, conflict tends to be unfocused, destructive, or indirectly aggressive, where attacking the people involved often holds precedence over addressing the issue. Conflict can be resolved only if the participants accept the concept of peacemaking. **Peacemaking** centers on understanding the concept that behaviors, not personalities, issues, not people, are involved.

Options for Conflict Resolution

There are three options for conflict resolution: win-lose, lose-lose, or win-win.

A **win-lose** approach centers on one person or company winning and another person or organization losing. For example, assume that your company has merged with another. This action necessitates selecting a new company logo. If you have proposed one insignia and someone else has proposed a different one, then a natural competition emerges because only one logo can be chosen. There will be a winner and there will be a loser as long as no other alternatives are possible.

Lose-lose takes place when one person feels so strongly that the other person is wrong, or so desires the other person defeated, that he/she is willing to lose in order to defeat the other person. Let's say that you and two others propose logos for the new organization. If you dislike competitor A, and there is a chance that your suggestion won't be chosen and that hers will, you might side with competitor C to make sure that your "enemy" doesn't win. Thus, you lose and your enemy also loses.

A **win-win** takes place when people are willing to work together through peace-making in order for both to feel that they have accomplished their goal. Using our example, if it appears that opinion is split between two proposed logos, one option would be for you to work with your competitor to design an insignia that both of you could take credit for and with which you would be proud.[32]

Styles of Conflict Resolution

Each person has a unique style for handling conflicts. The usual styles of conflict resolution are: avoidance, accommodation, smoothing over, compromising, competition, and integration.[33]

Avoidance   Some people choose to avoid dealing with the issue and settle for the status quo. This **avoidance** usually takes the form of attempting to withdraw from contact with the other person, or avoiding the issue of conflict when the possibility for taking some action is present. If, for example, someone has been asking for help with their work, the avoider may leave his/her desk if the person requesting help comes toward the avoider's desk. Or, if asked about really minding doing the extra work, the avoider may answer, "No," when really wanting to say, "Yes."

This avoiding method is rarely successful because the conflict does not go away by itself, even though the avoider wishes it would. Avoidance can be effective only if the conflict is short-lived or minor.

Accommodation   In **accommodation** one person puts other people's needs above their own. During conflict, an accommodating individual gives in and lets the other person have his/her way, feeling that the other person's needs are more important. If someone asks for a favor, the accommodating person will give in, even though he/she may not want to do so.

This style of resolution rarely solves the problem, for one person wins, while the other loses. The winner feels great; the loser often feels used. It does, however, give the accommodator peace and quiet—at all costs. If that is the most important thing, then accommodation is a positive method.

Smoothing-over   The end goal of **smoothing over** is to give the impression that everything is all right. The person who smooths over conflict usually lets the other person know what they want, but not in a forceful enough way to get the other person to take the required action. The major purpose of smoothing-over is to maintain the relationship. If a fellow employee asks you to help him with a report, you could smooth-over by saying, "Well, OK, but I've really got a lot of work of my own to do." You hope that the person will take the hint and withdraw the request. Usually, that is not the case. The desired assistance is available, so why should he be concerned?

If the relationship with the person is important, and the other person appears willing to end it if you don't act on his request, then smoothing-over may be appropriate.

Compromise   In **compromise,** concerns are identified and addressed. The advantage of this method over avoidance, accommodation, or smoothing-over is that the issue is discussed and, hopefully, resolved.

In its best form, compromise allows each person to understand the views and needs of the other. Each can then propose solutions to the problem and trade back and forth until an agreeable settlement is reached. Unfortunately, this style often results in both participants being dissatisfied, as neither gets exactly what he/she wants.

Competition   Power is at the center of competition. In **competition** the name of the game is winning. Someone must win and someone must lose. I get my way or you get yours. Whoever is stronger, more powerful, and more cunning is going to be the winner. Threats, abuse, and even blackmail are the tools of the competitor.

The competitive style gets the issue out into the open. And, one way or another, someone gets their way. If you win, you will probably feel good about the victory. Unfortunately, you may also be a loser. Competitive conflict resolution usually results in hurt feelings, frustrations, and destructive working relationships and friendships. In spite of the negative aspects of this method, an aggressive methodology is often applied regularly by some businesspeople.

Integration   The ideal method of conflict resolution is integration. In **integration** communicators confront the problem directly and work toward a solution that all parties can agree upon. This takes much time and a commitment that focuses on preserving the relationship and the dignity of all involved.

Integration centers on the concept that the most critical issue at stake in conflict resolution is the self-esteem of the people involved. Integration uses the following principles to preserve human dignity and to control psychological interference:

One or both parties refuse to put the conflict into a win-lose form. No one has to be victorious; no one has to be defeated. The objective of the confrontation is to resolve the problem and achieve a workable solution; not to win a war.

At least one of the participants will verbalize the need to preserve the relationship. You can disagree with someone without hating or destroying that person.

One or both parties will give evidence that they understand the other person's feeling, even though they find the other person's actions unacceptable.

They will restrain themselves from interrupting each other even if the effort is painful. An honest exchange of ideas takes place when there are listeners as well as speakers.

Honesty is an indispensable ingredient. Tell it like it is, why you feel as you do, what can and cannot be done, and why.

Both parties refrain from critiquing the other person's behavior and from blaming them for causing the conflict. No one can make you mad. You commit yourself to the act of anger. By blaming the other person, little can or will be accomplished.

Working Through a Conflict

In working through a conflict with a coworker or a supervisor, some individuals choose just to ignore the conflict, hoping that it will disappear. If it is a minor conflict, this indeed may be the result and both parties essentially will forget about the incident. It may not be so easy, however, to wish away the stress. Consequently, it may be more appropriate for the communicators to attempt to defuse the hostility.

Defusion of a conflict usually can be made more manageable by delaying any potential confrontation. If a person has a conflict with a coworker, for instance, it could be useful for both parties not to discuss the situation until tempers have cooled off and the conflict is put into its proper perspective. It may be difficult to achieve a defusion, however, because both parties may be sufficiently ego-involved in the incident and find it necessary to save face in the relationship.

Direct confrontation of a conflict may be the most open, effective communication strategy to employ in resolving conflicts, particularly if both parties to the conflict are able and willing to handle the confrontation. Some people tend to avoid confrontation because the risk is great—we can end relationships and stop communication as a consequence of dealing head-on with an issue. But, in the long run, most people who work with each other on a daily basis often are appreciative of the chance to "clear the air" and get on with their business. A continuing conflict can be disruptive to the communication climate and lead to distress and unhappiness on the part of all individuals involved in the situation. Holding grudges and unexpressed grievances takes effort and interferes with progress.

Direct confrontation, it should be recognized, probably is more realistic for individuals within any organization who have a peer relationship. Direct confrontation with one's own superior may well bring untold risks if the superior is unable to put the confrontation in the proper perspective. People have been fired from their jobs, demoted, and otherwise mistreated for openly challenging a superior, especially one who is unwilling to "lose face" and deal with the communication in a constructive fashion.

One of the most popular and destructive conflicts found in many organizations is the natural tendency to blame the boss for everything that is wrong with an organization. Workers who have direct dealings with an immediate supervisor and little contact with those at higher levels come to lay all their problems on the head of the manager. The manager then has the task of communicating why he or she responds and acts as he or she does, bringing workers to the understanding of the institutional constraints and procedures which may realistically define the manager's role in working with the employees.

Steps in Conflict Resolution   Unfortunately, there are no guaranteed solutions or surefire approaches for settling disputes. In fact, it must be understood that not all conflicts can be resolved. There are, however, some steps that can be useful in attempting conflict resolution.

1. Define the conflict.
2. View the conflict as a joint problem.
3. State the problem.

4. Check your perceptions.
5. Generate possible solutions.
6. Reach a mutually acceptable solution.
7. Implement and evaluate the situation.[34]

Assertiveness

Avoidance, accommodation, and smoothing-over are nonassertive methods of conflict resolution. They are **nonassertive** since they are a means of communication that does not directly attempt to resolve the problem. Competition is **aggressive** because it does not take the other person into consideration. When well used, compromise is an assertive act. Integration is always assertive. **Assertive** communication takes place when the individual accomplishes his or her task while taking into consideration the feelings and needs of others.

Effective conflict resolution requires that individuals learn how to be assertive communicators. Assertiveness training has become a popular workshop topic in organizations as individuals have come to recognize that an assertive communication style can be an asset to upward mobility in career paths. The assertive individual, who is neither aggressive nor retiring, usually can accomplish his/her objectives within the work force. The assertive person is one who: exhibits high-level energy; has courage and flexibility; has strong self-respect and the ability to deal with challenging situations; can handle confrontations; exhibits self-confidence; often establishes dominance in group meetings; is allowed the most talking time in meetings; and is able to command all the attention he/she wants or needs. Assertive persons stand out in group meetings because "their contributions receive more consideration than others' and the most significant points and remarks are usually addressed to them."[35]

In asserting, describe your perspective. Statements of "I feel . . . ," and "It makes me feel . . ." will get more positive results than "You are . . . ," and "You make me. . . ." An effectively assertive person is polite but firm; open to suggestions, but not namby-pamby; cooperative, but not gutless.

Being Assertive "Being assertive really means understanding yourself and being comfortable with who and what you are. It does not mean that you are impolite, irascible, uncouth, or defensive. It does not mean using abusive language, or daring someone to knock the chip off your shoulder."[36] The assertive individual considers his/her needs and decides if the consequences of asserting will be greater than those of not asserting. In most cases the answer will be to take a stand, get at the problem, and solve it. The major question in deciding whether or not to assert is, "What is the worst thing that can happen?" Usually the answer is that you will no longer feel like you are being **victimized,** or manipulated by others. No one but you is deciding what you will do, and when you will do it; no one is insisting that you take actions you don't want to take.

The assertiveness code is: Is it hurting anyone? Is it harming you? Do you enjoy it? If so, it's okay.[37]

To be assertive:

Clarify the situation and focus on the issue. (What is the goal? What do I want to accomplish?)

Determine how the assertive behavior will help you accomplish your goal. (Will explaining your needs or stating what you want resolve the problem and get the desired action?)

Determine what you usually do to avoid asserting yourself in this situation? (In the past, what did I do in similar situations? Did it accomplish my goal? Did it solve the problem?)

Why do you want to give that up and assert yourself instead? (Was I unsuccessful with my usual style of conflict resolution? If so, then a new methodology is in order. Is this issue important enough to risk the hurt or rejection, or loss of a friend or a job that I might suffer if I assert myself?)

What might be stopping you from asserting yourself? (Do I have irrational beliefs? Am I afraid to change the past? Is the person victimizing me to the degree that I am afraid to act?)

Do you have the information you need to go ahead and act? (Do I know what must be solved? Am I sure of my facts in the case?)

Can you let the other person know that you hear and understand him/her, let him/her know how you feel, tell him/her what you want? (Do I have the skills to assert myself effectively?)

Some basic principles that may help you to be effectively assertive include:

a. When expressing refusal, express a decisive "no". Explain why you are refusing but don't be unduly apologetic. Where applicable, offer the other person an alternative course of action.

b. Request an explanation when asked to do something unreasonable.

c. Look the person with whom you're talking in the eye.

d. When expressing annoyance or criticism, comment on the person's behavior, rather than attacking him/her. ("I feel taken advantage of when you ask me to do your work and then you go on a break," versus "You're not fair! You make me do your work and you go on a break.") An attack will usually start a conflict, while the "I" statement is less likely to elicit a defensive response.

e. Remember that no one knows what is going on in your head unless you tell people what you are thinking and feeling. Hoping doesn't bring about action or change; doing does.[38]

Effective assertion involves making statements concerning the situation, problem, or desired change. Assertive statements require thought and skill.

Assertive Messages　　There are three types of assertive messages: simple assertive statements, empathic statements or responses, and confronting responses. A **simple assertive statement** is a statement of fact. An **empathic statement/response** recognizes the other person's position but is stated in a way that expresses your own needs. It may follow a simple assertion, or be the first step in the assertive process. A **confronting**

response usually follows a simple assertion or an empathetic response. It describes the person's behavior and then states your position.

The type of assertion to be used depends on the situation in which you find yourself and the message you want to get across. Assume that you are waiting at the copy machine and someone from another department pushes in front of you.

Simple assertion: "I was here first." (This is said directly to the person, in a matter-of-fact way. The hope is that the person will move or wait until you are done, thus solving the problem.)

Empathic statement/response: "I know you're probably in a hurry, but I was here first." (This can be said as a follow-up to the simple assertion you just made, or it can be the opening statement. The intention is to recognize that the person may have a reason for doing what was done, but that you are not going to allow it to happen.)

Confronting response: "I was here first. You cut in front of me. I would like you to move." (The intent is to allow the person to know what is wrong and how he/she can correct it.)

Sometimes it is necessary to develop an in-depth message in order to deal with a major problem. As good public speakers have discovered, it is often a good idea to develop the message, rehearse it, and present it.

DESC Scripting   A method for planning an assertive message has been described as DESC Scripting.[39] **DESC Scripting** entails describing, expressing, specifying, and stating possible consequences.

This is the plan for a DESC script:

*D*escribe: Describe as specifically and objectively as possible the behavior that is bothersome to you. (Example: "I was told by you that my raise would be $65 a week. I only received $30 more in my paycheck.")

*E*xpress: Say how you feel and think about this behavior. (Example: "It makes me angry and confused because I was not given the amount that we agreed upon.")

*S*pecify: Ask for a different, specific behavior. (Example: "I would like my pay raised by our agreed upon amount.")

*C*onsequences: Spell out concretely and simply what the reward or consequences will be for changing the behavior. (Example: "If you make the change I will take on the extra work load that we agreed upon," or "If the increase is not given I will make a formal complaint to the union.")

Remember that in DESC Scripting you may stop at any time during the process when you receive satisfaction. If, following the description step, the supervisor shows you a copy of the order and indicates that she sent in the request, but that payroll may not yet have received it, then you need go no further.

If you go as far as the consequence step, be certain that you are willing to carry out your promise or threat. If you are not willing to quit, don't threaten to do so. If you aren't willing to sue, then don't propose that solution. If the union will not handle the matter, then threatening to complain to them is an idle bluff.[40]

THE CHANGING ROLE OF INTERPERSONAL COMMUNICATION IN BUSINESS

■ The American workplace will require new rules for the future, rules "to encourage people to channel their creativity away from themselves and back onto the concrete tasks that need doing in the new era . . . inventing new modes of self-help, making quality of life compatible with productivity, creating community through caring for others."[41] Such an objective will require new rules for our interpersonal communication at work, communication which brings with it a commitment to making individuals feel that they have an important role to play in the structure of the organization so that both the needs of the employer and the employee are satisfied.

SUMMARY

Interpersonal communication involves the exchange of messages and the development of a relationship based on the effect of those messages.

Most problems in communication occur in the relationship dimension rather than in the content dimension.

Interpersonal transactions are multichanneled.

Four components of interpersonal communication are (1) being aware of how and why interference takes place in communication, (2) selecting the most appropriate from a repertoire of communication acts, (3) implementing these communication choices effectively through verbal and nonverbal means, and (4) evaluating these communication attempts according to the elements of appropriateness and effectiveness.

The types of communicative interference are environmental, physiological, semantic, syntactic, organizational, psychological, and social.

Self-disclosure is the revealing of a person's private world to someone else.

Interpersonal communication is at the heart of most business dealings.

Businesses use the telephone to keep in touch, solve problems, deal with emergencies, and carry out many kinds of transactions.

The One-Minute Manager theory centers on the philosophy that almost everybody wants to be working in a meaningful way.

Managers are sometimes called upon to criticize or reprimand employees.

An important responsibility of the individual involved in management or supervisory roles is directing (order giving and direction giving).

One of the major interpersonal areas of concern with people working together is that of conflict.

Options for conflict resolution are win-lose, lose-lose, and win-win.

Conflict resolution styles include: avoidance, accommodation, smoothing over, compromising, competing, and integration.

A person may choose to be assertive, aggressive, or nonassertive in dealing with conflict.

Learning assertive behavior is an important interpersonal skill.

THINGS TO DO

1. Think back to the last time you were involved in a conflict. Were you arguing issues or personalities? Did you resolve the conflict? If so, how? If not, why not?

2. Bring in an object or a series of objects that have to be assembled (a neck tie; a shoe with shoelaces; a camera and film; a screw, screw driver, and a piece of wood). Plan the directions you will be giving to a member of the class. He/she is to carry out the task by following your directions exactly as given. If he/she is not successful, redo the directions and try again. Keep adjusting until the task can be done using your directions.

3. Think back to a strong verbal exchange (either a positive or a negative incident) you have had with someone you consider very close (best friend, parent, brother, or sister). What were the emotions of the interaction? Describe how the relationship had an effect on what happened. Discuss this based on the chapter's comments about relationships and their effects on communication.

4. Think back over the past twenty-four hours. Did you have a problem in interpersonal communications? Describe what happened. Analyze the breakdown by using the interference factors discussed in this chapter. How could the breakdown have been avoided?

5. Find an example of a letter to the editor of a newspaper or a magazine article that contains *bureaucratese*. Bring it to class. A discussion will take place concerning the use of jargon, acronyms, and euphemisms based on the articles the class members bring in.

6. Your instructor will divide you into groups of three. One person in each group is to teach the other two people a process using the direction-giving procedure described in the text. You may select any task that requires physical activity and three or more steps in the procedure. Each team of employees will demonstrate the process to the entire class in order to test the effectiveness of the order giving.

7. Using the vocabulary in this chapter identify the type of interference which caused the transactional problem in communication in each of the following situations.
   a. You tell your uncle about a course you are taking in computer math and he is confused because he does not understand the words you use.
   b. A friend tells you of an economic theory she has recently learned about, but the information is mixed up, and she keeps jumping back and forth in her ideas.
   c. You are speaking to a secretary in an office where there are three other people typing. The secretary has trouble hearing you.
   d. In discussing a new advertising campaign, the public relations firm representative uses television production terms you do not understand.
   e. You have been taught that swearing is wrong, especially in formal settings. One of the company executives swears throughout his report on improving the company image. You get upset and don't listen to what he is saying.

f. You have trouble understanding the representative of a Japanese firm who is trying to sell you equipment because the placement of his words in the sentences sounds strange to you.

g. Your secretary has had an operation which has caused a short-term loss of his hearing. It is difficult for you to converse with him.

h. You have been assigned to do a store inventory with another employee. She has just broken up with her boyfriend. In talking with her, you find her conversation is negative and she gives only surface attention to what you have to say. When you explain that it is difficult to work under these conditions, her anger is so great she stomps out of the room and refuses to come back.

8. Bring a bag or box to class which has five items in it that represent some value, belief, attitude, or personal attribute you have. The class members will show each of their objects and explain why they brought it. After the presentations, discuss the following:

a. Was it difficult to talk about yourself in public? If so, why?

b. Are there things which you could have brought that would have given some different insights into your belief/value/attitude system, but did not? If so, why didn't you bring those things in?

c. If you only had to share your thoughts with your best friend, rather than with the class, would you have displayed or stated different information?

NOTES

1. E. T. Klemmer and F. W. Snyder, "Measurement of Time Spent Communicating," *Journal of Communication* 22 (June 1972):142–58.

2. For an excellent discussion of relationships and power as a communication affector see Charles T. Brown, and Paul W. Keller, *Monologue To Dialogue,* 2nd ed. (Englewood Cliffs: Prentice-Hall, 1979).

3. Ibid., 96.

4. Based on a concept presented in K. J. Connolly and J. S. Bruner, *The Growth of Competence* (New York: Academic Press, 1974), 3–7.

5. Factors that cause communicative breakdowns are sometimes referred to as *noise.* The concept appears in Roy Berko, Andrew Wolvin, and Darlyn Wolvin, *Communicating: A Social and Career Focus,* 4th ed. (Boston: Houghton Mifflin, 1989). The term *interference* is suggested in Richard E. Crable, *Using Communication* (Boston: Allyn & Bacon, 1979).

6. "Gobbledygook," *Washington Star,* 8 November 1977.

7. Brown and Keller, *Monologue to Dialogue,* 165.

8. Edward Hall and Mildred Hall, "The Sounds of Silence," *Playboy* (June 1971): 140.

9. Sidney Jourard, *The Transparent Self* (New York: Van Nostrand Reinhold, 1964), 5–6.

10. Carl J. Armbruster, "Communication Aids Getting Ahead," *Elyria Chronicle-Telegram,* 30 July 1978, D3.

11. Ibid.

12. Abraham Maslow, *Motivation and Personality* (New York: Harper and Row, 1970).

13. William Schutz, *The Interpersonal Underworld* (Palo Alto: Science Behavior Books, 1966), 13.

14. Everett M. Rogers and Dilip K. Bhowmik, "Homophily and Heterophily: Relationships Concepts for Communication Research," in *Speech Communication Behavior Perspectives and Principles*, ed. Larry L. Barker and Robert J. Kibler (Englewood Cliffs: Prentice-Hall, 1971), 206–225.

15. Howard Muson, "Getting the Phone's Number," *Psychology Today* (April 1982):42.

16. Based, in part, on a series of handouts distributed by the Community Education Division, Lorain County Community College, April, 1982.

17. Richard C. Anderson, *Communication: The Vital Artery* (Watsonville, CA: Correlan Publications, 1973), 2.

18. *Effective Communication On The Job* (New York: American Manufacturing Association, 1963), 115.

19. A. Vogel, "Why Don't Employees Speak Up?" *Personnel Administration* 30 (May–June 1967):21.

20. Gerald M. Goldhaber, *Organizational Communication* (Dubuque: Wm. C. Brown 1986), 205.

21. *Effective Communication On the Job* (New York: American Manufacturing Association, 1963), 115.

22. James T. Yenckel, "Careers: Praise the Worker and Pass the Profits," *Washington Post*, 27 Sept. 1982, C5; based on interviews with Kenneth Blanchard and Spencer Johnson, authors of *The One Minute Manager* (New York: Morrow Publishing, 1982).

23. Ibid.

24. Eileen Mazer, "How To Really Say What's on Your Mind," *Prevention* (September 1981).

25. *Effective Communication on the Job, A Guide for Supervisors and Executives,* revised ed. (American Management Association, 1963), 223.

26. Ibid., 231.

27. John Hollwitz, "Difficult Personalities" (Paper presented at the Speech Communication Association Convention, Chicago, 1 November 1984).

28. Ron Walker and Daniel Barnes, "Communicating with the Difficult Personality: Problems in an Academic Setting" (Paper presented at the Speech Communication Association convention, Chicago, 1984).

29. *Effective Communication On the Job,* 207–9.

30. *Effective Communication On the Job,* 209.

31. Ibid., 169.

32. Lawrence Rosenfeld, "Conflict's NOT a Four-Letter Word," unpublished workshop manual, 1982, 5, as adapted from Deborah Weider-Hatfield, "A Unit in Conflict Management Communication Skills," *Communication Education,* 30 (July 1981):265–273.

33. For a complete discussion of conflict and resolution see: Ron Adler, Lawrence Rosenfeld, and Neil Towne, *Interplay,* 3d ed. (New York: Holt, Rinehart and Winston, 1983), 277–301.

34. The procedure presented was conceived by Richard Weaver, in *Understanding Interpersonal Communcation* (Glenview, IL: Scott, Foresman and Company, 1978). It is a variation of the Dewey problem-solving method as presented in John Dewey, *How We Think* (Chicago: D. C. Heath, 1910).

35. Eugene Raudsepp and Joseph Yeager, "Office Power," *Passages* (April 1981):8–10, 12.

36. Leah Curtin, "A Profile of Assertive Behavior," *Supervisor Nurse* (May 1979):7.

37. Based on L. Z. Bloom, et al., *The New Assertive Woman* (New York: Dell Paperback Books, 1976).

38. Ibid.
39. Based on Sharon Bower and Gordon Bower, *Asserting Yourself* (Reading, MA: Addison-Wesley Publishers, 1976).
40. Ibid.
41. Daniel Yankelovich, *New Rules* (New York: Random House, 1981), 264.

II

BUSINESS COMMUNICATION

7

☐

Communication in the Organization

Communication is the life flow of any human enterprise. **Business communication** *(the transmission of ideas, information, direction, or criticism) is essential to an organization's existence; without it, the enterprise would cease to function.*[1]

Business organizations are complex communication systems.[2]

The individual entering today's business organization must function in a dynamic communication system.[3]

Communication is a vital and intrinsic part of management. Delegation, control, measurement, and motivation cannot exist without it.[4]

OVERVIEW   Organizational communication may flow downward from administrators to workers or upward from the workers to the corporate leaders. Communication is the basis for recruiting, hiring, training, job maintenance, and job performance and appraisal. Unfortunately, there are obstacles to effective corporate communication within organizations.

KEY WORDS

business communication
external communication
internal communication
intradepartmental communication
interdepartmental communication
proprietory communication
confidential communication
grapevine
issues management

corporate communication department
theory of differentiation/integration
linking-pin concept
organizational climate
organizational culture
trait analysis
critical incident analysis
Management by Objective (MBO)

Whether examining the basis for human enterprise, the business organization as a whole, the individuals who participate in the organization, or the management role in an organization, the same general conclusion can be reached—communication is a very important and integral part of the world of business. Some business experts feel that it is *the* most important aspect of business success or failure.[5]

Organizations today are caught in a frantic race to recoup the competitive edge of productivity which many analysts believe has been lost to Japanese industry. As a result, management specialists are concerned with determining just what can be done to restore quality. "The reality is that quality is essential to survival," so American manufacturing and service industries are trying everything "from statistical measurement of manufacturing processes to answering the phone on the first ring."[6]

As today's organizations work to be competitive in the world market, they are also changing their nature and scope. Rather than the typical manufacturing company with its management layers and hierarchy, the future information-based organization will more likely resemble a hospital, a university, or a symphony orchestra. Management experts suggest that "the typical business will be knowledge-based, an organization composed largely of specialists who direct and discipline their own performance through an organized feedback from colleagues, customers, and headquarters."[7]

As a consequence of this change in scope, organizations have found themselves caught up in communication problems for which they are not prepared. An official with the Ford Motor Company expressed his concern over the unprecedented communication crisis in business which hampers both **external communication** (relations with customers, stockholders, and regulatory agencies) and **internal communications** (the flow of messages within a network of individuals and groups). He contends that communication "should be at the top of the list of skills developed by every careerist who wants to get anywhere near the top of most any institution in this country,"[8] and he speaks for many others in private industry: "American corporations now rank communication among their greatest developmental needs."[9] This same attitude was expressed in an advertisement (figure 7.1)[10] run at one time by the SONY corporation.

Survey results reveal that an overwhelming amount of a businessperson's time is spent communicating. About half of an executive's time is spent in listening.[11] The average manager spends between 50 and 90 percent of his/her time communicating by one means or another.[12] First-line managers may spend 60 percent of their time in communication.[13] A study of communication time use confirmed that both written and oral communication time are very important to persons in business and industry. The survey of respondents revealed that 62 percent felt that the ability to communicate in writing was important to their jobs, and 90 percent stressed that the ability to communicate by speaking was important.[14]

Not only is the amount of time spent communicating a concern, but the effectiveness of an individual or even an entire corporation may be directly affected by communicative skills. Eighty-five percent of the personnel officers in a recent survey indicated that an applicant's odds of success in their companies depends on the applicant's ability to communicate effectively.[15] Another study suggests that in the most productive departments every worker spoke highly of the communication skills of the

FIGURE 7.1

department head, while in the least productive departments only 26 percent of the workers rated the boss as highly skilled as a communicator.[16] Labor grievances, in which the largest issues are discipline and discharge, are often decided in favor of the employee. The major cause for a company's loss of cases centered on the poor communication abilities of management while handling the problem.[17]

Communication difficulties can contribute to problems in motivation, attitude, leadership, coordination, and control. These areas of employee-employer relations clearly center on communication. "Employers and employees live in different worlds. They work in the same building, dress similarly, and lend their efforts to the success of the same company. Yet they don't speak the same language or even think the same. Consequently, there is an ever-present danger that the crossed wires of poor communication will result in somebody blowing an emotional fuse."[8]

The Heisler Study,[19] the basis for new understandings of what it takes to get ahead in business, indicates that employees' promotions are based on their skills in problem-solving, self-direction, cooperation, and communication. Despite the hard work ethic, which perpetuates the idea that how well one performs a task serves as the basis for promotion and merit pay, promotions actually are based on the employee's ability to deal with unforeseen problems as they arise. The major criteria for promoting people to higher levels of management could center on "here's a problem, you solve it; then communicate about the solution." Regardless of the level, however, it is clear that communication skills are the key to organizational effectivenesss. "In the 1990's and beyond we will need more leaders at all levels in our organizations who can communicate effectively to influence and direct others' behavior toward improving performance. In such efforts, the communication skills of first-line supervisors and informal group leaders can be as crucial as the CEO's (company executive officer) communication competence."[20]

A recent study revealed that, in order to facilitate the flow of information and ideas, and to achieve an understanding of feelings and attitudes, businesses and industries should conduct programs to increase the communication skills of their employees.[21] If this is true, questions are raised about the ways in which business communication takes place and the specific skills and competency levels needed by those who are involved in business.

An understanding of the communication skills and competencies exhibited and those needed in organizations may be developed by briefly examining (1) ways in which businesses communicate; (2) the role of corporate communication; (3) organizational structure and communication climate; (4) communication as an activity function; and (5) obstacles to communication in the organization.

WAYS IN WHICH BUSINESSES COMMUNICATE

■ Large businesses and corporations tend to be organized by departments or operational groups. In these cases, the communication tends to be within departments, between departments, outside the company, in restrictive patterns (proprietary and confidential communications), and through informal channels.

Communication Within Departments

☐ **Intradepartmental communication** centers on such matters as the time by which a project is to be accomplished, the disseminating operating information to field personnel, generating proposals for new or improved methods or products, explaining procedures, instructions for task performance, updating procedures, evaluation sessions, and problem-solving/decision-making sessions. An example of communication within a department is a group of budget analysts meeting to discuss procedures for implementing a new computer process.

In a study of business communication skills for the 1980s, executives from 45 major American industrial corporations were surveyed. Executives, when asked to identify the relative importance of future business communication skills, rated dictation as an important skill for the future. The expanding use of word and data processors may require greater speed and efficiency in creating messages through dictation—particularly when word processors are designed to respond to vocal rather than keyboard signals.

Communication Between Departments

☐　　　**Interdepartmental communication** takes place when there are alterations of existing policies or methods that must be shared for reinforcement of the way matters are to be handled between departments and for coordination of actions regarding a task or project that is to be jointly undertaken by several departments. For example, a personnel officer may need to organize staff briefing sessions of all supervisors within the organization to explain a new personnel evaluation and reporting system.

Communication Outside the Company

☐　　　Information must sometimes be shared with those with whom the company has dealings such as customers, vendors, financial institutions, stockholders, supplemental groups (insurance companies, employment agencies, lawyers, auditors), and governmental agencies.

A corporation may have to explain a new system of billing to its customers. Such a need for communication outside the company may involve an entire public information campaign, including television and radio announcements, a speaker's bureau, and direct mail circulars. A survey of executives asked to anticipate important communication skills for the future discovered that corporate executives perceived external communication to be of growing importance in industry.[23]

The communication explosion during the last thirty years has made it necessary for corporations to be concerned with dealing with the general public as well as their employees and customers. Every aspect of the corporation is under examination. The very existence of an organization is sometimes based on how it communicates to the public. There must be concern over the recall of defective products, the ways in which employee relations are handled, and the protection of the corporation's reputation. A case in point is the way in which McNeil Lab Inc. handled the situation in which bottles of Tylenol that were suspected of being poisoned were found on pharmacy shelves. Through swift action and an excellent public relations campaign, the manufacturer was able to convince consumers that the fault was not that of the bottler.

Proprietary and Confidential Communication

☐ Certain types of information must be communicated in special ways because of the nature of the material. The message preparation regarding this information is referred to as **proprietary communication.** Such communication might involve personal information about individual employees, planning personnel changes and departmental reorganizations, future company plans and developments, company finances, projected changes in basic company practices, special customer relations, vendor relationships, or operating data.

When the Privacy Act was passed by Congress, it became necessary for personnel managers to develop **confidential communication** practices which established procedures to protect an individual's right to have her/his records kept private. Once formulated, these regulations had to be communicated as company policy. Existing laws regarding equal opportunity employment also require that a clear procedure be set up in hiring and firing practices. Again, this requires special handling of information and effective communication processing.

Informal Channels

☐ All organizational members engage in informal communication. This type of communication originates spontaneously outside the formal channels and is the natural response to the need for social interaction.

If an organization is not departmentalized (often the case in proprietorships, partnerships, and small corporations), the internal communication tends to flow with no particular structure. Individuals may feel no obligation to follow an upward or downward structure, but instead may go directly to the individual with whom they wish to communicate rather than to an immediate supervisor.[24]

Even in departmentalized structures, there are times when the informal flow of communication between supervisors and subordinates is most effective.

In spite of the prevailing emphasis on studying communication within organizational settings, one big factor management has tended to overlook is the informal flow of communication.[25] Much analysis has been done on formal structures, but little is really known about the informal patterns. A particularly neglected aspect of organizational communication is the grapevine.

The Business Grapevine

☐ There is no dodging the fact that, as a carrier of news and gossip, the grapevine often affects the affairs of management.[26] The grapevine cannot be abolished or stopped. No manager can fire it, because it was not hired. It is simply there. The **grapevine** is an informal network that spreads information from person to person.

Some managers regard the grapevine as an evil—a network that regularly spreads rumors, destroys morale and reputations, leads to irresponsible actions, and challenges authority. Others regard it as a productive element because it acts as a safety valve and carries news fast. Still others see it as a mixed blessing.

An informal carrier of news and gossip in an organization is the grapevine. (© Denver Post)

There are some significant characteristics that describe the grapevine in most organizations.[27, 28]

1. Speed of transmission. It does not take long for information to spread once it has entered the system. Whether it is about an employee's illness, a pending merger, a large order, or a new company policy, the grapevine tends to beat the official announcement.
2. Little or no selectivity. The grapevine acts without conscious direction or thought. It will carry anything, anytime, anywhere.
3. The grapevine operates primarily in the work place, and the spread of information tends to be confined to the job environment.
4. The grapevine tends to be most active in organizations in which there are very structured and closed lines of communication.
5. Most grapevine rumors within organizations can be traced to barriers in communication between management and employees.

A survey of U.S. and Canadian industrial organizations analyzed the effectiveness of internal communication channels. The results demonstrate the importance of communication in management. It also revealed the communication channels that employees used as sources of current information and indicated which information sources were preferred.

Survey respondents' major sources of current organizational information.[29]

Rank	Information Source	Percent of Employees Using This Source	Preference Rank
1	Immediate supervisor	55.1%	1
2	Grapevine	39.8%	15
3	Employee handbook/ other references	32.0%	4
4	Bulletin board(s)	31.5%	9
5	Small group meetings	28.1%	2
6	Regular general employee publication	27.9%	6
7	Annual business report to employees	24.6%	7
8	Regular local employee publication	20.2%	8
9	Mass meetings	15.9%	11
10	Union	13.2%	13
11	Orientation program	12.5%	5
12	Top executives	11.7%	3
13	Audio-visual programs	10.2%	12
14	Mass media	9.7%	14
15	Upward communication programs	9.0%	10

These results reveal the prominent role that the immediate supervisor plays as a communicator in the organization, while clearly showing the important role of the grapevine.

The grapevine is an ever-present communication channel as it " . . . cannot be abolished, rubbed out, hidden under a basket, chopped down, tied up, or stopped. If we suppress it in one place, it will pop up in another. If we cut off one of its sources, it merely moves to another one. . . ."[30]

THE ROLE OF CORPORATE COMMUNICATION

■

To better understand the status of corporate communication in American industry, we conducted a survey of Fortune 500 companies. They were asked to describe their communication activities.[31]

The Director of Corporate Communications for Aetna Life and Casualty Company stated that, "over the past ten years and in particular the last five years, there has been a steady and broadening increase in the role played by corporate communications."[32] To illustrate this growth, he cites:

1. More and more corporate communication specialists are involved in the development of operating divisions' plans and strategies.

2. Due to training and encouragement, there has been a dramatic increase in management dialogue (all levels) with the media.
3. There has been a significant increase in the use of audio-visual communications, for example slides, videotapes, and most recently, tele-conferencing.

Speaking Activities

The Chase Manhattan Bank illustrates the range of speaking activities typical of large organizations. The corporation has a Friday Morning Meeting each week for all officers of the bank. The meeting, which features a speaker from within the bank, includes a presentation on a selected company topic. The communication department helps the speaker develop the script, audio-visual aids, and presentation techniques. In addition, the department offers presentation consulting to officers in the bank conducting internal presentations such as staff meetings or Board of Directors meetings, or external presentations to banking associations, other financial groups, or perhaps to a non-banking audience.[33]

Issues Management

In many organizations there is a trend to provide issues management training within the communication management function. **Issues management** involves the development and presentation of corporate policy on issues relevant to internal and external publics. Mobil Oil Corporation, for instance, offers extensive communication on the issue of energy and natural resource conservation in their newspaper, magazine, and television advertising.

The need for professional management of issues was addressed by an officer of Continental Illinois National Bank when he stated, "Today, business organizations must find their way through a thicket of often conflicting interests, and speak clearly and carefully on public issues that can or do involve them. There is little doubt that continued success will demand greater integration of approaches to and positions on policy issues with basic business strategies and objectives. . . . Thus, we have been seeing the modern evolution of the discipline of 'issues management'."[34] To meet this need, Continental developed a public policy committee to handle the issues management process.

Other organizations have set up units within the firm to accomplish the difficult task of providing consistent, meaningful responses to complex issues affecting the organization. The Prudential Life Insurance Company, for example, surveys its employees to get perceptions of a variety of organizational issues, including communication. One of its regional offices used the results of one of these surveys to identify employee concerns in the areas of communication and then took specific actions to address these concerns. A follow-up survey showed improvements in employee perceptions of the communication process.[35]

Communication Skills

To prepare employees to handle media interviews and public communication, many organizations offer special training programs to develop speaking skills. Pacific Gas and Electric Company in San Francisco offers what they call a "Speak Easy" training program "to help these employees be more comfortable and effective as they appear before the news media or before official or civic organizations."[36] The company uses its own television studio and provides an entire day for students to practice press conferences and speaking techniques with feedback on their skills offered by trainers and fellow employees.

The preparation of employees to participate in corporate speakers bureaus which address groups within and outside the organization has become an important task of communication departments. Often, professional speech consultants are hired, to serve along with the corporation's own communication specialists, to prepare speakers for in-house briefings and public presentations in a variety of forms.

As part of an extensive range of communication activities, the J. C. Penney Company offers employees speaking development training for public appearances and presentations within the corporation itself. A presentation course is offered in the Management Training and Development Center, and employees are provided with the pamphlet, *Preparing An Oral Presentation,* "which establishes guidelines and standards for briefings."[37] Employees are encouraged to utilize the standards because "past use has proven their effectiveness,"[38] and the employees' audience has seen many other presentations and has come to expect that these standards will be followed.[39]

Other organizations are recognizing the importance of good listening skills at all levels. Consequently, listening training has become central to the communication skills development in many types of organizations. Federal agencies, for example, have developed some extensive listening training programs. Control Data and the Ford Motor Company include listening skills as part of their training curricula. Probably the most famous attempt at listening training was made by the Sperry Corporation which developed an entire advertising campaign based on the theme "We Understand How Important It Is to Listen" and backed up the theme with an extensive training program in listening skills.[40]

Communication Departments

☐

As the communication demands of an organization grow increasingly complex in today's information society, many firms are creating communication departments staffed with professionals to handle internal and external communication functions. These departments, which represent a fairly new approach to corporate communication, offer an organization a systematic, coordinated strategy for dealing with the communication needs and channels within the operation.

Much of the work of corporate communication departments focuses on public communication and public relations efforts. The Northwestern Mutual Life Insurance Company in Milwaukee has a vice-president for communication who is "responsible for initiating, establishing and promoting communications policies and programs to develop and maintain among the company's various publics favorable attitudes toward the company."[41] The mission of the **corporate communication department** is to "evaluate how various publics perceive the company, identify the actions of the company with the public interest, and plan and execute communications programs to earn favorable understanding for the company among the various publics."[42] To accomplish this mission, Northwestern Mutual's communication department is organized into three divisions: Advertising and Corporate Information; Public Relations; and Creative Services.

Southern California Edison Company has established a Corporate Communications Advisory Committee made up of officers and specialists from throughout the company. Noting the broad scale of internal and external communication in the utility industry, the vice-president of the firm feels that the Committee is an effective way to keep "tabs on changing communication projects and priorities on an on-going basis."[43]

Bank of America's communication department is responsible for a series of activities including generating news releases about the bank; training bank executives for television interviews; speech writing for the president and members of the managing committee; preparing position papers on important bank issues; training employees to express their needs, concerns, and problems to management; developing plain language standards for customer forms; facilitating teamwork and problem solving by providing meeting management training; publishing instructional materials; producing consumer education films; preparing speeches for speakers, as requested; preparing briefing packages about overseas visits for members of senior management; developing a multi-media program for high schools; and developing patterns for speech programs for overseas management.[44] To meet these objectives, the division is divided into sub-units (figure 7.2).

FIGURE 7.2

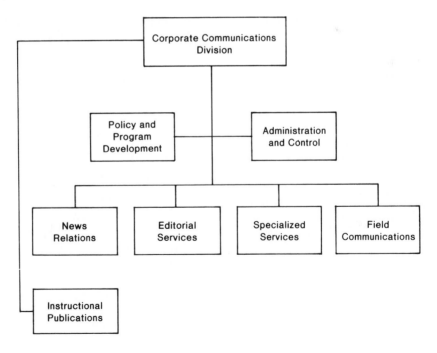

Sometimes the communication divisions have unique responsibilities for training and working with individuals who are fulfilling a specific situational need. Such was the case when the AT&T Company was confronted with a communication challenge after a consumer activist appeared on the Phil Donahue show and complained about AT&T's profits and pricing policies. In response AT&T trained several corporate officers who then appeared on a later broadcast of the Donahue show to explain the complicated rate structure and industry competition.[45]

In some non-profit organizations traditional communication department activities, such as internal and external communication functions, are combined with fund-raising efforts. The American Red Cross, for instance, recently merged the communication departmental functions with their development efforts. And the University of Maryland at College Park has an Office of Institutional Advancement headed by a vice-president to coordinate both development and communication.

Organizational Commitment

Our survey results suggest that an organization requires considerable commitment throughout the system to develop effective communication. Otherwise, concern about communication functions may end up limited to the corporate communication department staff. The identification of such a department may indeed signal the organizational recognition of the central role of communication and of the need for improving that communication at all levels. And that objective can be the key to increased productivity and even economic survival in these perilous economic times.

ORGANIZATIONAL STRUCTURE, CLIMATE, AND CULTURE

The structure of an organization depends greatly upon the mission of the organization—the goods or services of the organization has been established to provide. The organization may take the structure of a typical organization chart (figure 7.3).[46]

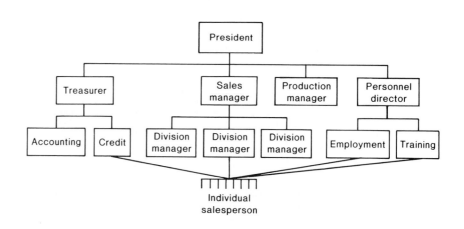

FIGURE 7.3 Functional organization. From *Elements of Managerial Action,* by Michael J. Jucius and William Schlander (Homewood, Illinois: R. D. Irwin, 1965), p. 189

Regardless of how the organization is set up, the structure requires both downward and upward communication in the system. Authoritarian managers tend to transmit orders downward. Elements of downward communication include: (1) job instruction; (2) explaining the rationale for an activity; (3) information about other aspects of the organization's policies, procedures, and benefits; (4) employee performance feedback; and (5) ideology to explain and support employees' commitment to the organization's mission.[47] The hierarchy of an organization has a great influence on the downward communication of information.

Likewise, the hierarchy can facilitate or inhibit the upward flow of communication. Upward communication usually concerns (1) job assignments; (2) fellow employees or managers; (3) organizational policies and procedures; or (4) tasks and their accomplishment.[48] One organizational communication researcher determined that "upward communication is rather ineffective."[49] The need for serious attention to upward communication in organizations is underscored by a study on communication satisfaction which determined that individuals received the greatest job satisfaction when communication dimensions such as personal feedback, good relationships with supervisor, and a positive communication climate were present.[50]

The **theory of differentiation/integration** describes organizational structure and climate. It suggests that organizations tend to become more internally complicated as they differentiate existing organizational units to take on more complex tasks. Organizations are shaped by the different cognitive and emotional orientations of the managers and the integration of departments to accomplish united efforts. Researchers suggest that organizations should differentiate units based on tasks and environments rather than attempting to combine different tasks in one unit. They also observe that organizations that "achieve these states of differentiation and integration will grow rapidly in size."[51] Since there is no one best way to organize a company internally, the communication styles and channels must be adapted carefully to maximize flexibility and coordination.

Employees are likely to function within a complex organizational structure using coordinating strategies—strategies which result from clear, direct communication by managers. Coordination by plan involves detailed rules and schedules to which a worker must adhere. Coordination by feedback, on the other hand, provides continuous response to an employee's efforts as they are coordinated within the organizational structure.[52] Testing these organizational structures revealed that coordination by feedback established an open, multi-directional communication climate.[53] To maintain coordination, the volume of communication must increase until horizontal communication flow results, especially through cross-departmental channels at the same status level.

Further, the **linking-pin concept** can be used to describe the manager within this information structure (figure 7.4).[54] The manager serves a critical role as the linking-pin between subordinates and superiors. Thus, the manager is a member of at least two groups—a superior in one (as a middle manager) and a subordinate in another (to the executive level)—and must be perceived as part of both groups to be effective. This perception of the role of the manager in the organizational hierarchy leads to the interaction-influence principle. This principle suggests that the more influence a manager has with superiors, the more effective he/she will be in managing subordinates.

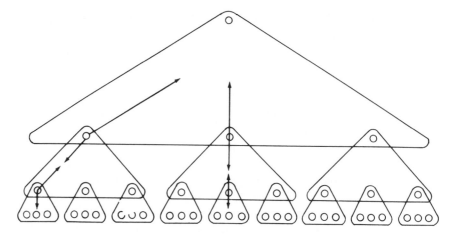

Likewise, the more the manager's decision making is influenced by subordinates, the more influence he/she, in turn, can exert on his/her superiors.[55] Such influence requires that the manager skillfully adapt as a communicator.

The structure of the organization, therefore, will facilitate or inhibit the downward, upward, and horizontal channels of communication. The **organizational climate,** the general atmosphere of supportiveness or defensiveness, is also a factor which influences the use of communication channels. A study of managers concluded that a supportive climate in which a worker has a sense of self-worth and importance usually occur in organizations in which (1) there is mutual trust and confidence; (2) superiors exhibit a willingness to help subordinates with job and personal matters; (3) managers are approachable and honest about company policies and procedures; and (4) managers are willing to give credit to subordinates' accomplishments and ideas.[56]

The structure and climate of an organization relates closely to the organizational culture. Wondering what makes an organization unique and gives it a personality of its own has led many analysts of modern organizations to look at the **organizational culture** (the company's traditions, rituals, values, history, interactions, and norms) as a key to understanding the effectiveness of the organization. Communication has been identified as the major ingredient for building and maintaining strong organizational cultures: "The companies and organizations that do the best job thinking through what they are all about, deciding how and to whom these central messages should be communicated and executing the communication plan in a quality way, invariably build a strong sense of esprit within their own organization and among the many constituents they serve."[57]

For all the theoretical perspectives on organizations, their workers, managers, structures, climates, and cultures, research clearly identifies one key to effectiveness: effective communication throughout the system. Indeed, it is especially advisable to maintain a communication perspective when studying organizations because "we need to look and listen to people talking about their work in their own words far more than perhaps some of us are inclined to do, if we are to avoid the danger of letting theory drive out good practice in the work environment."[58] It is the listening and talking that makes up the communication in the system.

COMMUNICATION AS AN ACTIVITY FUNCTION

■ Communication is also important within the context of the basic functions of an organization: recruiting, hiring, training, ongoing job maintenance, and job performance and appraisal.

Recruiting

☐ Prospective employees may search out employers, but employers also search for the individuals who will best satisfy the needs of the organization. To do this effectively, businesses plan recruiting techniques and strategies. They determine the procedures they will use, where to recruit, and how to disseminate information. Recruiting is carried out in indirect ways such as help-wanted advertisements and employment services. In addition, direct communication takes place between employees of the business and prospective employees at career days, open houses, and college visitations. Corporations interested in recruiting "high performance" college students spend a great deal of money having such individuals visit their headquarters, talk with people in the organization, and tour facilities in an effort to persuade them that they should choose to work with their organization rather than a competitor's.

Hiring

☐ Depending upon the perceived needs of the organization, employment interviews are conducted in order to select the best qualified candidates. Much time and money is invested in training personnel to be effective interviewers. A great deal of money and effort can be wasted by making errors in the interview and selection process, resulting in the hiring of poorly qualified individuals. Listening skills, interviewing skills, and effective interpersonal skills are needed by those working in the hiring areas.

Training

☐ No matter what the background of the individual, adjustments to new work settings are often eased by effective training programs. Introducing an employee to such factors as job assignments, the work station procedure, and rules for operation within the organization structure help increase an employee's productivity.

Training in communication skills is an important function in many organizations. With the recognition that effective listening and speaking are critical to the operation of an organization has come the realization that people entering organizations are poorly equipped with these skills. One training specialist, discussing training and development issues in the 1990s, observed that "we hire people for their technical skills and fire them for their lack of interpersonal skills . . . communication is a big issue, not because we haven't paid attention to it, but because we haven't paid attention to it in the right way."[59]

Many corporations invest a great deal of time and money in training employees in communication skills (H. Armstrong Roberts)

Job Maintenance

☐ Employees may find it necessary to obtain additional information, make inquiries, and express their desires and needs. To eliminate or at least to lessen job-related stress, such factors as the line of command and grievance procedures must be clearly communicated. Sharing information, squelching rumors, and explaining new or altered company policies must also occur. Major problems often stem from factors such as incomplete training, misunderstandings about the employee's place in the organization, and poorly defined procedures concerning promotion, pay and reward classifications, work station procedures, and environmental maintenance. Questions concerning these matters frequently arise following the employee's initial adjustment to the job. Unless channels are open for communication to clarify these matters, poor employee-employer relationships may result.

Job Performance

☐ Depending upon the type of job held, employees may require public speaking skills to inform or persuade others within or outside the organization. Salespeople need persuasive and interpersonal skills to deal with the public. The ability to work with individuals on the telephone requires effective listening and interpersonal skills. An individual with problem-solving or decision-making responsibilities ought to have a systematic approach to reach effective conclusions. Normal everyday contact with fellow employees necessitates interpersonal skills. And many organizations recognize that all employees—executive, manager, supervisor, worker—must be able to listen carefully in order to do the work of the organization.

Performance Appraisal

☐ The traditional method of employee appraisal centers on supervisors observing and recording the actions and attitudes of employees. Three common methods of appraisal are trait analysis, critical incident analysis, and management by objectives.

Trait analysis evaluates factors such as punctuality, general attitude, work ability, cooperativeness, and acceptance of authority. This usually occurs at a specified time.

Critical incident analysis occurs when an assigned superior makes a notation at the time of the incident. The notation can refer to a major occurrence of either a positive or a negative nature. During performance evaluation, employee records are checked for the number and the quality of the occurrences. Some organizations combine both trait and critical incident methods of analysis to evaluate employees.

Another method of evaluation currently being used by organizations is **Management by Objectives,** often referred to as **MBO.** In an MBO organization, subordinates meet with their supervisors to establish goals. The subordinate usually proposes specific activities that will be used as the basis for job improvement or increased output. These are clearly stated in terms of the expected outcome. If the goals are accepted by the supervisor, then a clear basis for evaluation and growth has been developed.

It is important that what is going to be done, how it is going to be accomplished, and how outcomes are to be measured are clearly communicated. A considerable amount of training on how to perform within this method is required. But the procedure does have an advantage over most other methods of appraisal because once real and meaningful goals are set, a reward or punishment system can easily be carried out.

OBSTACLES TO EFFECTIVE CORPORATE COMMUNICATION

■ Understanding the communication needs and functions of a corporation does not ensure effective communication. Sometimes obstacles get in the way of successful transactions. Some of these obstacles are a lack of a communication policy in the organization, the authoritarian attitude of management, too many levels of management, insufficient communication training, the nature of the change, and the lack of innovation.

Lack of a Communication Policy

☐ Many organizations assume that communication just happens. Officials give no thought to establishing policies governing how messages are to be sent from one work level to another, how ideas are to be generated, who is ultimately responsible for decision making, and how information is to be distributed both within and outside of the organization. As a result, the organization drifts, responding to the communication needs in an inconsistent, haphazard fashion.

Recognizing the need to establish carefully articulated communication plans, some organizations have developed thorough plans to handle the complex communication needs of the firm. One of the most highly developed communication plans belongs to the Honeywell Corporation. Their mission statement illustrates their commitment: "The Corporate Communications Department exists to express and clarify the position and resulting identity of Honeywell to people inside and outside the company."[60]

Ineffective Communication Networks

☐ Communication networks within an organization can sometimes be ineffective for any of a number of reasons. The networks can result in jamming rather than facilitating information flow. Too many managers look at communication as only a top-down process, never considering the use of bottom-up communication within their units. And organizations will attempt to function with some sort of centralized control of the communication which also can lead to a very slow, inefficient flow of information.

As we have seen, the communication structure of an organization is critical to its communication success. Communication networks—the flow of information upward, downward, horizontally across departments, and through informal channels—can facilitate the work of an organization. These networks or paths for the flow of messages, are centralized or decentralized. The more management controls the communication network, the more centralized it is. Prevailing theory suggests that an organization would do well to use a centralized network "when the problem is simple and it [the company] wants minimum messages and errors and is looking for a leader," while the decentralized network is appropriate "when the problem is complex . . . and high morale and flexibility are desired."[61]

Inability to Change

☐ One common characteristic of most organizations today is that they are experiencing tremendous change. Internal and external pressures have necessitated flexibility and adaptation to changes in missions, economic realities, and the workforce. Sadly, most individuals find change to be difficult and unsettling. As a result, there is a tendency to resist change and to want to hold on to existing ways of doing things for comfort and security, a clear deterrent to progress.

Management experts stress that an organization's effectiveness depends on management's ability to recognize and address changing realities.[62] Indeed, the ability to keep up with rapid change is seen as a requirement for management survival.[62]

The Authoritarian Attitude of Management

☐ In some organizations, the general attitude among employees is that expressing personal views will result in blocked promotions and reprimands—negative rather than positive rewards. If this is the case, then little or no innovative suggestions will come from employees. If management gives the impression that it is not interested in employee problems, there will be few, if any, solutions to those problems. Such distrust can fester and lead to work stoppages and the competitive attitude of employees versus employer.

Too Many Levels of Management

☐   If the decision makers are physically and philosophically removed from the workers, effective communication will be difficult, if not impossible. Little may be known about the needs of the employees, so distrust caused by rumors (the lack of direct communication) may result. Many organizations today have come to recognize the problems with bureaucratic layers and are making attempts to "flatten out" the management structure so that workers and managers have more direct, immediate access to each other in doing the work of the organization.

Insufficient Communication Training

☐   "The educational institutions, even those with very good reputations, do an abysmal job of training young people to communicate . . . 60 to 70 percent of the people who join corporations right out of American universities were not able to write well-constructed business letters and close to 80 to 90 percent of them "needed instruction on how to write a simple business report,"[64] concludes one observer of American industry. The same holds true for spoken communication skills. The end result is corporate problems, especially on the leadership level, since "If you can't communicate, you can't command."[65]

The Nature of Corporate Change

☐   Even after discovering that a major problem in an organization is based on poor communication, little may be done about it. The nature of corporations holds the key as to why this is true. Corporations are slow to change. There are many forces and ideas operating in the work setting. Deeply held beliefs, long-term commitments to a set plan of action, confusion over how to go about making changes, security from doing it the way it has always been done, fear of job loss due to discovery of new methods, and bruised egos influence decisions in every organization. It is often easier to just let things continue as they are rather than rock the boat.

Lack of Innovation

☐   An extensive study of this country's leading companies highlights eight attributes which allow organizations to be innovative and overcome the causes of poor communication.[66]

1. *A bias for action.* When these organizations needed action, they brought together a group of people to work in a group setting. Little concern was paid to anything other than the need for action. These groups had been trained to use decision-making skills and group techniques for reaching their goal, and they proceeded to get the job done.
2. *Close relations with customers.* Innovative companies realized the need to keep in touch with their customers. This meant communicating with, not just to, them. They were aware of the need to listen to and to learn from the people they served. They actively sought out information through interviews, ques-

tionnaires, focus groups, and even bringing customers into business meetings and planning sessions.

3. *Autonomy and entrepreneurship.* Training in leadership skills, communication skills, meeting management, and fostering positive self-concepts was an important part of the training program of many of the innovative organizations.

4. *Productivity through people.* The rank and file were treated as the source of quality and productivity gain. Encouragement was given for participation in discussions that dealt with production techniques, corporate policies, and health and welfare programs. To accomplish this, communication skills training in the areas of group action, public speaking, listening, and leadership becomes an important part of the corporate process.

5. *Hands-on, value-driven.* The innovative organizations consider value, quality, service, and cleanliness the norm. Again, the communication of these values to the public, as well as developing employee attitudes that encourage these values, centers on the effective use of both internal and external communication.

6. *Stick to the knitting.* Innovative organizations clearly understand what they are best at doing. They stay within their knowledge and experiential boundaries and, though they work for expansion, they communicate clearly within the organization the talents and skills that will allow them to succeed and the limitations they perceive in their own corporate abilities.

7. *Simple form, lean staff.* Most of the innovative companies studied had a very lean top-level staff. Emphasis was placed on simple organizational structures, leaving tremendous communicative flexibility for people to interact with each other instead of confining routes of communication. Often, corporate officers were found in close proximity to all levels of employees rather than in isolated offices. Some officers excelled at managing by mingling directly with the workers, thus developing a good understanding of all levels of employees and opening the avenues of communication.

8. *Simultaneous loose-tight properties.* People are the most important asset to the organization. "The excellent company lives their commitment to people."[67] The decision-making process involves "busy bands of engineers, salesmen and manufacturers hammering out problems in a conference room. Even a customer was there."[68]

While these qualities of excellence in corporations demonstrate the importance of good communication, unfortunately "the eight qualities are absent in most large corporations. American companies are being stymied not only by their staffs, but also by their structures and systems, both of which inhibit action."[69]

SUMMARY

In this chapter we have examined communication as an important part of business organizations. The major points were:

Communication is an integral part of the world of business.
An overwhelming amount of a businessperson's time is spent communicating.

Communication difficulties can contribute to problems of motivation, attitude, leadership, coordination, and control.

Businesses communicate within departments, between departments, outside the company, in restrictive patterns, and through informal channels.

All organizational members engage in informal communication.

The grapevine is an informal network that spreads information from person to person.

Issues management is an important aspect of corporate communication.

Many corporations have communication departments.

Organizations have structures which encourage either upward or downward communication and the horizontal flow of communication.

Communication plays a vital role in corporate recruiting, hiring, training, job maintenance, and job performance and appraisal.

Factors present in corporate structures and attitudes either create communication obstacles or encourage effective communication.

THINGS TO DO

1. Topics for discussion:
   a. Under which method would you prefer to be evaluated: trait analysis, critical incident analysis, or MBO? Why?
   b. Think of a job you have held. Identify several specific incidents when there were problems created by ineffective communication. What were they? What other problems were created by the ineffective communication? Were the problems ever resolved? If so, how? If you haven't had work experience, talk to someone who is presently employed and ask them the questions posed.
2. Make an appointment to talk with a personnel manager of a business. Discuss the major communication problems found in recent college graduates who have interviewed for jobs. Ask the manager to identify the difficulties these deficiencies have created for the candidates. Report your findings to the class.
3. Your class will be asked to collect organizational charts from textbooks and local businesses and organizations. Compare them. Try to ascertain similarities and differences in the flow of communication in these organizations. If possible, discuss communication structures with members of the various industries and try to find out if the flow works, and why or why not.
4. Your instructors may have you view a filmstrip entitled "The Rumor Clinic" which is distributed by the B'nai B'rith Anti-Defamation League. This film demonstrates how information is spread through the grapevine. Following the activity, discuss the implications of information spread through this informal system.
5. Class members will be divided into groups. Each group is to read a chapter of Peters and Waterman's *In Search of Excellence* and then discuss the material's relevance to effective corporate communication.

NOTES

1. Richard Anderson, *Communication: The Vital Artery* (Watsonville, CA: Correlan Publications, 1973), 2.
2. Vincent DiSalvo, David Larsen, and William Seiler, "Communication Skills Needed by Persons in Business Organizations," *Communication Education* 25 (November 1976): 370.
3. Daniel Katz and Robert Kahn, *The Social Psychology of Organizations* (New York: John Wiley and Sons, 1966), 16.
4. *Effective Communication on the Job* (New York: American Management Association, 1963), 110.
5. Stephen Madeline, address to the 1980 Midwest Regional Conference of the American Business Communication Association, 13.
6. Cindy Skrzycki, "The Quest for the Best: U.S. Firms Turn to Quality as Competitive Tool," *The Washington Post* (2 October 1988), H2.
7. Peter F. Drucker, "The Coming of the New Organization," *Harvard Business Review* (January–February 1988): 45.
8. Cf. Linda L. Putnam, "Role Functions and Role Conflicts of Communication Trainers," *Journal of Business Communication* (Fall 1979): 37f.
9. "It is Now Imperative that American Business Find a More Stimulating Way to Communicate with Itself," a series of ads run in various magazines by SONY Video Communications.
10. *Effective Communication on the Job, 16.*
11. Ibid., 60.
12. Ibid., 15.
13. Raymond Leisker, *Business Communication Theory and Application* (Homewood, IL: R. D. Irwin, 1972), 5.
14. Martha H. Rader and Alan P. Wunsch, "A Survey of Communication Practices of Business School Graduates by Job Category and Undergraduate Major," *Journal of Business Communication,* 17 (Summer 1980): 35.
15. James Melohlov, Paul Popp, and Michael Porte, "Communication: A View from the Inside of Business," *Journal of Business Communication* 11 (1974): 53–59.
16. *Effective Communication on the Job,* 114.
17. Ibid., 203.
18. Carol Armbruster, "Job Jottings," *Elyria Chronicle-Telegram,* 18 February 1979, B-4; quoted from W. J. Heisler, "Promotion, What Does It Take to Get Ahead?" *Business Horizons,* April 1978.
19. Ibid., B-4.
20. Allan D. Frank and Judi Brownell, "Preface" *Communication and Behavior for Improved Performance: 2 + 2 = 5.* (New York: Holt, Rinehart and Winston, 1989), vii.
21. J. E. Meister and L. L. Reinsch, Jr., "Communication Training in Manufacturing Firms," *Communication Education* 27 (September 1978): 239.
22. Dan H. Swenson, "Relative Importance of Business Communication Skills for the Next Ten Years," *Journal of Business Communication,* 17 (Winter 1980): 47.
23. Ibid.
24. For an expanded discussion of ways in which businesses use communication, see Richard Anderson, *Communication: The Vital Artery* (Watsonville: Correlan Publications, 1973).
25. Keith Davis, "Management Communication and the Grapevine," *Harvard Business Review* 31 (January–February 1952): 43–49.
26. Ibid., 43–49.
27. Ibid., 43–49.

28. *Effective Communication on the Job,* 119.
29. A study of internal communication channels conducted by The International Association of Business Communicators and the New York consulting firm, Towers, Perrin, Forster and Crosby.
30. Keith Davis, *Human Behavior at Work* (New York: McGraw-Hill, 1972), 263.
31. Survey conducted by Andrew Wolvin, University of Maryland, 1982.
32. Correspondence from Thomas J. Collins, director of Corporate Communications for Aetna Life and Casualty Company, October, 1981.
33. Correspondence from Gail W. Kslevitz, second vice president, Chase Manhattan Bank, 28 October 1981.
34. John V. Egan, Jr., "Continental's Public Policy Committee and the Life Cycle of an Issue," Continental Illinois National Bank, 1.
35. Opinion Survey, October 1977, Prudential Insurance Company of America.
36. Correspondence from Grant N. Horne, vice president, Public Relations, 12 October 1981.
37. *Preparing An Oral Presentation,* J. C. Penney Company, New York, p. 1.
38. Ibid.
39. Ibid.
40. David Clutterbuck, "How Sperry Made People Listen," *Interpersonal Management* 36 (February 1981): 23.
41. Correspondence from Robert O. Carboni, Vice President-Communications, 25 September 1981.
42. Ibid.
43. Correspondence from Edward A. Myers, Jr., 22 September 1981
44. List and organizational chart furnished by The Bank of America.
45. Jim McClure, "Our Side of the Story," *Bell Telephone Magazine* 2 (1981): 20–23.
46. Michael J. Jucius and William Schlander, *Elements of Managerial Action* (Homewood, IL: R. D. Irwin, 1965), p. 189.
47. Daniel Katz and Robert L. Kahn, *The Social Psychology of Organizations* (New York: John Wiley and Sons, 1966).
48. Ibid.
49. Allan D. Frank, "Trends in Communication: Who Talks to Whom?" *Personnel,* 62 (December 1985): p. 41.
50. Cal W. Downs and Michael D. Hazen, "A Factor Analytic Study of Communication Satisfaction," *The Journal of Business Communication,* 14 (Spring 1977): 63–73.
51. Paul R. Lawrence and Jay W. Lorsch, *Organization and Environment* (Boston: Harvard University Graduate School of Business Administration Division of Research, 1967), p. 239.
52. J. G. March and Herbert A. Simon, *Organizations* (New York: John Wiley and Sons, 1958).
53. Jerald Hage, Michael Aiken, and Cora B. Marret, "Organization Structure and Communicators," *American Sociological Reviews* 36 (October 1971): 860–871.
54. Rensis Likert, *New Patterns of Management* (New York: McGraw-Hill, 1961).
55. Ibid.
56. Rensis Likert, *The Human Organization: Its Management and Value* (New York: McGraw Hill, 1967).
57. Allan Kennedy, "Back-Yard Conversations: New Tools for Quality Conversations," *Communication World* (November 1984): 26.

58. Sylvia Shimmin, "The Future of Work" in *Changes in Working Life,* K. D. Duncan, M. M. Gruneberg, and D. Walls, eds. (New York: John Wiley and Sons, 1980) p. 5.
59. "Zenger on the 90's," *Syntax Newsletter,* 11 (Winter 1988): 1.
60. *Honeywell 1988 Communications Plan* (Minneapolis, MN: Honeywell Corp., 1988), p. 10.
61. Gerald M. Goldhaber, *Organizational Communication* (Dubuque, IA: William C. Brown, 1986), p. 289.
62. Peter F. Drucker, Managing in Turbulent Times (New York: Harper and Row, 1980).
63. Carol T. Schreiber, "Organizational Effectiveness: Implications for the Practice of Management," in Kim S. Cameron and David A. Whetten, eds., *Organizational Effectiveness* (New York: Academic Press, 1983), p. 258.
64. John Molloy, "Making Your Point, Not Burying It," *Self* (April 1981): 91.
65. Ibid.
66. Thomas Peters and Robert Waterman, Jr., *In Search of Excellence* (New York: Harper and Row, 1982), pp. 13–17.
67. Ibid.
68. Ibid.
69. Ibid., 17.

8

Communicators in Organizations

OVERVIEW American business, industrial, and governmental organizations are undergoing great changes. Effective communication is an important aspect of adapting to the changes. Communicators in an organization are the workers and the managers. Workers must be motivated and learn workable communication skills, management behavior techniques must be evaluated and management functions evaluated, and new techniques of organizational operation and communication must be investigated.

KEY WORDS

scientific management model
human relations model
immaturity-maturity theory
hierarchy of needs
Theory X
Theory Y
Motivation-Hygiene Theory
hygiene factors
motivator factors
ERG Theory
Acquired-Needs Theory

Equity Theory
Expectancy Theory
Goal-Setting Theory
Reinforcement Theory
Systems management
Managerial Grid
top-down process
bottom-up process
Theory Z
quality circles
Theory G

American business, industrial, and governmental organizations are undergoing profound changes. As our society finds itself in an information explosion (some experts suggest that our information now accelerates at such a rate as to virtually double every seven years), the structure and functions of an organization must necessarily adapt to these developments. It is predicted that as "the United States is rapidly shifting from a mass industrial society to an information society, the final impact will be more profound than the 19th century shift from an agricultural to an industrial society."[1]

At the same time that organizations must develop strategies to cope with an ever-expanding information base, we are experiencing a serious decline in American productivity. This lowering of productivity has had far-reaching economic implications, not just for Americans but for many nations throughout the world. Emphasizing the dramatic nature of these implications is the fact that "productivity in America [has] declined by 2 percent, while the Japanese saw an increase of 4.7 percent, West German productivity was up 3.7 percent, and the increase for Taiwan was 4.2 percent."[2] It is further predicted that "by the end of this decade, the United States will have lost its long-standing leadership role in productivity."[3]

Coupled with the decline in productivity and the information revolution, organizations are required to come to grips with expanding technological capabilities, particularly through sophisticated computer hardware and software. These advances in technology enable organizations to process vast amounts of information with speed and precision—provided the equipment and the operators are functioning effectively.

Another major impact is the United States' role as part of the global economy. Japanese autos and appliances are standard items in many American homes, and American business and industry finds a continuing need to broaden its base to deal, not just with the Japanese, but also with the developing nations of the Third World, Latin America, China, and the continuing relationships in the European Common Market. This global economy requires a truly international operation—facilities, services, and people who can function with people from and in other cultures.

THE WORK FORCE AND ORGANIZATIONAL CHANGE

■

The information and technological changes also have had an effect on and are affected by human relationships. Americans spend a great deal of time in front of their television sets. The self-help industry is thriving. People are concerned (through books, seminars, organizations) with physical development, weight loss, improved personal (and sexual) relationships, time management, assertiveness skills, stress management, and a host of communication strategies for effective parenting, loving, and living. We have grown more isolated in urban and suburban communities in which interaction with neighbors may be superficial at best. The extended family is spread across the map, so couples raising children no longer have the immediate support of relatives. And these relationships are further influenced by the increased amount of leisure time available to most Americans.

The result of these changes is a vastly changing work force. Workers in America are increasingly accustomed to the availability of leisure time. The traditional forty-hour week is under attack by some groups who want to offer employees more flexible work schedules. Some organizations, therefore, have offered their employees flextime, permitting varied schedules throughout the workday and even scheduling four-day, ten-hour work weeks. Other organizations have adapted worker schedules to permit individuals to do their work at home. Some word processor operators, for example, have equipment in their homes which is then fed by telephone lines to the central system at the organization's headquarters. It is predicted that in the 1990s 25 percent of the nonagricultural work force in the United States will be on flextime and on a shorter work schedule.[4]

In addition to the flexibility of schedules, the introduction of technology in the workplace has other implications. Computers are being used to create a paperless office, to monitor worker performance, to increase productivity, and even to determine pay and promotion. While computer technology has revolutionized industry, experts in office automation are the first to point out that workers "generally respond better to the personal control of human supervisors than the impersonal control of the computer."[5]

The information explosion also results in a more educated work force. People today must necessarily know more—have more information—and are involved in continuing educational experiences beyond secondary school. More and more Americans are going to two-year and four-year colleges, enrolling in employee development and training courses at work, and participating in a wide range of adult learning classes offered through schools and recreation departments within local communities. According to the U.S. Office of Education, the average length of schooling of the work force has reached twelve years. The schooling experience socializes people to become more individualistic, because in the school socialization process the inividual is paramount.[6] Educated workers, then, are going to be concerned about their personal development, their self-fulfillment, as part of an organization.

Further, the work force is changing as more and more women are entering the labor market and staying in it. Young couples often cannot afford the "luxury" of the wife staying at home to raise children, so working mothers continue to be a growing population in organizations—and bring with them increased needs for flextime, work at home, child care, and greater parent roles for fathers. In addition, more and more women are opting for careers outside the traditional home environment. The number of women entering business and engineering schools is increasing rapidly and they will, consequently, be entering the labor force in record numbers.[7]

Organizations also are adapting to continued efforts to recruit and retain minority (and handicapped) employees. Nationwide affirmative action programs call for special strategies to enable minority (and handicapped) persons to have a fair chance at success in an upwardly mobile society. "There are now some 1 million blacks in college, up from 282,000 in 1970. This population will not only diminish the number living at lower socioeconomic levels, but will bring people with higher expectation for upward-mobility into the work force."[8]

Likewise, our society is growing older. As Americans live longer, federal efforts to protect the rights of the elderly affect the work force. People no longer are required to retire at age 65 and, given the state of the economy and the limits of social security

More individuals than ever are choosing to remain in their professions past age 65 (Zefa/H. Armstrong Roberts)

benefits, more and more individuals will be choosing to stay in positions as long as possible. Consequently, new entries into the job market may have to adjust their aspirations for upward mobility as top-level positions are less readily opened up by retirements of senior executives. It may be necessary to abandon the idea that up is better and devise strategies to enable workers to enjoy a productive work life at the same employment level.

All of these significant changes in the American work force[9] will have a tremendous impact on how human resources are dealt with in organizations. To improve productivity, a company must develop "a sensitivity to what human beings are motivated by, what kind of feedback they respond to and how organizations can be structured so that individuals more effectively maximize their contributions."[10] In short, an organization must develop effective communication to best utilize human resources productively.

THEORIES OF WORKER MOTIVATION

Effective communication behavior in an organization can be understood as we recognize the behavior of workers and managers in the organization. It is helpful, therefore, to review some of the key theories which form the basis for our knowledge of how workers and managers communicate. Traditionally, organizations have dealt with their human resources through worker motivation.

Scientific Management Model

One attempt at dealing with motivation analyzes industrial efficiency with regard to equipment, procedures, and reward systems and develops a **scientific management model** for managers to deal with employees. This model stresses that workers need to have solid training and sufficient pay to perform effectively on the job.[11] Each job is reduced to a scientific process, and the workers are evaluated on how well they fulfill the process. Because the human psychology of the workers is not an important part of this approach to management, the role of communication, beyond order giving and taking, is diminished.

It has been increasingly apparent that though the scientific management model may be efficient in theory, in practice it has not been successful. The importance of dealing with workers as human beings by communicating *with* them rather than *to* them has resulted in other approaches to worker motivation. Thus, the human relations model was developed.

Human Relations Model

The **human relations model** focuses attention on the needs of the employees beyond their desire to accomplish the task and get paid for it. The Hawthorne effect, so-named because the experiments were conducted at Western Electric's Hawthorne plant, centers on the concept that workers perform more effectively when someone pays attention to them. Though there are now some questions concerning the validity of the testing method, the study continues to be a landmark in the humanizing of the work place and in finding more sensitive ways to motivate workers.[12] One of the most important outcomes of the human relations model was the effort to develop effective management-employee communication so that workers are understood, communicated with, and receive recognition as being a unique part of the production team.

The human relations concept, stemming from the early Hawthorne studies, has been reinvestigated and refined by a number of other theorists.

Early Motivation Theories

Four theories were formulated during the 1950s. Although their validity is now questioned, they deserve recognition as the forerunners of present day employee motivation concepts.[13] These are the Immaturity-Maturity, Hierarchy of Needs, X and Y, and the Motivation Hygiene theories.

Immaturity-Maturity Theory

The **immaturity-maturity theory** proposes that group behavior is a function of the interactions of personalities of the workers and working environments, and there is a basic incongruity between the needs of workers and the needs of a formal organization with all its bureaucracy.[14] To get the two factors to come together becomes a major challenge of any organization. Clearly, communication assumes a central role in such a challenge.

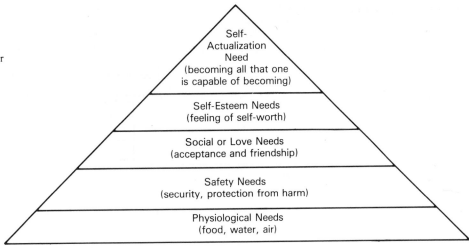

Hierarchy of Needs Theory

The research on organizational behavior and worker motivation led Abraham Maslow, the father of motivational research, to the conclusion that individual needs and motives combine with biological, cultural, and situational factors to determine behavior.[15] Maslow emphasized that these could be viewed as a **hierarchy of needs** (figure 8.1). Maslow's hierarchy suggests that a manager should understand at what need level workers are operating and attempt to satisfy the needs at that level. It is difficult to motivate a worker to self-esteem, for instance, if there are some basic physiological needs (food, shelter) which are not being met. There seems to be a need for workers to have a voice in decisions, to have information, and to feel involved in the organization. We fulfill these needs through communication.

Theories X

Theory X, as identified by Douglas McGregor, assumes that workers have a natural aversion to work. Therefore, the worker, lacking ambition and a sense of responsibility, while valuing security above all else, will work effectively only when ordered, threatened, or forced to do so.

Theory Y

Assuming a different approach is Theory Y. **Theory Y**[16] is based on the participatory approach which concludes that workers can be more effectively integrated—not ordered—into their work. Theory Y assumes that work is as natural a part of human behavior as play or rest. Individuals, therefore, can be motivated to work effectively if they are offered the opportunity to realize their own potential.

FIGURE 8.2 Comparison of Satisfiers and Dissatisfiers. From "One More Time: How Do You Motivate Employees?" by Frederick Hertzberg, *Harvard Business Review,* January–February, 1968, p. 57.

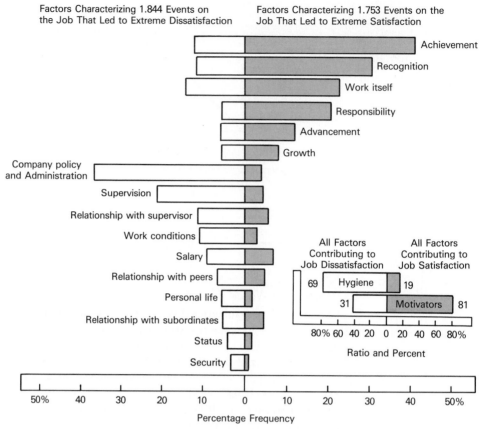

Motivation-Hygiene Theory

Psychologist Frederick Herzberg proposed the **Motivation-Hygiene Theory**.[17] Herzberg asked people to describe in detail, situations in which they felt exceptionally good or bad about their jobs. The responses were tabulated and placed into sixteen categories. A summary of these findings is shown in figure 8.2.

Herzberg concluded that the replies people gave when they felt good about their jobs were significantly different from the replies given when they felt bad about their jobs. He also hypothesized that certain characteristics were consistently related to job satisfaction, while others were related to job dissatisfaction. Intrinsic factors—factors related to oneself—were achievement, growth, advancement, responsibility and the work itself. These characteristics related to job satisfaction. Extrinsic factors—factors related to the environment of the job—were such things as company policy, the administration, working conditions, economic conditions, and interpersonal relationships. These are listed on the left side of figure 8.2.

Herzberg proposed that there was a dual continuum: The opposite of "satisfaction" is "no satisfaction" and the opposite of "dissatisfaction" is "no dissatisfaction."

FIGURE 8.3 Contrasting Views of Satisfaction-Dissatisfaction. From *Management,* 2nd ed. by Stephen P. Robbins (Englewood Cliffs, New Jersey: Prentice Hall, 1988), p. 343.

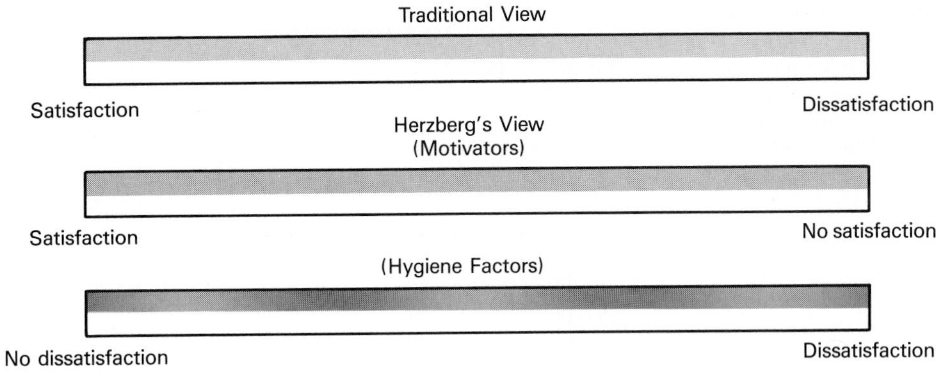

Traditional View

Satisfaction   Dissatisfaction

Herzberg's View
(Motivators)

Satisfaction   No satisfaction

(Hygiene Factors)

No dissatisfaction   Dissatisfaction

(See figure 8.3.) Factors that eliminate dissatisfaction were characterized by Herzberg as **hygiene factors.** Those that increase satisfaction were labeled as **motivator factors.**

According to Herzberg, the factors leading to job dissatisfaction are separate and distinct from those that lead to job satisfaction. Consequently, managers who seek to eliminate factors which create job dissatisfaction can lower dissatisfaction levels but not necessarily create motivation. Accordingly, Herzberg argued that managers should work at lowering dissatisfaction levels as best they can while emphasizing the motivator that can lead to increased job satisfaction.

Contemporary Motivation Theories

The early motivation theories were building blocks for contemporary concepts. Contemporary theories include the ERG, Acquired-Needs, Equity, Expectancy, Goal Setting, and Reinforcement theories.

ERG Theory

ERG Theory offers a way to understand and respond to the needs of people at work by categorizing three needs: existence, relatedness, and growth needs. Existence needs represent desires for physiological and material well-being. Relatedness needs represent desires for satisfying interpersonal relationships. Growth needs are desires for continued psychological growth and development.[18]

Acquired-Needs Theory

David McClelland, in his **Acquired-Needs Theory,** hypothesized the importance of the need for achievement. He designated achievement as MACH. MACH is the desire to do something better or more efficiently, to solve problems, or to master complex tasks. He indicated that people have a need for power. This need for power included a desire to control others, to influence their behavior, and to be responsible for other people. He also theorized that people have a strong need for affiliation. They desire to establish and maintain friendly and warm relations with other people.[19]

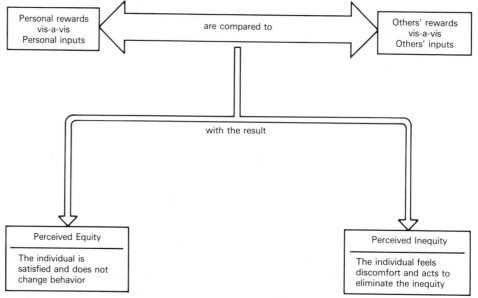

FIGURE 8.4 The Equity Comparison: Perceived Inequity as a Motivating State. From *Management for Productivity* 3rd ed. by John R. Schermerhorn, Jr. (New York: Wiley and Sons, 1989), p. 363.

Equity Theory

Developed by J. Stacey Adams, the **Equity Theory** states that an employee compares his job's input-output ratio to the input-output ratio of relevant others.[20] This equity comparison is shown in figure 8.4.

The Expectancy Theory

Developed by Victor Vroom, the Expectancy Theory is presently considered to be the most comprehensive explanation of motivation. **The Expectancy Theory** states that the tendency to act in a certain way depends on the strength of the expectation that the act will be followed by an outcome and on the attractiveness of that outcome to the individual.[21] In other words, "an individual will be motivated to perform effectively in an organizational setting when effective performance leads to rewards that the individual values. The challenge, then, is to create a work environment in which this condition will exist."[22] For a long period of time it was felt that increasing pay would fulfill this need.[23]

An analysis of worker motivation suggests that workers today indeed are not motivated by pay alone. Seventy-five percent of Americans surveyed no longer find acceptable the prospect of working at a boring job so long as the pay is good. Today's values center on such factors as more freedom to choose one's own life style; life as an adventure as well as an economic choice; leisure; self-expression and creativity; and a greater concern for past and future.[24] These new values suggest a need, perhaps, for new management communication strategies within American organizations. "The trick is to supervise and manage people in such a way that they want to do a good job."[25] A simplified model of Expectancy Theory is presented in figure 8.5.

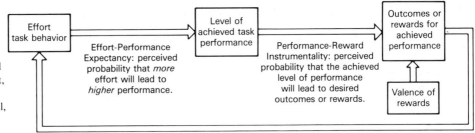

FIGURE 8.5 Simplified Expectancy Model of Motivation. From *Management Concepts and Effective Practice* 2nd edition by Michael A. Hitt, R. Dennis Middlemist, Robert L. Mathis (St. Paul, Minnesota: West Publishing, 1986), p. 326.

The Goal-setting Theory

Developed by Edwin Locke, the central premise of the **Goal-setting Theory** is that well-set goals provide an important source of motivation.[26]

Reinforcement Theory

The major premise of the **Reinforcement Theory** is that people will most likely engage in desired behavior if they are rewarded for doing so. Rewards are most effective if they immediately follow a desired response. In addition, behavior that is not rewarded—or is punished—is less likely to be repeated. Accepting this concept leads to the conclusion that if a worker does something right and is praised, then the worker is more likely to perform well than if the worker is caught doing something wrong and is punished. Psychologist B. F. Skinner was a leading advocate of reinforcement.[27]

THEORIES OF MANAGER BEHAVIOR

The primary role of communication in motivating workers is reflected not only in the literature on worker motivation, but also in the research on manager behavior. Several theories have studied the behavior of managers in an attempt to understand more clearly how one can go about motivating people to perform effectively at work.

Types of Managerial Behavior

One of the earliest works on management sets forth the five functions of a manager—to plan, to organize, to command, to coordinate, and to control.[28] For years, the directive view of what a manager does has held steady. Such a view suggests a one-way, "send down the order" view of communication.

Clearly the one-way view of communication is giving way to a variety of communication styles that are compatible with the multiple roles that a manager is required to fulfill. Table 8.1 presents a complete listing of Mintzberg's managerial roles which investigates the concept that managers at all levels find that communication skills take an increasing importance as managerial roles change and expand.[29]

TABLE 8.1 □ Mintzberg's Managerial Roles

Role	Description	Identifiable Activities
Interpersonal		
Figurehead	Symbolic head; obliged to perform a number of routine duties of a legal or social nature	Ceremony, status requests, solicitations
Leader	Responsible for the motivation and activation of subordinates; responsible for staffing, training, and associated duties	Virtually all managerial activities involving subordinates
Liasion	Maintains self-developed network of outside contacts and informers who provide favors and information	Acknowledgements of mail; external board work; other activities involving outsiders
Informational		
Monitor	Seeks and receives wide variety of special information (much of it current) to develop thorough understanding of organization and environment; emerges as nerve center of internal and external information of the organization	Handling all mail and contacts categorized as concerned primarily with receiving information (e.g., periodical news, observational tours)
Disseminator	Transmits information received from outsiders or from other subordinates to members of the organization; some information factual, some involving interpretation and integration of diverse value positions of organizational influencers	Fowarding mail into organization for informational purposes, verbal contacts involving information flow to subordinates (e.g., review sessions, instant communication flows)
Spokesperson	Transmits information to outsiders on organization's plans, policies, actions, results, etc.; serves as expert on organization's industry	Board meetings; handling mail and contacts involving transmission of information to outsiders
Decisional		
Entrepreneur	Searches organization and its environment for opportunities and initiates "improvement projects" to bring about change; supervises design of certain projects as well	Strategy and review sessions involving initiation or design of improvement projects

Role	Description	Identifiable Activities
Disturbance handler	Responsible for corrective action when organization faces important, unexpected disturbances	Strategy and review sessions involving disturbances and crises
Resource allocator	Responsible for the allocation of organizational resources of all kinds—in effect the making or approval of all significant organizational decisions	Scheduling; requests for authorization; any activity involving budgeting and the programming of subordinates' work
Negotiator	Responsible for representing the organization at major negotiations	Negotiation

From *The Nature of Managerial Work* by Henry Mintzberg (New York: Harper & Row, 1973), 93–94.

Analyzing Manager Behavior

☐ Another way of looking at the manager role is by analyzing the manager's performance on the job.

Systems Management

Systems management categorizes the manager according to one of four styles: (System 1)—the exploitative authoritative manager who controls and directs employees; (System 2)—the benevolent authoritative manager; (System 3)—the consultative manager who utilizes employee input for lower-level decision making; and (System 4)—participative managers who encourage employees to participate in decision making at all levels.[30] System 4 managers are those who would serve as facilitators, communicating with and encouraging communication among employees.

Managerial Grid

The **Managerial Grid**[31] (figure 8.6) charts managerial styles on a graphic representation of managerial concern for people and for production. In this system there are five distinct managerial styles noted on the grid and these are used for analysis of an individual manager's style.

The five managerial styles were described as 1,9—Country Club leadership style; 9,9—Team Leadership Style; 5,5—Middle of the Road Leadership Style; 1,1—Impoverished Leader; and 9,1—Task-Centered Leader. The team-oriented leader is considered to be the most effective style. Obviously, the team-oriented leader requires good communication skills.

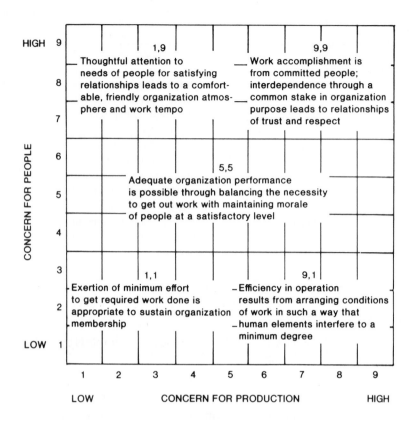

HIGH 9

1,9
Thoughtful attention to
needs of people for satisfying
relationships leads to a comfortable, friendly organization atmosphere and work tempo

9,9
Work accomplishment is
from committed people;
interdependence through a
common stake in organization
purpose leads to relationships
of trust and respect

5,5
Adequate organization performance
is possible through balancing the necessity
to get out work with maintaining morale
of people at a satisfactory level

1,1
Exertion of minimum effort
to get required work done is
appropriate to sustain organization
membership

9,1
Efficiency in operation
results from arranging conditions
of work in such a way that
human elements interfere to a
minimum degree

LOW 1

CONCERN FOR PEOPLE

1 2 3 4 5 6 7 8 9

LOW   CONCERN FOR PRODUCTION   HIGH

COMMUNICATION AS A MANAGEMENT FUNCTION

Communication can be viewed as an integral part of the management function. Though there are differences of opinion, it is generally agreed that the primary functions of managers are planning, organizing, leading, and evaluating. Certainly communication is at the core of any effective execution of these functions.

Increasingly, managers are encouraged to "open up the lines of communication between management and workers, so both sides can benefit from gripes and recommendations."[32] This is not just theory; it is being put into practice. The Pitney Bowes manufacturing firm, for example, has a program which includes yearly meetings between workers and corporate executives. A vice president for the corporation summarizes the program as one of interpersonal communication: "Management listens to employee recommendations and acts upon them."[33]

Planning

Much time and effort is spent by members of the management team in planning the concepts and establishing the procedures that will be used to carry out these plans. The ultimate operation of an organization and its success or failure may be dependent upon the plan agreed upon. Whether planning comes from the top-down process or the bottom-up process, a great number of interpersonal skills are needed.

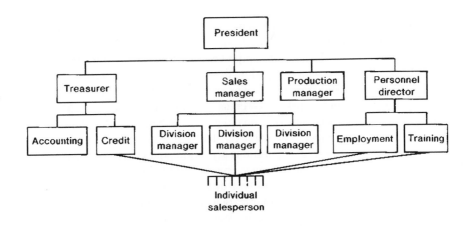

FIGURE 8.7 From
*Elements of Managerial
Action,* by Michael J.
Jucius and William
Schlander (Homewood,
Illinois: R. D. Irwin, 1965),
p. 189.

The Top-Down Process

The most common method of planning and carrying out plans in modern industrial
America is the **top-down process,** in which the individuals who have been given the
executive or upper-level decision-making positions determine the philosophy and procedures of the organization and inform those on the next highest level of their responsibilities. The information and orders continue to proceed down through the organization,
usually via a predetermined organizational flowchart (figure 8.7) until they reach the
level at which they are to be carried out.

The president may have decided to implement a new accounting procedure. The
president sends the recommendations down to the treasurer, who then informs accounting and credit departments of the new procedure. This is an example of the typical top-down process.

The Bottom-Up Process

As we have seen, one of the most important areas of concern in organizational communication is the need for motivation of workers within the organization. In addition,
job stress and job burnout are phenomena receiving increasing attention today. In some
occupations, burnout seems near epidemic in proportion.[34] To add to the problem is
the declining American productivity and the changing American work force. These
problems have led to a new analysis of "what's right" for American industry. And
what's right for American industry has led many experts to investigate Japanese management techniques.

"Japanese workers turn out 15 percent more products than their American counterpart workers."[35] They also seem more loyal to their companies and are absent less.
These factors have encouraged American industry to look carefully at the Japanese
management systems, including the bottom-up process, in hopes of better motivating
workers.

The bottom-up process is a communicative system. It differs from the top-down
process in that those at the lower levels get an opportunity to provide input in the
decision-making procedure. Effective communication skills become the basis for suc-

cessful planning and problem solving. There is a definite necessity for good listening skills.

The **bottom-up process** is based on the concept that change and initiative within an organization should come from those closest to the problem. Change is brought about from below. The sales force and distributors innovate in the marketplace, while hourly workers, foremen, and middle managers improve the production process.

The decision-making process begins with subordinates bringing proposals to the manager. The manager does not accept or reject the proposal, but instead questions are asked, suggestions are made, and encouragement is given to go back for more answers. The sequence reoccurs until the two ultimately either decide that the proposal has merit or it is discarded. If the proposal is accepted, the manager refers it to others higher in the organization. The same questioning process is repeated until the proposal is finally adopted or rejected. This process recognizes that in many cases there are numerous alternative solutions, none or all of which might work. The group decision creates commitment of all parties to the final chosen solution. The process, of course, is time consuming. The findings of behavioral science, however, suggest that often the quality of commitment to a decision, rather than the quality of some dimension of the decision itself, is the most critical factor in the fate of a project or accomplishment of a task. If productivity and positive employee-employer relations result, then the slow-down may be very productive and worthwhile.

Theory Z

William Ouchi's **Theory Z** approach to management builds on trust as a way of working together—"a way of communicating to people that they matter as people not as parts."[36] The result of establishing a trusting interpersonal relationship with employees is to give them a reason to feel committed to the organization, to feel good about working within it. The process is one in which "individuals who are accustomed to depending upon one another, who have a long-term commitment to their working relationships, and who work well together will form cohesive groups and naturally be more adept at tackling problems they all must face."[37]

This development of trust and worker participation is highly characteristic of Japanese manufacturing organizations. Japanese companies assume that persons at all levels within the organization can be trusted, that they are competent, and that they have the best interests of the organization in mind. Consequently, Japanese organizations do not have to have considerable layers of bureaucracy at the top to review everything done by the subordinate levels. Rather, "Japanese managers trust not only their workers but also their peers and superiors."[38]

Characteristics of the Theory Z approach include lifetime employment, employee participation in decision making, slow evaluation and promotion, collective responsibility for the work, and nonspecialized career paths. These employment aspects rooted in the Japanese culture are not easily transferred to American industry. In spite of this, some U.S. firms such as Hewlett-Packard, Dayton-Hudson, Rockwell International, and Intel have applied Theory Z approaches in their management systems.

Quality of Work Life and Quality Circle Movement

In order to encourage upward communication within the organization, **Quality Circles**—small work groups assigned to the task of establishing priorities, scheduling, and procedures before moving recommendations on up to management—have developed. These groups can determine such factors as work schedules, shift times, and production procedures. As one worker puts it, "It results in a lot more openness. You aren't afraid all the time. You aren't afraid to take something up with management."[39]

The key to achieving the goal of humanizing the workplace is to bring about a cooperative, constructive, nonadversarial effort through open, frank, and enlightened discussion between parties. This process recognizes that democratizing the workplace and humanizing the job need not be a matter of confrontation but of mutual concern for the worker, the enterprise, and the welfare of society."[40]

An effective quality circle should consist of a small group of employees (8 to 10) who do similar work and who voluntarily meet on a regular basis (usually one hour per week) on company time to identify and analyze work-related problems and recommend solutions to management. It also is suggested that the group is most effective if it has a role in implementing the solutions. Throughout the process, workers need to be trained in the use of the group discussion process and in presentation techniques to present their solutions to management.[41]

Such organizations as Dana Corporation, Kaiser Aluminum, General Foods, Exxon, and General Electric are using this system.[42] It is interesting to note that General Motors, adopting the Japanese approach, "has launched a mass program in 85 separate plants to try to create an environment that involves workers, that allows them to see how their tasks contribute to the goals of the total organization."[43]

Permitting small groups of employees to join together to discuss quality and production problems in an open communication system frequently yields substantial results. Quality circles at the Toyota Motor plant in Takaska, Japan have produced thousands of suggestions for improvement each year, and most are put into practice.[44] A similar system now operates at Ford's Lorain, Ohio plant and has resulted in quality improvement in their product line and working conditions. A Quality Circle operates in a process of steps:

1. Managers at all levels, especially at the top, should be committed to the concept and give it their unqualified support.
2. Only volunteers should be allowed to participate in the program.
3. Projects undertaken should relate directly—or at least indirectly—to participants' work.
4. Projects should be team efforts, not individual activities.
5. Participants should be trained in effective quality control and problem-solving techniques.
6. Circle leaders should also be trained in group dynamics and leadership of workers as a group.
7. QC groups should be given feedback regarding their recommendations and solutions.[45]

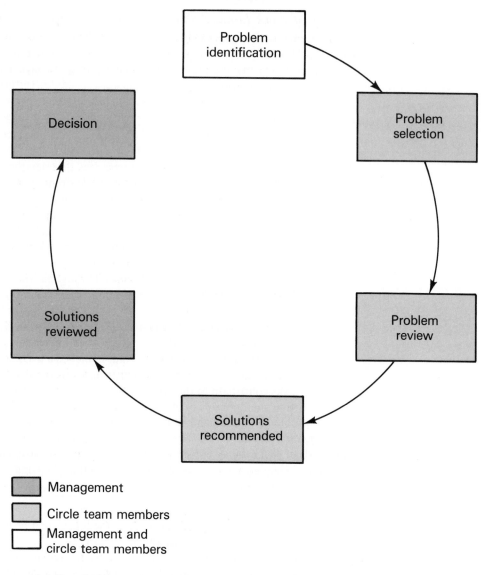

FIGURE 8.8 How a Typical Quality Circle Operates. From *Management,* 2nd ed. by Stephen P. Robbins (Englewood Cliffs, New Jersey, 1988), p. 602.

Quality circles are not established to become gripe or bull sessions. The groups usually receive training in decision-making techniques and are made aware of the process of group decision making and the responsibilities they have undertaken.[46] Implementing a quality circle is explained in figure 8.8.

While the concept offers the potential of improved interpersonal communication throughout the organizational system, experts caution that the quality circle should not be regarded as the panacea for all that ails corporate America.

In spite of their many advantages, quality circles may have limited usefulness in the United States. One survey cites that 60 of 176 companies that adopted quality circles in 1981 felt lukewarm or negative about their programs by 1984, and that 7 percent of the companies had dropped the technique. Interestingly, a 1981 survey revealed that of 238 Japanese businesses in the US, only 20 had established quality circles at their U.S. sites.[47]

Reasons given for the lack of success are inadequate employee training in quality circle operation before the program was instituted, union pressure encouraging the system to fail, and the limited education level of many of the workers who were given the responsibility of providing leadership and input. Japanese companies have been conservative in instituting the policies because of union difficulties, plus the perception that the American worker does not have the same dedication to the company as the Japanese worker. It is believed that this lack of loyalty leads to a lower desire for participatory input unless motivational rewards such as bonuses or added benefits are offered.

Though the quality circle concept has promise and appears to provide real quality and productivity improvements, it may have limited usefulness in this country unless there is an improvement in employee training and a change in union and employee attitudes.[48]

Implementing the Bottom-Up Process One of the difficulties with implementing upward communication is creating an open communication climate in which workers feel comfortable disclosing freely to their superiors. "A relationship with subordinates that promotes upward communication must be a supportive one so the subordinates feel that the superior will not take advantage of them if they fully speak their minds. The development of this trust will take some time and care on the part of the manager."[49]

The use of upward communication requires that managers be willing to receive the communication and to respond to it. An organization which has not utilized participative decision making must necessarily re-orient its workers to gain their trust and confidence before workers will be willing to participate. In urging executives to adopt this management style, it has been stressed that: "You can keep good people longer, and you can increase productivity, if you demonstrate clearly to them that you sincerely want their help and that you appreciate and reward those who willingly and thoughtfully bring their ideas and suggestions to you."[50]

Organizing
□

Management teams must decide on the structure of their organization, create job descriptions, determine the authority and responsibility that accompany jobs, and develop compensation practices. These factors are part of the organizing responsibilities of operation. Many hours of small-group meetings and one-to-one communications center on these matters.

By effectively communicating, information can be shared, duplication eliminated, conflict between people and departments limited, and fewer resources wasted.

Leading

☐

Those responsible for leading must learn to utilize the potential of the organization in order to generate the most desirable outcomes. Directing, requesting, telling, asking, persuading, soliciting, and motivating are all communication terms that describe the role of the leaders.

Anyone in a leadership role must deal with decision making and problem solving. Choices must be made; action must be taken. Learning a systematic approach to deciding on the choice or the action is a major communicative factor in effective leading.

Effective leadership training includes clarifying what are sometimes called the boundaries of authority and activity. These boundaries include learning how to tell the employee what to do, how to do it, where to do it, why to do it, and who is to do it.

Evaluating

☐

It is necessary to gather information so that measurement can be made of how well the organization is doing. This evaluation should be conducted on an on-going basis to ensure that agreed upon plans are being carried out. This evaluation will allow for adjustment of the operational plans so that the plans are appropriate. It may be determined that the plan is not working and should be replaced, or that everything is working well and the scheme is a success and should be continued unaltered.

The information collected serves to allow the management to use resources in the best and most productive way. Responding to the vast number of theories and formulas descriptive of modern management, a former chief executive officer of ITT describes his **Theory G** approach to management, an approach based on communicating with his staff:

> All the computers, reports, surveys, and staff analysis provided us with only one thing: information, faulty information, and, sometimes, misinformation. When it came time to make a decision, I would ask one, two, or several people, "What do you think?" From the interchange of ideas, one sparking the other, based upon the facts at hand, we would reach a decision, for better or worse.[51]

COMMUNICATION AS AN EMPLOYEE FUNCTION

■

Just as managers of organizations need effective communication skills, so, too, do workers in those organizations.

An examination of businesses and their methods of communication leads to the question of what specific communication skills are needed by those entering the field. A conference focusing on career communication education identified the following:

Small Group Facilitation: ability to develop and facilitate effective functioning of small groups within an organization, both in terms of accomplishing the group's task and establishing an atmosphere of cooperation with the group.
Interviewing: ability to assess individual capabilities and establish rapport with potential employees or those already on the job.

Problem-Solving/Decision-Making: ability to analyze a problem, to make decisions concerning specific strategies for solving the problem, and to evaluate the effectiveness of these solutions.

Public Relations: ability to establish communication that invites credibility, trust, and confidence between a firm and the public.

Listening: ability to receive, interpret, understand, and respond to both verbal and nonverbal messages from clients or employees, both in terms of the information given and the feelings expressed.

Persuasion: ability to persuade clients or employees (as individuals or groups) to accept a policy, believe a claim, or take a specific course of action.

Motivation: ability to motivate others in a given job situation by being sensitive and responsive to their needs.

Conflict Resolution: ability to handle conflict between individuals or groups within an organization by diagnosing the conflict and selecting strategies to achieve resolution of the conflict.

Speaking Competence: ability to think through, organize, and present information in a concise and coherent manner.

Relationship Building: ability to facilitate positive and productive relationships between coworkers and between members of various levels of an organization.

Questioning Techniques: ability to ask questions that are precise, clear, and logical for the purpose of securing relevant and in-depth information.[52]

A Control Data communication executive describes the centrality of communicating in the business of getting work done: "More and more of the resources and energies of organization members are being devoted to communication activities such as seeking information, reading, writing, listening to presentations, conversing with colleagues, maintaining personal contacts inside and outside the corporation, participating in various meetings, and dealing with routine paperwork."[53]

It is clear that organizations such as Control Data, which takes seriously the development of the communication skills of all of its employees, not just managers and executives, are on the right track. Likewise, it is evident that individuals who wish to succeed in organizations would do well to develop strong communication skills prior to entering the business world.

SUMMARY

In this chapter we have examined the role of communicators in organizations. The major concepts discussed were:

American business and industrial and governmental organizations are undergoing profound changes.

Information and technological changes have had an effect on human relations.

Traditionally, organizations have dealt with human resources through worker motivation.

The scientific management model stresses the need for workers to have solid training and sufficient pay to perform effectively on the job.

The human relations model focuses attention on the needs of the employees beyond their desire to accomplish the task and get paid for it.

Early motivational theories included immaturity-maturity, Hierarchy of Needs, Theory X, Theory Y, and Motivation-Hygiene.

Contemporary motivation theories include ERG, Acquired-Needs, Equity, Expectancy Goal-Setting, and Reinforcement.

Manager behavior has a great effect on worker productivity.

Quality Circles attempt to humanize the workplace.

Two styles of communication in organizations are the bottom-up and top-down processes.

Communication in business is both a management and an employee function.

THINGS TO DO

1. At present many Japanese organizations and some American companies work on the bottom-up process. Research the subject and report back to class with the results. A general class discussion should take place over the advantages and disadvantages of this practice. Your instructor may want to set up a formal debate between teams in the class, with one side taking the bottom-up process as the best method, while the other side defends the top-down process.

2. Do you think Americans can alter their work habits to accommodate the quality circle method of decision-making?

3. Why don't you think the scientific management model is working in present day U.S. industry?

4. Use the quality circle method for setting up rules of procedure for your class operation, including such factors as a grading system and assignment schedule.

5. Members of the class who are working, or who can interview people who are employed, are to make out a Managerial Grid. Discuss the outcomes of the results of the activity.

NOTES

1. John Naisbitt, "The New Economic and Political Order of the 1980's" (Speech presented to the Foresight Group, Stockholm, Sweden, April 17, 1980).
2. Mike Michaelson, "The Decline of American Productivity," *Success Unlimited* (October 1980):25.
3. C. Jackson Grayson, Jr.
4. "New Work Schedules for a Changing Society," Scarsdale: Work in America Institute Inc., 1981.
5. Peter Perl, "High-Tech Methods Boost Productivity, But At a Cost," *Washington Post,* 3 September 1984, Al.
6. Louis E. Davis, "Changes in Work Environments: The Next 20 Years," in *Changes in Working Life,* K. D. Duncan, M. M. Gruneberg, and D. Wallis, eds. (New York: John Wiley and Sons, 1980), 207.
7. George S. Odiorne, "Training to be Ready for the 90's." *Training and Development Journal* 34 (December 1980):14.
8. Ibid.
9. For an interesting book on the future of work, see Clark Kerr and Jerome M. Rosow, *Work in America in the Decade Ahead* (New York: Van Nostrand Reinhold, 1979).
10. Clara O'Dell, cited in Michaelson, "The Decline of American Productivity," 29.

11. Frederick W. Taylor, *Scientific Management* (New York: Harper and Brothers, 1911).
12. Berkeley Rice, "The Hawthorne Defect: Persistence of a Flawed Theory," *Psychology Today* 16 (February 1982):74.
13. Stephen P. Robbins, *Management Concepts and Applications* (Englewood Cliffs: Prentice-Hall, 1988), 339.
14. Chris Argyris, *Personality and Organization—The Conflict between System and the Individual* (New York: Harper and Row, 1957).
15. Abraham Maslow, *Motivation and Personality,* 2nd ed. (New York: Harper and Row, 1970).
16. Douglas McGregor, *The Human Side of Enterprise* (New York: McGraw-Hill, 1960).
17. Frederick Herzberg, Bernard Mauener, and Barbara Snyderman, *The Motivation to Work* (New York: John Wiley, 1959).
18. Clayton P. Alderfer, *Existence, Relatedness, and Growth* (New York: Free Press, 1972).
19. David C. McClelland, *Human Motivation* (Glenview: Scott-Foresman, 1985).
20. J. Stacey Adams, "Toward an Understanding of Inequity," *Journal of Abnormal and Social Psychology* 67 (1963):422–436.
21. Victor H. Vroom, *Work and Motivation* (New York: Wiley, 1964)
22. Edward E. Lawler III, "Motivation: Closing the Gap Between Theory and Practice" in *Changes in Working Life,* 541–542.
23. E. A. Locke, D. B. Ferren, V. M. Caleb, K. N. Shaw, and A. T. Denny, "The Relative Effectiveness of Four Methods of Motivating Employee Performance" in *Changes in Working Life,* 381.
24. Daniel Yankelovich, *New Rules* (New York: Random House, 1981), 152.
25. Jim Wendle, "And Still Nobody Gives A Damn," *Purdue Perspective* (Spring 1984):3, 4.
26. Edwin A. Locke and Gary P. Latham, *Goal Setting: A Motivational Technique That Works* (Englewood: Prentice-Hall, 1984).
27. B. F. Skinner, *Contingencies of Reinforcement* (New York: Appleton-Century-Croft, 1969).
28. Henri Fayol, *General and Industrial Management* (London: Pitman House, 1967).
29. Henry Mintzberg, *Then Nature of Managerial Work* (New York: Harper and Row, 1973).
30. Rensis Likert, *The Human Organization: Its Management and Value* (New York: McGraw-Hill, 1967).
31. Robert R. Blake and Jane S. Mouton, *The Managerial Grid* (Houston: Gulf Publishing Co., 1964).
32. Sylvia Porter, "Your Money's Worth," *Washington Post,* 22 September 1981, D9.
33. Ibid.
34. Jerry E. Bishop, "The Personal and Business Cost of 'Job Burnout'," *Wall Street Journal,* 11 November 1980, 33, 37.
35. Richard Johnson and W. G. Ouchi, "Management in America—Japanese Style," *Washington Post,* 3 November 1974, 3.
36. William Ouchi, *Theory Z* (Reading, Mass.: Addison-Wesley Publishers, 1981), 206.
37. Ibid., 207.
38. Claudia Deutsch, "Trust, the New Ingredient in Management," *Business Week,* (6 July 1981): pp. 104–105.
39. Derek Norcross, "Sweden's Newest Export—Industrial Democracy," *Washington Post Parade* (15 December 1974), 15, and Jonathan Wolman, "Taking Part in the Decision-Making Process," *Elyria Chronicle-Telegram,* 27 August 1978, D4.

40. Ibid.
41. Terri Lazarus in a talk to the American Society of Training and Development, April 22, 1982, Washington, D.C.
42. Jonathan Wolman, "Taking Part in the Decision-Making Process," *Elyria Chronicle-Telegram,* 27 August 1974, D4.
43. Jerome Rosow, "The Worker of the '80s: Manage Him Like An Asset," *INC 3* (February 1981):74.
44. "Adapting Japanese Management to American Organizations," *Training and Development Journal,* (September, 1982): 9–10.
45. Donald C. Mosley, Leon C. Meggison, and Paul H. Pietri, Jr., *Supervisory Management,* 2nd ed. Cincinnati: South-Western Publishing, 1989.
46. Leon C. Megginson, Donald C. Mosley, Paul H. Pietri, Jr., *Management Concepts and Applications* (New York: Harper and Row, 1989).
47. "The Trouble with Managing Japanese-style," (*Fortune* April 2, 1984): 50–56.
48. Merle O'Donnell and Robert J. O'Donnell, "Quality Circles: The Latest Fad or a Real Winner?," *Business Horizons,* (May–June, 1984): 48–52.
49. Gary Gemmill, "Managing Upward Communications," *Management Review* (May 1970):28.
50. Charles C. Vance, "How to Encourage Upward Communication from Your Employees," *Association Management* 28 (May 1976):59.
51. Harold Geneen, "Theory G," *United* 29 (November 1984):69.
52. Diane Lockwood and Sara Boatman, "Marketability: Who Needs Us and What Can We Do for Them?" (Paper presented at the Central States Speech Association Convention, 1975).
53. David G. Lee, "Improving Organizational Communication: A Role for Training and Development Within Control Data" (Paper presented at the Speech Communication Association Convention, Chicago, November 1984).

9

☐

Ethics and Business

OVERVIEW   The role of ethics in business and the kinds of value judgments made in the business community has become a very important issue. Some question whether or not there has been a demise of organizational ethics due to the pressures on business to be successful. One of the major questions currently facing businesses is whether or not they can nurture ethical behavior in the present-day competitive environment. As a result, business communications frequently encounter ethical choices.

KEY TERMS   philosophy   utilitarianism
             ethics   ethical analysis
             business ethics   ethical communicators
             consequentialism

THE ETHICAL DILEMMA

If society is "man writ large" as the Greek philosopher Plato claimed, then a society will be good and just only insofar as it nourishes those values which are recognized and practiced on a personal level by morally concerned individuals. "Rational and sensitive persons accept the role of ethics in private and personal relationships. What rational person, for example, would disagree with the view that it is morally wrong for one person to harm another innocent person? Or, who would disagree with the view that it is morally good for one person to promote the well-being of another?"[1]

If at least part of the rationale and purpose of business (some would say the whole of it) is its contribution to the well-being of society, then the ethics of business and the kinds of value judgments the business community makes ought to be similar to those governing personal and social situations in general.

Unfortunately, the morality of both people and businesses has come under strong question. In recent years, scandals seem to have become a growth industry. We read about them in tabloids and pulp newspapers available at the check-out counter of supermarkets. Television blares the news of defense contractors bilking the Pentagon, banks laundering cash for suspected crooks, and well-known brokerage firms admitting to kiting checks. Corporate embezzlement schemes, toxic waste dumping, insider trading, influence peddling, and industrial espionage are heralded on the front pages as are stories reflecting a growing crisis of conscience in America in general, and corporate America specifically.

With so many signs of unethical behavior, one may wonder if ethics has any place in the business world. Has the term "business ethics" become a contradiction in terms? Or, perhaps has the word *ethics* come to mean one thing within a business context and another in personal life?

What has brought about what may be called the nation's ethical demise? Historically, the change in our ethical structure seems to be rooted in the 1960s when our society was swept into a period of turbulence with such events as the Viet Nam War protests, and the assassinations of John F. Kennedy, Robert Kennedy and Martin Luther King. In this period, we started to question many accepted values. This trend continued into the 1970s when the questioning grew more intense with Watergate putting the spotlight on government ethics.

The ethical demise may have been caused by the breakdown of the traditional institutional support for moral teaching—religion and family life. It may have been stimulated by our being bombarded by information that is really *dis*information. Some of the cause may lie in the acceptance of the philosophical concept that all things are relative and that nothing is absolutely right or wrong, which may have fostered cynicism. Some blame the widespread falloff on the every-person-for-themselves ethic.

Whatever the cause, there is an awareness of an ethical crisis in society and the resulting ethical carryover into business and industry. The changed attitude of society may be reflected by a recent poll which shows that less than 50 percent of college freshmen list "developing a meaningful philosophy of life" as their main goal of life, while 71 percent see "being well off financially" as an important goal. These figures, when compared with those of previous decades, illustrates a steep drop in the emphasis on a meaningful philosophy of life as the basis for judgments and a sharp increase in financial security as a predominant motivator.[2]

ETHICS AND BUSINESS

In our free enterprise system, it is generally assumed that commerce and industry exist to make money. "In this age of satellite communications and computerized manufacturing, the competition isn't just the shop down the street. It's shops all over the world. Making money is hard, and so is resisting the temptation to make it any way you can."[3]

Nowhere is the temptation to breach business ethics stronger than in world of high finance. (H. Armstrong Roberts)

Businesspeople operate under enormous pressures. There is pressure to increase sales to clients, managers are urged to cut costs, stockholders demand higher profits, top-level management imposes pressures, upwardly-mobile families want more of the finer things of life. These economic pressures leave their mark on many corporate consciences, often creating a difficult atmosphere for encouraging ethical behavior.

Defenders of the capitalist system emphasize that our system allows individual freedom and individual choice. The defenders contend that under this system individuals are free to act as they wish so long as they do no harm to others. The people may use their money as they choose and register their preferences in their purchases. The second basic feature of the system is that each person entering into a transaction seeks to achieve personal goals or ends. A transaction is considered to be fair or just if both parties enter the transaction with appropriate knowledge and if they enter it freely.[4] Those who espouse that attitude believe that each person is responsible to do what he or she thinks is in his or her best interest, both as producer or seller and as consumer. They also feel that there has not been much of a change in the ethical system of businesses and industries, only that consumer groups and regulatory agencies are now keeping track of fraud and deception, and the press is much more vigilant today. This, they contend, makes us more aware of unethical actions, an awareness heightened by such movements as affirmative action, environmental concerns, and those directed against sexual harassment.[5]

ETHICS DEFINED
■

To understand ethics, we must understand that it is part of an ongoing philosophical enterprise. **Philosophy,** in its broadest meaning, is a systematic attempt to make sense out of our individual and collective experience. We do this through analysis, investigating actions and thoughts in detail to determine the meaning of terms, the validity of arguments, and the nature and status or presuppositions by discerning their components. Next, we synthesize by constructing a unified view which brings together all the parts of our experiences as intelligibly as possible.[6]

"**Ethics** can be defined as a systematic attempt, through the use of reason, to make sense of our individual and social moral experience in such a way as to determine the rules which govern human conduct and the values worth pursuing in life."[7] Ethics is not just the practice of individuals: it is a value shared by society as a whole. The word *ethics* comes from the Greek word *ethos,* meaning *custom* and *character.* Customs and characteristics pervade society—individuals, families, media, government, and business and industry.

An important aspect of any ethical system is the role of truth and lies. The theoretical societal rule regarding lying is not to lie. However, the reality of lying is extremely complex. There are many kinds of lies, from the white lie in which small untruths are told to spare another's feelings, to the big lies told to protect national security or other major areas of concern. "Probably most Americans accept white lies as a necessary evil. Without them, everyday life would have considerably rougher edges."[8] "But the edges of those 'acceptable' untruths are easily blurred, and there is a huge middle range of falsehoods that Americans have traditionally viewed as unjustifiable . . . lies of expediency or cowardice, lies that give the liar an advantage he would not otherwise have, such as inflating credentials to get a job, lies that allow the evasion of responsibility—perhaps laying the blame on others—and lies that manipulate others to achieve the liar's goal."[9]

BUSINESS ETHICS DEFINED

In dealing with ethics, the U.S. world of business finds itself coming to grips with general philosophical concepts applied to the free-enterprise system. The theory of **business ethics** attempts to describe how people should act within given business structures; a practical discipline with practical importance. The application of business ethics can help people approach moral problems in business more systematically and with better tools than they might otherwise. In addition, it can help people to see issues they might normally ignore. It can also impel business people to make changes that they might otherwise not be moved to make. However, business ethics will not change business practices unless those engaged in the practices that need moral change wish to change them.[10]

Historically, the country's initial mandate to business was rather simple. People wanted goods to be as plentiful, good, and cheap as possible. As problems developed, laws were introduced to regulate working conditions, protect children, prevent monopolistic practices, and preserve the environment. The regulations frequently represented moral concerns on the part of the people. "A business may ignore the moral demands of a whole society since it is part of that society and dependent on it at the same time that it serves it."[11]

The question of businesses and their ethics, therefore, is essentially a question of personal ethics based on both values instilled in the individual and the environmental background of the individual. Personal ambition greatly distorts sound judgment in such matters, as does the overriding quest for corporate sales and profits. Should individuals in management positions, where sales and the resulting profits are going to be impaired, always tell the truth? Should they alert the public to possible problems to the environment, their health, and their safety caused by the production of possible endangering products? Are they obligated to share information that may never be found out unless someone blows the whistle on the wrong-doing or wrong-doers? For example, are businesspersons required to come to the public with information about toxic waste dumping, nuclear meltdown coverups, and dangerous products? Are people involved in business and industry bound by the concept of **consequentialism,** which suggests that the consequences of human actions are evaluated in terms of the extent to which they achieve desirable results?

Is the desirable result of the free enterprise system to be profit, profit within the framework of societal and human safety, or a combination thereof?

"Given the lack of moral considerations in many decisions within the business community, a resuscitation of the ethical principle of **utilitarianism,** which states that an action is right or good if it contributes to the well-being of society in general, might be appropriate. The concern that opponents of utilitarianism have had has been that it does not adequately consider the rights of individuals, but with the safeguards provided by civil rights legislation during the past 25 years, the time may have come to apply this principle to current ethical abuses in business, much as it was used to correct abuses against industrial workers in the nineteenth century England."[12]

ETHICS IN BUSINESS

An investigation of the topic of ethics in business centers on such issues as whether or not capitalism encourages immoral acts, whether or not there has been a change in ethical practices and the nature of corporate responsibility.

Capitalism and Ethics

Some critics of capitalism charge that this system encourages unethical behavior—rewarding selfishness, dishonesty and greed. They contend that as long as we accept the cliche that "the business of business is business" and that creating profits is paramount in the system, then individuals and organizations will do whatever they must to gain those profits even if this includes immoral or unethical acts.

Changes in Ethical Practices

Has there been a breakdown in business ethics? Some theorists believe that while there has been a great deal of negative publicity concerning the breakdown of ethics in the business environment, there has not really been much of a change in the practices of industry regarding ethical actions. As stated by one expert, "Overall, I don't see any evidence of a sharp decline in corporate ethics. Rather I believe our expectations for corporate behavior has risen."[13] This view is further developed by the belief that because of Watergate and Iran-gate, the media has started to do a great deal more of investigative reporting. In addition, the advent of citizens groups, such as those headed by consumer advocate Ralph Nader, have alerted the general public to their rights and responsibilities regarding such matters as safety, product defects, and environmental protection.

CORPORATE RESPONSIBILITY

The bottom-line statement in corporate responsibility should be that *corporations should act morally*. But, is this practical? And is knowing what is morally required sufficient?

American business is faced with more competition than ever before, in all industries. Can business nurture ethical behavior in such a cut-throat environment?

Can American corporations compete on a world-wide level when their competitors are not governed by the same ethical standards? "In some countries, you have to pay someone before you can conduct business. They call it 'baksheesh'—which means 'a gift of money as a favor or reward'—and this payment is an accepted custom."[14] In our society, we view baksheesh as unethical because we believe that paying to do business corrupts honest competition. A few years ago, a clamor was heard when several American companies admitted to paying bribes abroad. The companies claimed that these payments were so much a way of life in some countries, they couldn't compete unless they went along.[15] Are our corporations expected to compete in the world market by world or by American ethics?

Whether or not dishonest business behavior is as old as humans or whether it is fueled by our fast-paced, self-centered society, the issue of business ethics is real, and lasting solutions must come from within the business community.

Ethics is a new frontier for the business community. Ethics traditionally has concerned itself with individuals and their actions. It is generally accepted that, ultimately, a corporation does not make moral decisions, but individuals within that organization make choices. Individuals make those decisions in keeping with their moral and ethical strength or weaknesses—their truthfulness or lack of truthfulness, honesty or lack of honesty, and integrity or lack of integrity. Individualism notwithstanding, corporations are responsible for the decisions that are made by its representatives. Organizations are increasingly recognizing that they must not be concerned only about the behavior of individuals, but also with the values that permeate the organizations.[16] "Corporations may limit the legal accountability of the persons who are incorporated, but insofar as they are simply a union of persons they still retain the ethical accountability of individuals."[17]

What is business doing about this? Corporations are implementing organizational codes of ethics, developing ethics training programs for executives and employees, evaluating and monitoring the organization's ethics, establishing ethics hotlines, doing ethics audits, and employing ombudsmen to oversee a corporation's ethics. This is not just an isolated pattern. "90% of Fortune 500 companies require employees to subscribe to a code of ethics. Such organizations as Union Carbide, Boeing, McDonnell Douglas, and Chemical Bank have set up programs to help employees deal with ethical conflicts."[18] A national teleconference on business ethics involving most of the major corporations was recently held. Colleges and universities have also accepted the challenge. "85% of all U.S. business schools offer courses in business ethics."[19]

This awareness of ethical accountability is starting to make corporations accept responsibility for their actions. For example, "when several people died after taking contaminated Tylenol capsules in 1982, Johnson and Johnson withdrew the product from the market and incurred a hefty financial loss. The firm was helped to make this ethically correct, but economically difficult decision, through its institutionalized ethics program. The corporate culture allowed someone to use the word 'safety' even if it meant a loss of millions in the short run."[20]

Corporations are also starting to insist on employee accountability. "Distortion of credentials by applicants for all levels of employment has increased substantially."[21] In an effort to weed out potential problem employees, many companies have tightened the screening process of job applicants. Fortune 500 corporations are increasing their background checks for entry-level and executive position applicants.[22]

Many corporations have also instituted employment civil rights and responsibilities programs. These are often based on the belief that employees are entitled to certain types of treatment regardless of race, sex, or age, and that each employee has a moral right to be treated like a human being. On the job, employees have the right to equality of treatment and the right of privacy. However, with these rights come obligations. Employees are obligated not to lie, not to spread false information, not to abuse or harass others, sexually or otherwise. They are obligated to fulfill the terms of their contracts.[23]

Some organizations have even encouraged a form of internal whistle-blowing as part of their procedure. Whistle-blowing has traditionally meant making known to some governmental agency, news reporter, or media personnel, actions or conditions within a firm that are either illegal or harmful to the public or that may cause harm to consumers of the firm's products or services. Since the consequences of whistle-blowing are often disastrous, such action is not to be undertaken lightly. The general attitude about whistle-blowing has been that it is justifiable if "the issue on which an employee intends to disclose information to the public concerns the infliction of serious harm on the public in general or on some members of it. The more serious the harm, the more serious the obligation."[24] In some instances, employers have set up a procedure through which problems of the organization are discussed in groups where employees are encouraged to share their views about the company's problems or problems of its product or services. In this way, the matter can be dealt with internally and corrected instead of becoming a public scandal. Auto manufacturers, such as Ford, have turned to this system with positive results.

USING ETHICS

■

Even in these days of questioning, there appears to be a truism concerning ethics: "We are not a perfect society. But that doesn't mean our society values unethical conduct. Ethical conduct is the norm—the custom."[25] Understanding your personal ethical system helps you make sense of your life, aids you to fulfill personal, professional, and social responsibilities, and make sound judgments.

While no universally accepted code of ethics exists, certainly driving forces are behind the way an individual applies ethics. Consider these forces:

1. *Each moral choice we make has repercussions for ourselves as well as for others.* For example, if you are working for a small business and the owner is not writing receipts for all of the sales and is taking the money for himself, thus avoiding having to pay taxes on the income, what is your course of action? If you decide to report the incident, it is very likely the owner will be arrested and you will lose your job, thus affecting both you and your employer.

2. *We must recognize ethical issues if we are to act on them.* "Recognition of ethical issues is an imperative for acting on them. Unlike other questions where we may decide on an answer without there being any requisite commitment of action, such as whether or not one product tastes better than another, ethical issues, since they involve human and societal well-being in a fundamental way, necessarily involve commitment and action as part of their resolution."[26]

When we are aware that we are making ethical judgments, we can start to identify hidden assumptions and determine whether or not there are reasonable grounds for making a judgment or for reaching a conclusion. For example, you can make the decision to report your employer for not acting ethically by pocketing money only if you are aware that this action is illegal and unethical.

3. *We must recognize that being moral is in our best interest.* Without even totally understanding the why of the matter, most people know the right thing to do. However, people often need the encouragement to be moral. If we accept the idea that we ought to be moral because we want to live in a certain kind of society and that society must be protected, then it is in our own best interest to be moral. "Thus, a person who reports that an employer is marketing an unsafe product is both acting morally and acting in his own self-interest in that he is contributing to the well-being of society, and in that his own well-being is inextricably interwoven with the well-being of society."[27] Consequently, a person who has determined to act morally in his or her own self interest would find it difficult not to report the tax-evading owner.

4. *We must develop analytical skills.* People have a need to examine and make distinctions among concepts that center on ethical principles and moral rules. We need to understand how we reach conclusions and the consequences of our decisions. Basic **ethical analysis** takes three steps: a) understanding what is happening, b) determining whether or not the action is moral or immoral (using personal criteria), and c) deciding if an action should be taken; and, if so, what the appropriate action should be. "This is not to say that analysis can always provide a clear cut answer to what is moral. Some moral issues, such as abortion, are so complex as to divide even professional philosophers. However, this is not the case with the vast majority of issue that arise in business ethics. These are issues for which, for the most part, ethical analysis can help determine the moral status and thus guide us to appropriate ethical action."[28]

5. *We must elicit a sense of moral responsibility.* It is important to understand that believing something is not the same as acting that way. Actions, not intentions, are the real issue. Believing that your employer is performing an immoral act and taking action to curb that unethical conduct are two different issues. "The major problem in business ethics is, in fact, not determining what is right and wrong, but increasing the awareness of ethical issues and developing a tendency to act in a morally responsible way."[29]

6. *Ethical certainty is usually not possible.* "Ethical certainty is not always possible. However, you can avoid the chaos and despair of subjectivity. If you thoughtfully arrive at some ethical principles that make sense to you and apply these principles in a logical and consistent way to ethical situations, then you can bring coherency to your decision making."[30] If you know how you reached your conclusion and accept that the system or method was logical to you, then there is consistency and coherence to your decision-making.[31]

ETHICS IN BUSINESS COMMUNICATION

It is a generally accepted principle that speakers should be ethical and this ethical quality be consistent. Unfortunately, this consistency is not always the case. An individual may be scrupulously ethical in personal relationships or activities. For example, a person who might not cheat or lie when playing in the weekly bridge game or in a golf match may knowingly make false or misleading statements to gain an advantage in a business situation and do so with a sense of pride and satisfaction because of the gains to be made, with none of the pangs of conscience that normally accompany personal moral deviations.

Ethical communicators are regarded as those who have a strong sense of moral awareness and a high degree of personal integrity. Though it is accepted that some problems may have more than one moral solution, and that no single definition of morality exists, an ethical speaker generally:

- Speaks with sincerity.
- Does not knowingly expose an audience to falsehoods or half-truths that cause significant harm.
- Does not deliberately alter the truth.
- Presents the truth as he or she understands it.
- Raises the listeners' level of expertise by supplying necessary facts, definitions, descriptions, and substantiating information.
- Conveys a message that is free from mental and physical coercion; a message that does not compel someone to take an action against his or her will.
- Does not fabricate statistics or other information intended to serve as proof of a contention or belief.
- Gives credit to the source of information and does not present that information as original when it is not.[32]

"The importance of truthfulness is fundamental to the whole area of ethics in communications. Confidence cannot be easily restored once it is lost."[33]

Likewise, the ethical listener takes seriously the responsibility for communicating. Just as we enjoy freedom of speech, our freedom to listen is based on the obligation to provide a fair hearing of the message and then to carefully analyze the strength of that message.

SUMMARY

In this chapter we have examined ethics and business. The major concepts discussed were:

The role of ethics in business ought to be substantially the same as those found in personal and social situations.

The morality of people and businesses has come under strong scrutiny.

Ethics is a systematic attempt to make sense of our individual and social moral experience.

Business ethics attempt to determine how people should act within given business structures.

The theories of consequentialism and utilitarianism affect business decisions.

Corporations should act morally.

While there are no universally accepted codes of ethics, there are driving forces behind the way an individual applies ethics as a communication.

THINGS TO DO

1. Do you feel businesses can be both ethical and profitable? Should anything get in the way of businesses making money?

2. Should a person doing business in a foreign country carry on business in the manner of that country, even if it is contrary to American ethical standards?

3. What would you do in each of the following situations? Be prepared to explain your answers:

    a. You are working for a corporation located on a river which is the source of drinking water for a town located downstream. You become aware that toxic chemical waste is being dumped into the river in such a way that the source of the waste will go undetected.

    b. You are the accountant for a small firm. You have been called before a governmental investigative panel and asked whether you are aware that the owner of the company is taking sales income from the business without recording it. You know it has happened. You will probably receive a jail sentence for being an accomplice if you admit the crime.

    c. You have taken approximately $600 in office supplies from the corporation for which you work to use in a home business you are operating. You are called into the manager's office and asked if you know anything about the depletion of the supplies inventory. The manager confides that he thinks John, a fellow worker, has been stealing them.

    d. You are dissatisfied with your present job. You have applied for a position with another company. You are called for an interview. You are told you must appear next Tuesday if you are to be considered. You will have to miss a day of work to go to the interview. You have no personal days off remaining. You don't want your present employer to know you are looking for another position because she would probably fire you.

    e. A fellow employee tells you in strict confidence that he has AIDS. You are employed in a high risk health care facility where it is possible for the employees to prick themselves with needles in the process of doing experiments, thus possibly contaminating the end product which is injected into patient's bodies, thus possibly leading to their being contaminated with the AIDS virus. On your monthly report, you are asked to reveal any information you have about health-risks.

    f. You are a lawyer. You are aware that your witness, a member of the executive board of the firm supplying 80 percent of your business, is lying during cross-examination.

    g. A member of your firm has found a way of entering into a competitor's computer operations. This allows you, if you so desire, to ascertain the competitor's bids on jobs which you both desire, in advance of the submission date. A large contract is up for bid. You and your competitor are the finalists for the job.

NOTES

1. Charles Buckalew, lecture at Lorain County Community College, Elyria, Ohio, January, 1989.
2. Wade, M. Euel, Jr., "The Lantern of Ethics," speech given at the University of Georgia, Athens, GA, November 5, 1987.
3. Leila Zogby, "Business Ethics—The Answers Lie Within," *Piedmont Airlines Magazine* (May 1988):122.
4. R. T. DeGeorge, *Business Ethics* (New York: MacMillan, 1982), 130.
5. "A Nation of Liars," *U.S. News and World Report* (23 February, 1987): 54–57; Wade.
6. DeGeorge, 10–11.
7. Ibid., 12.
8. "A Nation of Liars," 54.
9. Ibid.
10. DeGeorge, 15.
11. Ibid., 7–8.
12. Buckalew.
13. Charles S. McCoy, Senior Fellow of Trinity Church's Center for Ethics and Corporate Policy, New York, as quoted in Zogby, 119.
14. Wade.
15. Ibid.
16. McCoy.
17. Buckalew.
18. Wade.
19. Baruch, Jeffrey and Elisabeth Nicol, "Teaching Ethics in Business School," *Collegiate News and Views* (Fall 1980):5.
20. Zogby, 122.
21. Ibid.
22. Ibid.
23. DeGeorge.
24. Ibid.
25. Wade.
26. Buckalew.
27. Ibid.
28. Ibid.
29. Ibid.
30. Ibid.
31. Ibid. and "Applied Ethics: A Strategy for Fostering Professional Responsibility," *Carnegie Quarterly* 28 (Spring/Summer 1980):3–4.
32. Nelson, Thomas, *Ethics in Speech Communication* (Indianapolis: Bobbs-Merrill, 1966), 139.
33. "Jaksa and Pritchard Write Communication Ethics Book," *Communication Research Bulletin,* Department of Communication, Western Michigan University (April 1988):1.

10

☐

Decision-Making in Business

OVERVIEW   Systematic decision making and problem solving help business people to make more effective decisions, thus saving time and money for businesses. Two decision-making procedures are the Inductive Process of Decision-Making and the Practical Decision-Making Process in which prescribed procedures are applied to agreed-upon criteria.

KEY WORDS

communication barriers
systematic process
emotional pollution
decision
good decision
problem
situation
Inductive Process of Problem Solving
brainstorming
workable

desirable
practical
Practical Decision-Making Process
primary information
secondary information
criteria
procedure
assessing adverse consequences
assessment instrument

Communication barriers: common errors in reasoning; unsystematic and emotional thinking; source and receiver short circuits; influences that operate at conscious and subconscious levels—all these factors result in costly errors and considerable time loss for types of organizations and individuals. Decision making and problem solving are dependent upon effective and efficient communication patterns at each stage of the process.

THE IMPORTANCE OF DECISION MAKING

Skilled decision-makers are indeed scarce, and our changing environment will make effective decision-making even more valuable in the future. It is certainly to your continuing advantage to be able to follow a systematic decision-making process that will help you minimize the factors that frequently obstruct effective decision-making processes. By habitually following a practical decision-making process, you should find that the number of good decisions will increase and that your decision-making confidence will grow.

You must remember, however, that even though results will be better using practical and systematic processes, they will not necessarily be perfect. It is doubtful that any decision-maker using any one method has ever achieved the ability to make good decisions all of the time.

Practical and effective decision-making is not an easy and automatic job, but neither does it have to result in mental anguish, indecision, fear, and frayed nerves. The following guidelines might help you make future decisions more effectively.

Follow a systematic process. Certainly intuition ought not be ignored, but it also should not be confused with slipshod methods. If you use a **systematic process** and occasionally complement the process with intuition, you will be following and using a fundamentally sound basis for practical decision making. The systematic process selected will vary according to the decision situation and the decision maker. "The effective decision maker uses a decision making mode to fit the decision environment, and the decision maker's ability and personality. Rarely will effective decision makers use the same style for all decisions."[1]

Consult and check. Be aware that one can rarely know all the answers or have at hand all the information that would prove valuable. Learn to use the advice, opinions, research, and analyses of others. It often takes longer to investigate a problem and its possible solutions than to select the cure.

Try to avoid crisis decisions and stress conditions. Try to avoid getting into spots where you have to make split-second decisions. Try to anticipate and prepare for the future crisis, if at all possible. If the decision situation is of an extremely personal nature, try to put off the decision until a time when you are apt to be less emotional or emotionally involved. If quick decisions must be made, consider the consequences of a tentative solution, as the paramount factor is reaching a plan of action.

Be on guard against emotional pollution. Recognition that we are not ever perfectly objective human beings and insistence that we use checkpoints to minimize **emotional pollution** (emotional obstacles) will go a long way toward improving our decision-making process and the results.

Do not expect to be right all of the time. No one ever reaches this level of perfection. Be proud and satisfied in the knowledge that if you have followed a systematic process that is applicable to your personality and the decision situation, regardless of the outcome or result, you have given it your best shot and could not have done it any better, no matter how hard you tried.

MAKING THE DECISION

■

What is a decision? A **decision** is a practical, appropriate response to a situation or problem. We can then conclude that decision-making is the process of thought and deliberation that leads to a decision.

What is a **good decision?** A good decision is one you are perfectly comfortable with, the perceived best possible solution to a problem. It is the result of following some systematic step-by-step process which caused you to arrive at a particular choice. It must always be kept in mind that what represents a good decision for you may not necessarily be the best decision for someone else looking at the same set of data and arriving at a choice.

Some problems you confront may lend themselves to easy solutions. Some, however, will not and will require a great deal of deliberation. Deliberate decisions are not the kind of decisions we make every day. They tend to be complicated, and they tend to have important consequences or a heavy impact on our lifestyles. We generally face extended time frames in which to make these decisions, and the decision requires a good bit of data gathering. These decisions are generally quite difficult to make, but are very necessary to our sense of well-being. These decisions require objective and systematic analysis, for the cost of being wrong is very high. Either you personally or the company you represent may have to live with your mistake permanently or at least for quite some time.

Defining the Problem

□

One of the major factors in effective decision-making is clearly identifying the **problem**— what has to be solved. Unfortunately, in many instances, if the problem is inappropriately defined, the likelihood that the action will cure what is wrong is almost accidental. If the problem can be simply defined, there is no difficulty. However, it is often necessary to hold off making the recommendation for solution until the problem is ascertained. This delay may allow time for a clear definition of the problem. The following case study should point to the need to clearly identify the problem.

Assume you are the regional sales manager for Sassy Products. The sales in the area you are responsible for have dropped by 30 percent during the past year. A simplistic problem definition would be, "The sales in Lorain County have decreased." If this were your defined problem, you would now move toward developing alternatives aimed at correcting this problem. Unfortunately, this may not produce a solution to the real problem. The decrease in sales is, in fact, just a symptom. It is not the problem; it is just the **situation**—what is happening. The problem is yet to be defined. In order to define the real problem, we should take a systematic approach to ascertain the cause. We are trying to determine what is unique in this situation that would indicate the cause of the problem, and then apply this uniqueness to the decision-making procedure. By interviewing the salesperson for the district, interviewing the clients, interviewing competitors, examining the economic conditions of the area, and making a market-share comparison (comparing your sales to your competitor's), we may be able to determine a possible cause.

The results of the search for a cause may turn up a general economic depression in the district; a long strike by the employees of the major industry in the area, causing the loss of purchasing power by the population; or a severe decrease in population may have caused general decrease in all product sales. In these cases, the solution to the problem is beyond your control and there may be no need to go further in your attempt to alter the sales plunge. If, on the other hand, the search for cause reveals something you can deal with, you can plug this into the decision-making process and search for the best solution.

DECISION-MAKING TECHNIQUES

Now that we have defined the terms, we can proceed to examine techniques. Remember, it is our contention that the use of systematic techniques can assist you in making satisfactory decisions. Keep in mind, however, that "judgment is an essential adjunct of the effective use of any technique, the purpose of the technique being to sharpen the judgment, not replace it."[2]

The Inductive Process of Decision Making

One of the possible systematic approaches to decision making is the procedure described in the model **The Inductive Process of Problem Solving.**[3] The steps in the inductive process are:

1. identify the situation.
2. identify the problem.
3. brainstorm for possible solutions.
4. evaluate the solutions for workability, desirability, and practicality.
5. select the most workable, desirable, and practical plan and put it into action.
6. evaluate the results.

By investigating what is happening, or generally describing the sequence of the situation, we can often ascertain what is unsatisfactory. By making sure that we understand the background, or the cause, we may be able to avoid attempting to solve something that is not, in fact, the problem or a problem.

Identifying the Problem

Once we have ascertained that something is unsatisfactory, we must then determine exactly what the problem is and what has to be solved or done to make the situation satisfactory.

In the case of Sassy Products, we would have to investigate to find the cause for the drop in sales so that we could specifically define the problem. Assume that in the process of interviewing the salespersons and clients, examination of the economic conditions, and examination of the sales comparisons it was revealed that one of the salespersons had not been making calls on some of his clients. In addition, if he did receive orders, he had not processed all of them. It is now possible to define the specific problem as "What can be done about getting the salesperson to call on his clients and to process the orders placed?" (You will note that the drop in sales—the situation—was symptomatic of the real problem.)

Brainstorming

Before quickly selecting the first possible solution you may think of, it is advisable to try to search out as many possible ways to solve the problem as you can. At first some of these ideas may appear to be silly or unworkable, but after evaluation, the "dumb" suggestions may turn out to be the best possible cure. In **brainstorming,** do not evaluate; just generate as many solutions as you can.

In the Sassy Products case, our brainstorming results are (1) fire the salesperson, (2) meet with the salesperson and try to ascertain why he is not fulfilling his job responsibilities and devise a plan to assist him, (3) take away the salesperson's company-owned car and tell him that he will get it back when sales increase and (4) do nothing.

Testing the Solution

In order to narrow down the brainstormed solutions, a set of solution evaluation guides is applied. Is the possible solution **workable?** (Can it solve the problem?) Is the solution **desirable?** (Will it lead to greater evils?) Is the solution **practical?** (Can it be put into practice realistically?) By testing each of the proposed cures, we are usually able to eliminate those that will not solve the problem. In the Sassy Products case, we can test each of our brainstormed solutions as shown in table 10.1.

Selecting the Solution

Reapplying the criteria of workability, desirability, and practicality, we should now be able to find the most workable, the most desirable, and the most practical solution and put it into effect.

In the Sassy Products case, since solution B seems to have the most positive possible end results, this solution would be put into effect.

Solution	Workable (solve problems)	Desirable (greater evils)	Practical (can be put into practice)
A. *Fire salesperson*	Won't help	Yes, salesperson to sell products	Can be put into effect
B. *Meet with salesperson*	Possibly	No foreseen evils	Can be put into effect
C. *Take away the car*	Probably not	Yes, salesperson won't be able to get to clients	Can be put into effect
D. *Do nothing*	No	Possibly, continued loss of sales	Can be put into effect.

Evaluating the Results

It is usually advisable to follow up on the applied solution to see if it has solved the problem. It is not unusual for the proposed plan for implementation of the solution to include a follow-up procedure and a time schedule for accomplishment of this procedure.

In the Sassy Products case, after talking to the salesperson, an agreement would be reached about the plan of action to be followed. The agreement could include such conditions as these: (1) the salesperson agrees to make calls on buyers and prospective buyers and to relay all orders to the sales department; (2) sales must increase in the salesperson's territory by 15 percent within the next sixty days; and (3) an automatic termination of employment will be made if the agreed upon terms are not carried out.

Practical Decision-Making Process

□

Let us now focus on an alternate format for decision making: "The Anatomy of a **Practical Decision-Making Process.**"[4] It consists of a specific sequence of steps, which, if followed, insure that we take into consideration essential elements in the decision-making process at each appropriate step.

The decision-making process can be illustrated by applying a case-study to the model. In this case-study, some factual data is available, but there is also a need to involve reactions and feelings of people as decision-making factors.

Decision-Making Situation

You are a member of the management team at the Dawn Manufacturing Company. The company has decided to open a new plant in Grafton, Ohio. It is your task to select the individual who will head the plant. The person selected will be dealing with new equipment and new personnel and will not be able to rely on headquarters for much assistance during the start-up of operations, due to the distance of the plant from the home operations. The person hired will have to make a large number of decisions in a limited amount of time.

Decision-Making Procedure

Step 1: *Define the Problem, Situation, or Opportunity.* By examining the inputs and asking the appropriate check questions, you will be able to enhance and add to the total understanding of the problem, situation, or opportunity.

Many operative influences affect the decision process. Some of these are recognizable and function at a conscious level. All of these inputs and influences tend to condition the definition stage of the process. This stage of the decision-making process is critical because if we are in error concerning the inputs or are unduly influenced by the inputs, we adversely affect all of the stages of the decision-making process.

In the Dawn Manufacturing case the problem is apparent: you must select an individual to head a new plant.

It would be worthwhile to ask a number of check questions of yourself and others at this stage of the process. They are:

1. Do I have sufficient information to properly make a definition?
2. Can a definition be made?
3. Is it necessary to make a definition?
4. Have I asked for other opinions?
5. Are my facts and observations supported by evidence?
6. Have I recognized that which is heresay, inference, and assumption?
7. Will a simple definition be sufficient?

Seeking answers to all of these questions, plus other relevant ones you may develop, will enhance your total understanding of the problem, situation, or opportunity. Essentially we are attempting to bring the "big picture" into sharp focus at this stage of the decision-making process.

Step 2: *State Objectives.* During this stage of the process, the common inputs consist of personal constraints: resources (the number of people available) and ability (the abilities of the personnel). Environmental or external constraints (resources and ability) must also be considered. The constraints represent boundary conditions in that you are restricted to a fixed limit or extent. One rarely, if ever, has unlimited resources and unlimited abilities. A determination of these limits will aid us in structuring practical, meaningful objectives.

In the Dawn Manufacturing case, you will select a qualified person to fill the vacancy; you will select the best person to fill the post.

Worthwhile check questions to ask of yourself and others at this stage are:

1. What is my goal?
2. What will the outcome be when I have solved this problem, situation, or opportunity?

3. Which objectives are absolute and which are relative?
4. Is my objective worthwhile?
5. Is my objective attainable?
6. Is my objective measurable?

Essentially we are attempting to specify our goal or goals, which, if accomplished, will result in correcting the discrepancy between the desired conditions and the actual conditions.

> Step 2A: *Restate the objective.* During this stage of the decision-making process, we are attempting to sharpen further the general objective statements we developed in Step 2. Remember, the sharper the focus, the better the picture. Our initial efforts in Step 2 can very likely be improved upon. Rarely does one write a perfect first draft of anything. For example, although this chapter has been written and rewritten several times, it is very possible it could be further improved if it were rewritten again.

In the Dawn Manufacturing case, you will fill the vacant post by promoting a person from within the company who is the best decision maker available at this time. You will select this person by using specified data.

Worthwhile check questions to ask of yourself and others at this stage of the decision-making process are:

1. Have I tried to state several other versions of my objective(s)?
2. Have I stated the objective in the most extreme, unfavorable terms?
3. Have I stated the objective in the most reasonably favorable terms?
4. Have I restated my objective in a variety of ways in order to make it as clear and precise as is reasonably possible?

Now that we have redrafted our objective a number of times, we have hopefully achieved a realistic statement of our goal(s).

> Step 3: *Gather and evaluate the data.* During this stage of the decision-making process, the common inputs consist of gathering primary and secondary information and then evaluating this information on the basis of significance, relevance, and quantity. **Primary information** is original in nature. It is information which you develop. **Secondary information** has already been gathered and codified, such as in newspapers, books, and magazines. As in Step 1, it will be necessary to check all inputs regarding inference, assumptions, and fact. These inputs tend to condition the development of the alternative stage and the action and follow-up stage of the process.

In the Dawn Manufacturing case, you will check the following sources for information. (1) Check personnel records. (2) Ask peers, supervisors, co-workers, and subordinates for appropriate information. (3) Use previous observations that have been made about the individual being investigated. (4) Refer to the record of critical incidents (a file kept of behaviors and performances on an individual working in a company, which contains positive and/or negative incidents in which the worker was directly involved). (5) Refer to past performance appraisals (evaluations about the worker). (6) Submit the individual to psychological testing to ascertain such factors as stability, the ability to perform under pressure, and the ability to make decisions.

Useful check questions in Stage 3 of the decision-making process are:

1. What kind of information do I need?
2. Where is the information available?
3. How much information do I need?
4. What costs are involved in acquiring the information?
5. How much time do I have?
6. Who can I help?

You might consider using a three-by-five-inch note card technique to assist you in this stage of the decision-making process. List each fact that you have gathered for this stage of the process on a blank three-by-five-inch note card. You can then rearrange the cards and the facts on the cards so that you can begin to place some interrelationships of those facts in proper perspective in a very convenient manner. You can shuffle the deck of note cards and rearrange the facts in a multitude of ways. In Step 3 of the decision-making process, we are essentially gathering and evaluating data so that we can effectively perform the remaining steps in our decision-making process.

Step 4: *Develop alternatives.* During this stage of the process the common inputs will consist of analytical thinking processes and creative thinking processes. Our purpose in this stage is to develop as large a quantity of alternatives as is reasonably possible. We will use analytical thinking and creative thinking to accomplish this. It is also helpful to get ideas from other people when you are performing the development-of-alternatives stage. They will help brainstorm and they will probably suggest many more alternatives than you might come up with by working alone. The inputs at this stage are absolutely critical to the success of the total process. The greater the quantity and quality of alternatives you develop, the better your chances are of selecting the best course of action. If you are not aware of various possible choices simply because you haven't thought of them or remembered them, then it becomes impossible to select from that which is not there.

In the Dawn Manufacturing case, our probing has resulted in the following alternatives: (1) promote Harry, (2) promote Debbie, (3) promote Denise, or (4) promote George.

Useful check questions for this stage are:

1. Have I developed a number of logical alternatives?
2. Have I developed a number of creative alternatives?
3. Are some of my alternatives unique?
4. Did I ask others to suggest some alternatives?
5. Do certain of my alternatives sound "far out?"

Good decision makers search out as many possible alternatives as they can before deciding on a solution. (American Media, Inc., Des Moines, IA)

Step 5: *Assess alternatives.* During this stage of the process we determine the system we will use to measure the performance of each of the possible alternatives. We will set up some kind of screening device that will permit us to objectively and subjectively assess the pluses and minuses of each alternative to be examined. The screening device consists of setting up basic requirements (**criteria**) that the alternatives should be tested against and using an assessment basis (**procedure**) for rating each alternative against the basic requirements.

It is generally worthwhile to separately and specifically examine an alternative by looking at it from a very negative point of view. This is a technique called **assessing adverse consequences,** and it requires that we actively seek out possible drawbacks or negative aspects of all contending alternatives. It is advisable to carry out the function of assessing adverse consequences after you have gotten a basic performance rating for each alternative, if one is available. Many of the alternatives that you have developed will no longer be in contention at this time, and you can better deal with the contending alternatives that still represent possible choices. You can simply list all negative aspects of each alternative on a sheet of paper, or you could even set up a weighing system that would reflect numerical values for each adverse consequence. The real

Assessment Instrument for Dawn Manufacturing Case

Alternatives	Decision Speed	Contribution to Objective	Decision Accuracy	Interpersonal Skills
1. Harry	N	N	N	Y
2. Debbie	N	N	Y	Y
3. Denise	Y	N	N	N
4. George	Y	Y	Y	Y

purpose of assessing adverse consequences is to be totally aware of negative aspects so that we are in a position to take action to minimize or correct conditions in the event that the negative aspects do in fact occur. There will then be fewer surprises and we will be better able to cope with adversity.

In the Dawn Manufacturing case, we decide that the following basic requirements (criteria) are needed for successful operation of the position: (1) speed in decision making, (2) contribution to our objective, (3) accuracy in decision making, and (4) interpersonal skills (ability to work with and through people). Using these criteria we develop an **assessment instrument**—a form to guide us through the decision-making process (table 10.2), and we use the information collected in Step 3 to make judgments about each of the candidates.

Some useful check questions for this stage are:

1. Are my screening requirements adequate?
2. Are my screening requirements relevant?
3. Is my assessment system adequate in that it permits me to make a discriminatory judgment?
4. Have I assessed adverse consequences for all primary alternatives still being considered?

Step 6: *Action and controls.* During this stage of the process we select the alternative that appears to satisfy optimum conditions, on balance, and we then set up controls to insure that all the work we have done in the preceding stages does not go to waste. Implementing the decision choice is critical to the entire decision-making process. We must not fail to think through and set established controls to protect the decision we have so systematically derived. It is important to remember that "an effective decision is a commitment to action and results."[5]

In the Dawn Manufacturing case, George is the first choice based on his having achieved the highest standard of performance in each of the four criteria we identified as prime factors in carrying out the job assignment.

Some useful check questions for this stage of the decision-making process are:

1. Have I determined everything that now must be done in order to make the decision work?

2. Who has to be informed of this decision?
3. What action needs to be taken and who is to take it?
4. Do I have a plan for determining progress in adjustment stages?
5. Have I established a plan for reviewing and evaluating this decision?

CRISIS DECISION-MAKING

■

Business executives spend a great deal of their time in problem analysis and decision-making. Their success often depends on their ability to do these things well. Many of the decisions facing them have to be made quickly. Executives often argue that they never have enough time to apply any systematic method to problem-solving. They contend that they are put in a position of making snap decisions, and, therefore, they need to rely on intuition rather than systematic process. Ironically, it is when crisis decisions have to be made that managers most desperately need an efficient method of handling problems and making decisions. Otherwise, much of their efforts will be wasted, along with money, time, and human resources.

A good decision-maker is like a skilled detective who has to spot the relevant information and use it, point by point, to narrow down the search for the real culprit. Doing this efficiently under pressure is not easy. But it can be done, and the more systematic and logical the method, the faster and more efficiently it will work. A systematic way of doing something is always more efficient and less time-consuming than is a disorderly approach which may require doing the same thing over several times in order to get it right.

Figure 10.1 illustrates that the first step in crisis decision making, as in all decision making, is to specify the problem, to determine what is wrong. Next, the causes: determine what made it wrong.

Then, specify the purpose of making the decision—what do you want the decision to accomplish? Don't plunge into an action until you are sure you have considered the relevant alternatives.

Next, formulate some possible solutions and use the information available to determine the probability of the solution's solving the problem. Take into consideration the consequences of taking an action, such as possible costs.

Based on these steps, select a solution and execute it.

The process sounds time-consuming. It need not be. Ultimately, it will be less time consuming and lead to a higher degree of successful than wildly dashing into a solution and not being aware of what you are really trying to rectify.

Most poor decisions are reached because the decision maker has an unclear picture of his or her goals and where they are trying to go in analyzing the problem and making the decision. Further, the decision-maker needs an orderly and systematic process for the problem-cause-decision sequence.

FIGURE 10.1 CRISIS DECISION-MAKING MODEL

CRISIS DECISION-MAKING MODEL

IDENTIFY PROBLEM ——————}DETERMINE CAUSES —————— }DETERMINE PURPOSE

OF THE DECISION —————— }PROPOSE SOLUTIONS —————— }SELECT SOLUTION

SUMMARY

In this chapter we have examined decision-making as a business activity. The major concepts discussed were:

Decision-making depends on effective and efficient communication patterns.

Following a practical decision-making process should lead to the possibility of making good decisions.

A decision is a practical, appropriate response to a situation that requires action.

A good decision is one with which you are perfectly comfortable and which is perceived as the best solution to a problem.

One of the major factors in effective decision making is clearly identifying the problem to be solved.

Two decision-making procedures are the Inductive Process of Decision Making and the Practical Decision-Making Process.

In the inductive process of decision making, the evaluation guides for solution selection are workability, desirability, and practicality.

In the practical decision-making process, the basis for decision making is following the prescribed procedure and applying the agreed upon criteria.

Crisis decision-making is an integral part of business.

THINGS TO DO

1. For discussion:
   a. It has often been said that the purpose of business is the solving of problems and the making of decisions. Do you agree? If you agree, name some examples that prove your contention.
   b. Define decision making.
   c. Of what value is using a systematic approach to decision making?
   d. Do you feel that a systematic approach to decision making is really necessary for effective solutions to problems, or is it really just a form of academic game-playing?

2. (a) The members of the class are each to interview a person who is in a management position for a business or corporation and is part of the decision-making process. A specific instance in which a decision was made concerning the business is to be described. The businessperson is not to reveal the outcome of the decision-making experience. (b) The class is divided into small groups (approximately 5 to 7 students) and is to select a decision-making project from those collected by the members of the group and then reach a conclusion for action. (c) Each group is to write a report and make an oral presentation to the class on the project. Before reporting to the class, the businessperson should be further questioned on the decision made and the process used to reach the decision.

3. The New Truck Dilemma[6]
   You are the supervisor of a crew of repairpeople for the telephone company. Each member of the crew drives a small service truck to and from his/her various jobs. A new truck has just been allocated to you for distribution. The new truck is a Chevrolet. You must decide who gets the new truck.

Facts about the trucks and the people in the crew that report to you:

George	17 years with the company, has a 2-year-old Ford truck
Betty	11 years with the company, has a 5-year-old Dodge truck
Jane	10 years with the company, has a 4-year-old Ford truck
Charlie	5 years with the company, has a 3-year-old Ford truck
Hank	3 years with the company, has a 5-year-old Chevrolet truck

Most of the people do all of their driving in the city, but Jane and Charlie cover the jobs in the suburbs and surrounding areas.

You ask each person to submit a statement explaining his or her reasons for getting the new truck. Here are their reasons:

GEORGE: When a new Chevrolet truck becomes available, I think I should get it because I have the most seniority and don't like my present truck. I own a Chevrolet car, and I prefer a Chevrolet truck, which I drove before I got the Ford.

BETTY: I feel I deserve a new truck and it certainly is my turn. My present truck is old, and since the more senior person has a fairly new truck, you should give me the new one. I have taken excellent care of my present Dodge and have kept it looking like new. A person deserves to be rewarded if she treats a company truck like her own.

JANE: I have more driving to do than most of the other people because my work is in the suburbs. I have a fairly old truck and feel I should have the new one because I do so much driving.

CHARLIE: The heater in my present truck is inadequate. Since Hank backed into the door of my truck, it has never been repaired to fit right. The door lets in too much cold air, and I attribute my frequent colds to this. I want to have a warm truck, since I have a good deal of driving to do. As long as it has good tires, brakes, and is comfortable, I don't care about the make.

HANK: I have the poorest truck in the crew. It is 5 years old, and before I got it, it had been in a bad wreck. It has never been good and I've put up with it for three years. It's about time I got a good truck to drive, and it seems only fair that the next one should be mine. I have a good accident record. The only accident I had was when I sprung the door of Charlie's truck when he opened it as I backed out of the garage. I hope the new truck is a Ford, because I prefer to drive one.

You are to decide on your own who should get the new truck. Use the advice given in the chapter about how to reach conclusions. Write your decision and criteria and bring them to class. The instructor will divide the class into small groups. Each group will meet and decide who should receive the truck. Each group is to report back to the class on who was selected and the procedure and criteria used in making the selection. A discussion on decision making should follow the group reports.

4. Businesses are often faced with situations where they must make decisions that center on ethics. Discuss the following:

You are in a decision-making management position for a small company that your family owns. Your company is polluting a stream that is used for feeding cattle. Due to the procedure you are using, there is little or no chance that you will ever be caught as the polluter. Many cattle who feed from the stream are dying because of the pollution. It will cost a great deal of money to change your filtering process and might even result in having to lay off many employees or closing the company. What should you do?

NOTES

1. William F. Glueck, *Management* (Hinsdale, IL.: Dryden Press, 1977), 402.
2. P. G. Moore, "Technique vs. Judgment in Decision Making," in *Organizational Dynamics* (New York: AMACOM, 1973), 27.
3. The theory presented is a modification of John Dewey, *How We Think* (Boston: D. C. Heath and Company, 1910), 68–78.
4. Ray Curtis, *Practical Decision Making: A Qualitative Approach* (Elyria, OH: Lorain County Community College, 1978), Chapter 9.
5. Peter F. Drucker, *An Introductory View of Management* (New York: Harper's College Press, 1977), 402.
6. Based on a handout used in The Speech Communication Teacher's Workshop, Pennsylvania State University, 1971.

III

BUSINESS COMMUNICATION SKILLS

11 □ Interviewing as a Business Function

OVERVIEW   An interview is a person-to-person communication with a decision-making purpose. Types of business-related interviews include informative, problem solving, persuasive, employment, performance appraisal, counseling, reprimanding, and stress. An interview follows an opening, body, and closing format. During the interview, both the interviewee and the interviewer have responsibilities for the development and satisfactory completion of the interview process.

KEY WORDS
interview
interviewer
interviewee
informative interview
problem-solving interview
communication audit
persuasive interview
employment interview
résumé
performance appraisal
counseling interview

reprimanding interview
stress/interrogation interview
press conference
talk show
open question
closed question
minor question
probe question
leading question
funnel schedule
inverted funnel format

A s people make decisions at all levels within the organization, they are aided in the process by one-to-one interpersonal communication. Indeed, most communication within an organization occurs in face-to-face interactions throughout any typical workday. We decide such issues as who to hire, how to accomplish a task, what tasks to accomplish, what the organization's goals are, who to fire, and who to train or retrain, often on the basis of interpersonal communication.

The face-to-face decision making frequently takes the form of formal or informal interviewing. An **interview** is a person-to-person communication (usually between two persons, but sometimes three or four persons may be involved) with a basic decision-making purpose. In the interview, one person assumes the role of initiator or questioner (the **interviewer**) while another person serves as the respondent (the **interviewee**).

As you read through the descriptions of the types of interviews, you may be surprised that some of these transactions are even called interviews. Many people, upon hearing the word *interview,* think only of the employment interview. However, there are many other types, some formal and some informal. Many times, people participate in interviews without even recognizing that they are actually taking part in one. If this is the case, they may not follow good interviewing techniques and thus fail to be successful in reaching their intended goal.

TYPES OF INTERVIEWS AND HOW TO PREPARE FOR THEM

■

We conduct interviews within an organization for a variety of decision-making purposes. These purposes characterize the various types of interviews that may be used: informative, problem solving, persuasive, employment, performance appraisal, counseling, reprimanding, and stress. Since the employment interview and the performance appraisal are so important to all workers, an extended discussion of these types of interviews will be presented.

The Informative Interview

☐

When we seek information, an **informative interview** structure may serve the purpose. A manager who needs to communicate information about a new personnel procedure, for example, may want to conduct personal interviews with each supervisor individually so that the information is clearly disseminated throughout the plant.

Communicators in an informative interview should try to be careful to distinguish fact from opinion so that the information transmitted can be as accurate as possible. It is important to develop rapport at the outset of an informative interview so that the interviewee will feel comfortable with the interviewer and be willing to open up and provide substantial information.

Informative Interview Outline

Purpose: to interview a young part-owner of a successful catering business in order to learn about his educational background, the evolution of his business, the functions of his business, the experiences he has had while in the business, and his conjectures concerning businesses.

    I. Introduction
        A. Establish rapport
        B. Explain purpose
   II. Education
        A. What was your major in college?
        B. How has your overall college education (including classes that were not in your major) benefited you in your field of work?
        C. Are there any specific classes you can recall that have helped you the most?
        D. Do you feel it is necessary for a person interested in owning a business to have a degree in business?
  III. Evolution of the business
        A. How did you become interested in owning your own business?
        B. How did you get involved in this particular business?
        C. How long did it take before you knew your business was successful?
  IV. Functions of the business
        A. How many people do you employ?
        B. What is your relationship with the people you employ?
        C. What type of people do you come in contact with most often?
        D. What skills does your position require?
    V. Experience
        A. What was your biggest shock when you entered the real world?
        B. Now that you have owned your own business, would you consider working for someone else?
        C. What are the biggest pressures you face in owning your own business?
  VI. Observations/Conjectures
        A. What suggestions would you have for a college student interested in owning a business?
        B. Do you feel a person has to have any specific type of personality to own a business?
        C. What do you think has been your greatest asset leading to your position as a successful businessperson?
        D. Would you be open to expanding the business, or would you rather sell it and get into another area?
 VII. Closing

The Problem-Solving Interview

☐   Another type of interview crucial to the decision-making function of an organization is the **problem-solving interview.** If a corporation is faced with a problem (e.g., is there a need for expansion), it may be useful to interview a variety of employees to determine what and where the problems are with an eye to locating some solutions to the problems. Personnel departments are finding the communication audit a useful decision-making technique. In a **communication audit,** employees are interviewed about their perception of communication problems—and their solutions—within the organization.

A good problem-solving interview should be structured carefully so that problems are thoroughly discussed before solutions are suggested. Such a structure can insure that both the interviewer and the interviewee understand just what are the problems to be solved. Otherwise, you may find yourself discussing a variety of solutions that do not really tackle the specific problem at hand.

Problem-Solving Interview Outline

Purpose: to decide whether your organization should convert from standard electric typewriters to electronic typewriters or to a word processing system. An office management consultant is being interviewed.

    I. Opening
       A. Establish rapport
       B. Explain purpose
   II. Statement of the problem
  III. What are the advantages of:
       A. Retaining the present system
       B. Converting to a word processing system
       C. Converting to electronic typewriters
   IV. What are the disadvantages of:
       A. Retaining the present system
       B. Converting to a word processing system
       C. Converting to electronic typewriters
    V. What recommendation would you make?
   VI. Why?
  VII. Closing

The Persuasive Interview

☐   In addition to informative and problem-solving types of interviews, you may find it necessary to conduct an interview in which you desire that some type of action takes place: the **persuasive interview.** Selling products on a one-to-one basis represents a typical type of persuasive interview. Again, it may be necessary to impart information about your product or proposal before you get into the actual advocacy of it.

An employment interview is the final step in screening in or screening out a candidate. (© James Shaffer)

It is helpful in persuasive interviewing to make a careful analysis of the interviewee so that you can adapt your motivational appeals directly to his or her interests or needs. For example, you might want to tap a government procurement officer's interest in saving money in the federal budget by pointing out how your new computer system can be cost-effective.

Overall decision making within the organization can be facilitated by persuasive, problem-solving, and informative interviews. Issues can be tackled and new procedures implemented at all levels through these structured interpersonal communications. Organizations also use a variety of personnel interviews to achieve a wide spectrum of decision-making functions.

The Employment Interview

□

"It's the wish of every job-seeker that the invitation to an (employment) interview will ultimately result in a job offer. The **employment interview** is usually the employer's final step in either screening in or screening out a candidate."[1] Since each of you probably will be going through the interviewing process in an attempt to find employment, it is helpful to review the regulations concerning interviewing, how to prepare for the interview, participate in the employment interview, and the role of the interviewer in the process.

Regulations Governing Employment Interviewing

The Civil Rights Act of 1964, and its supporting regulations, have led to a considerable overhaul in the hiring process in business and industry. Equal opportunity employment laws now specify that employers must hire people for their ability to do the job rather than for their ability to simply get the job.

Despite this new focus in the selection process, the process still depends very much on the employment interview. Applicants are screened through a review of **résumés** and then through, perhaps, a series of interviews by the personnel staff assigned to the task of making the hiring recommendations. The process, at best, is highly subjective in that the impression an individual makes even before beginning the interview can have a profound impact on the success of the interview.

All individuals who participate in the employment interview process should be aware that the equal opportunity employment regulations specify that certain questions are not legal, so that an employment interviewer may not ask the questions and an employment interviewee is not obligated, nor should be, to answer the unlawful questions. A summary of the regulations enumerated the *unlawful* inquiries as:

1. Asking the applicant if he or she has ever worked under another name.
2. Asking the applicant to name his or her birthplace.
3. Asking for the birthplace of the applicant's parents, spouse, or other close relatives.
4. Asking the applicant to submit proof of age by supplying birth certificate or baptismal record.
5. Asking the applicant for his or her religious affiliation, name of church, or religious holidays he or she observes.
6. Asking the applicant if he or she is a naturalized citizen.
7. Asking the applicant for the date when he or she acquired his or her citizenship.
8. Asking the applicant if he or she has ever been arrested for any crime and where and when.
9. Asking the applicant how he or she acquired his or her ability to read, write, or speak a foreign language.
10. Requesting the applicant to provide names of three relatives other than father, spouse, or minor-age dependent children.
11. Asking the applicant for his wife's maiden name.
12. Asking the maiden name of the applicant's mother.
13. Asking for the full names of the applicant's brothers and sisters.
14. Asking the applicant for a list of the clubs, societies, and lodges to which he or she belongs.
15. Asking the applicant to include a photograph with his or her application.
16. Asking the applicant to supply addresses of cousins, uncles, aunts, nieces, nephews, grandparents, etc., who can be contacted for references.[2]

On the other hand, it *IS* legal to ask the applicant if he or she is a citizen of the United States; to indicate what foreign language he or she can read, write, or speak fluently; and about his or her past work experiences.

An interesting approach to obtaining the employment interviews is for a person to decide which organizations he or she would like to work for and then set up informational interviews with the personnel department to find out more about the company and its employment picture. After conducting these informational interviews to learn about the career field, one selects those organizations which appear to offer the greatest potential and return to them for employment interviews.[3] Such a strategy can provide the individual with useful information about the career field, practice in interviewing, and a good idea as to which organizations do have interesting positions available. (We have a sense, however, that this strategy is overused, and it would appear that you should be very forthright about taking a personnel officer's time to learn about the company and the field when arranging the interview.)

Getting Ready for the Interview[4]

"About two out of 100 job hunters are prepared for the interview. Preparation means doing your homework on the company you're applying to, and, if possible, the people to whom you are going to talk. It's just impossible to wing it."[5] Some of the most common complaints by interviewers about interviewees are that they have unrealistic attitudes, have vague interests and goals, lack the preparation for the interview (they are poorly informed about the job or the organization), are ignorant about work life, possess poor communication skills (the answers are trite, there is a reticence to speak up, they have difficulty expressing themselves in specifics), project undesirable personal factors, and have poor scholastic records.[6]

A national study indicates the following order of factors lead to favorable hiring decisions:

1. Communication skills
2. Grade point average
3. Work experience
4. Appearance
5. Extracurricular activities
6. Location preference
7. Academic accomplishments

The following are steps you should take to prepare yourself for an employment interview:

1. Locate employment sources.
   Any interview must first be preceded with locating an organization which might be interested in hiring you and in which you are interested in possibly working for. Locating the organization may be done by contacting an employment agency. These services are either generalists, which supply information about various types of occupations, or specialty agencies which center their efforts only on one type of service (secretarial, or accounting, or sales). Other sources are college or university placement bureaus. Organizational placement services may also be of assistance. For example, if you are looking for a job as a theatrical business manager, the placement services of the Speech Communication Association might be your best sources. Friends, college advisors, newspaper help-wanted ads, and state employment services might also provide information.

FIGURE 11.1 Résumé.

Barbara Finegan
1210 F Street
College Park, Maryland 20742
Telephone (301) 555-1234

CAREER OBJECTIVE: To utilize skills in communication analysis in a corporation.

Special interest in international communication, having lived in southern France for three years while father was in Foreign Service.

EDUCATION: B.A. in Communication, University of Maryland, College Park, May, 1989, Cumulative grade point average: 3.2 on a 4.0 system.

Focus in major was on Organizational Communication. Prepared to analyze communication problems between/among employees and supervisors; to develop training programs in communication audits; to design communication strategies for implementing change.

Fall, 1989, internship with the Lee Company in the personnel training office. Participated in needs analysis and design of communication training program for managers.

Editor of student University of Maryland newspaper. The Diamondback, 1988-89.

Summer camp counselor, Amherst, Ohio Recreation Department, summers of 1986-87.

COCURRICULAR ACTIVITIES: Debater and President, University of Maryland, Calvert Communication Union forensic and debate club, 1985-89.

President, Student Government Association, 1985-89.

Member, Alpha Epsilon Phi social sorority, 1985-89.

HONORS/AWARDS: Debater of the Year, Delta Sigma XI Award, 1988.

SPECIAL SKILLS: Fluent in French. Typing at 80 wpm.

REFERENCES: Dr. John Doe, Director of Speech Communication, University of Maryland, College Park, Maryland 20742.

Dr. Mary Smith, Director, Communication Research Center, Speech Communication, University of Maryland, College Park, Maryland 20742.

Mr. Tom Johnson, Manager, Amherst Recreation Department, Amherst, Ohio 44001.

2. Prepare a résumé.

As shown in figure 11.1, a **résumé,**[8] or typed information sheet, that you either send in advance or bring with you to the interview, should include:

a. Personal data: name, address, telephone number.

b. Career objective: kind of job you are seeking.

c. Education: list your formal education by giving high school and higher degrees, degrees or certificates received, major and minor subjects, other courses related to your job goal, scholarships and honors, and extracurricular activities.

d. Experience

(1) By job: most recent one working backward. For each job list dates of employment, name and address of employer and nature of business,

position you held, specific job duties and scope of responsibility, and accomplishments.

(2) By function: describe briefly the work you performed.

e. Additional information: knowledge of foreign languages; volunteer or leisure-time activities; special skills, such as typing, or shorthand; ability to operate special equipment; membership to professional organizations; articles published; patents; inventions; special awards; and recognitions.

f. References: give the names, positions, and addresses of at least three persons who have direct knowledge of your work competence. Some résumé specialists[9] recommend that the job seeker should not list references on the form, but should state, "Available upon request." If you do this, make sure you bring along their addresses, and phone numbers.

Some general principles that can be followed in résumé writing include:[10,11]

a. There is no set standard length; however, one typed page is usually enough for recent graduates.

b. Emphasize the positive by focusing on those things in your past which stand out favorably.

c. Use words and phrases that you are familiar with and type your résumé accurately, making sure that all words are spelled correctly and that proper grammar is used.

d. Vary the résumé according to the job for which you are applying. A printed document, though it looks professional, may not be a good idea as it is impossible to alter for each position.

e. Avoid the word *résumé* on the top. That's what it is; they know that. Your name should be the first thing they see.

f. Avoid long statements of career objectives. The objectives, if included, should be specific, such as: "Management trainer in a financial institution."

g. Assume that your résumé is not going to please everyone. Adopt a style and tone with which you are comfortable. Take into consideration the profession. If you are trying to get a banking or accounting job, you would probably do well with a conservative approach. For the advertising or public relations field, a touch of clever salesmanship and flair might be appropriate.

3. Find out specific information. Make certain that, after making the appointment for the interview, you get the full name and address of the company. Know your interviewer's full name and find out how to pronounce it. If you aren't sure how to pronounce the name, call his or her secretary in advance of the session. Do some research about the company. Talk to former or current employees or look up information in such sources as *Thomas' Register of American Manufacturers, Moody's Manuals, Fitch Corporation Manuals, MacRae's Bluebook, Standard and Poor's Corporation Records, Dun and Bradstreet Reference Book,* or any company's annual report.

4. Prepare questions you might have before you go in for the interview. Make sure you are aware of the operation of the company. You might want to find out: exactly what the job entails; the goals of the organization (they should be compatible with your own); the types of benefits given (insurance, travel expenses, stock options); the people you'll be working with; if you'd be covered by unemployment insurance; what type of retirement plan is offered; and any special information about employee-employer relationships that makes this organization unique.
5. Think through some questions that might be asked and prepare tentative answers. Topics often covered include: type of position you are interested in; courses taken in college; general training, qualifications for the specific job; extracurricular offices held; restrictions on geographic location placement; personal characteristics which will aid you in this field; positive and negative personal characteristics; evaluation of your scholastic work; why the profession was chosen; long-term plans (where do you expect to be in 5 years? 10 years?); special abilities; personal habits (liquor use, smoking, drug use); and what type of work interests you.
6. Bring a pen that writes neatly and have an inconspicuous notebook with you. You may need to fill out additional forms, or take notes about some phase of the interview (name of someone to contact or a phone number, for example).
7. Plan to arrive at the designated place at least 10 minutes early.
8. Dress accordingly.[12]

Participating in the Employment Interview

"When you arrive for the interview, be as calm, confident and assured as possible. Be properly dressed for a business situation, be prepared to present your history in an orderly and organized manner and—above all—be affable and gracious about answering the same question several times."[13]

Procedure for an Interview   There is no way to anticipate exactly what will happen during an interview; but, in general, the following suggestions will probably help you in most interview situations.[14,15]

1. Greet the interviewer by name.
2. Take your cues from him or her at the start—where to sit, if you should shake hands.
3. Don't chew gum or smoke unless you are invited to do so.
4. Be ready for any type of question. Listen carefully to what the interviewer asks. Sample opening questions are: "What can I do for you?" "Tell me about yourself." "Why are you interested in this company?"
5. Don't just answer *yes* or *no*. Give examples, clarify your ideas.
6. Be prepared with some questions that he or she might answer for you. Insert these when it appears that he or she is finished asking you questions, or when you are asked "Do you have any questions?"

7. Sit up in your chair and look alert and interested.

8. Look your interviewer directly in the eye, and keep doing it from time to time during your conversation. This is very important: interviewers look for this.

9. Make sure that your good points get across to the interviewer. Point them out on your résumé and tell him or her important things that are not on the résumé.

10. Most interviews will follow a rather simple question-and-answer formula. The greatest preventive against contradictory answers is to tell the truth. Frankness is admired by many people, so don't fudge your answers. Avoid the following clichés as interviewers are tired of hearing them and they are meaningless and often misleading: "I'll take anything," "I want a challenging position," "I'm looking for a rewarding experience," "I like people," "The salary should be commensurate with my experience."

11. Conduct yourself as if you are determined to get the job you are discussing.

12. Know about what salary the job is worth and what you will accept. The interviewer is likely to ask what salary you would accept. Be prepared with a figure.

13. Most interviews last between 20 and 30 minutes. Try and anticipate that in timing your answers and asking questions.

14. Make sure as the interview comes to an end that you understand what will happen next: they will call you, you should contact them, you are to send them a copy of something. Whatever the next step, be sure you know. Repeat this to the interviewer to make sure that you are in agreement.

15. At the end, thank the interviewer for his or her time and consideration.

16. Usually, a thank-you note is not necessary.

Screening a Prospective Employer[16]   Remember that before and during an employment interview you are screening the employer as well as being screened by him or her. Often people accept jobs out of haste, or to be sure they get something, and pay for it later. You are going to spend a period of time at that job. Be sure it is what you really want, or can aid you to get where you really want to be before accepting the position. Is it where you want to live? Is the salary enough for you to live on? Are the working conditions those you can feel comfortable with?

You might want to find out the reputation of the organization in the field. Is this the kind of company you want to work for? Examine the physical environment. Will you be comfortable working there? If your interview is with an interview service rather than a representative of the company, or away from the work site, make a personal trip to the company before accepting the position.

Ask questions concerning living conditions in the area if you are going away from a familiar area. Such factors as cost, social and cultural opportunities, religious institutions, and climatic conditions may be important to you. Consider these factors.

Role of the Employment Interviewer

The state of the American economy is such that many individuals are facing or have faced unemployment. Because organizations have had to cut back budgets, they have usually had to cut back on personnel, so organizations just do not have the number of openings they may once have had. Consequently, more individuals are applying for fewer positions. Employment interviewers have a more difficult task than ever sorting through résumés and making recommendations based on a considerable number of positive interview experiences.

Employment interviewers must be careful, however, to remember that part of their role, as representatives of the corporation, is to "sell" the corporation by providing a positive experience in the interview for the applicant. Attention to communication details, even if the chances for hiring are very slim, is a key to providing a positive employment interview experience.

To be effective communicators, employment interviewers should consider the following recommendations:[17,18] (1) Be courteous. (2) Don't give the person the third degree unless you mean to interrogate. Use questions that help the other person to think. (3) Ask questions that make the respondent go into detail. Ask for examples or explanations to discover reasons behind the person's thinking. (4) Avoid irrelevant questions (e.g., "Who do you think will win the World Series?") unless you are trying to set an informal tone for the session. (5) Avoid illegal questions (e.g., "To what church do you belong?" "Does your spouse work?"). (6) Ask "suppose" questions (if you are interviewing for a farm implement company, "What do you suppose would happen if the government withdrew farm price supports?"). This type of question often allows you to probe the interviewee's perceptions and knowledge in the field. (7) Ask the respondent if he or she needs time to think. (8) Ask "W" questions: what, why, when, where, and who. These questions will secure the facts and information you need. (9) End the interview by indicating when and if the interviewee will hear of the decision made. As a follow-up, provide the applicant with a response as soon as possible.

The Performance Appraisal

☐

Once hired, the employee undoubtedly will be faced with periodic **performance appraisals** in which his or her work is evaluated. Federal law now mandates that all federal employees must be systematically evaluated in their job performances according to the specifications set out for the job. Many other organizations, due to court orders and governmental restrictions, also must follow clear, preset procedures. Consequently, managers and supervisors must be carefully trained in the handling of performance appraisals.

Methods of Appraisal

There are three methods of conducting the performance appraisal interview:

(1) tell and sell
(2) tell and listen, and
(3) problem solving.

Tell and Sell   In the tell and sell method, the supervisor plays a role similar to that of a prescribing physician. An evaluation is made, it is communicated, and the supervisor convinces the subordinate to accept it. The method requires considerable skill in persuasion and motivation. It can be an unpleasant experience for the interviewer and the interviewee if the evaluation is negative. An atmosphere of defensiveness and hostility may develop, which interferes with achieving the immediate and long-term objectives of the interview. The supervisor provides both diagnosis and remedy, and the procedure allows little or no upward communication from the subordinate to the superior. It is generally felt that this is the most time-saving method, for the presentation is basically one-sided. It is often frustrating for the employee, as he or she is restricted to a passive participant role. The tell and sell method is also very specific regarding what the employee is to do and what is expected.

Tell and Listen   In the tell and listen method, the interview is held in order to communicate the evaluation to the employee and then to let the employee respond to it and suggest needed alternatives. The supervisor plays the role of "judge" by communicating the evaluation, but does not try to convince the subordinate of the evaluation. The method rests on the supervisor acting as a nondirective counselor in the second part of the interview. Necessary strategies include active listening, encouraging the interviewee to talk, and reflecting feelings to show that the interviewer understands. Both parties are less likely to need to "save face" in this approach, because the supervisor feels no need to defend the evaluation while the interviewer does not fear reprisals for displeasing the supervisor. There is encouragement of upward communication. The major disadvantage of this method is that the employee may need an agenda for improving his or her performance. Because of this problem, participants may not actually reach a very helpful procedure for performance improvement.

Problem-Solving Method of Appraisal   The problem-solving method of appraisal is the only method that changes the interviewer's role from "judge" to "helper." The employee is invited to make a job analysis; to review progress that has been made since the last appraisal; and to discuss problems, needs, innovations, and satisfactions and dissatisfactions that have been encountered. An agreement is reached as to what changes should be made, the methods to be used, and how they will be evaluated.

Change is actually stimulated because the method assumes that change is an essential part of business and that participation is essential to healthy growth. The general disadvantage of this method is that the time involved tends to be great. In addition, employees and supervisors with poor interpersonal communicative skills may find it difficult to articulate their ideas.

Effective Appraisal Interviews

Effective appraisal interviews, no matter which method is used, depend upon effective communication skills. Some suggestions to supervisors to make appraisal interviews a positive experience are as follows:[19]

> Discuss the job; make sure there is agreement on what the worker is supposed to be doing.
>
> If the subordinate's self-appraisal is more favorable than your appraisal, invite the person to tell you specifically why. Often in trying to explain, the subordinate

will see that the self-appraisal is not accurate, or you might see where you are wrong.

Evaluate the job, not the person, unless the effectiveness of the work performance is based on identifiable personal habits. (Clothing style may be important for the consultant who represents the company via contact with the public, but the machinist's clothing may be of no concern unless it is either dangerous or so distracting that it interferes with other workers' efficiency.)

If you are partly at fault, admit it.

Acknowledge that both of you could wholly or partly be wrong in your evaluations and that by listening to each other there might be a change in either or both of your attitudes, thus working for mutual benefits.

If the subordinate is truly deficient and must be corrected, indicate exactly where he or she stands, what can be done to achieve a satisfactory evaluation in the future, set up a procedure for aiding in the improvement, and clearly indicate the consequences of continued negative performance.

Remember that evaluation involves more than pointing out negative aspects of the job performance. Positive comments interwoven with negative comments tend to make the negative more acceptable and to reinforce the positive behaviors.

A good performance appraisal should follow a clear procedure in order to avoid organizational interference. The steps of an interview are usually rapport building (welcome, personal comments), orientation (background of the need for the interview), recall of previous objectives (any prior evaluations and agreements are discussed), subordinate gives accounting, supervisor gives his or her views, and plans and goals for the next evaluation period are discussed.

Just as the interviewer who conducts the performance appraisal should keep an open mind and develop a supportive communication climate for the interview, so, too, should the interviewee approach the appraisal process with a positive attitude.

Some helpful suggestions for individuals who participate as interviewees in performance appraisals are:[20]

1. Answer all questions as completely as possible.
2. Offer explanations but do not make excuses or lay blame.
3. Ask for clarification as appropriate.
4. Ask for specific suggestions for improvement.
5. Ask for help for improving performance.
6. Ask how much time is available to solve a particular performance problem.
7. Do not try to improve everything at once: set priorities.
8. Avoid getting angry or overreacting.
9. Reiterate the problem or solution for clarification and understanding by both parties.
10. Maintain a positive relationship with the interviewer.
11. Correct any false impressions or assumptions which may be held about performance.
12. Close the interview with an open mind.

Performance appraisals, if conducted on a regular basis, can be of tremendous value to the supervisor, the employee, and the organization. They provide the opportunity for workers and managers to deal in-depth with the employee's work habits, productivity, and human relationships within the organization. The University Research Corporation in Bethesda, Maryland, developed an appraisal process which illustrates how the plan can be implemented. Employees are first asked to write an initial self-analysis, evaluating their work against their own standards and expectations. Supervisors offer ways that employees might improve their effectiveness and then subordinates communicate what help they need from their managers to do a better job. In the final stages of the plan, workers and managers review employee career objectives. The process increases worker-boss communication, providing a basis for regular discussions of goals and performance strengths and problems.[21]

While thorough appraisals can be quite time consuming, the results can be well worth the effort. An employee who has no sense as to how he or she is doing on the job is not going to be particularly satisfied or effective in that work.

Performance Appraisal Outline

    I. Greet employee
        A. Establish rapport
        B. Explain purpose of interview
    II. Discuss employee's job
        A. What are all the things you do on your job?
        B. Which do you think are the most important?
        C. Which take most of your time?
        D. Are there ways in which you think we could use your talents and time more profitably?
    III. Discuss employee's self-perceptions
        A. What do you think are your greatest strengths?
        B. Where do you feel less competent?
        C. Do you feel that you are growing more competent or less competent as time goes by?
            1. In what ways?
            2. How?
            3. Why?
        D. Is there any way in which you think that I, or someone else, could help you to make yourself more valuable to the company?
        E. Do I do anything that makes your job harder?
    IV. Evaluate the person
        A. State positive aspects of his or her performance
        B. Criticize the person's performance
            1. Explain exactly where he or she stands
            2. If the subordinate appraised himself more favorably than you did, invite him to tell you why
            3. Tell him or her specifically what you think can be done to improve

4. If he or she shows desire to improve, offer aid
   a. On-the-job aid
   b. In-organizational aid
   c. Out-of-organization aid
5. Set up a plan of action to aid in changing the behavior. Include a specific procedure, deadlines, and the re-evaluation procedure
V. Closing

The Counseling Interview

A special type of personnel problem-solving interview is the **counseling interview.** In this interview, the interviewer serves as a "sounding board" to let the interviewee talk through his or her own problems and come up with his or her own solutions to that problem. If a manager, for example, discovers that the employee has some job-related problem and that he or she probably could solve it if given the opportunity to talk it out, this interview form can be quite effective.

To handle the role of sounding board once the interview is started, the interviewer should use only those verbal and nonverbal responses that can serve to keep the interviewee talking. Nondirective responses, such as a nod of the head and verbally reflecting what the interviewee has just said, are appropriate.

Understanding how to identify and help resolve human problems in the workplace is a sensitive and complex task. It's not surprising that many supervisors prefer to ignore subordinates' problems, as if to say, "that's not *my* problem." In fact, it *is* the supervisor's problem. If these problems are left unattended, the economic and emotional results can be painful for the organization, the other employees, and the troubled person.[22]

Many supervisors and managers are not trained to handle psychological problems. They, in fact, could do more harm than good if they attempt to play amateur psychologist. Many organizations have experts such as psychologists, counselors, or human resource specialists to handle more difficult situations. If an organization does not have such a support staff, referrals to social service agencies or professionals should be made rather than having an untrained person attempt to assist.

In the case of minor problems, someone who is called in to participate in a counseling interview should handle the situation much like an informative interview. The following generalized outline can be used to structure a counseling interview.

Counseling Interview Outline

Purpose: to make Employee X aware that his/her behavior is of concern and to offer assistance in helping her/him handle the situation.

    I. Introduction
   II. An explanation of the expectations and objectives of the interview
  III. Encouragement to the troubled person to explain what he/she perceives to be wrong

IV. An investigation is made of the ramifications of continuing the behavior or activity
V. An examination of the difference in perception between the interviewer and the interviewee as revealed in III and IV (if any exist)
VI. The interviewee's options are discussed
VII. A decision is made as to what course of action will be taken

The Reprimanding Interview

If, after performance appraisal and even counseling interviews, an employee still has problems on the job, it may be necessary as a last resort to conduct a **reprimanding interview.** The reprimand assumes a performance problem and begins at the point where it is necessary to come up with a specific solution to that problem.

One key to effective communication in a reprimanding interview is to maintain a controlled emotional level. It is never effective to discipline an employee in a fit of anger, because one runs the risk of making statements which are emotional rather than logical. While the reprimand must be conducted at the appropriate time to have an impact on changing a person's performance behavior, a wise manager will take time to "cool off" before initiating any disciplinary communication.

While some persons responsible for reprimanding simply spell out the problem and the way to correct it for an employee (much like a parent scolding a child), a more constructive approach would be to use an adaptation of the counseling format. Once it is clear what the problem is (and at this point it has been a recurring problem or a problem of a severe nature), the interviewee should be given the opportunity to discuss the resolution of the problem. Most people can handle their own problems if permitted to discuss them with someone who can help put the problem in perspective.

Reprimand Interview Outline

I. Introduction
II. Explanation of what the employee did wrong
III. Explanation of why it was wrong
IV. Statement of the penalty
V. Explanation of the reason for selecting this reprimanding action
VI. Explanation of what will happen if there is repetition of the performance or behavior
VII. Explanation of what can be done to improve the person's performance or behavior
VIII. Discussion with the employee as to why the problem persists and what can be done to overcome it
IX. Solicitation of employee commitment to correcting the problem immediately

The Stress or Interrogation Interview

☐ In addition to personnel, persuasive, problem-solving, and informative interviews, some organizations may make use of a special type of **stress,** or **interrogation, interview.** This form requires that the interviewer create a communication climate of psychological stress in order to get the interviewee to reveal information and to observe how the interviewee handles himself/herself under stress. Some use this to check the prospective employee's ability to respond under stress. This is done in an attempt to ascertain how an individual will operate if the future employee is being considered for a position that is stress-oriented. Some people feel that this practice is unethical. Others, however, believe that this is the only way to screen out those who cannot perform under pressure and, therefore, would not perform effectively if hired. Other organizations must use this form for security purposes—interrogation of shoplifters, for instance. Often professional interviewers who are experts in stress analysis are hired by firms to conduct this type of interrogation.

Effective handling of stress interviews requires special verbal and nonverbal techniques to create the necessary climate of stress. It is important to anticipate what the interviewee would perceive as stressful (loud vocal tone, standing up, rapid-fire questioning, etc.) and adapt accordingly.

Stress Interview Outline

A follow-up interview is being held for the position of production director for your organization's television studio. Purpose: to ascertain whether the candidate can work well under stressful conditions, which is a requirement for this position.

I. Introduction

II. What do you consider your strengths as a candidate for this position?

III. What do you consider your weakest skill in television production?

IV. How do you expect us to turn over a three-quarter of a million dollar investment in media equipment to someone who is incompetent in (repeat the weakness the candidate has stated)?

V. A member of the public relation's department gives you a script to produce that you feel is poorly written, does not well represent the firm, and has some material that may be in poor taste. What would you do?

VI. What would you do if, after taking the action you just explained, your immediate supervisor said to go ahead with the project, exactly as it was submitted?

VII. After you have been here for two years another television production person is brought in and given a position of higher rank and pay. What would you do?

VIII. Closing

The various forms of interviews that we have been discussing are all performed within the organization, thus fulfilling internal decision-making needs. As a means of internal communication, the interviews can lend purpose and structure to the functioning of the business or corporation. It may be necessary, however, for some spokespersons of the organization to participate as external communicators in public interviews. These public interviews usually take the form of press conferences, television talk shows, or radio call-in interview shows.

The Press Conference

☐ The executive press conference has become a basic responsibility for most governmental and corporate CEOs, for the reactions of a leader are important news stories in and of themselves. It is noted that "the press conference is an institution which is still evolving" and that it is not "at all clear just what constitutes a satisfactory press conference."[23]

A **press conference** is typically characterized by a number of interviewers—reporters—who ask a variety of questions. The interviewee controls the interview in that he or she must time the conference and must be sure to allow a number of the reporters to ask questions. In a structured press conference, the person to be interviewed may give a short speech to be followed by a question-and-answer session. In some cases the questioners are restricted to asking questions only about the subject of the speech that

A press conference is characterized by a number of interviewers who ask a variety of questions.

has just been presented. A spontaneous press conference isn't too structured, so questions may move from one topic to the next. In this format the reporters present are allowed to ask any questions they desire. It is a good idea to anticipate the general line of questioning in advance and even to rehearse some responses so that you will be an articulate spokesperson for the organization. It is also useful to repeat the question before responding so that you are sure everyone has heard and understood the question being asked.

The Talk Show

☐

With the growth of the talk show format on radio and television, more and more businesspersons are being invited to defend their company's policies, explain new products, and clarify the actions being taken by their organizations. Many of the same characteristics of the press conference are contained in the **talk show** format. Questions are asked, answers are expected, and judgments are made.

A television show host may set up a general line of questions in advance so that you will be able to prepare for the appearance. It's important to maintain composure and to be responsive at a conversational level while on the air.

A good talk show will often function as if it were a relaxed "chat," while operating under the time constraints and subject limitations, which should take some of the pressure off you.

A popular radio format is the call-in show, where the interviewee, as the expert guest, appears with the show's host and fields phone-in questions. Many of these shows do not prescreen the phone calls, so you might encounter some negative, irrelevant, or unclear questions. It is wise for a business representative to anticipate the types of questions to be asked and to have such materials as corporation reports and statistical information available for quick reference.

It is important that you consider the ramifications of what you say and not get trapped into saying something that can be embarrassing to you or your company.

STRUCTURING THE INTERVIEW

■

Regardless of the type of interview in which you may participate, it is helpful to give the interview, even the informal interview, a basic structure. Careful organization can insure that all of the points that need to be covered in the interview have certain essential characteristics.

The Opening

☐

The opening of an interview ought to accomplish two objectives: (1) to establish rapport between the communicators and (2) to establish the overall purpose of the interview.

Establishing rapport is a crucial step at the beginning of any interview (except, perhaps, the interrogation interview). The interviewer and the interviewee need a comfortable communication climate in which to respond openly and honestly. Thus, it's important that the two people recognize each other as human beings and create some type of common bond. An interview should not be regarded as a debate confrontation in which there are winners and losers.

Certain key host functions on the part of the interviewer—like offering to take the interviewee's coat and offering a cup of coffee or a place to sit—are part of this initial step. It can also help to discuss any personal elements that might be appropriate. You might share an interest in sports, in plants, in children, or have attended the same college. Whatever is done at the outset, it should be done sincerely; otherwise, the opening will be reduced to strained small talk.

Your authors sometimes consult with marketing and sales representatives who must sell products or service to institutions. We have noted how frequently the salespeople neglect to start out by building rapport with the purchaser, or attempting to deal with him/her as a person rather than as "the institution" in the abstract. Establishing rapport can help to cut through the stereotypes of "Here Comes XYZ Corporation" or "Today I have to sell books." Ignoring this first step often turns off potential buyers or clients. It does not take long to develop a comfortable communication climate. Most people appreciate the effort to create a common bond. Once the rapport is established, you can move on to defining the purpose of the interview.

Purpose Statement

□

The purpose of the interview usually is predetermined, and usually both the interviewer and the interviewee have understood this purpose when the original appointment was made. It is helpful, however, to reiterate that purpose at the onset to make sure that both parties understand the objectives. The purpose determines the type of interview conducted, so it is a good idea to spell out the objective. Sample purpose statements are:

Informative: "I'm interested, Mr. Smith, in learning more about your invention."

Problem Solving: "We've noted a decline in worker morale, so I thought it would be useful to get your reactions on how we might solve the problem."

Persuasive: "Our company has just marketed a new product, and I'd appreciate the opportunity to introduce it to you."

Employment: "I'm interested in the opening you have for a junior accountant."

Performance Appraisal: "You've been with us six months, Miss Jones, so I'd like to take the time to discuss your work as a clerk typist."

Counseling: "I've sensed that you're not very comfortable as a receptionist, and I wonder if you'd like to talk about it."

Performance Appraisal: "We've discussed your absenteeism on previous occasions, Mr. Green, and we have to work out a plan to stop the problem."

Interrogation: "You were observed taking this merchandise."

The Body of an Interview

☐ Once you set the purpose and establish rapport at the opening of the interview, you can move to the body of the interview. The body of the interview is the heart of the discussion in which you handle the questions and responses to those questions.

Types of Questions

Five basic questions can be useful to the interviewer in structuring the content of the interview.

The Open Question provides for an alternative of responses, giving the interviewee room to elaborate a response. "How do you feel about the new Management By Objectives system?" "How would you characterize your management style?"

The Closed Question narrows and structures the responses you will receive. It is useful if you need a direct, to-the-point answer. "Do you agree with the affirmative action policy?" "Was there time to fully implement the new program?"

The Mirror Question reflects the content of what the respondent has just said. At times, particularly in counseling interviews, it may be useful to reflect on the emotion being communicated as well. "You say you disagree with that particular operation?" "You feel strongly about this, don't you?"

The Probe Question is designed to get more specific, more detailed information or opinions from the interviewee. It is a good follow-up to open questions. "You have indicated that you prefer zero-based budgeting. Could you elaborate on that?" "You feel that the new promotion system can be more effective. Why?"

The Leading Question literally leads the interviewee to a response. It is a manipulative form of communication that could make the interviewee say things or agree to things he or she really does not believe, and the ramifications of asking such a question should be considered before using this. A sample of a leading question is, "You don't really feel that tax shelters are justified, do you?"

Format

It is a helpful technique to set up the questions in advance as a general interview schedule; make a basic outline of the questions you want to ask. This schedule might take the funnel or the inverted funnel type of format.

The **funnel schedule** structures the questions from the more general to the more specific. Thus, if you want to gain more information about a new system, this formal schedule might be suitable.

General: "Could you describe for me the basic procedures of the new evaluation system?"
More Specific: "How does the evaluation operate? When does it occur?"
Specific: "Why was the system instituted? Do you think it will work? Why?"

On the other hand, it may be necessary to start out with specifics and move to the general—the **inverted funnel format**—as in a reprimand interview.

Specific: "Are you aware that your productivity has continued to fall off significantly in the last month?"

More General: "You realize that we've discussed this before?"

General: "Why does this continue to be a problem?"

An interview schedule must, at best, be a general guide for the questions to be covered in the body of the interview. The best interviews are structured but spontaneous enough so that the two parties can adapt to each other and to what is said. You will want to listen carefully and even allow the interview to go in a different direction if you find that other points are more interesting or more relevant to the purpose. Thus, you don't want to adhere slavishly to your prepared checklist of questions if it is not accomplishing the purpose. On the other hand, your question can give a general direction to the body of the interview so that you will accomplish your purpose.

The Closing

☐

Once the body of the interview has been completed and you are satisfied that the material has been covered, you should move into the closing. The closing should tie together what has been covered in a short summary. The summary can reiterate what has been accomplished in the interview, but it isn't necessary to rehash every minute point that's been discussed.

Further, an effective closing should provide the opportunity for both parties to clear up any last questions, to agree on what has been accomplished, and to agree, if necessary, on what next step should follow. It's wise not to leave the interview until the final step is clarified, especially if you want to close a sale, know when to hear about employment decisions, or how to implement a solution. The closing is the time to make a final, lasting impression with the interview partner. Consequently, the closing deserves as much care and attention as the rest of the interview process. Sample closings are:

Problem Solving: "Then we're agreed that you will train the new operators before they are allowed to work the machinery."

Persuasive: "We will deliver the model 32 XYZ calculator on March 23rd. The total price is $550 including shipping and taxes."

Employment: "I'm very interested in your coming to work for us. I will let you know by next Tuesday whether the Board has approved the recommendation."

COMMUNICATION RESPONSIBILITIES IN THE INTERVIEW

■

Within the framework of the opening, body, and closing, the interviewer and the interviewee have certain communication responsibilities.

Interviewee Responsibilities

☐ As the interviewee, your essential responsibility is to research and to prepare in advance so that you can articulate your responses clearly, directly, and substantially, and so that you can adapt to the interviewer and the line of questions. Thus, your background research should extend to analyzing the interviewer and the organization he or she represents as well as to the content of the interview itself. An interviewee who has "done his or her homework" often impresses an interviewer.

Likewise, the interviewee should be a good listener in order to field the questions and in order to adapt throughout the interview. Careful listening is the key to effective communication within the interview. Focus your attention on *what* is being said so that your responses will be adapted to the substance of the interview.

Attention to how you dress and to the image you project can serve to increase your communication effectiveness in any interview. Your background research should enable you to make careful decisions about what you wear and the image you wish to communicate. If you plan to attend an employment interview for a professional position, for instance, you would want to dress as a professional. Persons interviewing for blue-collar positions, on the other hand, have found that a polished executive image can be distracting. Marketing specialists take the need to project a suitable corporate image seriously. The "corporate image" changes, so it is wise to observe what individuals in the field of business are wearing at the particular time you are being interviewed. You may not feel that clothing is important, but most corporations do, and that becomes the basis for what is done in the field of business.

A checklist of the interviewee's responsibilities, in an attempt to insure effective communication within the interview, include the following points:

1. Prepare carefully to have background on the subject area and on the interviewer.
2. Dress appropriately.
3. Arrive for the scheduled interview on time.
4. Establish rapport with the interviewer at the onset of the interview.
5. Listen to the questions and comments of the interviewer carefully.
6. Respond clearly and appropriately, both verbally and nonverbally.
7. Be honest and forthright in the discussion.
8. Adapt to the line of questioning of the interviewer.
9. Ask questions and secure necessary information from the interviewer.
10. Participate actively in the close of the interview to review and sum up what has been accomplished in the interview.

Interviewer Responsibilities

☐ In addition to the research and communication skills, the interviewer has specific interview responsibilities to perform, such as the necessary host functions of setting the time and place and the physical arrangements. In addition, the interviewer should have a prepared schedule of questions to serve as a guide for conducting the interview. Remember, however, to adapt to the schedule, so that the interview can go in the direction that seems most appropriate for this interviewee. The same set of questions, even for a similar circumstance, may be inappropriate for any given interviewee.

The interviewer usually takes the lead in the opening and closing of the interview. As you use the schedule of questions, provide some transitions and internal summaries so that both you and the interviewee can stay tuned in to the sequence of the interview. Transitions can be helpful as internal checks to be sure that both parties understand what has been said and where the interview is going next. "I have a good understanding, then, of your educational background. Could you also tell me what experience you have had?"

An effective interview can fill the decision-making needs of the organization with a variety of interpersonal communication objectives. To be effective, the interview ought to have a clearly defined purpose; be carefully structured; allow open, spontaneous communication between the interviewer and the interviewee; and most important, fulfill its purpose statement.

SUMMARY

In this chapter we have examined interviewing as a function of interpersonal communication within the business or organization. The major concepts discussed were:

An interview is a person-to-person communication with a decision-making purpose.

Types of business-related interviews are informative, problem solving, persuasive, employment, performance appraisal, counseling, reprimanding, and stress.

An informative interview seeks to search out information.

A problem-solving interview is used for decision making.

A persuasive interview attempts to change opinions or obtain a specific type of action.

The employment interview is based on securing a job or finding the best candidate to fill a job.

Performance appraisals often include an interview in which managers or supervisors evaluate employees.

A counseling interview centers on aiding an employee in solving a personal problem that is related to his or her job performance.

A reprimanding interview has as its purpose the correcting of a problem by correcting some attitude or action.

Stress or interrogation interviews attempt to find out how an individual will react under stress.

The press conference, a special type of interview in which businesspeople are sometimes involved, is characterized by a number of interviewers asking a variety of questions for the purpose of information gathering.

The parts of an interview are the opening, body, and closing.

Both the interviewer and the interviewee have responsibilities during the interview.

THINGS TO DO

1. Each student is to select an individual who is involved in a specific occupation he or she wishes to pursue. Make an appointment to interview the person. The student is to prepare a list of questions that will be used during the interview.

The student's purpose in the interview is to find out as much about the job as possible (educational necessities, job description, working conditions, etc.). The student is to report to the class on the interview, including the questions used, the results of the interview, and perceptions of the interview process.

2. An expert in a specific field of business will be invited to the class. The students are to interview the businessperson in order to find out about the field. This could be conducted as a press conference, where the guest gives a short presentation first and then the questions are asked, or the members of the class can ask appropriate questions.

3. Students with different majors are paired into dyads. Through the interview process, students are to find out as much as possible about each other's major. This can be done in or out of class.

4. You are a personnel manager of a corporation looking for employees for the following positions: secretary to the company's treasurer, assistant to the director of data processing, advertising manager, and a salesperson. Prepare a list of questions you would use as a guideline for interviewing the people applying for each of the jobs. Compare your lists with those of other students during a class discussion.

5. Those students in the class who have applied recently for a job should relate the procedure followed during the interview. Students could also relate any other type of interviewing situation in which they have been involved.

6. Listed are three sets of interviewing situations. Two students are selected for each role and are told to portray the person described.

Interview 1

WORKER: You have been working for this concern for over three months, and you were told you would certainly get a raise in salary in a relatively short time if you concentrated on "giving it your all." This you have done, putting in much overtime. No one seems to have noticed, however, and feeling that you are entitled to more pay, you have asked for an appointment with the boss to state your case.

BOSS: You begin this interview with the standard statement, "Can I help you?" You know very well what the worker wants. You have, indeed, been watching over him or her, and planned to grant a raise, but wanted the worker to be able to express clearly *why* he or she should have it rather than John, Bob, and Alice—all of whom have been there at least three months longer than he or she has. You also want to find out if the worker is willing to continue to accept additional responsibilities and overtime.

Interview 2

INTERVIEWEE: You are applying for a job as a receptionist in an office. You really want the job, and your qualifications are excellent. You are, however, a rather shy person. Explain why you would be best suited for this position, and try to make a good impression.

INTERVIEWER: This is the fifteenth applicant for the job you advertised in the local paper. So far, no one has impressed you as being able to communicate under stress. This applicant doesn't seem too promising either, and you are tired after a long day. Open your interview with the standard question, "Why do you think you are particularly qualified to handle this job?" If the applicant comes up with satisfying answers to your questions, hire the person!

Interview 3

COMPLAINER: You have what you consider a legitimate gripe about working conditions where you are employed. A male coworker who has been with the company six months less than you has been recommended for a promotion. You sincerely feel that you should have been promoted, and that the only reason you weren't is because you are a woman.

SUPERVISOR: You were forced to employ this woman in order to fulfill the minority requirements, although you were certain a man would have been better for the job. You personally feel that "a woman's place is in the home." You are, however, concerned that she will go to the American Civil Liberties Union with her grievance. Try to keep her from taking that step and convince her that she doesn't *deserve* a promotion, but that the other worker does.

7. The class will be divided into dyads, with one person designated the interviewer and the other person the interviewee. Each dyad will be assigned a magazine article dealing with some phase of business. Without consulting one another, the interviewer will conduct an informative interview concerning the article.

8. Repeat either assignment 3 or 7, but instead of conducting the interview in front of the class, tape-record it. Treat the experience as if it were a radio interview.

9. Each member of the class is to write five items an interviewer might ask in order to find out about that person. The class is to be divided into groups of three (interviewer, interviewee, and an observer). The interviewer is to use the five questions as the basis for finding out as much as he or she can about the interviewee. After a ten-minute interview, the observer will state what he or she believes the interviewee communicated and comment upon the interview conducted, critiquing the participation of both the interviewee and interviewer. Switch roles until all three people have played each role.

10. Your instructor will give you a pamphlet entitled *What Students Should Know about Interviewing.* Use the pamphlet as the basis for a discussion of the theme "The rest of a student's life can depend on a 30-minute interview."[24]

NOTES

1. Carole Carmichael, "Questions to Ask Before You Take a Job," *Fort Lauderdale News,* 14 December 1980, Lifestyle Cl.
2. Robert Minter, "Human Rights Laws and Pre-Employment Inquiries," Personnel Journal, 52 (June 1972):432.
3. Richard Nelson Bolles, *What Color Is Your Parachute?* (Berkeley: Ten Speeds Press, 1989).
4. This section is based on the combined suggestions of *Making the Most of Your Job Interview* (New York Life Insurance Company) and *What Students Should Know About Job Interviewing* (General Electric Corporation).
5. James Yenckel, "Careers: Facing the Interview," *Style, Washington Post,* 20 October 1981, D5.

6. Donna Goodall, and H. Lloyd Goodall, Jr., "The Employment Interview," *Communication Quarterly* 30 (September 1982):116–122.
7. Ibid., 120.
8. Based on *Merchandising Your Job Talents* (Washington, D.C.: U.S. Department of Labor-Employment and Training Administration, 1976).
9. Caroline Donnelly, "Writing An Advertisement for Yourself," *Money* (January 1974).
10. Ibid.
11. "How to Write a Resume," *Progressive Forensics* 1 (March 1984).
12. See the section of this book dealing with clothing (chapter 4) and John Molloy, *Dress for Success* (New York: Warner Books, 1978), and *The Woman's Dress for Success Book* (Chicago: Follet, 1977).
13. "Get Organized for Your Job Interview," *Cleveland Plain Dealer,* 22 February 1976, sect. 4, 2.
14. Based on *Merchandising Your Job Talents.*
15. "How Do You Talk to A Job Interviewer," special recruitment advertising supplement to the *Washington Post,* 7 October 1984.
16. Based on the concepts of Carole Carmichael.
17. Peggy Scherretz, "If You Ask Me: Nothing Personal," *Washington Post,* 15 February 1982, B5.
18. Lawrence G. Muller, Jr., "Straight Talk," *Security Management* (January 1982):25–26.
19. For a complete description of these points, the reader might be interested in reviewing Robert Hoppock, "Seventeen Principles of Appraisal Interviews," *Effective Communication on the Job* (American Management Association, 1963): 242–245.
20. Charles Stewart and William B. Cash, *Interviewing Principles and Practices* (Dubuque: Wm. C. Brown, 1982), 228.
21. Describe in James T. Yenckel, "Careers: The Ratings Game," *Washington Post,* 25 March 1982, B5.
22. John Meyer and Teresa Meyer, "The Supervisor As Counselor—How to Help the Distressed Employee," *Management Review* (April 1982):44.
23. Charles Paul Freund, "Whose Press Conference Is It, Anyway?" *City Paper* (29 January 1988): 12.
24. The pamphlet *What You Should Know About Interviewing* is available free of charge by writing to General Electric Company, Educational Communications, Room 901, 570 Lexington Avenue, New York, New York 10022.

12

□

Group Communication in the Business Setting

OVERVIEW   Many of the decisions made within businesses and organizations are the result of small-group action. Groups work with a defined purpose. Groups within an organization usually meet in private but may also appear in public. Groups operate with a leader, with some groups also having leadership. Members of a group should know the plan or rules by which the group will operate so that they can assume their responsibility for participation in the decision-making process.

KEY WORDS

small-group communication	maintenance function
small group	task function
purpose	leader
group structure	authoritarian leader
cohesion	democratic leader
private discussion	laissez-faire leader
informal discussion group	leadership
round table discussion group	procedure
brainstorming group	agenda
planning meeting	hidden agenda
buzz session	parliamentary procedure
1-3-6 Decision-Making Technique	vote
quality circle	majority
study circle	motion
self-managing work team	plurality
teleconferencing	part-of-the-whole voting
audio teleconferencing	consensus
video teleconferencing	criteria
computerconferencing	participants
focus group	followership
public discussion	risky shift
panel discussion	group polarization
symposium	groupthink
forum	communication network
conference	

Many of the decisions made within businesses and organizations are the products of group action. The old adage, "Two heads are better than one" reflects the benefit of handling organizational issues through analysis and discussion within a group rather than by one person.

Small-group communication is a major vehicle for decision-making for most organizations. The **small group** usually contains five to seven people.

THE NATURE OF COMMUNICATION IN SMALL GROUPS

A corporation faced with the need to automate its payroll system will have to decide what to do with the staff of accounting and bookkeeping personnel. The chief executive usually prefers not to handle decisions of such magnitude alone. Input can be provided through small-group conferences with other officers and the management staff.

A key advantage to the use of small-group communication is the opportunity for participation. If an organization can allow those people who will be most affected by a decision to participate in the decision-making process, those affected are more likely to feel a sense of commitment to the decision. Thus, those payroll staff members who must be reassigned to other departments may be more amenable to transfers if they have had some opportunity to participate in the decision process. Likewise, small-group communication has the advantage of giving voice to various points of view. A manager may decide on one way to rearrange the payroll office space, but other opinions, brought out in discussions, might lead to an even better method for the physical arrangement.

While small-group communication certainly offers advantages to organizational decision making, managers should recognize that the process has some limitations. Most important, it is time consuming. While two heads are better than one, it may take much longer for them to come up with a workable conclusion. Thus, the process can be effective only if time is available. Certainly, an effort should be made to take the necessary time, but if a decision must be immediate or if time is too costly, other decision-making procedures may be warranted.

It also is important to recognize that the small-group process will provide the benefits of participation and commitment only if management is prepared and equipped to carry through on decisions. We have known business groups, for example, that discussed new production procedures and submitted a plan for their recommended system to the company's management, only to receive no response. When asked to deal with other issues, the same group perceived a lack of real commitment on the part of management and would not make decisions on the other issues. If it is not possible to actively deal with group decision-making within an organization, it is much better to dismiss the idea of forming the groups than to let them "spin wheels" to no productive end.

Setting a Purpose

To derive benefits from a small group, the group communication process must be effective. To that end, the group should have a clearly-defined communication purpose. The **purpose,** the overall objectives of the group—why it is meeting and what purpose

To be effective, a small group needs to have a clearly established purpose that is understood by all members. (© Frank Siteman/Taurus Photos)

it needs to accomplish—ought to be understood and agreed upon by all members within the group.

Group discussions may be utilized to accomplish a variety of purposes. Groups serve a social function by giving the members an opportunity to interact and get to know each other. Organizations find this to be a useful first step in putting together a new group of employees.

A second objective of groups may be therapeutic—to allow individuals within the group the opportunity to express their feelings, frustrations, and problems. Industrial psychologists sometimes use therapeutic groups to get at the problems of employee morale.

A group may form for the purpose of sharing information. Members of a task force designed to study competitive marketing practices, for example, might get together to share information about their findings.

Yet another function of groups may be value analysis—using group communication to determine, the worth of something. A group of publishers, for instance, might want to discuss the value of publishing books by politicians who have been convicted of high crimes while in office.

The purpose most related to decision-making is problem-solving. This function serves to identify issues facing an organization and to arrive at solutions or to establish policy. A government agency facing an impending budget cut, for instance, may need to bring its mid-level managers together to discuss how best to continue the missions of the organization despite limited resources.

Group Structure

☐
In addition to purpose, an effective group needs a **group structure,** a basic plan for accomplishing its objectives. The proper organization of the discussion can maximize the opportunity for all members to participate, regardless of their points of view.

Cohesion

☐
The opportunity for participation should lead to another important characteristic of an effective group—**cohesion.** Members must feel a sense of commitment to each other and to the objective of the group. Cohesion is important for creating a comfortable, open communication climate. We are all members of various groups. The group to which we belong at any one time can affect what we say, the beliefs we hold, and the actions we undertake.

These characteristics of cohesion, structure, and purpose describe any type of effective group discussion, whether private (for the benefit of the participants) or public (for the benefit of an audience).

PRIVATE DISCUSSIONS

■
Groups within an organization most commonly meet in **private discussion.** No audience observes the actions of the group; therefore, attention centers on the proceedings and the participants. The group members speak to each other, use visual aids that can be seen by the group, and use language that is appropriate for those taking part in the discussion. If an audience is present, as in public discussions, participants must be certain that the observers can see and hear what is transpiring while still maintaining the group interaction.

We can identify eight different formats for private group discussions: the informal discussion; a round table discussion; a brainstorming session; the planning meeting; a buzz session; the Quality Circle; self-managing work teams; and teleconferencing.

Informal Discussions

☐
A group of construction workers at lunch might get into an extended discussion on the best schedule for the new subway system they are building. This is an example of an **informal discussion group,** as it lacks formal structure or designed leadership, but it can provide the participants with a chance to voice their opinions and to feel a greater sense of belonging to the group as a whole. Such informal groups, when they go beyond casual conversation, can play an important role in the communication network of an organization. These informal groups can function as the grapevine to pass information (and misinformation) through channels of communication. All organizations have these informal groups, and when used to their advantage by management, information can be communicated quickly and efficiently to all levels in an organization. However, such groups also run the danger of transmitting gossip and rumors through these same informal channels.[1]

Round Table Discussions

□ A more task-oriented type of private group is the **round table discussion.** This takes the form of conversational interaction within a small group of people to accomplish a specific objective. The group usually follows some agenda or outline to give it a basic structure. A group of managers brought together to discuss what could be done to increase worker productivity may follow a round table discussion format to conduct their meeting.

Brainstorming Sessions

□ Organizations also frequently use the **brainstorming discussion** to come up with solutions to management problems. In this type of discussion, participants meet to suggest—brainstorm—solutions to the problem. No evaluation or analysis of the proposed solutions is permitted. Thus, creativity is given full reign, allowing participants to bring up any solutions, regardless of how radical they might be. Usually the suggestions will be referred to a committee for analysis, selection, and implementation after the brainstorming session is completed.

Planning Meetings

□ Most organizations use the **planning meeting,** an effort to bring together a group of people to make plans for handling any of a vast number of company policies or procedures. Unfortunately, planning meetings are often called once a crisis has been identified and the group must decide how to solve the problem with little or no advance preparation. One management consultant observes that planning meetings are made up of too many members who are "too busy putting out fires to think about the future and afraid to nail down a decision that would mean accountability."[2] Since the purpose of the planning meeting is to generate recommendations which will be reported to executive officers, it is suggested that the planning meeting result in a document which addresses: (1) the plan; (2) why the plan is recommended; (3) the goals of the plan; and (4) the time and dollars it will cost to implement the plan.[3]

Buzz Sessions

□ At times, a group may be too large to accomplish much, so it is useful to turn to the **buzz session** strategy. In this format, a large group is broken down into smaller groups to conduct discussions on the same issue. The smaller groups then report back their conclusions to the larger group as a whole. This technique is especially useful if you want to give people in a large group a sense of participation and if you need a general sense of the ideas of the group as a whole.

A systematic buzz group format is based on the nominal group decision-making technique[4] and is known as "The 1-3-6."

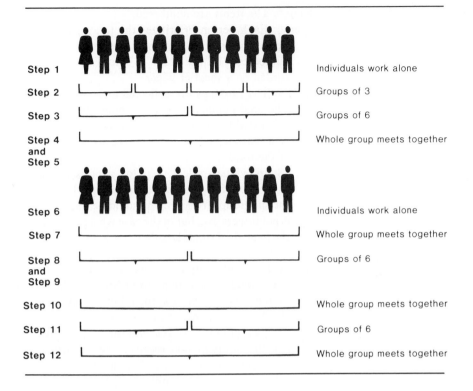

FIGURE 12.1 The 1-3-6 decision-making technique.

Step 1   Individuals work alone
Step 2   Groups of 3
Step 3   Groups of 6
Step 4 and Step 5   Whole group meets together
Step 6   Individuals work alone
Step 7   Whole group meets together
Step 8 and Step 9   Groups of 6
Step 10   Whole group meets together
Step 11   Groups of 6
Step 12   Whole group meets together

The 1-3-6 Decision-Making Technique

Having determined the specific decision to be made or the problem to be solved, the group is ready to work toward solution.

The steps in **"1-3-6 Decision-Making Technique"**[5] are as follows (figure 12.1):

Step 1: All individuals in the group list what they feel should be done to solve the problem or the best possible decisions regarding the issue. This is a self-brain-storming session. All ideas generated should be listed, with no evaluation made of the suggestions.

Step 2: Participants are divided into subgroups of three. Each group combines its members' lists. No items are deleted, but possibilities are combined and solutions or decisions are reworded. There should be no discussion of the value of the ideas in this step.

Step 3: The group is divided so that two subgroups of three people each meet and combine their lists. Again, duplicate ideas are eliminated and solutions or decisions are reworded. No evaluations are made.

Step 4: The total group reassembles. A spokesperson for each subgroup reads aloud the subgroup's list. Items are written on a long sheet of paper or on a black-board. (It is important that everyone in the room be able to read the lists, so large writing is imperative.)

Step 5: The items are numbered.

Step 6: Each person prioritizes the total list. The participants rank in order all items, with no ties. The most important or best solution or decision should be numbered "1," the next "2," etc. Each person's individual rankings are recorded on a sheet of paper.

Step 7: The rankings are collected and tallied. The top ten items are identified. The final number to be used should be in proportion to the number of items generated from Step 4. If 30 or more items were generated, the top 10 would be a reasonable final list. If there are fewer, select about one-half to one-third of the total.

Step 8: Individuals select their top choices and then are randomly divided into subgroups of no more than six persons. If possible, a representative of each of the subgroups from Step 3 should be in each of the newly formed units. (This is not imperative, but in the case where there is a lack of clarity of a statement, the individual from the subgroup that generated the idea may be able to clarify its meaning.)

Step 9: Each subgroup is to select what it considers to be the best solution using the individual selections from Step 8.[6] At this step, evaluations are made. Statements may be reworded, but no new solutions may be introduced.

Step 10: Spokespersons for each subgroup report on the decision of the subgroup. If all subgroups have selected the same solution, the process is completed. If not, the solutions that received the support of at least one subgroup are retained and the others are eliminated.

Step 11: Subgroups reassemble and select the best solution from the list available.

Step 12: A spokesperson for each subgroup reports on the selection of his or her subgroup.

Steps 11 and 12 are repeated until a single solution is chosen.

Some smaller groups adopt an alternative approach, using only Steps 1 through 6 and then having all members meet together to reach a final solution. This approach may be used for groups of less than ten people.

Quality Circle

□

Probably no issue in contemporary American management is of more concern than that of worker participation in relation to productivity. The successes of the Japanese use of the Quality Circle, and the Scandinavian use of the Study Circle, have led American managers to study the procedure in depth and to implement such a process in American industry. Many American industries have now used this concept. General Electric, General Motors, Kaiser Aluminum, Exxon, and Westinghouse are only a few of the corporations instituting quality circles in recent years.[7]

Essentially, the **Quality Circle** is a small group of workers (typically eight to ten in a group) who meet together regularly for group discussions about commonly-agreed-upon problems and their solutions. In the Scandinavian system, Study Circles, personal as well as employers' needs and interests are discussed. **Study Circle** participants decide what they will discuss, where to meet, the materials, the resources, the learning plans, and the problem-solving methods. Study Circles do not employ structured discussion or an authority figure.

The success of these groups requires considerable commitment throughout the organization so that managers and executives will be open to the recommended solutions from the groups and be able to implement those solutions likely to be effective in meeting organizational problems. Such an approach involves the worker in the decision-making process so that she or he has a voice in the operation and thus a greater commitment to seeing that the operation is accomplished. The process has generated increased productivity for the organization and greater worker satisfaction.

The Quality Circle and Study Circle, widely hailed in management today, should not be viewed as the "quick fix" for all that ails industry. It must be recognized that the use of Quality Circles in Japan constitutes a different purpose in a very different corporate culture than we find in American firms.[8] Those companies in America that have been unsuccessful in using circles report several negative factors and causes:

1. Employees disliked the management. They saw Quality Circles as a management ploy to reduce overtime and perhaps cut the work force by increasing productivity.
2. Companies did a poor job of selling Quality Circles. They have to tell employees what's in it for them.
3. The foremen or supervisors picked to lead the Quality Circles received some training in human relations and group dynamics, but they felt that little of it applied to the specific ends of their own departments.
4. Most companies regarded the Quality Circle programs as merely a way of improving production techniques.[9]

Developing an effective group and arriving at clear understanding of the problem, much less coming up with meaningful solutions, takes a considerable amount of time. All those involved in the process must recognize that the time to accomplish actual results can be costly and consuming. But the results, according to those who have observed Quality Circle groups in operation, are well worth the investment of time, resources, and management commitment.

It was observed, for example, that the Japanese automobile productivity (which increased at a phenomenal 9.3 percent rate between 1975 and 1980 in contrast to the U.S. rate of 1.6 percent for the same period) results from a commitment to quality work and from Japanese workers "who regard themselves as 'members of the company' as well as members of the union."[10] Contrasting these worker attitudes with their American counterparts, it has been noted that "one really big difference on the labor-management front . . . is that there is an attitude of cooperation rather than confrontation."[11] This attitude results from the democratic, participative management style perfected by Japanese industries, allowing workers to participate in decisions and to give them a voice, through the group process, in what they do and how they do it.

The usual Quality Circle process involves the following agenda:

    I. Identify and select a problem
    II. Analyze the problem
      A. Set criteria
      B. Gather data
    III. Brainstorm for solutions. (See previous discussions in this chapter on brainstorming and the 1-3-6 Decision-Making Technique.)
    IV. Select and plan for solution
      A. Solve the problem. (Note: Use one of the structured problem-solving techniques at this stage.)
      B. Establish a satisfactory solution to the problem. (Some groups will have to stop here as their agreed-upon responsibilities may stop at establishing a solution. If they are also responsible for implementing the solution, they can proceed to the next step.)
      C. Decide how to implement the solution
      D. Determine what resources are available and needed
    V. Implement the solution

Self-Managing Work Teams

☐

Teamwork has come to be recognized in many industries as a key to creating a successful workforce. A recent hospital study revealed, for example, that "whether patients survive in the intensive care unit depends less on the amount of high-tech equipment available than on effective coordination between doctors and nurses."[12]

Given the changing nature of the workplace and the efforts to "flatten out" management structure, it just will not be possible for everyone to move up to management positions. This requires that individuals find their "niche" in the organization and work with others in that role to be "self managers," assuming much greater responsibility for their own work skills and performance. These efforts to develop more of a "team" perspective in getting the job done are integral to organizational development. To date, team-building has been focused primarily on management team-building, but it is clear that the creation of **self-managing work teams** in the workplace will be necessary throughout an organization. Stressing the need for secretaries to assume an important role as part of the office team, for example, some specialists recognize that without teamwork, "communication breaks down, coordination slips, resources are wasted, effort is duplicated, target dates and goals are missed, and people get frustrated."[13]

Teleconferencing

☐

Many businesses are in search of ways to increase management productivity and are paying more attention to methods of making more effective use of management time and cutting travel costs. It is estimated that "managers spend an average of 46 percent of their time in meetings and meeting-associated travel."[14] But consider that "20 million meetings are held every day in the U.S.: 80 percent of all meetings last less than 30 minutes; 60 percent of all meetings could be handled by voice communications; and

35 percent of all meetings are for the exchange of information only."[15] With this proliferation of meetings, **teleconferencing** (audio, video, and computer teleconferencing), has become of increasing interest to business organizations.

Types of Teleconferencing

"Teleconferencing means conferring, discussing, or communicating by telephone or other media between two or more people at two or more locations."[16] This process is sometimes known as an electronic meeting.

"**Audio teleconferencing** is voice communication among three or more individuals or groups participating simultaneously over a telephone line."[17]

Video teleconferencing is audio plus full visual conferencing for groups separated by distance. Cable, satellite, or microwaves are used to send the signal. This process allows participants to see and hear each other. Electronic blackboards may be used to transmit sketches, diagrams, maps, or similar material which is drawn on the blackboard by one of the participants."[18]

Sessions can also be held via **computerconferencing** in which computer terminals transmit information and can be accessed immediately by all conference participants, or the material can be stored for later action.

More and more corporations are using teleconferencing as a means of conducting small group meetings with people from different parts of the country.

Uses of Teleconferencing

Two questions arise: How can teleconferencing be used? And is it being used?[19,20]

The uses of the process include announcements or status reports, giving instructions or disseminating information, planning and scheduling activities, crisis management, problem solving, and training.

Teleconferencing is becoming popular because it:

- can improve productivity through reduced travel time, allow for faster decision making, and increase the availability of personnel because they are in the office more and out on travel less.
- tends to result in shorter and better organized meetings than those that are held face-to-face.
- reduces travel costs because 50 to 60 percent of all meetings can be held technologically. It is estimated that for every dollar invested in teleconferencing about $4.00 in travel expenses are avoided. Aetna Corporation indicates that in one year teleconferencing saved it $322,000.[12]
- provides additional, convenient opportunities for professional education and training.
- increases cooperation and participation among employees, heightens their commitment, makes possible decentralization of larger organizations, and bring in resource people not otherwise available or accessible.

Teleconferencing Problems

Teleconferencing is not necessarily the solution to all business problems. A few objections to electronic meetings have been registered.

Some critics feel that there is an undue emphasis placed on the technology and that people regard the entire process too lightly since it is similar to the entertainment or leisure time activities of television and conversational telephone use. Many also feel that face-to-face interactions are more effective and that the mechanical nature of the technology can create emotional distance.

In some instances, participants feel uncomfortable being on camera or in front of a microphone. Participants also must make adjustments and learn some new skills based on this contemporary mode of communicating.

The amount of investment necessary to get an organization involved in teleconferencing is also a concern. In order to cut down on individual organization's teleconferencing costs, hotel chains such as Hilton and Holiday Inn have installed teleconferencing facilities in their city properties to enable groups to use the equipment. In some cities, AT&T also has fully-equipped public meeting rooms and studios for rental to organizations.[22]

Participating in a Teleconference

Many of the guidelines for face-to-face meetings apply to teleconferencing, but some principles are unique to electronic meetings:[23]

Speakers should be close enough to the microphones to be easily heard.

Participants must be careful to control noise of papers, tapping on tables, and other distracting habits that the microphones will pick up.

High-quality graphics must be prepared to fit the television format when using videoconferencing.

Handouts should be provided in advance for a meeting using audioconferencing.

Participants should be introduced at the beginning of the meeting and continue to identify themselves as they proceed through an audio conference.

Unannounced departures and entrances should be avoided.

Participants, especially in videoconferencing, will have to wait until the cameras are turned to them before they can participate.

The conference should be limited to no more than an hour; if longer, a break should be scheduled.

Teleconferencing appears to be an accepted part of organizational practice, so individuals should develop an understanding of and skills for participation in teleconferences.

Focus Group

□

An organization might very well want to test representative consumer reactions to a new product line, a new service, or even a new advertising campaign. In such instances, one area of market research proving useful in industry is the focus group. A **focus group** brings together a small group of representative consumers (usually offered some sort of honorarium) with a discussion moderator to look at the company's proposed effort and react to it. The reactions are carefully cataloged to be used as part of the research to make necessary changes. Most marketing research firms today use this technique. They have found that the effective focus group requires qualified participants and a well-prepared, sensitive moderator who leads the group through a series of questions to generate all possible reactions from the participants.[24]

PUBLIC DISCUSSIONS

■

Public discussions, while maintaining conversational informality, are usually more structured because they are presented for an audience. The presence of observers necessitates control of time, vocal projection, and audience-directed physical action. Typically, a moderator is in charge of public discussions. Forms of public discussion include the panel discussion, the symposium, and the forum.

Panel Discussion

□

One popular form of public discussion is the **panel discussion** which is characterized by interaction among the participants. The members follow an agenda, guided by a moderator. The television public affairs show "The McLaughlin Group" is an example of the use of the panel discussion. It is a good form for the presentation of viewpoints to employee groups, especially if a number of people might wish to be involved in the presentation.

Symposium

☐

A more structured and less interactive type of public discussion is the **symposium.** In this format, participants present short speeches, reports, or remarks. A moderator introduces the program and makes transitions between the speakers. The speakers do not actually interact with each other, so the symposium technically is not a true discussion, but it is a public group presentation. The format is useful for presenting information if a variety of people have related aspects of information on a common topic.

For instance, a major insurance company presented information about a new plan to all employees at a small company. One individual describes the firm's vision care program, another the prescription drug program, and another the dental care plan. The format was effective, as each participant was a specialist and could field detailed questions and give answers about each feature of the plan.

Forum

☐

The question-and-answer session is still another form of public discussion: the **forum.** The forum is that part of any public presentation in which the audience participates. It could be combined with a lecture, a film, a symposium, or a panel. If it is possible logistically, the forum should be built into almost any public presentation, because it offers the opportunity for audience participation and enables speakers to clear up any points or get at other issues that may be important to the audience.

The symposium, panel, and forum can combine quite effectively for some public presentations. For instance, this format was used for the discussion of organizational communication training practices at a national conference of communication educators. Three communication trainers, representing government, industry, and private consulting, presented short talks on their work and then interacted as a panel with a moderator on more specific issues in organizational communication training. Finally, the moderator opened up the session for questions from the audience.

CONFERENCES

■

In addition to small group discussions, individuals may participate in larger conference groups. Professional societies and associations often feature conferences over the course of one or several days.

Participants in a **conference** convene to share information, discuss issues, and conduct business. The agenda for a larger conference might include a variety of activities: panel discussions, round table discussions, speeches, technical reports, committee meetings, and large group business sessions. For many organizations, the annual conference serves as an important vehicle for getting all of the members together to share professional interests and information and to complete the necessary business of the organization.

Conferences have become an important part of the functioning of many groups (trade associations, management groups, marketing groups). Indeed, the importance of annual, semi-annual, or even quarterly conferences is reflected in the development of career positions for persons who are skilled in meeting management. Meeting planners work to arrange all of the logistics of the gatherings: lining up themes and speakers, publicizing the events, booking hotels, and arranging food and activity functions.

The International Listening Association is an example of a group that holds conferences. This association of business executives, educators, counselors, researchers, and other persons interested in listening behavior holds an annual spring conference. The three-day session opens with welcoming speeches and a keynote speaker at a luncheon, followed by a number of panels and workshops on a variety of listening research, instruction, and application issues. Association committees hold meetings to deal with their business during this time, and the Executive Board of officers conducts business meetings. The members elect their officers. The conference concludes with an awards banquet. The meetings provide an excellent opportunity for members to interact about matters pertaining to the field of listening and to get to know each other on a personal level.

GROUP MAINTENANCE AND TASK FUNCTIONS

Regardless of the type of small-group discussion used, either public or private, certain general functions must be handled for a group to be successful. These general functions of groups are characterized as **maintenance functions** (meeting the interpersonal needs of the group members) and **task functions** (getting the job done).[25] These functions can be handled by the same people or by different people through the course of any discussion.

Task questions often asked about groups include: How do we start? How do we go about making decisions? Are there any keys to effective group operation?

Getting Started

One of the major problems confronting groups is getting together for the first meeting. If the committee is appointed, the individual making the committee selection should either set the time, date, and place of the first meeting or designate one of the appointees to take the responsibility for getting the group assembled. If no one has been assigned to assemble the group or no specific procedure for assembling the group has been set, one of the members of the group should initiate the process. All too often everyone waits for someone else to take action; consequently, no meeting is called.

After the group is assembled, it is advisable that an operational procedure be established by the members. The procedure might include identifying the leader's role, defining the task, and setting up criteria for decision-making.

Leader and Leadership

☐ The **leader** is the person who guides the group through the decision-making process (see figure 12.2).[26] The leader may be elected, be appointed, or emerge from the group itself.

In many organizations, a procedure has been set up for a democratic selection of the leader of any committee operating within the company. If this is the case, the first group action should be electing the leader.

Some organizations operate through an appointment system: a supervisor appoints a member of the group or the committee to serve as the leader. Sometimes a position, based on the job description, includes responsibility for leading certain committees or groups. The treasurer, for example, may chair the Finance Committee. If this is true, usually calling the first meeting and making of preliminary decisions on the operational procedures are handled by the appointed leader.

Still another method of providing guidance for the group is the self-emergence of the leader. When a group of people get together for some type of task accomplishment and no leader has been appointed or elected, it is not unusual for some person to take charge. This individual has emerged as the leader and until someone else assumes the guiding functions will continue to aid the group in carrying through its tasks.

The leader should facilitate the communication process. The person or persons taking responsibility for the communication process are obligated to be certain that the group functions according to its agreed-upon procedures as well as progressing through its agenda. This can best be accomplished by making sure that the rights of the members of the group are respected. Clarifications and internal summaries as well as transitions tying up a point that has been covered and then introducing the next item on the agenda aid a group in accomplishing its task. These structural aids—summaries, transitions, clarifications—are particularly valuable in keeping the group on track and moving forward to its objective.

In group operation, conflicts may arise over the leader's function and role. A leaderless group, a group in which there is a fight for control, or one in which the leader does not function effectively, is likely to have difficulty in fulfilling the group's task. Members of the group should be aware of this potential problem and take action to correct the situation if problems occur. Possible actions could include the selection of a new leader, confronting the situation through an open discussion of how to solve the conflict, appealing to a supervisor for aid, or dissolving the group.

There are various approaches to studying and understanding a leader. The trait theory suggests that leaders are born with inherent leadership characteristics so that they will emerge as natural leaders in almost any group. The function theory takes the opposite viewpoint, suggesting that leaders perform key functions that can be learned by anyone who wishes to facilitate the group's task and maintenance responsibilities.[27] Considerable attention to leadership styles as they interact with a leader's functions can be useful to understanding the complexities of being a leader.

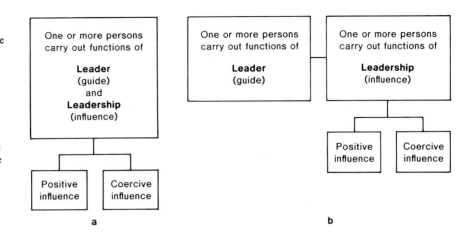

FIGURE 12.2 Berko-Wolvin-Wolvin model of the leader/leadership relationship. The leader is the group's guide. Leadership is the ability to influence, which can be used either positively or coercively. Both leader and leadership functions can be carried out by (a) the same person(s), or (b) separate persons. From *Communicating: A Social and Career Focus,* by Roy Berko, Andrew Wolvin, Darlyn Wolvin, Copyright © 1977 by Houghton Mifflin Company. Reprinted by Permission of the publishers.

Leader Style

Early work concerning leader style identified three basic styles:

Authoritarian leaders dominate and direct the group according to his or her own goals

Democratic leaders allow members to form their own goals.

Laissez-faire leaders allow members to do whatever they wish[28]

It is generally recognized that different leader styles might be appropriate to meet the needs (both task needs and maintenance needs) of various groups. It is possible that one group may require more of an authoritarian approach to accomplish what must be done, while another unit may function very well in a more democratic situation. Further, the same group may require different leader behaviors, depending upon the task it must accomplish. A good manager must learn when to assume responsibility for making decisions or implementing a procedure or process alone and when to delegate that responsibility to the group.[29]

It is difficult to describe the leader style most appropriate to American industry today. Many feel that the answer lies in the tremendous success of the Japanese management style, which establishes the manager as a facilitator whose "primary role is not giving orders but facilitating action, bringing about the cooperation and consensus among dissident viewpoints, and providing people with the information and resources they need to do their jobs."[30] Others feel that we should look for "leaders who combine a tough-minded understanding and pragmatism with compassion and interest in people. That means involving employees in making decisions and developing an organization that allows the utmost individual development and responsibility."[31]

Whatever the style, it is clear that the leader must be an effective communicator as well as an effective leader. "In short, nothing serves an organization better . . . than leadership that knows what it wants, communicates those intentions accurately, and knows how to stay on course and when to change."[32]

Leader Roles

The leader of the group usually performs the roles of coordinator, facilitator, trainer, observer, gap filler, and monitor.[33,34]

Coordinator The leader arranges the time and place for meetings and for secretarial help and secures an operator for any audio-visual equipment that will be used. The leader usually plans and distributes the order of business—the agenda—for a meeting. The role also includes acting as a clearinghouse for any questions or problems confronted by the participants before the sessions, as well as acting as the liaison between the group and other people in the organization.

Facilitator Once an agenda has been developed, the leader is responsible for helping the participants to follow this agenda as the meeting progresses. The leader should assist members in identifying problems, defining issues, and working together. In addition, by giving the necessary background to the matter being dealt with, and filling in the limits of the decision-making power of the group, the leader can help to avoid problems.

Trainer It is often assumed that members of groups automatically know how the meetings are run, the rules of order, how to work toward reaching decisions, and how to work together to accomplish mutual goals. This is often not the case. Frequently, the leader must directly or indirectly instruct meeting participants in these matters. Training sessions concerning group processes, problem solving, and group actions may be needed. Even while the meeting is in progress, the leader might need to clarify the voting process, the decision-making procedure, or even strategies of participation.

Observer As the meeting progresses, it may be necessary to aid the group in functioning effectively, to identify areas in which change might facilitate its work, and to describe to members what is happening in terms of the group process. Some specific areas to watch for include digressions from the topic, personality conflicts which cause the decision-making process to grind to a halt, members who want to speak or have not spoken, compulsive talkers who should be controlled, and the failure to think creatively. This role might entail drawing out silent members with such questions as "Does anyone who hasn't spoken care to comment?" or "Roger, what is your opinion of . . . ?"

The leader might suggest the need for sharing personal experiences by asking questions. "Does anyone know of instances where this has worked?" The leader might want to call attention to a point that may not have been considered by asking, "Does anyone have any information on this point?" The leader also may keep the discussion focused on the subject by suggesting "That's interesting, but just how does this point fit in with the issue we're considering?"

To use conflict constructively, the approach might be to ask, "Since we do not seem to be able to resolve this difference now, could we move on to the next point?" Or "What aspects of the opposing views are acceptable to all of us?"

Suggesting the need for additional information can also be accomplished by asking questions. "Do we have enough information to decide now?" "Is it agreeable to the group if we ask a subcommittee to bring back the necessary information to our next session?"

To prevent a few individuals from monopolizing the discussion, the leader could request, "May we hear from someone who hasn't expressed an opinion?" Another approach may be, "Jim, since we have only a few minutes left, could you summarize your remarks so that we may hear from the others?"

Gap-Filler At the conclusion of a discussion, or at the end of the meeting, it is necessary to remind everyone what has transpired. The leader should summarize what has been discussed, clarify his or her perceptions of what has happened or is about to happen, and facilitate compromise so that a decision can be reached.

Leadership Role

Some individual or individuals may assume a leadership role within a group. **Leadership** is exemplified by those persons or even one person whose comments and actions ultimately influence the outcome of the group's decisions. These individuals may emerge from the group itself. In some instances they assume their role due to a position they have within the organization. They may, for example, hold a major office in the organization or may have much experience and knowledge about the subject being discussed.

Monitor Once the conclusion has been reached or a solution to a problem has been decided upon, a plan must be developed to carry it out. The leader should be certain that each person clearly understands his/her responsibilities, assignments, and functions. This might include giving out schedules and assignment sheets.

An individual is usually most successful in the leadership role if the members of the group perceive that person in a positive way. The membership does not necessarily have to agree with the leader, but it must respect that individual's method of dealing with matters as well as with people in order to have a positive effect. Sometimes, because of positions, an individual has influence over the group, but the other members may resent the decision(s) reached or fail to fully participate because they feel that their input will be of no value in the final decision. Unless they exert the authority of their position, persons who do not have the support of the group members will not be very successful in assuming leadership roles. A person can be a leader of a group only if she or he is perceived by the members of the group to be a leader. Recognize, too, that the leadership functions in a group may shift from person to person. You may even find several leaders in a group rather than a single leader.

As organizations become more involved in the team-building concept, the nature of leadership is changing. Some organizational specialists have suggested that as organizations become more decentralized and more often linked by computers and other information technologies, the leader role will be shared or even rotated among team members within the organization.[35]

Procedures

☐

The members of a group should know the **procedure,** the plan and the rules under which they will operate. In order to avoid confusion and chaos, the importance of setting up an agenda, the rules of operation, and voting procedures should be clear to the membership.

Agenda

The accomplishment of group objectives is most effective through agenda setting. An **agenda** is an outline, or a plan, indicating the order in which the group will conduct its discussion.

An information-sharing discussion should follow an agenda which sets up basic questions dealing with the factual information to be covered. The agenda is limited to information—no effort should be made to evaluate or to advocate a point of view.

A management group might discuss the question, "What is zero-based budgeting?" with a three-step agenda:

1. What are the purposes of zero-based budgeting?
2. What are the key characteristics of zero-based budgeting?
3. What are the advantages and disadvantages of zero-based budgeting?

An agenda for a value-analysis discussion goes beyond sharing information to assessing the worth of the topic under discussion. Executives might deal with the question, "Is there value in management leader leadership training?"

1. What are the goals of leader/leadership training?
   a. Is identification of potential leaders an objective?
   b. Is the purpose to develop leadership in present managers?
2. Are the goals being accomplished?
   a. Are the goals achieved in the current training program?
   b. Are the goals maintained on the job?
3. Are the goals worth achieving?
   a. Are they valuable in terms of personal development?
   b. Is leader/leadership training justified in terms of increased worker or manager productivity?
   c. Is leader/leadership training justified in terms of cost benefits?

A problem-solving discussion moves from a discussion of the problem to an analysis of various solutions to the problem. A careful problem-solving agenda should cover the problem thoroughly before leading participants to a discussion of the solutions.

A management group might want to deliberate the question, "What can be done to solve the problem of poor internal communication?"

1. Locating and defining the problem
   a. What constitutes internal communication?
   b. What is "poor"?
2. Exploring the problem
   a. What are the causes of the problem?

b. What are the effects of the problem?

c. What goals do we need to accomplish?

3. What are possible solutions to the problem?

    a. Is a communication training program a solution?

    b. Should we hire a communication consultant?

    c. Do we need an office of internal communication?

4. What is the best solution?

5. How should the solution be implemented?

The last item (and sometimes even the last two items) on the problem-solving agenda may not be the group's responsibility. Instead, the group may refer all solutions to management for evaluation and implementation.

Regardless of the purpose of the discussion, a well-planned agenda can be useful to participants as a general guideline for their discussion. It can help the group to accomplish its task expediently and enable the members to stay within the necessary framework to meet its objectives.

Hidden Agenda   The members of the group should recognize one maintenance problem that can debilitate the efforts of the group—the hidden agenda. Certain members may have unstated, underlying objectives—**a hidden agenda**—and be willing to sacrifice the good of the whole group for these selfish interests.

For example, an employee might have a personal interest in maintaining a procedure that should be changed. Under these conditions the employee would not state his view by saying, "That change would make me have to leave for work at 6 o'clock in the morning, and I don't want to get up that early." Instead, the employee will present many reasons, none of which are his true reason, in order to stop approval of the action. He might suggest that changing the starting time will make for difficulties in employee carpools or put a burden on those individuals who are commuters and take trains to work. He may be embarrassed to say that he doesn't want to get up earlier, or he simply may feel that it is no one's business but his own. Whatever the reason, he is not going to reveal it, instead placing smoke screens before the group in order to obscure his reason.

Sometimes such factors as the fear of repraisals or the possibility of financial loss may be the cause of a hidden agenda. Whatever the reason, a person operating on this level often obstructs progress through such tactics as delay, changing the subject, and advancing irrelevant arguments.

If you recognize this type of behavior, you may need to act assertively by posing the question, "What is your real objection?" Another approach is to show the individual that you are aware of his or her actions and then ask the person to explain these actions.

Rules of Operation

Most formal organizational meetings will operate under parliamentary procedure, most commonly *Robert's Rules of Order*. **Parliamentary procedure** consists of a set of rules that explains how groups should carry on their official actions. It is helpful if the leader of the group that operates under these regulations is familiar with parliamentary procedure. Typically, businesses and organizations have training sessions for those who will be in leader roles, or they will have an expert (a parliamentarian) available to attend meetings to aid in conducting them.

Voting Procedures   One of the primary procedures to be established is decision-making. The most common method is for a proposal to be presented and a **vote** to be taken to determine the number who favor the proposal. Since there are various methods of voting or reaching agreement, this, too, should be decided upon before starting to carry on decision-making. The most common methods of voting or reaching agreement are by majority, plurality, part-of-the-whole, and consensus.

According to *Robert's Rules of Order,* "when the term **majority** vote is used without qualifications it means more than half of the votes cast by persons entitled to vote, excluding blanks and abstentions."[36] For example, if a group consists of seven people and four vote *yes* and three vote *no,* the motion passes because more than half have voted in favor. (A **motion** is a statement indicating what action should be taken.) A vote of three in favor and four against would defeat the motion. If only five of the people voted, then it would take three *yes* votes to pass the motion. Deciding by majority rule is the most standard form of voting in organizational decision making.

Yet another method is **plurality.**[32] This is a common approach when more than two options are available. Since plurality means *most,* if three candidates are running for an office, the one who receives the most votes is declared the winner. If three different ideas have been presented to the advertising department for selection, and it has been agreed that a plurality voting system will be used to decide on the theme for the new advertising campaign, the idea getting the most votes is selected. One of the disadvantages of this procedure centers on the fact that selection can be made with less than a majority. If Idea A gets three votes, and Idea B and C each get two votes, Idea A is chosen with less than a majority. In spite of its drawbacks, most of our governmental as well as union elections are by plurality.

Sometimes a **part-of-the-whole voting** method is used. In this form a part or a percentage of those voting is agreed upon as the minimum needed for taking action. Most commonly, two-thirds or 66.67 percent is the amount selected by groups wanting to use more than a majority. Any percentage may be selected as the minimum needed for approval.

Another method of voting or reaching conclusions is consensus. In parliamentary procedure, **consensus** signifies all.[38] For an action to take place, everyone in the group must agree to the proposal. Obviously, it is very difficult to get everyone to agree, so this method is used only when very important decisions are to be made. Juries, for example, operate under the consensus system. Some organizations using committees for hiring at the executive level use consensus in their election process, since the decision is so critical to the welfare of the entire group.

Criteria

In some cases, agreement must be reached on the criteria to be used in the selection or the choice of an action. Confusion can be avoided if members know in advance what **criteria,** what measurement tool, will be used. For instance, in organizations where personnel are to be hired, it is common to develop a job description. A job description should indicate the minimum education, skills, and experiences needed to carry out the job, and set up an instrument for evaluating the candidates, selecting the one who receives the highest total points on the evaluation scale. This procedure is extremely important in implementing an affirmative action program in an organization. Because of legal implications, organizations are required to show how and why certain candidates were or were not hired. Without an agreed-upon procedure and clear criteria, this proof is almost impossible.

Participants

☐

It is the right, and often the responsibility, of the **participants** (the group members) to take an active part in the decision-making process. Since one of the major responsibilities of management, middle management, and supervisory personnel is decision making, the maintenance of your job and the possibility for advancement may well depend on your participation in group matters.

Keep in mind that if you are a member of a group and do not participate actively in determining the action taken, you may be thought to be incompetent or shirking your responsibilities. This does not mean that you should dominate the group, but you must be aware of your responsibility to be prepared and to participate when it is appropriate for you to do so. Your participation should reflect your position and areas of expertise.

As a group member, you should research the topic thoroughly so that you can discuss the question intelligently. Be prepared to support your comments, when necessary, with research data—statistics, examples, and testimony. A good participant also uses his or her own experience with the topic, personal research, and expertise, as support for contributing to the group. Poor preparation by the participants can undercut the group's effectiveness, especially if the discussion functions at just the superficial "I think" level. Little would be accomplished except pooling group ignorance.

The discussion facilitator should also practice good communication skills. It is quite important to listen carefully so as to understand the comments of others and to respond meaningfully to them. Make sure others can hear you as you speak. Try not to dominate the discussion. If you notice others not participating, you may want to draw them into the conversation. Even a "What do you think, John?" may help to break the ice and encourage participation. Remember, however, just as it is everyone's right to participate, it is also his or her right to choose not to participate.

Participation Activities[39]

Individuals participating in a group should realize that the success of the group depends on each person in the group, not just on the leader. Following are some behaviors that will enable you to function effectively as a participant in group discussion:

Initiate ideas. Having an idea is of no value unless you share it with others. Your idea may help the group reach the best solution.

Seek information. Asking for facts, clarifying ideas, and suggesting what information is needed will aid the group.

Give information. Offer facts, experiences, and evidence that add to the group's knowledge.

Elaborate. Add to the information of others. You may have facts, experiences, and perceptions that the idea's originator may not know.

Energize. Try to keep enthusiasm in the group by encouraging others to speak and reminding all of the importance of the issue.

Support others. Agree with and praise others for participating and offering information.

Harmonize. If disputes erupt, you may want to step in and encourage the combatants to see that the issue at stake is the purpose of the group and not the personal needs of any individual person.

Listen actively. The majority of your time in any group discussion is normally spent listening to others.

Followership

Just as there is so much current interest in developing leadership in organizational development, so, too, is there a new-found interest in understanding and dealing with the concept of **followership,** the group of people who are not in positions of leadership. Organizations have come to realize, as we observed in our discussion of self-managing work teams, that not all individuals are going to be able to move up the corporate ladder to positions of management leadership. Thus, it will be necessary for many members of the work force to find their particular "niche" in an organization and develop their own individual self-management and self-leadership skills. In our investigation on the subject identified individuals need "superleadership" skills to develop self-leadership as organizational followers.[40] Urging that followers receive organizational training just as managers do, one organizational consultant recommends that organizations adapt a partnership concept so that employee followers can contribute their ideas and assume responsibility for the company's effectiveness and success.[41] As an indication of how the followership concept is reaching American industries, one major Washington, D.C. advertising agency has recently put the names of *all* the firm's employees on the door!

To accomplish the maintenance and the task functions in a group discussion, the members must serve as communicators in both participant and leadership capacities and must be aware of other factors affecting the outcome of the group dynamics.

Risky Shift and Group Polarization

Research in group dynamics has identified what has come to be known as the risky shift phenomenon. The desire to build group cohesion can lead to considerable pressure to conform. The **risky shift** concept suggests that decisions reached after discussion by a group are more likely to be based on greater experimentation and will be less conservative. Thus, more risky decisions are likely to be made by groups than by individuals working alone.[42] Other research contradicts the risky shift point of view, however, with results that indicate that there is a tendency for group discussion to enhance the initially dominant point of view held by members before the discussion takes place. Investigators determine that this **group polarization** phenomenon suggests that the average inclination of group members before discussion is generally strengthened by the discussion itself.[43]

Groupthink

Another phenomenon identified in the research has an important impact on the results of group dynamics. It is clear that the pressure for conformity can be overwhelming in a group. The principle of **groupthink** has been defined as "the mode of thinking that persons engage in when concurrence seeking becomes so dominant in a cohesive in-group that it tends to override realistic appraisal of alternative courses of action."[44] Individual members of juries sometimes reveal the tremendous group pressure that can be exerted to reach consensus in a jury decision. Specifically, the tragic Challenger space shuttle disaster reflects an example of the influence of groupthink by NASA's scientists, engineers, and contractors.

Communication Networks

☐ The pressures to conform and the building of group cohesion through task and maintenance functions all affect the dynamics of the group as individuals attempt to communicate with each other in any sort of group discussion. Another significant variable which affects the communication efforts is the **communication network,** the pattern of information flow, that the group utilizes. Early research on communication networks identified five basic forms, as illustrated in figure 12.3. Each of the dots represents an individual communicator. In general, the centralized networks such as the chain and the wheel are most effective for a group to deal with simple problems, while the decentralized networks such as the circle and the all-channel are more effective for solving complex problems. The decentralized networks often can be faster, more accurate, and result in greater member satisfaction.[45] The influence of communication networks would suggest, therefore, that careful attention to seating arrangements can enhance the communication flow in groups.

Time and Place

☐ When and where the group meets may have an effect on the decision-making process. Meetings held very early or extremely late in the day can cause problems. If people feel inconvenienced, they may react negatively, make quick and unfounded decisions,

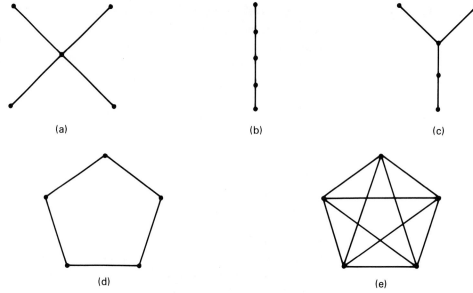

FIGURE 12.3
Communication networks:
(a) wheel, (b) chain, (c) Y,
(d) circle, and (e) all-
channel.

(a)   (b)   (c)

(d)   (e)

or avoid participation. The length of a meeting can also have an effect, for as time drags on, people can become irritated, distracted, and bored. It may be more effective to have several short meetings rather than one very long one. It is often wise to schedule a coffee break during long sessions. Even a physical break to allow participants to stand up and stretch can be helpful. A leader of a group should watch for such verbal and nonverbal signs as temper flares and fidgeting as indicators that the meeting has gone on for too long.

As the communication networks demonstrate, seating arrangements can create either verbal interaction or verbal vacuums. Placing chairs in a circle or in a U can encourage communication. When people can see each other, can directly confront each other, or do not have to speak around someone else, they are more likely to participate. A long, narrow table can divide people—the left side of the table against the right side, or one end of the table against the other. The table can make the chair placement such that we can directly see and contact only those to our right, our left, and across the table. This may be an effective arrangement for a formal session but not for one in which great interaction is desired.

The place of the meeting can also contribute to the results. Having a session in any area where people can be disrupted or interrupted may create difficulties. Some businesses purposely take their groups to hotels or other off-sites for special meeting sessions so that the normal routine of the office will not create disturbances. The corporation's cafeteria may be a great place to have lunch or a casual conversation, but it won't lend itself well to a task-oriented meeting.

Taking into consideration the time of day, the time available, where the meeting is to be held, and the seating arrangements of the participants can help ensure a more effective task-oriented session.

SUMMARY   In this chapter we have examined group communication in the business setting. These are the major concepts discussed:

Many of the decisions made within businesses and organizations are the products of group action.

Small groups usually contain five to seven people.

A sense of commitment is a positive result of allowing individuals to work in groups to make business decisions.

To derive benefits from a small group, a clearly-defined communication purpose must be agreed upon.

Purposes of groups include social activities, therapeutic sessions, information sharing, value analysis, and decision making.

Groups within an organization most commonly meet in private.

Private group discussions can be informal, round table discussions, brainstorming sessions, or buzz sessions.

A structured buzz session format is the "1-3-6 Decision-Making Technique."

The Quality Circle is a small group of workers who meet on a regular basis to discuss work-related problems and possible solutions.

Teleconferencing is becoming a popular business meeting process.

Conferences are large groups which meet to share professional information, discuss issues, or conduct business.

Forms of public discussions include panel discussions, symposiums, and forums.

The general functions of a group are characterized as maintenance functions and task functions.

The leader is the person who guides the group through the decision-making process.

There are three types of leader styles: authoritarian, democratic, and laissez-faire.

Leader roles include that of coordinator, facilitator, trainer, observer, gap-filler, and monitor.

The leadership is the individual who influences the group in the decision-making process.

The members of a group should know the plan or the rules under which they will operate.

An agenda is an outline, or a plan, indicating the order in which the group will conduct its discussion.

Most formal organizational meetings will operate under parliamentary procedure, most commonly *Robert's Rules of Order*.

The most typical methods of voting or reaching agreement are by majority, plurality, part-of-the-whole, and consensus.

It is the right and the responsibility of group members to take an active part in the decision-making process.

A hidden agenda is the underlying objective of a member of a group that may hinder effective group action.

The time and place of a meeting may affect its outcome.

THINGS TO DO

1. You have participated in small-group discussions (club meetings, for example). Think back to an occasion. What problems did you encounter? Make a list of problems that plagued your group and caused difficulty in accomplishing your tasks. In class, discuss your observations and share conclusions on how the obstacles might have been overcome.

2. You have read about effective group discussion. What is meant by "effective" as it relates to task-oriented groups?

3. Many companies are attempting to act as the primary group source for their employees. Through research in business journals, magazines, and newspapers, and discussion with businesspeople, try to find specific instances in which the companies are accomplishing their primary group source role. Do the same for the social group role of companies.

4. Each student in the class should decide on a business-oriented topic that lends itself to a discussion (e.g., What is Management By Objectives?). Students should bring the topics to class. You will be divided into smaller groups. Each group, using the suggestions of its members, should decide on a topic it feels the class will be interested in learning more about, develop an agenda, and conduct a twenty-minute class discussion, following that agenda.

5. This text discusses four different methods of voting commonly used by groups. What are the advantages and disadvantages of each of the methods? Discuss the method you would prefer in the following situations:
   a. The employees' credit union is electing its officers.
   b. The president of the company's Board of Directors is to be elected.
   c. A proposal has been made to your union for a new salary and fringe benefits package.
   d. The executive board of a union to which you belong recommends a strike. The membership must decide whether or not to honor the call for the work stoppage.
   e. A vote is being taken on whether or not the corporation for which you work will merge with another corporation.
   f. A decision is being made by the executive management team on whether or not to phase out an entire product line.

6. Your class should adopt a project in decision making. You are to develop a realistic project and then carry out the decision agreed upon. Use the "1-3-6 Decision-Making Technique" to decide on the project to be undertaken. After making the project selection, carry it out and test the results.

7. Conduct an interview with two persons in business who hold positions of leadership. Focus your questions on finding out the most common communication problems they encounter, how the communication problems are dealt with, and how they could be prevented. Based on your interview, meet with members of the small group your instructor will select. Plan for a discussion based on the topic, "Communication problems confronted by persons in business leadership positions."

8. Formulate ten commandments that would aid individuals who will participate in small-group discussions. Share these with the class. If your instructor de-

sires, you may use the 1-3-6 method to formulate "Ten Commandments for Effective Small-Group Discussions" with the entire class participating.

9. You are in a leadership position in a company.
    a. Do you feel that it is good practice to present the conclusion you want the group to reach and then guide its members to that conclusion? Why or why not?
    b. You have recently been appointed to your position. How do you go about establishing yourself as a leader at your first meeting with those who are directly below you in the corporate structure?

10. The class will be divided into small groups. Each group is to pick one of the following business-oriented topics and prepare an outline for a discussion. Each group is to carry out and tape-record the discussion. Submit the tape to your instructor. Your instructor will listen to the discussion, meet with each group at an assigned time, and critique the material covered and the techniques used.
    a. Automation and the worker.
    b. The role of labor unions in business and industry.
    c. White collar theft.
    d. Data processing in industry.
    e. Outlawing strikes.
    f. Spiraling costs-of-living and how they affect industry.
    g. Advertising as a means of product sales.
    h. The morality of advertising.
    i. Television as an influence on business image.
    j. The effect of clothing on employee perception.
    k. Women in business and industry.
    l. Reverse discrimination as a problem in corporations.
    m. Internal and external communication in the organization.
    n. Mergers and their effects on the organization.

NOTES

1. See the discussion of the grapevine in chapter 1 of this text for a more detailed explanation of the effect of informal channels of communication in the organization.
2. Paul O. Lovett, "Meetings That Work: Plans Bosses Can Approve," *Harvard Business Review* 6 (November–December 1988): 38.
3. Ibid, 39.
4. The nominal group technique, developed by Andre Delbecq and Andrew H. Vande Ven, is described in Joseph Conlin, "Who's Running This Show Anyway?" *Successful Meetings* (December 1987): 43.
5. Adapted by Roy Berko from Eileen Breckenridge, "Improving School Climate," *Phi Delta Kappan* (December 1976): 314–318.
6. In our definition of small groups, the size of the group was described as "usually 5–6." Since the 1-3-6 procedure was designed for groups ideally divisible by 3, we recognize there may be some difficulty in getting exactly 3 into each group. Minor modifications will not affect the outcome of the process.

7. Arnold Kanarick, "The Far Side of Quality Circle," *Management Review* 70 (October 1981): 16–17.

8. Gregory P. Shea, "Quality Circles: The Danger of Bottled Change," *Sloan Management Review* (Spring 1986): 33–43.

9. Berkeley Rice, "Square Holes for Quality Circles," *Psychology Today* (February 1984): 17, as based on a study done by Woodruff Imberman.

10. Hobart Rowan, "The Japanese Advantage," *Washington Post* 11 October 1981, G2.

11. Ibid., G3.

12. "Success of Intensive Care Depends on Teamwork," *Washington Post "Health"* (15 March, 1986): 5.

13. "Liaison: Key to Effective Teamwork," *The Office Professional,* 7 (15 November, 1987): 1.

14. Carl McDaniel, "Focus Groups—Their Role in the Marketing Research Process," *Akron Business and Economic Review* (Winter, 1979): 14–19.

15. Kathleen Wagoner and Mary Ruprecht, *Office Automation: A Management Approach* (New York: John Wiley and Sons, 1984), 157.

16. Ibid.

17. Mary Bergerud and Jean Gonzalez, *Word/Information Processing,* 2nd ed (New York: John Wiley and Sons, 1984), 157.

18. Ibid., 226.

19. Ibid., 228.

20. Bonnie Roe White, "Teleconferencing: Its Potential in the Modern Office," *Century 21 Reporting* (Fall 1984): 5.

21. For an extensive discussion of teleconferencing, see Eleanor Tedesco and Robert Mitchell, *Administrative Office Management—the Electronic Office* (New York: John Wiley and Sons, 1984), 388–407.

22. Wagoner and Ruprecht, 158.

23. Ibid.

24. White, "Teleconferencing," 6.

25. Kenneth O. Benne and Paul Sheats, "Functional Roles of Group Members," *Journal of Social Issues,* 4 (1948): 41–49.

26. Roy Berko, Andrew Wolvin, and Darlyn Wolvin, *Communicating: A Social and Career Focus* (Boston: Houghton Mifflin, 1989), 329.

27. For a review of approaches to leadership, see Stewart L. Tubbs, *A Systems Approach to Small Group Interaction,* 3rd edition (New York: Random House, 1988), 148–155.

28. Ralph White and Ronald Lippitt, *Autocracy and Democracy* (New York: Harper and Row, 1960).

29. Fred Fiedler, *A Theory of Leadership Effectiveness* (New York: McGraw-Hill, 1967).

30. William H. Franklin, "What Japanese Managers Know That American Managers Don't," *Administrative Management* 49 (September 1981): 52.

31. Alvin P. Sanoff, "Who Will Lead 'This New Breed' of Americans?" *U.S. News and World Report* (15 March 1982), 80–81; and Michael Maccoby, *The Leader: A New Face for American Management* (Washington, DC: Project Technology, Work and Character).

32. Warren Bennis, "The Artform of Leadership," *Training and Development Journal* 36 (April 1982): 45.

33. Based on Patricia Bradley, "Effective Questioning—Group Discussion," unpublished paper, Indiana University.

34. Ernest Stech and Sharon Ratliffe, *Working in Groups* (Skokie, IL: National Textbook Company, 1976), 220–221.

35. Lynda M. Applegate, James I. Cash, Jr., and D. Quinn Mills, "Information Technology and Tomorrow's Manager," *Harvard Business Review,* 6 (November–December 1988): 128–136.

36. Sarah Corbin Robert, *Robert's Rules of Order,* newly revised. (Glenview, IL: Scott Foresman and Company, 1970), 339.

37. Ibid., 343.

38. The term *consensus* has been accepted in everyday communication to mean *generally agree.* Specifically, in such instances as murder trials and in specialized situations, it takes its official meaning of *unanimity,* or *all of those participating.*

39. John Brilhart, *Effective Group Discussion,* 4th ed (Dubuque: William C. Brown, 1982,) p. 100.

40. Charles C. Manz and Henry P. Sims *Superleaders: Leading Others to Lead Themselves* (Englewood Cliffs: Prentice-Hall), 1989.

41. Pam Carroll, "Good Followers Are Worth Training," *Nation's Business* (September 1988): 54–55. See also Robert E. Kelley, "In Praise of Followers," *Harvard Business Review* 6 (November–December, 1988): 142–148.

42. J. A. F. Stoner, "Comparison of Individual and Group Decisions Involving Risk," (M.A. thesis, Massachusetts Institute of Technology, School of Industrial Management, 1961).

43. David G. Meyers, *Social Psychology* (New York: McGraw-Hill, 1987), 337–346.

44. Irving Janis, *Victims of Groupthink* (Boston: Houghton Mifflin, 1972), 8.

45. H. J. Leavitt, "Some Effects of Certain Communication Patterns on Group Performance," *Journal of Abnormal and Social Psychology* 46 (1951): 38–50.

13 □ Planning the Public Speech Presentation

Individuals in the field of business often give speeches before groups of people. Each speaking situation has participants, a setting, and a purpose. Audience analysis is an important consideration in all speeches. Speakers must find and use various types of information to develop the presentation.

KEY WORDS

participants
setting
place
time
emotional climate
purpose
purpose statement
function
structure

self-knowledge
research information
interview
citations
oral footnote
bibliography
quote
paraphrase

Individuals involved in the field of business often find themselves speaking before groups of people. These speeches may be presented to members of their own organization (referred to as a presentation), to groups with whom the company carries on business, or to public groups who have requested information about business-related matters. If the speaker is successful, the company may benefit from increased sales, good public relations, or better products or policies. The speaker also benefits, especially if the outcomes are promotions, increased sales, increased pay, positive self-concept, or the praise from others for successful accomplishment. The odds of an individual being a successful speaker increase as the person becomes aware of how to plan and present a speech effectively.

PARAMETERS OF SPEAKING

■

Every communicative situation contains three parameters: the participants, the setting, and the purpose. In public communication, the speaker should know and consider these factors, or the goal(s) of the speech may not be accomplished.

Prospective speakers who have had little exposure to audiences and the ways in which they respond (or do not respond) to speeches often overlook the vital step of analyzing the audience, the setting, and the purpose. People pay little attention to presentations that don't interest them or which they don't see as relevant to making their lives better or more complete. Therefore, it is imperative that the topic selected be of interest to the audience.

Speakers must also be sure that the speech topic selected and the channels to be used are appropriate for the place where they will speak. If a room cannot be darkened, then a speech which depends upon the use of slides is not going to be possible.

In some cases, knowing the setting will allow the speaker to make arrangements for equipment not usually available in the speaking area. It may be necessary to order or bring in machinery such as a slide projector, film projector, or tape recorder. Is there a blackboard if one will be needed? Is there a stand to hold any graphics that may be used?

To analyze the audience and the setting, you should consider the following questions when planning a speech:[1]

1. Who is your audience?
2. What does the audience need or expect from the presentation?
3. What do you know about your audience?
4. As a source, what impressions does the audience already have of you?
5. What impressions will you try to create or modify?
6. What channels will you use?
7. What kind of feedback do you expect based on the topic and your intended purpose?
8. If you are giving a persuasive speech, is there something you should know about the members of audience in order to fit your appeals to them?
9. Based on the audience analysis, what kind of personal background, definition

of terms, and historical information will you have to include in order to make sure the audience will understand the presentation?

10. Are there any special materials, seating arrangements, or equipment you will need for the presentation?

The Participants

☐

The **participants** in a communicative event consist of those persons who are taking part in the message-sending and receiving: the speaker and the audience members. In analyzing the audience, the speaker might want to consider age, sex, religion, cultural background, intellectual level, occupation, race, political affiliations, and social and economic levels. An analysis of these factors helps the speaker select the topic, the language, and the types of examples and clarification that will be needed to accomplish the goal.

If you are representing your organization at a career-planning seminar for teenagers, the topic you select would be quite different than if you were speaking to a group of senior citizens. Speakers often select or reject examples that appeal to an audience based on its religious or ethnic beliefs. Using examples of Israeli business successes might be very appropriate in a speech about business practices in emerging countries presented to a primarily Jewish audience, while using that same example before a group composed largely of Arabs might bring about negative reactions. The educational and intellectual background of a certain audience might allow for assumptions that it is familiar with the topic you are speaking about and needs little background, while another audience might require extensive historical information and numerous definitions of terms. Speaking to a group of certified public accountants about the legal aspects of accounting principles is not the same as speaking to prospective college accounting majors. Speaking about the long-range effects of stock and bond investment to a group of wealthy businesspersons may be quite appropriate, but that same topic would be unsuitable for an audience composed of welfare recipients.

It is important to know something of the values of your intended listeners—what it is that they consider to be important, of worth to them personally and as a group. For example, in speaking to a group of fairly representative Americans, it might be helpful to know the results of a survey in which a representative group of Americans were asked about their hopes and fears. The researchers discovered the following categories (according to the percentage of respondents who referred to each topic):[2]

Personal Hopes
Better or decent standard of living 39%
Good health for self 22%
Economic stability in general; no inflation 13%
Happy family life 11%
Peace of mind, emotional maturity 11%
Own a home or live in a better one 9%
Peace in the world 8%
Aspirations for children 8%

Good job; congenial work 8%
Wealth 7%
Employment 7%
Good health for family 6%
Be a normal, decent person 5%

Personal Fears
Lower standard of living 32%
Ill health for self 18%
War 16%
Economic instability in general; inflation 15%
Unemployment 14%
Ill health of family 6%
Crime 5%

National Hopes
Economic stability; no inflation 37%
Peace 28%
Employment; jobs for all 26%
Improved standard of living; greater national prosperity 18%
Law and order 10%
Better world 6%
Resolution of energy crisis 6%
National unity and political stability 5%
Friendly relations with countries 5%

National Fears
War 41%
Economic instability; inflation 33%
Unemployment 15%
Lack of law an order 11%
Threat of communism 8%
No improvement in, or inadequate, standard of living 7%
National disunity or political instability 5%
Energy crisis 5%

People will listen to topics which are of direct interest to them or that affect them. They are most likely to want to listen if they think they can gain information, lead a better life, save money, or gain spiritually. If the language used is at a level they can understand, they are more likely to listen. If the examples given are vivid, clear, and aid in holding their attention, they are likely to listen. In other words, it is no accident when public speakers are successful. They work at it by analyzing their audiences and trying to figure out ways to make those assembled want to listen to what they have to say. Before going out to speak or even planning the presentation, find out as much as you can about the audience.

The Setting

☐

The **setting** of a speech consists of the place, the time, and the emotional climate.

Place

The **place,** where the presentation is given, is another factor affecting a speech. The size of the room, the temperature, the furniture arrangement, and the number of people present may make a difference in what is said and how it is presented. Before going out to speak, ask questions about the place.

It may be difficult to hear in a large room, so you may need a microphone. Plans usually have to be made in advance to get a microphone. It is very difficult to create a feeling of intimacy in an auditorium. If your topic and presentation would be ineffective if presented in a large setting, then you may need to select an alternate subject.

The use of visual aids may be difficult if the room is very large, there are no electrical outlets, or the room cannot be darkened. Demonstrating something that must be viewed by everyone may be very difficult if everyone cannot assemble within seeing distance. Again, this might necessitate a change in topic or method of presentation. Unless the speaker knows and takes into account the setting, the effectiveness of the presentation may be diminished or destroyed.

Be aware of the temperature of the room. It is difficult to concentrate when you are overly hot or cold. If possible, try to have the temperature adjusted to make it comfortable in the room. Opening windows and turning on or off heat and air conditioning, though not usually the responsibility of the speaker, may be necessary. If the temperature is a problem and nothing can be done about it, it might be wise to shorten your presentation.

If you feel that the placement of the furniture in the room will affect your speech, request the suitable arrangement. You may have to ask members of the audience to move around, form groups, or communicate with each other as part of your speech. If they are sitting around tables or on chairs that are attached to the floor, it may be impossible for the audience to fulfill your needs. Do you want interaction? People sitting in a circle tend to interact more than those sitting in straight rows. People seated at tables with their backs to you may be in awkward positions to create eye contact with you, causing frustration for both you and the audience members. It is wise to check on the seating configuration, for it may affect your topic choice, the types of activities you request from the audience, and the types of visual aids you use or had hoped to use.

The number of people present also should be considered. If you are planning on having audience participation and a large number of people are present, chaos may result. People jammed into a small, confined area respond differently than that same number of people comfortably seated in a room with suitable space. As you proceed through your speech, watch the audience for feedback that would allow you to shorten the presentation if you find those present are getting uncomfortable because of the crunch of human bodies, poor ventilation, or inadequate sound or lighting.

Time

There are two considerations concerning **time:** how long and what time of day. A popular speaker's adage is: the mind can only absorb what the seat can endure. This suggests that an audience will sit still for only so long before it becomes inattentive, uncomfortable, and sometimes outwardly hostile. We have all sat through speeches, sermons, or tributes that were just too long. There is no set rule for how long a speech should be. The basic guide is that it should effectively cover the material that must be presented in order to accomplish the goal. It should be long enough not to frustrate the listener by failing to develop the ideas and, therefore, cause irritation because of the lack of understanding. That, of course, is very little help in deciding exactly how long to speak. A basic rule might be that each major subject you are dealing with should be covered in about fifteen or twenty minutes. If you are taking more time than that, you may be trying to say too much. Remember that the listener's attention span is actually quite limited and probably affected by the need to take a "commercial break" every 7 to 10 minutes.

One specific consideration is whether there is an agreed-upon time limit to which you should adhere. If the group to whom you are speaking has one-half hour set aside for you, make sure you keep within that limit. Many clubs and organizations that invite businesspeople to speak are set up as lunchtime groups, for example. Going over the time limit and stopping these people from getting back to their places of employment might cause long-term hostility toward you and the organization you represent. Or, if your supervisor has allotted you ten minutes to explain a new procedure and you ramble well beyond that time, the "brilliant" proposal may be ignored out of negative reaction to your time usage. Some professional speakers suggest that there is no such thing as a bad *short* speech. Consider this and try to be as short as possible while being aware of your end goal. Don't be brief just to be brief, but do be brief if you can accomplish your goal quickly.

The time of day may likewise influence topic selection and the length of your speech. Speaking very early, just before lunch, at the end of the workday, or very late at night could all cause attention problems. Again, take this into consideration in planning and use the clock and general attitude of the audience as cues in deciding how long to speak and when the audience is reaching its listening limit.

Emotional Climate

Taking into consideration the **emotional climate,** the attitude of the people you are going to address, may allow you to be more successful in accomplishing your goal. Usually audiences are open and receptive to an effective speaker. Sometimes, however, the topic selected, the affiliations of the listeners or the speaker, or the circumstances under which the speech is being given may create a negative climate.

With present public distrust of certain large corporations (such as utility, petroleum, and automobile manufacturers), representatives of those firms may encounter hostile audiences. Salespersons, because of their reputation for manipulative practices, are also sometimes suspect. You may be presenting information about a subject that will negatively alter the way of life, the environment, or the livelihood of your audience.

The emotional attitude of the audience members can have an effect on the effectiveness of the speech. (© Bob Coyle)

In all these cases, careful planning to try to alleviate fears, develop a positive rapport with the audience, and diffuse the potential attackers becomes necessary.

One of the best methods of handling negative perceptions is to recognize them and to try to explain your organization's or your point of view. If rumors are circulating concerning some matter, try to confront the issue rather than skirting it. There is an old saying about not being able to fool all of the people all of the time. With television coverage, consumer activism, and general public distrust of big business, many people simply are not going to be fooled by avoidance of the issues or double-talking around the issue.

The Purpose and Purpose Statement

☐ Once the general topic has been decided upon, the speaker may want to set a clear **purpose,** the response he or she wants from the audience. If you are not exactly sure what you want from the audience, the odds of accomplishing much are very doubtful. Speakers sometimes appear before an audience, aimlessly wander through a presentation, and then wonder why the audience did not get the message or take the desired action. There probably was no message to get, no clear idea of the action to take. Most successful speakers word a **purpose statement** that specifically indicates the exact topic of the speech and what the speaker wants from the audience. The two parts of a purpose statement are called the function and the structure.

The **function** of a speech is the desired response wanted from the audience—a value change, an attitude alteration, or a behavior confirmation. The general purposes of a speech are to inform or to persuade. The **structure** of the speech is a statement of the exact topic and sometimes the method to be used for developing the body of the presentation. Samples of purpose statements are:

> To inform the Executive Board of the three phases of advertising to be used in marketing our new product, Sassy Soap, by investigating the newspaper, magazine, and television campaigns.
>
> To persuade the members of the Vehicle Recommendation Committee of the Harlan Manufacturing Company to purchase their new fleet of trucks from XYZ Auto Sales because of our special leasing policy, twenty-four hour service guarantee, and thirty-day delivery plan.

In both of these purpose statements, the audience, the specific nature of the desired audience response, and the exact topic are clearly stated. All material included in the presentation should lead to gaining the stated effect.

In preparing the purpose statement, the speaker should attempt to analyze the audience so that he or she can be guided in the approach to take in developing the material, the type of approach to take, and the language to be used.

Stating the exact purpose, whether it is to inform or persuade, allows the speaker to focus on the way in which the speech will be developed so that it is clear to the listeners.

It is wise to use an exact word in the purpose statement to key the method you are going to use to develop the speech. Key words for informing are: analyze, compare, contrast, demonstrate, describe, discuss, explain, identify, list, show, state, and summarize. Persuasive terms include: to accept, to agree, to buy, to contribute, to defend, to disagree with, to follow, to help, to join, to lend, to participate in, to react to, to select, to serve, to support, to switch to, to volunteer, to vote for.

This narrowing of the subject allows for a treatment of an exact topic and prevents the speaker from wandering off into areas not specified in the purpose statement. The clearer the purpose statement, the clearer the speech probably will be for the listeners.

SOURCES OF INFORMATION

■

Self-knowledge

☐   In most instances, business speakers select a topic or are asked to present information about areas with which they are familiar. If this is the case, the speaker should list all of his or her **self-knowledge,** the information known about the topic. It is not a good idea to start writing out sentences and paragraphs at this point: simply list the ideas you want to include. Many speakers find it advisable to collect their ideas over several sittings, if the time is available. In this way, you often can add ideas you had not thought about the first time. If, after sorting through your ideas, you feel that there is enough information present to proceed, then you should start organizing your thoughts. If, however, you feel that you have to turn to outside sources for more information, then start doing some research before actually structuring the speech.

Research Information

☐   If you are not an expert on your topic, you may have to turn to **research information,** sources who or which provide information about the topic.

Print and Recorded Sources

Since most individuals do not have extensive collections of resources in their homes, they may turn to the library as their research source. Having working knowledge of what is contained and how things are placed in the library may allow you to find information you may not have otherwise been able to unearth.

Theories on how to begin researching a topic abound. One concept is that if you are dealing with an unfamiliar topic, you should start by looking in an index. Indexes list ideas in alphabetical order, usually in summarized form. By referring to an encyclopedia, you can obtain general information about a subject. If it is knowledge about a person, one of the *Who's Who* sources could give you ideas. Geographical information is found in an atlas. Statistics are available in such sources as *Facts on File, Book of Facts,* and *American Statistics Index.*

Many researchers go immediately to the card catalog. Since the card catalog lists the book sources held by the library, this may be a good place to start. Unfortunately, since the card catalog is organized by book titles, authors, and subject areas, it may be difficult for you to find what you are looking for unless you have specific information to use as a basis for your search. A good strategy is to make a list of all possible headings under which you might find information on the topic in the card catalog. You might find material on personnel management, for instance, under such topics as *personnel, management, human resource development,* and *employment.*

The researcher should pay attention to the publication dates of books. If you need current information, it may be impossible to find books that are up-to-date enough about the topic. If this is the case, magazines may be a valuable source. General magazines (*Time, Newsweek, People*) are listed in the *Reader's Guide to Periodical Lit-*

erature. By looking under the subject area, the specific article title, or name of the author, you will be able to find the name of the magazine, date of publication, and page number. However, not all magazines are listed in the *Reader's Guide to Periodical Literature.* Business and related information can be found in *Business Periodicals Index, The Applied Science and Technology Index,* and *The Public Affairs Information Service.* Magazines containing business-oriented information include *Fortune, Forbes, Business Week, Nation's Business, Harvard Business Review,* and *Management Review.*

Numerous professional organizations publish pamphlets and informational documents. Those specifically dealing with business topics include the American Management Association and the Society for Advancement of Management.[3] Many libraries order documents published by these and other organizations. If not, information may be obtained by writing directly to the publisher or organization.

Newspapers contain current information. They are published daily, weekly, or bi-weekly. Because of the speed with which they are written, and the fact that much of what is contained in newspapers is biased by publication policies or the attitudes of writers, one must be careful in using this source. Copies of many newspapers are currently kept in libraries on microfilm. In order to be able to use the information, you must have the name of the newspaper and the dates when the articles appeared. This can be obtained for the *New York Times,* for example, by referring to the *New York Times Index.* Indexes of most widely circulated newspapers are available in large libraries. For local news sources, a phone call or a visit to the desired newspaper's office may get you into their morgue, which is the library at the newspaper where past articles they have printed are stored.

The federal government, as well as state and local governments, print information concerning legislative actions as well as general information. The United States Government Printing Office, which has branches in many large cities, distributes information at a minimal charge. The publication *Monthly Catalog of U.S. Government Publications* lists all materials produced. If there is no office in your area, information can be obtained by writing to the Superintendent of Documents, United States Government Printing Office, Washington, D.C. Many members of the House of Representatives and the Senate have offices in the districts they represent. A telephone call to that office may result in obtaining the desired materials or information.

Special interest groups publish data concerning various topics. The names of some of these organizations appear in the yellow pages of local telephone books. A phone call or letter to the group will usually result in their forwarding information or leading you to other sources.

Besides printed materials, information is available via nonprint media. Libraries and audio-visual departments of colleges and universities and local school district libraries have catalogs that list films, records, videotapes, and filmstrips from commercially and locally prepared sources covering various topics. Many businesses and industries produce their own training materials and public relations materials and are often willing to lend them or rent them.

Interviews

Besides print and nonprint materials, it is often advisable to conduct an **interview** by speaking or corresponding with individuals who are knowledgeable in a specific field. Indeed, these persons may provide you with the most helpful, current information. A source file of "experts" to whom you can turn for information may save you considerable time and effort when you have to develop a speech. Another excellent source is the telephone book. The yellow pages have listings of various organizations, businesses, and clubs that may provide the information you need. These interviews may be in person, over the telephone, or through a letter or questionnaire. The main purpose of this approach is to allow you to obtain direct access to specific information that has not been published, needs to be expanded upon, or to get clarification of published materials.

Research Note-Taking

☐ It is important as you are taking notes while researching that you record **citations** (the sources of the information). When putting the speech together, it is often necessary to include oral footnotes, especially if you feel that you, as the source, need to enhance your credibility by references to other authorities. Often these authorities must be identified for the listeners, as the audience may be unfamiliar with them.

An **oral footnote** identifies the source of the materials. It usually includes the writer's or the speaker's name and where the statement was made or written. In addition, the speaker may choose to credit the credentials of the source. An example of an oral footnote would be "Sandy Linver in her book, *Speak Easy: How to Talk Your Way to the Top,* advises business speakers that the major cause of stage fright is that most people feel that their public speaking situation demands that they be another person, someone who's perfect." If the speaker felt that Ms. Linver needed to be more completely established as an authority, the oral footnote might have been "Sandy Linver, who heads an Atlanta, Georgia, firm that teaches business executives to become more effective speakers, has recently published a book entitled, *Speak Easy: How to Talk Your Way to the Top.* In the book Ms. Linver advises that the major cause of stage fright is that, "Most . . . perfect."

It is wise to keep a **bibliography** that lists the source used, the name(s) of the authors, and the place and date of publication. Some speakers, in doing research, list their sources on a sheet of paper as they use them. They identify each source by a number and, on each note card or piece of paper that contains a reference to the source, identify it with a number. A sample of that is on the following page.

As you take notes, the information you find in a source would be designated by the number on the bibliography list, followed by the page on which the information appears. A "1–15" would indicate that the material was found in the Makay book on page 15. If the material is a **quote** (taken from the source word for word) quotation marks would appear around the entry. If it is put in your own words (a **paraphrase**), then no quotation marks would appear.

BIBLIOGRAPHY

1. Makay, John. *Speaking with an Audience*. New York: T.Y. Crowell, 1977.
2. Berko, Roy, Wolvin, Andrew, and Wolvin, Darlyn. *Communicating: A Social and Career Focus*. Boston: Houghton Mifflin, 1977.
3. Ochs, Donovan and Winkler, Anthony. *A Brief Introduction to Speech*. New York: Harcourt Brace Jovanovich, 1979.

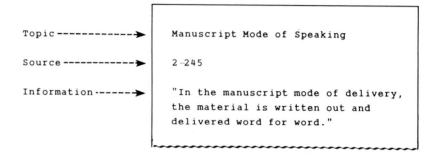

Topic ————————➤ | Manuscript Mode of Speaking

Source ———————➤ | 2–245

Information ———➤ | "In the manuscript mode of delivery, the material is written out and delivered word for word."

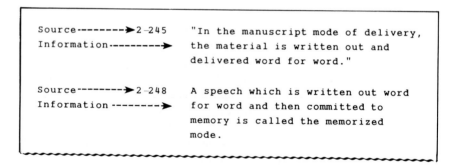

Source ————➤ 2–245 | "In the manuscript mode of delivery, the material is written out and delivered word for word."
Information ———➤

Source ————➤ 2–248 | A speech which is written out word for word and then committed to memory is called the memorized mode.
Information ———➤

Many researchers like to use three-by-five or four-by-six-inch cards for taking notes. They put one major idea on a card and identify the card with the general topic on the first line, followed by the source, then the information. A note card would look like this:

Other researchers prefer to take notes on sheets of paper, identifying the source in the left-hand margin, and then cut the paper into strips for use later. This form would look like this:

Whatever method you use for recording information, careful research is often an important step for any speaker in developing a substantial, effective presentation.

SUMMARY

In this chapter we have investigated the planning of a public speech. The major ideas presented were these:

Individuals involved in the field of business often find themselves speaking before groups of people.

Every communicative situation contains three parameters: the participants, the setting, and the purpose.

In analyzing the audience, the speaker might want to consider the factors of age, sex, religion, cultural background, intellectual level, occupation, race, political affiliations, and social and economic levels.

Setting considerations are the place, the time, the time available, and the emotional climate.

A speaker should set a clear purpose—the response he or she wants from the audience.

The two ideas present in a purpose statement are the function and the structure.

Information presented in a speech may be derived from self-knowledge, research information, or interviews.

A working knowledge of what is available in a library and where to find it is invaluable to a researcher.

It is important as you are taking notes during research that you record citations (the sources of the information).

An oral footnote is used during a speech to identify the source of the research materials used in the presentation.

A bibliography lists the sources used in preparing a speech.

THINGS TO DO

1. Using your class as your audience, write an audience analysis that could be used as the basis for planning a speech. Use the suggestions given in the text for audience analysis as the basis for your conclusions.

2. Write a purpose statement for a speech to inform the class about some phase of your college major or a business-related topic. Go to the library. Find quotations from the following sources regarding the topic: three quotations from different books; two quotations from magazines; one index quotation or diagram; and one quotation from either a newspaper, a government pamphlet, or a professional organizational document. Record your findings, using the running bibliography note card method described in the chapter.

3. Write two oral footnotes, using the information you collected doing the research for question 2. Hand these in on note cards with your research from question 2.

4. Find two research sources in which you can find material on each of the following topics. Indicate the author of the material, the title of the source, the publication date, the publisher, and the page number.

   a. Management By Objectives.
   b. The merger of the AFL and the CIO.
   c. The history of General Electric Company.
   d. The population of the United States according to the last census.

e. The population of the United States (estimated) as of last year.

f. The United States Gross National Product of last year.

g. The effect of the grapevine on business and industries.

h. A description of a personnel director's job in a typical large corporation.

i. The name of the chairman of the Board of Directors of General Motors, United States Steel, and IBM.

j. Scientific Management (sometimes called the Classical Theory of Organization) is a movement which began before World War I.

k. Where the Wharton School of Business is located.

l. A description of *downward communication* (sometimes called the top-down process).

m. The names of last year's ten largest corporations in the United States, according to net incomes.

NOTES

1. Mary Vielhaber, J. Janelle Shubert, "Communication Coaching for the Executive: A Process Analysis" (Paper presented at the Speech Communication Association Convention, Chicago, November, 1984).

2. William Watts, "Americans' Hopes and Fears: The Future Can Fend for Itself," *Psychology Today* (September 1981):36–48.

3. The address of both the American Management Association and the Society for the Advancement of Management is 135 West 50th Street, New York, New York 10020.

14

□

Preparing the
Public Speech
or Presentation

OVERVIEW   A public speech has four parts: introduction, statement of the central idea, body, and the conclusion. Speeches should be developed with supporting ideas and, when necessary, supplementary aids. Properly prepared notes aid a speaker in being effective.

KEY WORDS
introduction
statement of central idea
body
conclusion
attention-getter
exposition
chronological order
spatial order
topical order
causal arrangement
contrast
comparison
comparison-contrast
problem-solution format
motivated sequence
critical reasoning structure
comparative advantage reasoning
transition

illustrations
specific instances
clarifiers
statistics
analogies
testimony
expert
didactic method
method of implication
oral footnote
supplementary aids
visual aids
audio aids
audio-visual aids
summary
clincher
working outline

The speaker has analyzed the audience, chosen the general topic, narrowed the topic to a purpose statement, completed the research, and assembled the necessary information. Now it is time to start putting the speech together. There are four basic parts to a public speech: introduction, statement of central idea, body, and conclusion. The **introduction** gains the audience's attention and may include exposition, or general background material. The **statement of the central idea** allows the audience to know where the speech is going. It sometimes forecasts the pattern for the speech. The **body** develops the major points of the speech in some logical order. The **conclusion** summarizes the major ideas by pulling the thoughts together.

THE INTRODUCTION

■

How long does it take for you to decide you don't want to watch that television show or listen to that radio station? It doesn't take very long, and once you have changed the show or the station, it is nearly impossible to get you back again. This same idea illustrates the importance of the introduction, the first part of a speech. Members of an audience quickly decide whether they are going to like, dislike, or even listen to a speaker. The decision may be based on something as simple as the speaker's clothing, the expression on the speaker's face just before starting, the speaker's stance, or the speaker's use of eye contact while delivering the first line. Yet believe it or not, these things turn us on or off and will be dealt with when we discuss the speech presentation. One of the most important factors, however, is what the speaker says during the first several seconds. If the speaker does not get the listener's attention almost immediately, everything that follows may be lost. If a listener does not understand what is being said because of a lack of background, confusion may result and the speech may be turned off or tuned out.

Attention-Getter

☐

In order to avoid these problems, the speaker should start the speech with an **attention-getter,** a type of introductory devise which grabs the attention of the audience.

Types of Attention-Getters
Personal references, humorous stories, illustrations, references to the occasion or setting, rhetorical or action questions, unusual or dramatic devices, and quotations are types of introductory devices used to get an audience's attention.

Personal Experience   The speaker may want to tell why a particular topic was selected and present some personal background, connection, or feelings about the topic. A time-study person who has discovered a new method for production might start out explaining how involvement in the project began, which then brought about the discovery. An accountant might want to share a special educational background and training in tax law with the audience before explaining what effects the new governmental regulations will have on corporate accounting procedures.

A listener may become confused if a speaker does not organize the speech clearly. (© Robert Eckert)

Humorous Stories   Humorous stories are often an effective way to start a presentation. People like to laugh, and humor creates a nice, relaxed atmosphere. Remember, however, that if you are giving a serious speech, you might get a negative reaction later in the presentation if your opening indicates that you are going to be funny. You should also be careful to select a story that fits the audience and will not insult or belittle its members, unless this is your intent. You do not have to be a comedy writer to use humor. Many good books have been developed to help people who want to include jokes or humorous stories in their presentations. Morris Mandel, author of *Stories for Speakers,* has written several volumes intended to add spice to a speech. Other sources are H. V. Proshnow's *The Public Speaker's Treasure Chest* and *The Speaker's Treasury of Stories for All Occasions.*

Illustrations   Stories, anecdotes, pictures, and slides, as well as a story that creates a vivid image, can be used at the start of a speech to get the audience's attention. These devices are called illustrators. Showing a series of pictures of a proposed new office building complex can pique the attention of an audience that has been assembled to hear what your company can do to improve its community. Telling a vivid story of how someone's life was saved because of a product developed by your pharmaceutical company may be a vivid way to illustrate the effectiveness of your products. The more you can get your listeners to actually see or be able to visualize a subject, the clearer it often becomes to them.

References to the Occasion or Setting   A speaker can get audience members involved in the presentation if he or she can build a bond with them. By getting the audience to identify with the speaker through a similar experience, a common belief, or a mutual cause, the speaker can make the audience part of the speech. The sales manager who can quickly grab the staff's attention by showing how a renewed effort on increased sales will make it possible for all of them to have pride in themselves and their company will have a good chance of getting increased motivation. The pollution control expert who starts the speech by reinforcing the idea, "we have all come together to cure a problem that affects all of us" may be well on the way to making that audience take some action.

Questions   Two types of questions may be used as introductions: the rhetorical question and the action question.

Rhetorical questions are presented in such a way that the speaker does not expect a response from the audience but wants it to think about the subject. "Have you ever thought about what effect the elimination of advertising would have on your life?" This rhetorical question asked at the start of a speech concerning the effect of advertising on consumer purchasing patterns would get the audience thinking about the subject.

An action question is posed in an attempt to find out something about the audience's attitudes, experiences, or knowledge. It requests the listeners to respond. "Advertising has a direct effect on what brand of products a shopper buys. Is that statement true? Would you please raise your hand if you feel that the statement is accurate." The speaker then would use the information obtained to develop the next idea. It is important that the information obtained from an action question be used. Some speakers ask the question and than go on their way believing that just because people raised or didn't raise their hands is enough to get them involved. Be sure there is a reason for the inclusion of this introductory device and that the questions have substance.

Unusual or Dramatic Devices   A woman once started her speech by showing the audience two pairs of pajamas. She took out a cigarette lighter and proceeded to try to set both pairs of pajamas on fire. One burned quickly; the other would not catch on fire. Her audience was a group of children's clothing manufacturers and her purpose was persuading the audience of the effectiveness of a fireproofing material developed by her company.

A member of the board of directors of a corporaton started a stockholder's meeting by saying, "This company lost money last year and I'm proud of it." The response, of course, was shocked horror. He went on to explain that the company had been placing funds in new investments that would, within a short period of time, result in tremendously increased profits.

Both of these are examples of introductions in which the speaker used an unusual or dramatic device that directly pertained to the topic of the speech in order to gain the audience's attention.

Quotations   Quoting an expert or reading a part of a book or magazine are devices intended to get the audience's attention and to introduce it to the topic. It is a very popular form of introduction and can be quite effective. Quoting from the Surgeon General's report on the dangers of smoking to nonsmokers would be an excellent start for a speech on why the company is proposing a ban on smoking at work stations.

Exposition

☐

The second part of the introduction, the **exposition,** allows the speaker to give the audience members the necessary information they will need in order to understand the basic concepts of the speech. Included in this section is any historical background about the subject that may help the receiver. For example, in presenting a speech to persuade the financial board of a small company to switch to automated payroll depositing, it might be wise briefly to discuss the present system being used.

Also included here might be definitions of terms you will be using throughout the speech and which you believe the audience must understand. In the case of the speech topic described in the previous paragraph, such a term as *automated payroll depositing* would have to be understood by the members of the audience.

Another expository factor might be the speaker's connection with the topic. In the automated payroll deposit speech, if you inform your listeners that you are an independent financial consultant, having no interest in any bank in the area, this information might eliminate the doubts of the financial board who may be suspicious that you are trying to sell the system just to make a profit.

The speaker who started by burning pajamas followed the action by telling the audience that legislation had been passed by a department of the federal government compelling fireproofing of garments to be sold for children. She proceeded to read the important section of the code. Since some people in the audience might not have been familiar with the action, this device allowed for a common understanding on the part of the listeners.

STATEMENT OF CENTRAL IDEA

■

Following the introduction, speakers should tell their audiences exactly what the speech is going to be about. This statement is the statement of the central idea. It provides a bridge between the introduction and the body of the speech. The statement of the central idea is often a paraphrase (a restatement) of the purpose statement. It suggests the purpose of the speech and often previews the structure of the presentation.

The speaker who started by telling how someone's life was saved because of a pharmaceutical company's product could follow the story with this preview: "Our company is in the business of service, and I would like to share with you today information about three of our lifesaving products."

The pollution control expert who told the audience that by working together they could cure the problem could preview with the statement: "By sharing with you some concepts of what each of us can do, I hope you will become part of the cure of pollution and not part of the cause."

In both of these cases the audience is aware of the speaker's topic and purpose. You may decide, for some specific reason, that it would be best to hold part of your statement of theme until later in the speech. For example, if you are going to propose a specific plan of action, you may not want to reveal it until the appropriate time during the speech. In the statement of the central idea you might want to mention only that you are going to probe into the problem and present possible solutions. Later in the presentation, you could insert a transitional statement such as, "Now that we have examined the problem and some of the solutions, I'd like to share with you my proposal for solving the problem."

THE BODY
■

The purpose of the body of the speech is to develop the major points. Since listeners tend to understand ideas that are clearly structured, it is advisable that the body of a speech follow a specific type of issue arrangement. The types of issue arrangements are chronological, spatial, topical, causal, comparison-contrast, and problem-solution.

Types of Issue Arrangements
□

Chronological Order
Some things lend themselves to presentation in a **chronological order,** either according to what came first, second, and third; by what has to be done first, then second, then third, etc.; or according to the dates when something happened, starting with a date and proceeding either forward or backward in the order of happening. A speech about the history of a corporation or explaining the step-by-step directions for putting together a piece of machinery fits this order of development.

Consider this example of the body of a speech developed with the chronological order method of issue arrangement:

Purpose statement: to inform the secretary pool of the procedure for using the new word processing equipment by listing the steps from inserting the floppy disks to bringing up the program.

III. Body
    A. Insert the program disk in drive A.
    B. Insert the blank formated disk in drive B.
    C. Turn on the machine using the on-off button on the right side of the machine.
    D. When the information appears on the screen follow the written directions.

Spatial Order

Another method of development is **spatial order.** In this structure the explanation follows some geographical format. Describing the company's headquarters by telling where the offices are, the manufacturing facilities, and then the shipping area is spatial development. Describing the location within the United States of the production facilities owned by a large corporation could be done by referring to those in the North, then the East, then the South, and then the West.

This speech body was developed by following the spatial order method of issue arrangement:

Purpose statement: to inform the personnel of the physical layout of the newly-relocated public relations department offices.

III. Body
- A. Offices on the left side of the corridor
    1. Department manager
    2. Public relations director
    3. Television production supervisor
    4. Audio-visual designer
    5. Speechwriter
- B. Offices in the center section
    1. Supply room
    2. Dark room
    3. Electronic editing lab
- C. Office on the right side of the corridor
    1. Television studio
    2. Graphics laboratory

Topical Order

Topical order arrangement is used when a general subject can be broken down into parts. In speaking about the products made by an electrical manufacturing company, it might be advisable to talk about the large appliance (refrigerators, stoves) then small appliances (toasters, mixers), replacement parts, and then their special items (sunlamp bulbs, heat coils).

Detailing the types of insurance sold by your agency could be accomplished by telling about all the types of life insurance, then the varieties of homeowner's policies, and then the health care coverages. By covering all the material in one topical area before going on to the next, it makes it easier for the receiver to understand the message without getting the various subjects mixed up.

This is an example of the body of a speech which follows the topical order method:

Purpose statement: to inform the newly hired members of the Personnel Department of the operational divisions of the secretarial staff.

III. Body
- A. Administrative assistants
- B. Executive secretaries
- C. Management secretaries
- D. Department secretaries
- E. Secretarial pool

Causal Arrangement

In explaining to the union grievance committee the step-by-step happenings that resulted in an industrial accident, the injured employee would be using a method of development referred to as causal. In **causal arrangement,** one may describe what happened and what resulted (cause-to-effect) or tell the outcome and how it came to be (effect-from-cause). This would be a good method for explaining the results of a scientific or chemical process or the reasons for profits or losses. It should be remembered that in using this structure of organizing, the source should develop the ideas step-by-step and not jump back and forth between ideas, thus avoiding confusing the receiver as to what happened or what caused this happening.

This speech lent itself well to the causal arrangement method of issue arrangement:

Purpose statement: To inform the service personnel that there is a shortage of operating vehicles by listing the three causes that brought about the shortage.

    III. Body
        A. Because of:
           1. Elimination of several repair personnel.
           2. Limited budget for replacement parts.
           3. Bad weather conditions.
        B. There is a shortage of operating vehicles.

Comparison, Contrast, and Comparison-Contrast Arrangements

We often can describe something by relating the similarities between ideas, the differences between matters, or both similarities and differences. These methods of development are **contrast** (differences), **comparison** (similarities), or **comparison-contrast** (similarities and differences). A speaker might describe the similarities of two manufacturing processes. Another speaker might contrast the fringe benefit programs of two industrial firms. An insurance salesperson could discuss the similarities and the differences between two different policy plans.

The comparison-contrast method of issue arrangements was used to develop this speech:

Purpose statement: to inform the business staff of the similarities and differences between electric and electronic typewriters.

    III. Body
        A. Similarities
           1. Ease of key operation.
           2. Adjustable identing.
           3. Dependability.
        B. Differences
           1. Centering procedure.
           2. Erasing procedure.
           3. Storage ability.
           4. Availability as a printer for a computer.

Problem-Solution Arrangement

Yet another method of development is **problem-solution format.** In this means of organizing ideas, the source structures the presentation by explaining the problem and then discussing the possible solutions, finally leading to the best possible plan of action for solving the problem. A water pollution expert could describe the present condition of the water system and then propose several plans of action to alter the pollution, finally recommending what is considered to be the best system for solving the problem.

There are basically three methods for dealing with the problem-solution format: The Motivated Sequence, Critical Reasoning Structure, and The Comparative Advantage Reasoning System.

Motivated Sequence   A specific format for problem solution is the five-step pattern known as the **motivated sequence.** The five steps are:

1. *Attention:* secure the audience's attention and focus that attention on the message.
2. *Need:* explain the nature, scope, and implications of the need or problem.
3. *Satisfaction:* provide a solution that will eliminate a significant portion of the problem you discussed in the Need step.
4. *Visualization:* mentally picture the future as it will be if your solution is adopted or if your solution is not adopted.
5. *Action:* call for specific adoption of your solution. Let the audience members know specifically what they need to believe or do in order to realize the benefits or avoid the perils that you have just visualized for them.[1]

Critical Reasoning Structure   Another method for organizing the persuasive problem-solving speech is through the **critical reasoning structure.** In this method, the speaker develops the body of the speech by stating the standards used for making a judgment and why the proposal is the one that best meets those standards. Only the one solution is discussed, and the speaker stresses all of the positive aspects of this solution.[2]

The Comparative Advantage Reasoning System   With the **comparative advantage reasoning** system, you begin by stating the possible solutions—including status quo (not making any change). Then the speaker lists the advantages and disadvantages of each possible solution. The last step of the body would be to compare the advantages and disadvantages of each possible solution and demonstrate how the proposal you are setting forth is the most workable, desirable, and practical, since it offers the most advantages and the fewest disadvantages.[3]

All of the methods described have one basic purpose; to structure ideas in such a way that the receiver will understand the message of the source.

The changing of ideas or proposing of beliefs often lends itself to problem-solution issue arrangement:

Purpose statement: to persuade the marketing department that a new line of cat food should be named Purr-fect.

III. Body
    A. Statement of problem.
    B. Names suggested from brainstorming session.
    C. Positives for each name.
    D. Negatives for each name.
    E. Reasons for recommending Purr-fect.

Transitions

☐

The structure of a speech is enhanced by the speaker's careful use of transitions. A good **transition** provides a bridge for the listener from one point of the speech to the next concept. The speaker, at the end of a point in the presentation, summarizes the idea discussed and then makes a transition to the next idea.

Examples of transitions would include:

> "Now that we've analyzed the revenue-sharing plan, let's determine why it's an appropriate procedure."
> "To clarify this point, let's look at an example from the field."
> "You can see how this computer system has created difficulties for the company, so let's look at some alternatives to eliminate the difficulties."

Transitions are critical to the presentation of ideas for listeners so that they can follow the sequence of ideas.

Forms of Support

☐

Since the purpose of the body of the speech is to develop the major points, it is important not only to structure the information in a pattern that allows for clarity of the ideas, but to make sure the concepts are clear, documented, and interesting. Forms of support, the methods available to hold the audience's attention and develop the message, are illustrations, specific instances, clarifiers, statistics, analogies, and testimony.

Illustrations

☐

Illustrations are stories, pictures, or slides that help develop the idea being presented. A story that is used could be hypothetical (made-up) or real. Hypothetical stories are usually introduced by saying, "Let us all imagine that . . ." or "Suppose you were. . . ." In developing an idea about the importance of wage increases, a speaker might hypothetically say, "Suppose you worked forty hours a week and didn't even make enough money to pay for your basic necessities. There are, in fact, many people in this country who are in that position." A real story, photos of actual events, or slides allowing us to clearly see the ideas being developed can all have a positive effect on our understanding and also in holding attention.

Specific Instances

Specific instances are included in a speech in order to give an example of what you are talking about. In speaking about how governmental regulations have caused your company to increase the cost of automobiles, you could cite the increases caused by required seat belts, impact bumpers, shatterproof glass, and exhaust emission systems. Without these specific ilustrations, the audience might not believe you or even know what you were specifically talking about.

Clarifiers

It often is necessary to use **clarifiers** to define terms, explain similarities between ideas, give historical information, and bridge the relationship between the speaker and the topic. If in giving a speech about management procedure, you are going to use the initials *MBWA,* you might assume that an audience composed of nonbusinesspeople will not know to what you are referring. Not only should you use the entire name, "Management By Wandering Around," the first time you mention the concept, but you should probably give a brief explanation of what it is.

These are all examples of clarifiers. If you feel that your listeners need some information that will aid them to better grasp what you are saying, insert a clarifier.

Statistics

Many speeches require the use of numbers to develop the purpose. **Statistics** are numerical collections of information that represent trends, theories, or actual amounts. They can be expressed in percentages, dollars, or numbers. Any time that numbers are used, the speaker should try to remember that not all numbers are accurate and should carefully be examined to make sure they represent what they are supposed to represent. A way of testing statistics is to ask:

1. Who says so?
2. How does he or she know?
3. What's missing?
4. Did somebody change the subject?
5. Does it make sense?[4]

Make sure also to keep in mind that it is difficult for listeners to grasp a quantity of numbers. It might be an advantage to make copies of the statistics and hand them out, display them on a blackboard, or make a flip chart. It also helps, if possible, to round the numbers off so that they can be easily understood. Nine million is an easy number to grasp, while nine million three hundred twenty-two thousand three hundred and sixteen is not easy to comprehend. Use statistics where necessary to aid the audience in specifically understanding any idea that requires numerical representation.

Analogies

Analogies are ideas presented by a speaker comparing or contrasting something with which the audience is unfamiliar to something with which it is familiar. In speaking about the Management By Objectives system of business operations, the speaker could say: "Many of us set goals before undertaking a task. We do this in order to evaluate how well we did, so we can have something to measure against. MBO is a system requiring that goals be set before starting a task. And like your situation, it makes it easy for businesspeople to evaluate whether they have accomplished their task."

When using analogies, it is important that you remember that the audience's understanding of the information depends upon its familiarity with the object, idea, or theory that is used as the basis for comparison.

Testimony

Testimony is a direct quotation (an actual statement) or a paraphrase (a reworded idea) of an authority. Speakers use testimonies to clarify ideas, back up ideas, and reinforce concepts. If a speaker feels that someone else's words would aid an audience to understand or be persuaded to believe, then the presenter will turn to a testimony for idea development. Audiences will often be impressed by ideas of a well-known person or someone they consider to be an expert. An **expert** is someone (or some group) who has knowledge or skill in a specific area, has gained respect in the field, or is an eyewitness to a happening. In presenting a speech about the new management theory, "Industrial Democracy," in which employees are involved in the decision-making process, the speaker could quote Pehr Cyllenhammer, president of Volvo Motors. Since he was in charge of the company at the time the plan was instituted and was in on the development of the process, he would be a knowledgeable person to quote.

Will the listeners be able to respond affirmatively to the testimony you present? In selecting testimony ask these basic questions.

1. Is the material quoted accurately?
2. Is the source biased because of position, employment, or affiliations?
3. Is the information relevant to the issue being discussed?
4. Is the source competent in the field being discussed?
5. Is the information current, if currency is important?[5]

Tests of Forms of Support In selecting materials to clarify or back up your ideas, the following checklist can be used to ascertain whether you should use the material or not.

1. Is the support accurate?
2. Is the support directly related to the contention?
3. Is the support relevant to the needs of the audience?
4. Is the support information the audience can understand and accept?
5. Is the support information I can understand and accept?
6. Is the support the best available?
7. Is the contention sound because of the support?[6]

Incorporating the Support The forms of support should be carefully incorporated in a speech. It is the objective of any type of communication to develop a clear message. The forms of support define, explain, and clarify the statements you make.

In the **diadactic method** you state your conclusion, then present the proof, and finally restate your conclusion. In outline form this would be:

    A. State your point.
    B. Make it clear by explanation, comparison, illustration, or definition.
    C. Support it by additional factual illustrations, specific instances, statistics, or testimony.
    D. Restate your point as the conclusion.

For example:[7]

    A. *Point:* There is a value to a liberal arts degree for all students, including business majors.
    B. *Explanation:* The liberal arts education stresses a broad background of experiences and thinking skills in contrast to specializing in a specific skill. Liberal arts students usually receive training in English, mathematics, science, social studies, speech and the arts and humanities.
    C. *Support*
        1. The U.S. Department of Education, in a 1984 report, warned that "we are in danger of becoming a . . . society devoid of renaissance men and women."
        2. William H. Eells, chairman of the Advisory Council for College Preparatory Education, stated, "The humanities provide for a business person a whole concept: the ability to develop interpersonal relationships, communication between management and employees."
        3. Eells, who is a Ford Motor Company executive, also said, "We would rather have a well-rounded person than someone who has expert training in computers alone."
    D. *Restatement:* there is a value to a liberal arts education.

The **method of implication** centers on presenting the facts first and then stating the conclusion based on those facts. (This is most effective in persuasion because it does not appear that you are pushing something down the throats of the listeners.) The outline form of the method of implication is:

    A. Present an analogy or illustration which implies the point you wish to make.
    B. Present a clarification of terms and illustrations, figures, and testimony which point inevitably to this conclusion without stating it.
    C. Show how these facts lead unavoidably to this conclusion; use explanations if necessary.
    D. Definitely state your point as a conclusion.

For example:

    A. *Implied point:* one of the questions often facing college students is whether or not there is a value to a liberal arts degree.
    B. *Explanation:* the liberal arts education stresses a broad background of experiences and thinking skills in contrast to specializing in a specific

skill. Liberal arts students usually receive training in English, mathematics, science, social studies, speech, the arts, and humanities.

    C. *Support*
        1. The U.S. Department of Education, in a 1984 report, warned that "we are in danger of becoming a nation of not very interesting specialists, a society devoid of renaissance men and women."
        2. William H. Eells, chairman of the Advisory Council for College Preparatory Education, stated, "The humanities provide for a business person a whole concept: the ability to develop interpersonal relationships, communication between management and employees."
        3. Eells, who is a Ford Motor Company executive, also said, "We would rather have a well-rounded person than someone who has expert training in computers alone."
    D. *Point:* Therefore, it appears that there is a definite value to a liberal arts education.

Oral Footnotes   When a speaker quotes an expert or uses statistics or other information from a source it is necessary to give credit to that source. This spoken credit is called an **oral footnote.** Oral footnotes call for the speaker to state the name of the person who presented the ideas. In addition, you may want to include the place the material was found (the name of the book or magazine), the date of publication, and something about the source that establishes that person as credible in the field being discussed. Sometimes all of these factors are included; at other times only one or two of the ideas. You have to determine how much information the audience members need in order to accept the information presented. Examples of oral footnotes are:

> Kathleen Edgerton Kendall, a professor of Rhetoric and Communication at State University of New York-Albany, in a survey she conducted, notes that 46.5 percent of the general public indicated that many workers had spoken to groups of ten or more people at least once in the last two years. This, she contends, does support the idea that real people do give speeches.[7]

> "Of all our allies, West Germany is the worst security risk." This is the conclusion reached by the CIA and reported in its report, "Documented Unauthorized High-Technology Diversion to the USSR."[8]

Supplementary Aids

Though the ideas we present with words and gestures may be enough to insure audience understanding, in some instances it may be necessary to supplement those ideas. In these cases **supplementary aids,** in the form of audio, visual, and audio-visual aids may be necessary.

    Supplementary aids are used to clarify. As a salesperson of business machines, you might be able to explain the operational process of a new model of a copying machine; however, bringing the machine in and demonstrating it to the audience would make the entire process much clearer. A time-study person explaining a new procedure of operation would have an easier time if a flowchart showing the step-by-step operation was displayed to the audience during the presentation.

Supplementary aids are also used to reinforce. As you make major points in a speech, you might want to display the major ideas so that when you get to the conclusion of the speech, you can review by going back over the displayed ideas to reinforce the concept. You might want to list the causes leading to the recommendation you will be making for changing company policies. If you have listed them on a blackboard as you were speaking, you could then use this listing to show how the conclusion was reached.

The major questions that should be asked in using supplementary aids are (1) whether the aid is relevant to the presentation and (2) whether the audience will better understand the material if the aid is used. If the answer to either or both of these questions is *yes*, then use the aid.

There are three types of supplementary aids: visual, audio, and audio-visual.

Visual Aids **Visual aids** appeal to our sense of sight. Examples include the following:

Real Objects To demonstrate how the new copy machine works, you bring in the actual machine. In order to show what happens because of a newly developed formula, you mix the chemicals before the audience.

Models At times it is impossible to bring real objects into the speech setting. A *scale* model, in exact proportion to the dimensions of the real object, or a *synthetic model,* which represents the real object but is not in exact proportions, may be used. To illustrate what a new industrial complex would look like, you might use a model of the project or incorporate into the presentation a scale model of a proposed new machine.

Photographs, Pictures, and Diagrams A photo of the present land site and a drawing of the way the plant your company wants to build will look after the construction is completed is an excellent way to demonstrate the idea before the city's planning commission. Or, a display of the proposed company identification insignia will aid the audience to see specifically what is being recommended.

Charts Charts are visual representations of numerical and statistical data giving information in numerical or diagram form. In explaining the financial condition of a company, the financial officers can illustrate the statistics by showing copies of the financial statement or by having graphs drawn to represent the numbers. A comparison or contrast of the production versus sales costs can be made by using a chart.

Cutaways A cutaway allows the viewer to see what is below the surface of an object. For example, in presenting its plans for construction of a new building, an architectural firm could let prospective clients see inside the building by having drawings with transparent walls to allow for viewing inside the facility. Or, to show how insulation is installed in a home, a salesman could have a drawing made showing a cross-section of a wall with the material packed in.

Mock-up A mock-up is used to show the building-up or the tearing-down of an article. A printing company could print each of four colors on pieces of plastic and then by placing one sheet on top of the other could illustrate the four-color process. Or, a piece of machinery can be constructed for assembly or disassembly in order to allow the audience to see the process.

Using Visual Aids Some basic suggestions for using visual aids in a speech are these:

1. The use of a visual aid in a speech takes as much careful planning as any other part of the presentation. Preplan your use of the aide. If you have not decided when and how you will use the aid, you may forget to insert it into the speech or attempt to display it at the wrong time.
2. Practice with the materials you are going to use. If it is a mechanical aid, make sure that you know how it works. Many speakers have assumed that they could operate devices and then been embarrassed when the object simply could not or would not work.
3. Prepare the audience for the aid. Just showing the audience something may be of very little value. Tell the audience what the aid is for and what it rep-

Visual aids appeal to the sense of sight.

resents: "By examining this chart you will see that. . . ."; "With the aid of this model, I would like to demonstrate for you the step-by-step process used. . . ."

4. Display the aid when you need it and then put it away. If you display the visual aid too early, its impact may be lost. If you leave it up too long, it may distract the audience from what you are saying.

5. Talk to the audience, not to the visual aid. There is a tendency for speakers to look down at the object or at the chart as they speak. Try to create as much eye contact with the audience as possible. Turning your back to speak to a graph will cause your voice to be projected away from the audience, thus making it difficult for the audience to hear you.

6. Do not stand between the visual aid and the audience. If the audience cannot see the aid, then there is no sense in using it. Try to display the aid in front of you or make sure that you are standing to the side of the aid as you refer to it. By using a long pointer rather than your finger, it will be less likely that you will block the aid.

7. Point to a chart, model, or object at the particular place to which you are referring. Do not make the listeners search for the information. Show them exactly where you want their attention focused.

Preparing Visual Aids. Visual aids, other than the actual objects, must be constructed, drawn, or prepared. One of the first considerations in preparing a visual aid is to determine what type of aid will be used and if there is any special machinery needed. Visual aids can be made of posterboard and markers, written on flip charts, displayed on magnet boards, created on a computer, written on blackboards or placed on or into such mechanical devices as opaque, overhead, filmstrip, or slide projectors.

Guidelines for using posterboards, computer-generated graphics, the blackboard, or flip charts include the following:

1. Are the lines or drawings heavy and large enough to be seen throughout the entire room?

2. Are the colors, shapes, and blending distinct enough to be seen?

3. Are there so many details that the aid is confusing? In general, one or two points only should be included on a single chart or diagram.

4. Is the aid artistically appealing?

5. Are all important parts labeled or titled?

6. Is the source of the information identified if necessary?

7. Does the aid communicate specifically what I intended to clarify or illuminate?[9]

8. Is the material accurate (e.g., words spelled correctly, numbers copied accurately)?

9. Flip charts are a series of large sheets of paper sealed together in a packet form. They are usually attached to a tripod and can either be written on in advance of the presentation or used like a blackboard during the session. A wide-tipped felt marker should be used for writing on them so that the audience can clearly see the writing.

10. Posterboards should be made of heavy cardboard and diplayed on an art easel. Do not roll up the charts on the way to the presentation, as they will most likely curl and fall off the easel during the presentation.

When using mechanical devices, make sure that you know how to work the equipment and that it is in operating order. Also, check to make sure that extension cords, screen(s), and room-darkening equipment are available.

An overhead projector uses either prepared sheets of clear plastic imprinted with charts or diagrams or blank sheets of plastic on which one can write with felt markers or grease pencils before or during the presentation. Opaque projectors project photographs, pages from magazines or books, and material written on sheets of paper onto a screen in a magnified form.

While these preparations are necessary to make for an effective presentation via visual aids, it should be noted that many companies provide entire audio-visual departments to design and prepare graphics for you. You will need, however, a clear idea as to what you want and how it is to fit into the presentation so that you can explain it carefully to the graphics staff who will construct the material for you.

Audio Aids   Sometimes seeing is just not enough. We may have to hear something in order to understand it. **Audio aids** appeal to our sense of hearing. An acoustical engineer could demonstrate the effect of a sound process by contrasting what the sound is like without the special treatment and then with it. Stereo equipment manufacturers commonly use audio aids to demonstrate the quality of their equipment when presenting their new product line to a conference of their distributors. A tape recording of a message given by a safety expert may be played for company supervisors as part of a speech on improvement of plant safety. You reading the words would not be as effective as the audience hearing the expert himself or herself speaking.

Audio-visual Aids   **Audio-visual aids,** such as films, videotapes, and tape-slide presentations, combine the dimensions of sight and sound. A videotape, as prepared by a national sales manager, can be inserted into a speech concerning a new line of products. Showing a series of slides about the new state building code accompanied by a pre-recorded tape may supplement the proposal being made by a company's safety engineer on what changes have to be made to increase safety in the plant.

THE CONCLUSION

■

The conclusion includes two elements: the summary of the major thoughts of the speech and the clincher.

Summary

☐

In the **summary,** the speaker repeats all of the points that he or she wants the audience to remember. This should be done specifically, not with a statement such as "I've told you the four parts of a speech." Instead, the statement should be, "The four parts of the speech are the introduction, statement of the central idea, the body, and the conclusion."

Clincher

☐

The second part of the conclusion is the **clincher.** The clincher creatively ends the speech. It is like the bow on the top of a present. It makes the entire process complete.

Types of Clinchers

Personal references, humorous stories, illustrations, answers to a rhetorical or an action question, unusual or dramatic devices, and quotations are types of clinchers used to conclude a speech.

Methods of Summary   One of the most common is restating the major ideas presented in the body of the speech. This usually consists of repeating the major headings in the outline of the body of the speech. It often is advisable that these be listed on a blackboard, a flip chart, a felt board, or on a sheet of cardboard. Allowing the audience to see as well as hear them may result in a more lasting effect.

Personal References   The accountant who established himself as an expert at the start of the speech may want to reestablish his authority in the conclusion so that the recommendations he made will be regarded as those of an authority in the field.

Humorous Stories   A joke or a story summarizing the points made in the speech could be used to wrap up the presentation. Again, caution is raised as to the appropriateness of the story or joke to the topic and the audience.

Illustrations   Repeating the pictures of the construction projects that your company could produce for the community could reinforce your speech on accepting your firm as the city's consultant. Or, showing the before-and-after pictures of skin-graft patient's recovery because of chemical products produced by your company is a good way to wrap up a speech on the progress made in medicine because of your organization's research techniques.

Answers to the Rhetorical Question   If you started out your speech with one or more rhetorical questions, one of the ways to end the speech would be to answer those questions. If, for example, you started by asking whether the audience members had ever thought about the effects of advertising on their lives, the body of the speech should have developed answers to that question. For a conclusion, you could repeat each of the ways in which advertising does have an effect.

Action Question-Statement   You may have set as the purpose of your speech the desire for a specific action from your audience—signing a petition, purchasing a product, or subscribing to a service. The effectiveness of the speech can be measured by asking the audience to take the desired action right now. If you get their signatures, money for a purchase, or the subscription, you have been successful.

Unusual or Dramatic Devices   A speaker talking about the effects of inflation ended her speech by ripping up a $10 bill to show the worthlessness of money caused by increased costs. A speaker for an air cleaner firm ended a speech about the need for installation of the equipment by setting off a smoke bomb, letting the mist filter through the room, and then turning on the equipment, which quickly cleared the smoke. It was an effective way to dramatically show the efficiency of the equipment.

Quotations   The reading of material from an expert, a report, or a piece of literature that wraps up the major idea of the presentation can be an effective way to conclude a speech.

PUTTING THE SPEECH TOGETHER

■

There are various approaches to the best way to put the speech together after you have analyzed the audience, selected a topic, decided on the purpose statement, and done the research. One procedure is to start by deciding on the type of introduction you will use, and develop it. Proceed through the speech by developing a statement of the central idea. Then, decide on what method of organization will be used for the body of the speech, and develop the body by selecting the major points and the exposition, illustrations, examples, statistics, and analogies that will be needed to complete the body. Finally, prepare the conclusion; summarize by choosing the type of clincher to be used and developing it.

Another approach is working on the statement of the central idea first, going to the body from there, then to the introduction, and finally to the conclusion. As an example, here is a completed outline for a speech, the purpose of which is to inform the audience of the step-by-step process which begins with finding job openings and ends when you are hired.

I. Introduction
   A. Are you thinking of applying for a job?
   B. Many people think about getting a job, but are unaware of the procedure to follow.
II. Central Idea: Applying for a job involves a step-by-step process which begins by finding job openings and ends when you are hired.
III. Body
   A. Learn about job openings
      1. Newspapers
      2. Trade publications
      3. Counselors
      4. Personnel agencies
      5. Friends and relatives
   B. Prepare and forward personal information to potential employers
      1. Letter of introduction
      2. Résumé

C. Call potential employer
1. When to call
2. What to say
3. Make an appointment
D. The interview
1. Promptness
2. Appearance
3. Personal presentation
4. Ask questions
IV. Conclusion
A. Follow these important steps: learn, prepare, call, and make a good impression.
B. I should know—I interviewed for five jobs and landed five jobs![10]

Working Outline

□

In preparing a speech, first develop a working outline. To develop a **working outline,** go back over the material you know or have researched. List the major ideas you wish to present. From these ideas you should be able to determine what method of issue arrangement you will use for the body of the speech. Then go back through your major ideas and number them according to the order in which they will be presented. Sort through your other materials and arrange them as part of the major ideas. Anything that does not fit within one of the major ideas is outside the purpose of the speech and can be put aside.

Your purpose statement is "to inform the audience of the ways in which businesses communicate." Your working outline might look like this:

I. Introduction
II. Statement of Central Idea
III. The body
A. Proprietory and confidential communication
B. Within departments
C. Between departments
D. Outside of the company
E. Informal flow
IV. Conclusion

Next you have the major headings you could sort through the material you have collected for the subheadings:

I. Introduction
II. Statement of Central Idea
III. The body
A. Proprietory and confidential communication
1. Personnel information
2. Future company plans
3. Company finances

    B. Within departments
      1. Project accomplishment
      2. Dissemination of operating information
      3. Proposals for new methods
      4. Explanation of procedures
    C. Between departments
      1. Altering existing policies
      2. Coordination of a common project
    D. Outside of the company
      1. Customer relations
      2. Vendor contacts
      3. Stockholder reports
    E. Informal flow
      1. No upward or downward pattern
      2. Direct contact between employee and employer
IV. Conclusion

Now you would start to develop secondary and, if appropriate, tertiary points. For example:

  III. Body
    A. Proprietory and confidential communication
      1. Personnel information
        a) Salary proposals
          (1) Administrative salaries
          (2) Midmanagement salaries
          (3) Hourly employee's salaries
        b) Personnel changes
          (1) Reorganization of departments
          (2) Elimination of positions
      2. Future company plans
        a) Expansion of plant facilities
        b) Transfer of production operations
        c) Purchase of equipment

After completing the body of the working outline, you could then develop the introduction, the statement of the central idea, and the conclusion as follows.

  I. Daniel Katz and Robert Kahn make a vital point about businesses and communication in their book *The Social Psychology of Organizations*. The authors state, "The individual entering today's business organization must function in a dynamic communication system."[11] Today, businesspeople in this country are searching for more effective ways to carry on the business of communicating. By understanding that the process is both dynamic and multidirectional, a breakthrough in understanding might take place and therefore improvement might result.

II Let us examine the five ways in which businesses communicate in order to gain an understanding of the dynamics of organizational communication.

III. Body

IV. Whether looking at the proprietory and confidential nature of communication, or how it takes place within departments, between departments, outside of the company, or in the informal flow, it should be obvious that there is, in fact, a dynamics of communication within the organizational structure.

Some speakers prefer to write out the introduction, statement of the central idea, and conclusion in sentence and paragraph form even if they are using an extemporaneous form (notes or outline) for the body of the speech. This plan allows the speaker to have a clear way in and out of the presentation and often reduces the initial fear some speakers have of forgetting their beginning. It also forces the speaker to develop a conclusion, a common oversight by amateur speakers.

The Speech-Planner Model

☐ Using the ideas presented in this chapter, the person who plans a speech should be able to develop a meaningful and well-structured presentation. A model that might help you in the future, which summarizes the ideas presented in this chapter, is:

Purpose statement:

    I. Introduction

        A. Attention getter

        B. Exposition

    II. Statement of central idea

    III. Body

        A. First major heading

            1. Subheading

                a. Subpoints

                    (1) Sub-subpoints

                    (2) Sub-subpoints etc.

                b. Subpoints etc.

            2. Subheading etc.

        B. Second major heading etc.

    IV. Conclusion

        A. Restatement

        B. Clincher

Wording the Manuscript Speech

☐ The speaker who decides to write out the speech has a unique challenge in developing the material. While it is a written manuscript, it must *sound* like a speech. Thus, the speaker who writes out his or her speech needs to develop a sense of spoken style—to write for receivers' ears, not their eyes. The sense of spoken style stems from the choice of words, sentences, and rhetorical devices.

The wording of a speech should be clear, direct, and colorful. The effective speaker strives for vocabulary easily understood by the listeners. Avoid using technical terms without definitions and other language that is not part of the general background and experience of the intended audience. A speaker presenting a briefing to the internal staff of a particular office can use the technical language of that group. However, that same speaker addressing a local social club must be careful not to assume that the listeners will have the same vocabulary as the office staff.

In addition to clarity, oral style ought to be colorful. A good sense of vivid wording can make a speech memorable. Phrases that can be repeated by the speaker two or three times are helpful in achieving vivid language. Frankin D. Roosevelt's phrase, "The only thing we have to fear is fear itself," is an example of vivid style that became a memorable rallying cry for Americans during World War II.

While clear, colorful wording is important to spoken style, effective speech style also is characterized by short, direct sentences. Most people who have gone through our public school systems are trained as essay writers. They are trained to write sentences of compound or complex structure, which are appropriate for the reading eye. But the listening ear cannot handle a large number of words in any one sentence. The speaker must use shorter, more direct sentences so that the listener can immediately comprehend the sense of the sentence.

In analyzing sentence length it has been determined what number of words would be comprehensible to the reader.[11] The research revealed levels of difficulty:

WORDS	EASE OF COMPREHENSION
8 (or less)	Very easy
11	Easy
14	Fairly Easy
17	Standard
21	Fairly Difficult
25	Difficult
29 (or more)	Very Difficult

These levels of difficulty were determined for the reader. Since the listener cannot go back and reread, he or she must get the point the first time it is presented. Thus, the comprehension of sentences by listeners is probably even less than the reading comprehension figures, so the speaker should remember to keep the sentences short for ease of listener comprehension. (This is also for the ease of presentation. It is difficult, without proper breath control, to read aloud a long, involved sentence so that it makes sense to the listener.)

Scholars of rhetorical style have characterized differences between written and spoken styles. Spoken style includes:[12]

1. More personal pronouns.
2. More variety in kinds of sentences.
3. More variety in length of sentences.

4. More simple sentences.
5. More sentence fragments.
6. More rhetorical questions.
7. More repetition of words, phrases, and sentences.
8. A higher ratio of monosyllabic to polysyllabic words.
9. More contractions.
10. More interjections, retractions, and self-corrections.
11. More indigenous or colloquial language.
12. More connotatively used words.
13. More euphony, alliteration, and other acoustical devices.
14. More figurative language.
15. More direct quotations.
16. More words that are widely familiar.

An additional hint for writing a speech: as you write the manuscript from your working outline, talk it aloud to make sure you are using spoken vocabulary and style that is easily understandable to your audience and easy for you to read. It is helpful for the manuscript speaker to keep these differences in mind when developing a speech manuscript and to write for the ears, not for the eyes.

PREPARING YOUR SPEECH NOTES

Not only a structured sequence but also well-developed notes can help a speaker. Some hints for preparation of the materials you will carry before the audience include the following:

1. Use standard or heavy typing paper or four-by-six-inch note cards. Thin paper sheets crinkle and if you are using a microphone will cause distracting noises. Also, thin pages can be seen through and may cause ideas from the next page to blend through onto the page above. Do not use erasable bond paper. The typing often smears as pages rub against each other or as damp hands touch the sheets. Avoid three-by-five-inch cards as they are small and so little material can be placed on them that you will need a whole stack for a speech. A pile of cards is difficult to hold in your hand.
2. Double or triple space the outline, notes, or manuscript. It makes it easier to read as you glance up and down.
3. In a manuscript speech (a totally written-out presentation) do not divide sentences between the bottom of one page and the top of another. Some very confusing ideas can be presented as you turn from one page to the next and pause in midsentence.
4. Use capital letters or *orator's pitch,* the special large-sized type available on some typewriters and computer printers, in preparing the manuscript.
5. Number all pages in order to avoid getting the pages mixed up. If you are using note cards, be sure to number each card.
6. Do not write on the backs of pages or cards. It can get quite confusing to find your place as you flip the cards from side to side, even if they are numbered.

7. Do not staple the pages of your script together. They are more difficult to control, and flipping the pages over the front of the podium can be distracting.
8. If you are going to be moving during your speech or won't have a podium, place your material on note cards. Most speakers prefer the four-by-six inch-size, as they are large enough to contain a sufficient amount of material, yet are easy to handle.

The structure of the speech is a major key to an effective presentation. Listeners have very limited attention spans and certainly need all the help that they can get from speakers in staying "on track" with the sequence of ideas in a speech. These structural elements assist that process and enable listeners to follow the speaker's ideas with some ability.

SUMMARY

In this chapter we have discussed the steps to be taken in preparing a speech. The major ideas presented were:

There are four basic parts to a public address: the introduction, statement of the central idea, body, and conclusion.

The introduction gains the audience's attention and may give general background material, referred to as exposition.

The statement of the central idea lets the audience know the direction of the speech.

The body develops the major points of the speech in some logical order.

The conclusion summarizes the major ideas by pulling the thoughts together and clinches the audience's understanding.

The types of introduction are the personal reference, humorous story, illustration, reference to the occasion or setting, rhetorical or action questions, unusual or dramatic device, and quotation.

The types of issue arrangements are chronological order, spatial order, topical arrangement, causal arrangement, comparison, contrast, comparison-contrast, and problem-solution.

Forms of support used in speeches include illustrations, specific instances, clarifiers, statistics, and analogies.

Supplementary aids are used to clarify what the speaker's words and gestures may not be able to make clear.

The major questions that should be asked in using supplementary aids are whether or not the aid is relevant to the presentation and whether or not the audience will better understand the material if the aid is used.

The three types of supplementary aids are visual, audio, and audio-visual.

Examples of visual aids are real objects, models, photographs, pictures, diagrams, charts, cutaways, and mock-ups.

It is important to know how to use and how to make visual aids in order to enhance a speech.

Audio aids include recordings, tapes, and real sounds.

Audio-visual aids include films, videotapes, and tape-slide presentations, which combine the dimensions of sight and sound.

Methods of conclusion include the statement of summary, personal reference, humorous stories, illustrations, answers to the rhetorical question, action question-statement, the unusual or dramatic device, and quotations.

A working outline aids the speaker in placing his or her ideas in an order for further development of the speech.

Care must be taken in wording a manuscript speech to insure oral style and clarity.

Properly prepared notes aid a speaker in being more effective.

THINGS TO DO

1. The following questions deal with speech structure. Answer each question or solve each problem, being as precise as possible. You may use your textbook.

   A. A public communication message is usually divided into what four parts?
   B. What is the purpose of the introduction?
      (1) Write two different introductions you could use if you were giving a talk on your favorite hobby.
      (2) Write an introduction that you could use if you were giving a speech with the purpose statement: to inform the audience of the effect of advertising on consumer buying.
   C. What is the purpose of the statement of the central idea?
      (1) Write a statement of the central idea that would follow the first introduction in B.1. above.
      (2) Write a statement of the central idea for B2 above.
   D. The body of a message develops the major points of a speech. It may be organized in a variety of ways. Arrange the following according to the method indicated:

      (1) Arrange the following in *CHRONOLOGICAL* order:
         a. Thanksgiving Day   1. _____
         b. Halloween   2. _____
         c. Easter Sunday   3. _____
         d. Christmas Day   4. _____
         e. Labor Day   5. _____
         f. Valentine's Day   6. _____
      (2) Arrange the following in *CHRONOLOGICAL* order:
         a. The invention of television   1. _____
         b. The invention of the lunar module 2. _____
         c. The invention of the automobile   3. _____
         d. The invention of the wheel   4. _____
         e. The invention of the steamboat   5. _____
      (3) Arrange the following in *SPATIAL* order. (reference point—Cleveland, Ohio)
         a. Denver, Colorado   1. _____
         b. Chicago, Illinois   2. _____
         c. Honolulu, Hawaii   3. _____
         d. Cleveland, Ohio   4. _____
         e. Los Angeles, California   5. _____

E. Indicate which of the following are *COMPARISON* and which are *CONTRAST:*
   a. Mary is as sweet as a rose.   _____
   b. He is as brave as a bull.   _____
   c. The red earth of Georgia, as opposed
      to the white sands of Hawaii.   _____
   d. The sun is as golden as butter.   _____
   e. The stormy Pacific, unlike the placid
      Red Sea.   _____
   f. She is as pretty as a picture.   _____

F. Match each of the following by *CAUSE-EFFECT:*
   a. Nuclear fallout   Death and grief   ( )
   b. Pickles and whipped cream   Pollution   ( )
   c. Serious infection   Indigestion   ( )
   d. War   Pneumonia   ( )
   e. Overeating   Energy Crisis   ( )
   f. Dog bite   Obesity   ( )
   g. Lack of all resources   Rabies   ( )

G. Name two topics that could be effectively developed in the topical pattern of order:
   1. _____
   2. _____

2. What method of development, as described in this chapter, would best be used for organizing a speech on each of the following topics:
   A. Describing the historical development of the RAR Corporation.
   B. Assembling a snow blower.
   C. The various production divisions of a corporation.
   D. RAR Corporation's procedure for increasing its sales during the past year.
   E. The results of RAR Corporation's new sales procedure.
   F. Why RAR Corporation decided to use a paticular sales campaign.

3. You are going to present a five-minute speech to your class.
   A. Analyze the audience and yourself. Pick a topic.
      (1) What topic did you pick?
      (2) Why did you pick that topic? Explain your answer by indicating the audience analysis used to select the topic.
   B. Write a purpose statement for the topic you selected.
      (1) Submit the purpose statement to your instructor.
      (2) Once the purpose statement is approved, proceed.
   C. Develop a working outline for the speech.
      (1) Turn the working outline in to your instructor.
      (2) Once the working outline is approved, proceed to D.
   D. Expand the working outline by adding the essential points and subpoints. Write a statement of central idea, an introduction, and a conclusion.
      (1) What method of introduction did you use?

(2) What type of issue arrangement was used for the body?

(3) What method of conclusion was used?

Turn your expanded working outline in to your instructor along with your answers to D.1. through 3.

E. After you have read and discussed chapter 13, your instructor may want you to present the speech you have just prepared to the class. Decide on the mode of presentation you will use and whether you will need visual aids. Then, using the principles discussed in chapter 13, give the speech to the class.

4. You are to select a topic that requires a supplemental aid to ensure understanding on the part of the audience. (The test of the subject chosen is that if the supplemental aid was eliminated, the speech would make no sense.) Give to the class a presentation of no more than five minutes using the supplemental aid.

5. You will prepare a five-minute speech in which every major topic and subtopic of the body of the speech is represented by a picture, word, or diagram on a flip chart. As you speak, you will use the flip chart to clarify or reinforce the point being made.[13]

6. You are to present a speech to the class. Every major idea must be introduced with a visual, audio-visual, or audio aid. At no time during the speech is the speaker to present a new idea unless it is accompanied by a supplemental aid. The topic selected must deal with some phase of the world of business.[14]

NOTES

1. Alan H. Monroe and Douglas Ehninger, *Principles and Types of Speech Communication* (Glenview, IL: Scott, Foresman and Company, 1974, 355.

2. Based on principles of persuasive arguments developed by Richard Crable, Purdue University.

3. Ibid.

4. Darrell Huff, *How to Lie with Statistics* (New York: W. W. Norton and Company, 1954), 123–42.

5. Roy Berko, Andrew Wolvin, and Darlyn Wolvin, *Communicating: A Social and Career Focus,* 2nd ed. (Boston: Houghton Mifflin, 1985), 311–312.

6. John Makay, *Speaking with an Audience* (New York: Crowell, 1977), 104.

7. Kathleen Kendall, "Do Real People Ever Give Speeches?" *Central States Speech Journal,* 25 (Fall 1974): 235.

8. Jack Anderson, "Big Leak in West Germany," *Elyria Chronicle-Telegram,* 28 January 1985, C-10.

9. Berko, Wolvin, and Wolvin, *Communicating,* 315.

10. Berko, Wolvin, Wolvin, *Communicating,* 1981, 290.

11. Daniel Katz and Robert Kahn, *The Social Psychology of Organizations,* 2nd ed. (New York: John Wiley and Sons, 1978), 16.

12. Rudolf Flesch, *The Art of Plain Talk* (New York: Harper and Row, 1946), 38.

13. John F. Wilson and Carroll C. Arnold, *Dimensions of Public Communication* (Boston: Allyn and Bacon, 1976), 195–196.

14. Instructors wishing a more detailed explanation of this assignment may refer to Ronald Fetzer, (September 1977):262–70.

15. Roy Berko, Andrew Wolvin, and Darlyn Wolvin, *Handbook of Instructional Options, Communicating: A Social and Career Focus* (Boston: Houghton Mifflin, 1977), 159.

15

☐

Presenting the
Public Speech
or Presentation

OVERVIEW   A speaker may choose one of four modes in which to present a speech: impromptu, extemporaneous, manuscript, and memorized. It is important in presenting a speech that it sound like an oral rather than a written presentation. Oral and physical elements are important for successful speech presentation. A speech given on radio or television is prepared in the same way as a live audience-directed speech but the speaker must be aware of the technical differences of the media. It is extremely common for speakers to have speech anxiety before and during a presentation. Assistance programs and treatment are available to control speech anxiety.

KEY WORDS

impromptu and ad lib
extemporaneous
manuscript
memorized
gestures
vocal elements
pitch
volume
rate

pause
monotone
virgules
speech anxiety
speechophobia
visualization
skill deficit
systematic desensitization
negative cognitive appraisal

The speaker has analyzed the audience, chosen the general topic, narrowed the topic to a purpose statement, completed the necessary research, selected a method of issue arrangement, constructed the body of the speech using the necessary major headings, selected the method of development, and prepared an attention-getting introduction, a clear statement of the central idea, and a summarizing conclusion. What's next? Presenting the speech!

MODES OF PRESENTATION

■ Four modes are used in the presentation of a speech: impromptu, extemporaneous, manuscript, and memorized. Let us look first at the method requiring no previous preparation and then examine the prepared speech modes.

Impromptu Presentation

☐ The **impromptu** mode of presentation, sometimes referred to as **ad lib,** takes place when a speech is made with little or no preparation. If you are asked a question following a planned speech you have just given, the response would be an impromptu speech. When you are called upon to clarify an idea or explain a proposal you have made, you are ad-libbing. When you decide, on the spur of the moment, to rise and give a response to an idea presented by someone else, or at a meeting make a proposal about which you had not thought previously, you are giving an impromptu speech.

People are almost never asked to make impromptu comments about something they know nothing about. Usually, requests for impromptu comments are made because a person has already done research, is currently working on the topic, or is perceived as a credible source on the topic. Indeed, if you do not feel comfortable with the topic or in doing such a presentation, it is wise to decline the invitation.

Preparing an Impromptu Presentation

If you find yourself in a situation where you are to ad-lib, use the principles that you have been taught regarding the development of a speech.

Depending on the situation, ask yourself your point of view, or the major ideas you want to stress, or those concepts that will answer the question asked or the problem to be solved. Next, if time is available, make a quick list of the major ideas you will be including and put them in one of the types of issue arrangement (chronological, spatial, etc.). Ask yourself how you are going to start. Again, think back quickly to the types of introductions discussed in this text. The easiest one to quickly come up with is the rhetorical question. Then try to figure out how you will end the presentation. Most ad-lib speakers choose to end by restating the major points made. When you go to orally present the material, give the introduction, the statement of the central idea, develop the major ideas of the body with explanations, illustrations, exposition and the other methods of support discussed, and then conclude.

If you don't have time to write the ideas down, quickly search through the same process, or as you speak, keep the structure of the speech in mind and continue to think in a sequential order.

Here is a way you might think through an ad-lib speech:

At a meeting of account supervisors, the advertising manager asks you, his assistant, "Would you tell us which of the advertising designs you prefer?"

You think: "Of the three designs, I like Design 2 the best, then Design 1, then Design 3. I like 2 because of the color blends, clear product identification and contemporary feel of the emblem. Design 1 has one positive aspect; it is more easily remembered. Design 3 is not well-conceived."

This, of course, is much more detailed than you could quickly write down, but asking yourself how and why the conclusion was reached allows you to develop the presentation as outlined.

The process appears difficult, but in reality, it is not as difficult as it appears. The more you practice giving any type of speech, the more comfortable you will become in developing ideas and quickly thinking in a sequential order.

Extemporaneous Presentation

☐ The speaker who uses notes or an outline when going before an audience is said to be speaking extemporaneously. The positive aspects of the **extemporaneous** mode are that you have time to prepare, you have the security of having notes to refer to as you speak, and you can talk to, rather than read to, an audience. There also are some potential problems, such as the possibility of getting lost if you do not practice sufficiently with the material, not being able to exactly time the presentation, and putting down too much information (which may result in reading to the audience). Despite these problems, the extemporaneous mode is used most often by effective speakers. It tends to allow for a presentation that encourages the speaker to have natural gestures, speak in a normal voice, and have consistent eye contact with the audience.

In order to ensure that you are comfortable with the outline or notes, practice aloud with them. By speaking, rather than just thinking through the material, you will find out if there are words you cannot pronounce or ideas that just won't develop. It also will give you an opportunity to judge approximately how long the speech will be. As you work with the material, you will find out whether you need all that you have written down or you can eliminate some. The general guideline for how much to take to the podium with you is that there should be enough so that you feel comfortable that you will not get lost, but not so much that you will wind up reading to the audience. Only you can be the judge of this, and you will able to decide only after much practice.

Manuscript Presentation

☐ In the **manuscript** mode of delivery, the material is written out and delivered word-for-word. Many inexperienced public speakers turn to this mode because they feel secure in having every word before them. This can be an advantage to speakers, but they fail to realize that most people do not read well orally and that often what results is a "flat" presentation which lacks gestures, eye contact, and the dynamics necessary to make an audience want to listen. Besides having exact wording there are two other advantages: the speech can be timed almost exactly and, if you are going to be quoted, there is no chance of someone turning the words around.

In manuscript speaking, the presenter must be so familiar with the text as to be able to maintain consistent eye contact while speaking to the audience. Rehearse with the script and become familiar enough with the material so you can grab a group of words on a line and then look up to convey the content of the entire line. Phrase the material so that you pause naturally at the ends of ideas, not the end of typed lines. Ex-president Carter often sounded so choppy in his presentations because when using a manuscript, he paused at the end of printed lines rather than at the end of thoughts.

Memorized Presentation

☐ There is practically no time when a public speaker should **memorize** a speech. Sometimes rules of speech contests require memorization, but other than that, the opportunities are rare. Though there is security in knowing exactly what you are going to say, a memorized presentation is a manuscript speech committed to memory, and the disadvantages far outweigh the advantages. Most memorized speeches sound orally flat. Speakers are so concerned about the exact word that is coming that they often forget that the words mean something. Speakers presenting memorized material tend to use little or no vocal variation. A common difficulty with the memorized speech is that you run the risk of forgetting. If you forget one word, you may not be able to remember anything else. In spite of these warnings, there are some people who insist on memorizing and do a very good job. But the odds are against it.

THE PHYSICAL ELEMENTS OF A SPEECH

■ Once you have selected the mode of presentation, you are ready to rehearse and present the speech. Presenting a speech encompasses physical and vocal elements. The physical elements of a speech include gestures, physical movements, posture, eye contact, and control of the aids you are using during the speech.

Gestures, such as the use of hands, body movements, and facial expressions, are important in holding an audience's attention. Researchers have determined that those who use hand movements when they talk appear freer, more open, and more honest to an audience than do those who do not use animation.[1] This does not mean, however, that simply throwing your hands around will make the audience listen to you. A speaker who uses natural gestures is likely to make the audience feel comfortable. Preplanned movements often appear artificial and give the audience the feeling that you are not being real or are trying to be something you are not. They may get very suspicious about you. Try to speak as you normally do.

Almost all of us gesture as we speak and use our faces and eyes to express ourselves. If you are using the extemporaneous mode of presentation, you are likely to be more natural as you speak than you would reading from manuscript. Emotional involvement affects your physical delivery. When you get excited and involved, your whole

A speaker who uses natural gestures is likely to make the audience feel comfortable. (© Steve Takatsuno)

body reacts. Notice people talking on the telephone. No one can see their gestures, but they gesture anyway. These are natural movements that result from animation. The more involved, excited, and dynamic you are as a speaker, the more likely you are to gesture.

These suggestions might help your physical presentation:

1. Arrange your papers on the podium so that you won't have to play with them. If you have two pages, place them next to each other rather than on top of each other. This will eliminate having to handle the papers during the speech.
2. Address the first line of the speech to the audience, not the podium. Remember, potential listeners rapidly determine whether or not to pay attention. If they think you are going to read to them, they are likely to tune you out.
3. Plant your feet on the ground several inches apart, with one foot slightly in

front of the other. This will stop you from swaying and also make it nearly impossible to lean on the podium.

4. Do not grasp the podium; let your hands lightly rest on the edges. That way, if you want to gesture, you can easily do so.

5. Look at the members of your audience as you speak. Avoid looking over their heads or at their feet. Watch their faces. You will get feedback from them that can aid you during the speech. Eye contact makes the audience members feel like you are speaking to them, and they are much more likely to pay attention to you.

6. Be familiar with the materials so that you look at the audience rather than at the pages as you go from one sheet to the next. If you are looking at the sheets, so will your listeners, and they will see you changing from one sheet to the next. Though there is nothing wrong with the audience knowing you are referring to notes, there is no sense in drawing attention to it. The audience may start watching for such things rather than listening to you.

7. It is not always necessary to stand behind the podium. If you want to create an informal mood, stand next to or in front of the podium. Some speakers like to sit casually on the corner of a desk or table. Though this is not recommended for formal presentations, it may work well before a small informal group.

8. If you are going to leave the podium and move to flip charts or to other visual aids, determine if you are going to need your cards or notes. If so, you may want to have that part of your speech outlined or written on four-by-six inch cards and take them along with you.

VOCAL DELIVERY

Oral presentation is important. Jody Powell, the White House press secretary during the Carter administration, used to grumble that television networks refused to carry the president's speeches. A CBS executive responded, "If the president delivered better speeches, the networks wouldn't hesitate to carry them . . . either Carter doesn't care or doesn't know what to do."[2] Carter's successor, Ronald Reagan, on the other hand, was so polished in his delivery style that he came to be known as "The Great Communicator."

Pitch, volume, rate, and pause are the **vocal elements** of a speech. These culminate in animation (the liveliness of a presentation). **Pitch** is the tone of the sounds, ranging from high (or shrill) tones of soprano to low (or deep) tones of bass. **Volume** ranges from loud to soft. **Rate** is the speed at which words are spoken. The average rate of speed is 150 words per minute (the equivalent of a double-spaced, typewritten page). **Pause,** stopping oral flow, is used by speakers for emphasis, dramatic effect, and to provide time for listeners (and the speaker) to "catch up" and regroup thoughts before moving on to another point.

A speech is most interesting for a listener if the speaker is animated and uses a variety of vocal pitch, volume, rate, and pause.

Some Hints Regarding Vocal Delivery

☐

1. Speak loudly enough so that you can be heard in all parts of the room.
2. Speak rather than read. There is a tendency for readers to fall into a flat vocal **monotone** (no change of volume and pitch).
3. Stress important words.
4. Adjust the pitch and the rate to the mood of the material. If it is exciting, then your rate should increase. If it is dramatic, the rate will slow down.
5. Group words together so that they make sense. Do not read or speak words; read or speak ideas.
6. Try to fit the rate to the complexity of the material. Complex ideas need a slow rate. Ideas that the audience is already familiar with probably could be presented more rapidly.
7. Speakers who use manuscripts sometimes <u>underline words to be stressed</u> and place **virgules** / (slash marks) / to indicate where they want to pause.
8. Pause before and after major ideas to stress their importance.
9. Emphasize the transition from one idea to another. Key words for this are *moreover, but, nevertheless,* and *however,* as they usually signal transitions to other ideas.

Some speeches are presented via the media (radio and television) in addition to or instead of a live presentation. There are some specific differences which a speaker should know about.

MEDIA APPEARANCES

■

Although a speaker should feel comfortable, he or she should recognize that a television studio is a high-pressure environment. An important aspect of media presentation is the time constraint. Shows are on for specified times and must stay within those time limits. In addition, the lights are hot and the director and crew have to maintain a tight schedule. Consequently, you probably will not be in a very relaxed interpersonal climate.

Pay attention to what the director asks you to do—even suggestions for what colors to wear, make-up, where to sit, and vocal levels. General television hints include not wearing white (it glares); not wearing heavily patterned clothes (they create blurs); not leaning into the microphone (as you speak, the technicians will adjust the microphone levels for you); and not wearing glaring or noisy jewelry. If time is available, try to practice on camera with whatever aids you will be using: script, cue cards, or mechanical prompters. Ask the director to give you suggestions for their use. During the speech, try to look directly into the camera.

A radio show omits the visual impact of your appearance, so your vocal control is the key to being understood. It is necessary to be conversational and fluent. Vocalized "uhs," and "well-ahs" and other disfluencies such as "you know" stand out on the air.

A popular type of radio show—the call-in interview show—allows the guest to present a short speech or explain his or her idea, and then allows for phone calls from the listeners. As with interview-type television shows, there may be no prescreening of the phone calls, so you might encounter any type of negative, irrelevant, or unclear question. In ad-libbing your answers, try to maintain your composure. You may want to pause and collect your thoughts before answering. You also might want to keep a pad and pencil next to you so that you can jot down ideas quickly and put them in some organizational pattern in order to avoid organizational interference.

Speak directly into the microphone. If you are using a script, try to keep it away from the microphone so it does not create noise. Remember, the audience cannot see you, so do not depend on gestures (e.g., head nods, smiles) to convey your answers. Be aware of the time restraints: arrive at the appointed time and remember that you cannot "add just one more thing" once the time is up, as there is no flexibility in program ending times.

SPEECH ANXIETY (SPEECHOPHOBIA)

■ **Speech anxiety** refers to the fears or anxieties speakers feel before and during speaking. If the person has a fear only about presenting material in a public speaking situation, it is called **speechophobia**.[3] Almost everyone suffers from some form of speech anxiety. Sixty-one percent of the United States population lists speaking before groups as its major fear, far ahead of such things as height, insects, financial problems, and even death.[4] "One of the top executives' greatest fears is public speaking."[5] Very few people escape the so-called "butterflies."

Speech anxiety is fear of a negative response from others as well as from ourselves. When people say they are afraid to give a speech, it must be understood that they are not really afraid of giving the speech, per se, but are instead afraid of the negative reaction they will get, both interpersonally and intrapersonally.

There is a difference between normal anxiety and extreme or disabling anxiety With the former, the speaker can remain calm and function. With extreme fear, the person becomes befuddled, goes off in all directions at once, and panics to the degree of dysfunction.

What are the reasons for this anxiety? There appears to be three major factors: (1) lack of ability to think of what to say and how to say it; (2) uncertainty over what to do with the body while speaking (e.g., "What do I do with my hands?" "How do I gesture?" "What do I do about being out of breath?"); (3) fear of losing the audience (i.e., "What do I do if they don't listen?").

We must realize that speech anxiety may be part of a larger problem than just the fear of public speaking. Some individuals are so communicatively apprehensive that they simply cannot function at *any* communicative level. Major researchers in the field[6] have analyzed such individuals and have developed programs that often assist in overcoming the problems of generalized communicative apprehensiveness. In the discussion that follows, we will look only at ways of assisting individuals who are fearful of public speaking situations.

It would be nice to be able to say that by reading the next several paragraphs you will overcome the fear, if you have it, of getting up and speaking before a group. Unfortunately, this is not exactly the case. There is no definitive research available to prove that any activities and programs will work for all individuals, but they have been used successfully for aiding some people.

Four plans of assistance and treatment are currently used:

1. learning to control anxiety through certain practices and devices
2. skill deficit training
3. systematic desensitization, and
4. negative cognitive appraisal.

Practice and Devices

☐ Having an activity or device to use before speaking makes some speakers feel that they can overcome their nervousness. Though some communication theorists totally disregard this as being a successful or realistic approach to speech anxiety, some people swear that these gimmicks work for them.[7]

Some speakers find that before they come forward to speak, it helps them if they take several deep breaths and totally expel the air. Others like to shake their hands at the wrists in order to 'shake out the nervousness.' Some people favor grabbing the seat of the chair with both hands, pushing downward and holding the position for about five seconds, then repeating this movement about five times. This movement tightens and then loosens the muscles, which causes a decrease in bodily tension for some people.

One of the best ways to avoid excessive nervousness is proper preparation. If you feel comfortable with your topic and your material, confident in your ability to accomplish your purpose, and you have practiced sufficiently, the normal nervousness that you feel should not cause any major problems as you speak.

A Gestalt therapy concept centers on letting the anxiety go as far as it can go. What usually happens is that anxiety reaches a peak and then goes away. Try this: Sit in a chair. Place your hands, one inside the other, with the palm of one hand resting on the palm of the other hand, and with the fingers of one hand wrapped around the back of the other. Take a deep breath and hold it. Force your hands together and keep forcing them. Don't let them move. The force should make your hands start to shake. You will then reach a point where the shaking will stop and you are forced to take a deep breath and you'll find you're relaxed and somewhat exhausted. You can use this activity to release tension immediately before you get up to speak.[8]

Another suggestion is to thoroughly prepare and practice your speech and use visualization. **Visualization** is an activity in which you sit or lie quietly and picture yourself going through the speech. See yourself get up from your chair, go forward, put your papers on the podium, look up at the audience members; see them look back pleasantly, and then give your first sentence. Go through the entire speech, noting the appreciative smiles and agreement of the audience, give the conclusion, hear the audience's applause, and walk back to your chair and sit down. During the entire process, do not see or feel any negative images or emotions. Keep running this positive image-tape over and over in your mind. Believe that it is true! The more you expect positive results, the more likely you will be to get them.

The more you think of yourself, the more nervous you may become. Therefore, a device that experienced speakers use to relax is trying to take the focus off themselves.

One way to do this is to concentrate on the head-nodders.[9] You will find that in speaking to those people, you get the feeling that someone is really listening to you. Knowing that someone is listening is reassuring, and it helps you to concentrate on the message rather than on the process of delivering the speech.

As for gestures, just do what comes naturally. If there is a podium, lightly rest your hands on it. One of the highest paid trainers of business executives gives the following advice: to control tension, face your psychological fears. Try to understand just what it is that is making you nervous. You should also monitor your posture. Stand up straight, with your feet slightly spread apart, one foot slightly in front of the other. This will stop you from swaying and make you feel comfortable. She also suggests that you should spend time making sure that your speech is well organized and that you should practice until you can recall the basic points you are going to make. And she recommends that as you speak, make eye contact with the audience.[10]

Skill Deficit

☐

Another assistance plan recognizes that being **skill deficit,** not having the ability to skillfully manage communication situations, results from the person not having a clear understanding of the skills that are necessary for effective performance. The course you are taking now is probably based on the skill deficit theory. Your instructor is attempting to teach you the skills necessary for effective speaking. There is usually a six-step process:

1. Teaching the basic skills—audience analysis, setting a purpose, research procedure, organizing, presentation.
2. Modeling—involves the observation of people who perform the desired activity well (watching video tapes, attending speeches, or instructor observation.)
3. Goal setting—establishing goals that are specific and attainable such as asking a question in class, developing an outline for a speech.
4. Covert rehearsal—practice giving speeches.
5. Behavior rehearsal—practicing in a simulated classroom or before a selected audience with whom you feel comfortable.
6. Live practice—actually implementing the behavior: giving a speech before an audience.[11]

Systematic Desensitization

☐

Systematic desensitization consists of three steps. In the first step, the subjects learn to totally relax their bodies by systematically tensing and relaxing various muscle groups. This is usually done by listening to a series of audio tapes. In some instances discussions concerning the process take place. The next step is visualization in which various scenes are pictured in the subject's mind which involve preparing and giving speeches, and then learning to relax when thinking about the tension-involving situation. The final stage is carrying out a speech and using the relaxation skills that have been mastered.[12]

Negative Cognitive Appraisal

☐   **Negative cognitive appraisal** teaches an individual to monitor and identify the negative self-talk that often accompanies the anxiety over preparing and giving a speech (e.g., "Everyone will think I'm foolish"; "That will really sound stupid"; "I'll probably get sick right in front of the audience"). Once the subjects have learned to identify negative self-statements and to evaluate the impact of these private thoughts on their actual comfort and behavior in or before communicative situations, they are then taught a number of procedures to reduce or modify their negative feelings through self-talk (literally talking themselves out of the negative feelings).[13]

If you are so severely traumatized by giving a speech that you feel you could benefit from more than just the skills training you are receiving in the course you are taking, check with your instructor to see if there is a communication apprehension program on your campus. If not, you might want to purchase a set of relaxation tapes and try to overcome the problem by following the procedure.[14] In reality, most of you reading this book will probably find that by learning the skills you are being taught and by practicing those skills, you will reach the level of manageable nervousness, which, as indicated earlier, is a typical reaction to the speaking situation.

Maybe the key to the whole problem is asking yourself, "What is the worst thing that can happen?" The answer is usually nothing so drastic that the anxiety is worth the effort.

A FINAL WORD ON PRESENTING THE SPEECH

■   The presentation of a speech requires a considerable investment of preparation time for the speaker to plan and rehearse. But the rewards of presenting a good speech with dynamic, polished delivery will pay off. You can accomplish your objective and leave a strong and lasting impression upon your listeners. In a business environment, this could mean a promotion, a raise, a sale, or a positive image for yourself and your organization.

SUMMARY   In this chapter we have looked at the presentation of the public speech. The major ideas presented were these:

    The four modes used in presenting a speech are impromptu, extemporaneous, manuscript, and memorized.

    An impromptu speech is made with little or no preparation.

    The speaker who uses notes or an outline when going before an audience is speaking extemporaneously.

    In the manuscript mode of delivery, the material is written out and delivered word for word.

    In a memorized speech, the speaker commits the materials to memory.

    It is important that a speech sound like an oral presentation and not be prepared or presented in a written style.

    Physical elements of a speech include gestures, physical movements, posture, eye contact, and control of the supplemental and speaking aids used during the presentation.

Pitch, volume, rate, and pause are the vocal elements of a speech. Animation is the liveliness of a presentation.

In making speeches on radio or television, it is important to be aware of the differences between the media requirements and those of a live presentation.

Speech anxiety refers to the fear speakers feel before and during speaking.

Almost everyone suffers from some form of speech anxiety.

Speechophobia is the fear of presenting material in a public speaking situation.

Assistance and treatment plans can be used to control speech anxiety.

THINGS TO DO

1. Submit to your instructor a list of three topics you feel you can speak about for a minimum of three minutes. Pick topics that you have experienced, have experiences in, or have learned about in some way: hobbies, special talents, academic interests, travel experiences. Your instructor will pick one of these topics as the basis for an ad-lib speech. The first speaker in the class will be given three minutes to get ready, the second speaker will get his or her topic as the first speaker starts to speak. As soon as the first speaker is done, the second speaker will go, and the third speaker will get his or her topic, etc.

2. Your instructor will prepare a list of controversial business issues. Topics will include such subjects as:

   A business's first obligation is to its stockholders.

   Advertising's major purpose is to sell products, and whatever means the advertiser uses, as long as they are not illegal, are justified.

   No corporation should be allowed to gain a monopoly position.

   The subjects will be placed in an envelope. Following the procedure described in assignment 1, you will select a topic and give an ad-lib speech on the topic.

3. Using the same topic you selected for assignment 2, you are to prepare an extemporaneous speech for presentation to the class. Following both the ad-lib and the extemporaneous presentations, students are to discuss the difference in the presentations and the advantages and disadvantages of each mode.

4. "One of the common problems facing individuals who are experts in or are training to be experts in a field is explaining to a layperson the concept, operation, or processing of an activity in their area of specialization. You will select an activity or concept directly related to your field of study and prepare a speech, approximately five minutes in length, in which you explain the activity or concept to the class. Carefully consider audience analysis."[15] Use the manuscript mode of presentation.

5. Read an article relating to some field of business in which you feel the class will be interested. Prepare a speech, approximately five minutes in length, that includes at least three long quotations (twenty words or more). Your instructor will be listening very carefully to your ability to read the quoted material well.

NOTES

1. M. L. Clark, E. A. Erway, and L. Beltzer, *The Learning Encounter* (New York: Random House, 1971), 52–65.
2. "Critics Fault Carter's Oratorical Style," *Cleveland Plain Dealer,* 19 February 1978, 1–4.
3. Lynda Gorov, "Speechless Over Speech! Relax," *Cleveland Plain Dealer,* 17 April 1983, E-1.
4. Tony Rodriguez, "Update of the Bruskin Study" (unpublished study, Cerritos College, California).
5. Ralph Prordian, "One Challenge Many Executives Fear: A Speech," *Wall Street Journal,* 28 September 1981.
6. Three researchers who have worked extensively in the area of speech anxiety (also called communication apprehension, reticence, and shyness) are James McCroskey, Gerald Phillips, and Phillip Zimbardo.
7. There is no definitive research available to prove that any of these activities will work for all individuals, but they have been used successfully by some individuals. These activities and references to additional means such as chemicals and physical conditioning were summarized in a presentation by Martin Freedman at the Eastern Communication Association Convention, Ocean City, Md., May 1980, and reported in Roy Berko. Andrew Wolvin, and Darlyn Wolvin, *Communicating: A Social and Career Focus,* 4th ed. (Boston: Houghton Mifflin, 1989), 432–436.
8. Based on concepts presented by Dr. Les Wyman, Gestalt Institute, April, 1983.
9. "Stage Fright, Reticence, Communication Apprehension, Shyness and Social Anxiety: Competing or Compatible Constructs?" (Panel discussion, Speech Communication Association convention, Chicago, IL), November 3, 1985.
10. Maureen Early, "Fear of Audience? Speak for Yourself," *Washington Post* 8 April 1979, F–12 as based on ideas developed by Sandy Linver, author of *Speak Easy: How To Talk Your Way to the Top.*
11. Susan Glaser, "Oral Communication Apprehension and Avoidance: The Current Status of Treatment Research," *Communication Education* (October 1981):333.
12. Lauren Ann Vicker, "The Speech Anxiety Program: Implementation of a Large-Scale Program for Reducing Fear of Public Speaking" (unpublished paper, presented at Eastern Communication Association, Hartford, May, 1982).
13. Glaser, "Oral Communication," 329–332.
14. A cassette tape recording entitled, *Deep Muscular Relaxation,* as prepared by James C. McCroskey, is available from the Speech Communication Association, 5105 Backlick Road, E, Annandale, Virgina 22003.
15. Roy Berko, Andrew Wolvin, and Darlyn Wolvin, *Handbook of Instructional Options, Communicating: A Social and Career Focus* (Boston: Houghton Mifflin, 1977), 165.

16

☐

Informative
Speaking

OVERVIEW   Employees in organizations are called upon to present informative speeches of various
                types. It is important to recognize the characteristics of these informative speeches in
                order to be effective in such presentations.

KEY WORDS   public communication   information speech
                public speaking   informative briefing
                informative speech   technical report
                description   professional paper
                direction giving speech

The public communication responsibilities of individuals in organizations have grown increasingly complex in recent years. Organizations have come to recognize the value of having employees from all levels of the agency, not just executives or public relations staff members, appear in public speeches and on television and radio to communicate company positions, issues, products, and services. An airline, for instance, once ran a series of television commercials in which various employees (a stewardess, a mechanic, a ticket agent) told viewers how much they are committed to doing a good job. A public utilities company established a speakers bureau to send out engineers, chemists, meter readers, managers, secretaries, and executives to speak to groups on energy conservation issues.

A retired Southern Bell vice president has suggested that all executives today must have public communication skills and develop "the ability to represent the enterprise to its customers, to the press, to the public, to the government—in short, to friends and even aggressive adversaries."[1] Much of this public representation takes the form of speaking to an audience.

When a speaker stands up to present material to an audience (**public communication** and **public speaking**), there is a purpose—something the speaker wants to accomplish. Traditionally, the purpose of speeches or presentations[2] has been considered to be either informative or persuasive. However, some communication experts contend that *all* speaking is persuasive in that there is an attempt to get the audience to do something in any speech. For the purposes of our discussion, we will accept that all communication does contain elements of persuasion. "The audience in the traditional informative speaking format must be persuaded to accept the information presented by the speaker. On the other hand, it is acknowledged that the structure of a message and the types of appeals used in the persuasive format differ in that they extend beyond those used in preparing a traditional informative speech."[3]

With that perspective, we present material on both informative speaking and persuasive speaking (the following chapter) so that you will have an understanding of the tools and techniques for both types of presentation. As we have seen, organizations have become increasingly information-based, shifting from the organization of departments and divisions, "the command-and-control organization, to the information-based organization, the organization of knowledge specialists."[4]

Some experts suggest that we double the amount of information in our society approximately every five years. To handle the vast amount of information, all workers in an organization must become knowledge specialists, capable of being effective informative communicators. Thus, informative speaking of various types will become increasingly vital to the functioning of these new, information-based organizations.

PURPOSES OF INFORMATIVE SPEAKING

The primary purpose of an **informative speech** or presentation is to enhance the listeners' understanding about some particular topic. The information may be either descriptive or directive.

Description

□   **Description** is used to explain the causes, the meaning, or the operation of some thing or some concept. Description illustrates happenings or events for the listener.

In describing, the speaker offers an account of what happened. For example, you would be using a descriptive topic if you are informing the audience about the history of the company for which you work, how a particular advertising campaign was developed, the principles of Management By Objectives, how an air brake assembly works, or the basic accounting procedures used by your company.

Direction Giving

□   When a speaker aids others in understanding some process or procedure that can be accomplished in a series of steps, he or she is presenting a **direction-giving speech.** To make an effective speech of this type, the speaker should define any terms with which the listeners are not familiar, describe objects to be used, explain their functions, and give directions for their use. The speaker should compare and contrast objects and steps with ideas, materials, and processes with which the audience is familiar, explaining the steps in the order in which they are to be carried out.

Direction-oriented speech topics might include how to read blue-prints, how to conduct a business meeting, or how to operate some new computer software.

CHARACTERISTICS OF INFORMATIVE SPEECHES
■

Adaptation to Audience

□   The effective informative presentation must be carefully targeted to the needs and interests of the intended listeners. The informative speaker will need to know something about the demographic characteristics of the audience and what those characteristics suggest for preparing and presenting an effective informative message.

It is important to ascertain if the listeners know anything about the topic you intend to address. Are the listeners experts in the field? Are the listeners without much background on the topic? You also want to determine their interest level. Do they share your interest in and commitment to the material you intend to cover? And it is important to know at what level they hold their information. Are they novices, or are they considerably experienced with the information you intend to present? These types of questions can guide you in making decisions as to what level to pitch your message, both in terms of the vocabulary you will use and the development of supporting details to clarify your points. You would want to tailor the message to the level of knowledge and interest appropriate to your listeners.

Supporting Details

☐   As you understand the level of knowledge and interest of your listeners, you can then make some decisions as to the appropriateness of the supporting details you plan to incorporate into your informative message. A good informative speech should be clear and concrete, providing sufficient supporting data to enhance the understanding of the listeners. Thus, the selection of statistics, examples, testimony, analogies should be guided by your perception of what will be truly informative and interesting to your audience.

One of the risks that informative speakers tend to take is the over-reliance on the use of explanations. While it is necessary to explain basic concepts and procedures in an informative presentation, the incessant use of explanation will grow monotonous for even the most sophisticated listeners. It is more effective to break up the discussion of the process or procedure with some of the other types of supporting details so that your listeners will have some variety and remain interested throughout.

Level of Interest

☐   One of the great occupational hazards which informative speakers face is the "so what?" or "ho hum" response from listeners. As one management communication specialist puts it, "It doesn't need to be dull to be good."[5] It is important to incorporate interest materials throughout the presentation or you won't actually reach your intended audience with your information. Based on your careful audience analysis, you can ascertain the listeners' level of involvement in your subject. Then you can select the supporting details to get and keep the attention of your listeners.

Listeners have been found to be more attentive to speakers who use a variety of familiar, concrete, humorous, novel, and vivid materials. Find information that is compelling to your audience or that can be made compelling by your treatment within the discussion of the points in the body of your presentation. A speaker who can compare and contrast, for instance, will enhance understanding of something that may not be readily familiar to a group of listeners.

Structure

☐   A major key to effective informative presentations is a solid structure. We have determined that listeners cannot maintain concentration and attention on any one stimuli for more than a short time frame; thus it is necessary to provide within the structure as many hooks as possible to enable the listener to stay involved with you as you develop the materials in your presentation. The partitioning structure is especially effective for any of the various types of informative speeches, as it offers a considerable degree of redundancy to reinforce the basic points the speaker wishes to cover. Forecast what you intend to cover, discuss it in the body of the speech, and conclude with a summary of the points to give the listeners three possible opportunities to grasp the basic points of your information.

Audio-Visual Materials

A well-developed informative presentation ought to incorporate some audio-visual aids to involve the visual channel in the process of communication. Since the visual channel can reinforce the verbal message, you can enhance the listeners' understanding by selecting and using visual aids carefully. Incorporate visual aids to highlight the points you are making. Avoid the tendency to over-use visuals (some technical briefers want to put the entire outline of their presentation on an overhead projector for listeners to follow), for they will lose their impact.

The use of the overhead projector with some well-designed and illustrated transparency projections improves any type of informative speaking. Indeed, the use of the overhead has become almost a convention in most informative speaking.

TYPES OF INFORMATIVE SPEECHES

Just as informative speeches have overall purposes, they may also be classified according to specific types. In addition to lectures (traditionally found in educational institutions), informative speeches can be categorized as the information speech, the informative briefing, the technical report, and the oral presentation of the professional paper.

Information Speech

In an **information speech,** the speaker assumes that the audience has little or no knowledge of the subject. It is the responsibility of the speaker to make sure, upon completion of the presentation, that the description or directions have been given in such a way that the listeners now understand something that they previously knew little or nothing about.

Since the listener may be relatively uninformed, the speaker must be very sure to give basic ideas. Exposition in the form of background ideas, definition of terms, and examples must be used in developing the presentation. In speaking to a high school group about management techniques used in business, for instance, it would be necessary to define such terms as *management, management techniques, Management By Objectives,* and *organizational chart.* After careful audience analysis, the speaker would assume that the listeners would not know these terms.

The information speech deals with the basic ideas of a topic. Repetition—restating main points so the listeners can remember them—is an important part of the information speech. You want your listeners to understand your information, so they need assistance in remembering the points you are making. If you repeat the major ideas, the listener should be able to acquire the necessary information.

Informative Briefing

The **informative briefing** is presented to an audience that already has knowledge about the subject area. Much communication in government, business, and organizations takes the form of briefings.

A technical report is a statement that explains a process, details a technique, or discusses new elements; it usually conveys more specialized information than a conventional informative speech (© Eric Kroll/ Taurus Photos)

Briefings are one of Washington's growth industries. There is an increasing trend for government agencies and corporations to offer public press briefings as well as internal employee briefings.[6]

The speaker, after analyzing the audience, concludes that its members have at least a basic knowledge in the field. Quite likely, the audience will be a group of professionals in the same field as the speaker. This suggests that the amount of exposition necessary in the presentation is limited. A speaker appearing before an audience composed of business managers for the purpose of briefing them on new methods of management would not have to define basic terms such as *management* and *organizational chart*. The speaker can assume that since people share expertise in a field, they can handle more detailed information. This requires careful analysis, however, as the listeners could be very confused if the speaker assumes that they have more background and familiarity with the topic than they do in actuality.

Briefing techniques are an inherent part of the quality circle concept as well. The team must put together a presentation for management which details the problem studied and the recommended solutions, with strategies for implementing them. Often organizations will engage consultants to assist the quality circle team to prepare and rehearse these extensive briefing presentations.

Technical Report

☐

Technical reports are the backbone of much decision-making in organizations. A **technical report** is a "concise, clear statement explaining a process, detailing a technique, or discussing new elements either to individuals within a business or industry or to people outside the organization."[7]

Individuals and groups should have as much background as possible on technical details before coming to conclusions about any sort of new process, procedure, equipment, or direction an organization may take.

As does any other informative speech, a good technical report offers enough background to clarify the proposal before the group. Again, careful audience analysis is the key, for the speaker should know how much background information may be appropriate for the intended audience.

It may be helpful to supply handouts of any technical drawings or statistics so that each member of your audience will have that information for immediate and for future reference to your proposal. And audience members appreciate the opportunity to participate in a thorough question-answer session following a technical report so that points can be clarified and other possible viewpoints explored.

Professional Paper

☐

A variation of the technical report is the presentation of a professional paper. A **professional paper** is usually a research-based, comprehensive written analysis of a topic in one's professional field. For most professionals in organizations, participation in professional societies (the American Management Association, the Society of Professional Engineers, etc.) is expected as part of the role we assume in our careers. Consequently, individuals are called upon to present their research and findings in professional papers at annual meetings and conventions of such societies.

The listeners are often given copies of the actual paper (which may be sent to the editor of a professional journal for review for possible publication), but the presentation of the paper, to be effective, ought not be a reading of the paper. The most impressive approach is to present an extemporaneous report of the contents of the paper. Careful structure, variety of support, and dynamic delivery will be welcomed by most any conference audience. Thus, thorough preparation of the presentation of the paper will enhance the speaker's effectiveness.

INFORMATIVE SPEECH FORMAT

■

This sample speech illustrates the way in which an informative purpose can be developed into a clear message.

Purpose: to inform the audience how to prepare a résumé.

I. Introduction
   A. Let's look into the future. You have graduated from college and you are now going out to make it in the real world. No matter what your training and qualifications, you could easily be passed over for that job you want if you do not pay careful attention to the way in which you compose your résumé.
   B. A résumé is a document which allows a prospective employer to examine your background and preparation for a job in order to determine if you are the best candidate for the position.

II. Central Idea
    A. Today I'll share with you some ideas on planning a résumé.
    B. By following these suggestions, you should be able to prepare a good document.
III. Body
    A. List your accomplishments
        1. Jobs and schooling.
        2. Honors and awards.
        3. Sports and hobbies.
        4. Volunteer work and military service.
        5. Review the list from an employer's point of view and decide which items you will include.
    B. Lay out your résumé.
        1. Design it to show the details of your qualifications as clearly as possible.
        2. Experiment with different formats and spacing until you find one that pleases you.
        3. Try to make it visually appealing, but make it easy to read and easy to understand.
        4. Purchase a good quality of watermarked paper; it's a small price to pay for the great improvement it will make in the appearance of the finished product.
    C. Heading the résumé.
        1. Full name, address, and phone number.
        2. Center on the page.
    D. Experience.
        1. List in reverse chronological order, starting with the most recent experience.
        2. Company name and full address.
        3. Job title, length of time employed there, unusual promotions, accomplishments or commendations, and functions.
    E. Education.
        1. List in reverse chronological order, starting with the most recent degree.
        2. School name, city, and state.
        3. Specific courses that apply to the field you are entering.
        4. Degrees you have received and the date you received them, or degrees you expect to earn and the anticipated dates of completion.
        5. Mention your high school only if you did not attend college.
        6. Mention a strong grade point average.
    F. Personal Data.
        1. Special skills such as foreign language, typing, computer operation.
        2. Relevant research interests.

G. References
   1. Most experts recommend stating only that they are available.
   2. There is some dispute about the advisability of including the references on the résumé.
IV. Conclusion
   A. In preparing a résumé, first list your accomplishments, decide on a layout, head the document, and list your experiences, education, and personal data.
   B. Writing a résumé is actually writing an advertisement for yourself. Ruth Blau, a publication and public information consultant, indicates, "Let your paperwork say something about you. Let it reflect your personality and your ability. Let it tell prospective employers that you are the kind of person they are looking for."

SUMMARY

In this chapter, we have looked at informative speaking from a business perspective. The major points included:

Traditionally, the purposes of speeches have been to inform or persuade.

An informative speech or presentation is one in which the primary purpose is to give information. The information may be descriptive or direction-giving.

The two main types of informative speeches are the information speech and the informative briefing. Speakers in business and industry are also called upon to present technical reports and professional papers.

In an information speech, the speaker assumes that the audience has little or no knowledge of the subject. The speaker therefore must provide basic information with clear exposition.

The informative briefing is presented to an audience having some knowledge of the subject.

The technical report is a clear and concise presentation of detailed information on a specific topic.

The presentation of a professional paper should be made extemporaneously to highlight the main points of the paper.

THINGS TO DO

1. Attend an informative presentation and observe what techniques the speaker uses in order to be effective. How did the audience respond? Were there many questions? Was the speaker clear and interesting? Was the audience involved throughout the presentation?

2. As a group, discuss current uses of informative speaking in the business world. How do individuals depend upon informative speakers in contrast to television as a source of information?

3. Interview a person who holds a position similar to one you wish to eventually have (e.g., accountant, security analyst, corporate lawyer). Give a three- to five-minute speech to the class which informs about the post. Include the nature of the position, the financial rewards, the communication skills needed for the job, the working conditions. You may do research beyond the interview if necessary.

4. Select an issue which confronts businesses. Topics could include safety regulations, employee health care, unionization, air or water pollution, white-collar stealing, Japanese competition, Japanese management techniques, or ethical responsibilities of businesses. Give a three- to five-minute speech which explains the nature of the problem and various approaches being taken by organizations to deal with or eliminate the issue. *Do not present your views. Do not take a stand on whether businesses are right or wrong.* Inform the audience.

5. Present a two- to four-minute direction-giving speech demonstrating how a piece of equipment operates or how a process works.

NOTES

1. Jasper Dorsey, "CEO as PR Man," *Sky* 9 (February 1980): 50.
2. The term *public speaking* traditionally is applied to speeches made to audiences outside of the specific business or organization while *presentations* are given within the organization. For the discussion in this text, the words will be used interchangeably, as many of the same principles apply to the development and the presentation of both of these.
3. Roy M. Berko, Andrew D. Wolvin, and Darlyn R. Wolvin, *Communicating: A Social and Career Focus* (Boston: Houghton Mifflin, 1989), 442.
4. Peter F. Drucker, "The Coming of the New Organization," *Harvard Business Review* (January-February, 1988): 53.
5. Lee Lescaze, "And Have You Had a Briefing Today?" *The Washington Post* (6 January 1982), A21.
6. Richard Wiegand, "It Doesn't Need To Be Dull To Be Good: How to Improve Staff Presentations," *Business Horizons* (July-August, 1985): 35.
7. Communicating, 447.

17

Persuasive Speaking

☐

OVERVIEW   A persuasive speech is designed to influence the beliefs and actions of others. The persuasive speech is widely used in various forms in organizations, and the persuasive speaker must demonstrate his or her credibility, build strong, substantial arguments with solid evidence, and use motivational appeals.

KEY WORDS

persuasive speech	deductive argument
persuasive speaker	enthymeme
conviction	inductive argument
actuation	sales talk
attitudes	sales approach
persuasive strategies	probing
credibility	motivational speech
psychological appeals	testimony

A persuasive speech is intended to influence the opinion or behavior of an audience. Its materials are drawn from problems about which people hold differing beliefs and opinions such as controversial matters that call for decisions or action. The **persuasive speaker** tells listeners what they ought to believe or do.

Within the organization, persuasion generally would involve an employee making a proposal for action such as a new procedure, a change of policy, a reorganization, employment of additional staff, etc. Outside of the corporation, the organization's representative might be attempting to get the audience to take an action that directly affects the company he or she represents, such as approving a zoning change to permit plant construction, relaxing pollution control standards, or purchasing the company's products.

GOALS OF PERSUASIVE SPEAKING

A persuasive speech or presentation may have as its end goal either conviction or actuation.

Conviction

In a speech with **conviction** as its objective, the speaker is attempting to get the listener to believe as the speaker does. Topics which might fall into this category could include such points as "There is real danger of nuclear fallout from atomic plants," or "XYZ Corporation has developed a clear set of equal opportunity guidelines." If after these presentations the members of the audience agree with the speaker's contention, then the presenter has accomplished the intended purpose of convincing the listeners.

Actuation

A speech of **actuation** should move the members of the audience to take the desired action that the speaker has proposed: buy the product, sign the petition, go on strike, or adopt the plan presented. Many of the activities of a business center on speeches of actuation. In fact, the success of the business may depend upon the success of the speaker in motivating the listener to take a desired action.

ACHIEVING PERSUASION

Audience Adaptation

In order to succeed in your persuasive mission, you may present claims explaining why you feel that you have developed the best plan of action for a pending decision. In addition, you should offer good reasons for adopting your proposal.

Good Intentions

☐ In reality, there is no reason that will be a *good* reason for *all* members of the audience. People tend to attach the label *good* to those reasons that are most suitable for them or that make sense to them whether or not they are actually the most appropriate for the people involved. It is virtually impossible that all members of the audience share the same concept of what is in their own best interests.

Recognize that the appeals will be effective only if you can get the audience to agree with you that they should take the action you propose. Your strategy, then, must be to develop ideas widely appealing to as many members of the audience as possible.

Decision-making Analysis

☐ You might consider three basic levels of decision-making analysis in putting together a persuasive message:

(1) field-related standards
(2) group standards; and
(3) individual standards of judgment.[1]

Field-related Standards

Field-related standards of judging are based on the idea that different types of businesses, and the employees of those businesses, have varying concepts as to what constitutes good reason. Profit tends to be a good reason for a business to do something. Speed, efficiency, community service, employee welfare, safety, job security are specific, field-related good reasons.

Group Standards

The particular group to which you are speaking may have specific standards for making decisions. If it is a group within your own organization, you would be wise to examine what factors have influenced its members in the past or to examine their past patterns of decision-making standards.

Questions you might ask about the group could include: Do they consistently accept or reject certain types of ideas? Do they positively or negatively respond to specific things time and time again? When they have made similar decisions in the past, were they consistent in the reasons for reaching these conclusions?

Individual Standards

Is there a strong leader in the group? Is there a person who has a great deal of influence in the group's decision making? Is it possible to identify what will influence that person? Is the person liberal or conservative in attitude? Is the person more affected by strong, logical appeals or psychological appeals? If there is such a leader in the group, it may be best to attempt to direct your reasons toward that individual.

Attitudes

☐

In order for your persuasive message to be effective, you must overcome listener **attitudes** (predispositions to respond) opposing your solution and develop positive attitudes toward your stand. There are some basic sources of resistance to attitude change. They may be understood by examining the following conclusions from the research on attitude change:[2]

1. Attitudes that are developed early in life and have been held for long periods of time are more resistant to change.
2. Attitudes that have been successfully held or rewarded and reinforced are more difficult to change.
3. Attitudes that are of strong personal concern are difficult to change. Ego involvement means that someone has a personal stake in maintaining the attitude.
4. Attitudes that have been expressed publicly are more resistant to change. When people have gone on record in support of something, they are reluctant to change position.
5. Attitudes are more resistant to change if the attitude is seen as a central attitude related to other attitudes and beliefs held by the person.
6. Attitudes are more resistant to change if the change seems inconsistent with either a person's logic or experience.
7. Attitudes are more resistant to change if the change is called for by a source of low credibility.
8. Using a strong fear appeal may make attitudes more difficult to change. That is, arguing for a change with strong threats or references to what might happen may backfire.

PERSUASIVE STRATEGIES

■

After having determined the initial attitude of your audience, you then want to select the **persuasive strategies** which will aid you in accomplishing your goal. A combination of your credibility as the speaker, your use of psychological appeals, and the strength of your arguments are important considerations.

Speaker Credibility

☐

The persuasive message that you present can be made compelling through the development of your own credibility as a speaker. You can demonstrate your **credibility** (that you are a believable source of information) by establishing your trustworthiness and competence.[3] Through demonstrating your credibility, you can increase the chance that your message and you, as the source of that message, are accepted.

A credible speaker is one who is perceived to be believable. Some speakers demonstrate how their past record should lead the audience to have faith in them. Showing how your persuasive plan is in the best interests of your listeners can also enhance your credibility.

Credible speakers are those recognized as authorities or experts and can more easily persuade their audiences. (UPI/Bettman Newsphotos)

Credible speakers are those recognized as authorities or experts on a subject or who can show that they are well researched in their subject. If you are basing your arguments on your expertise, it is helpful to reiterate your authority throughout the speech. Connect yourself to your topic with reference to your personal experiences, accomplishments, or observations. Citing sound research, statistics, and authorities who agree with your views further your image as a credible speaker.

Psychological Appeals

The credibility of the speaker can be further enhanced with **psychological appeals.** As you analyze your audience, try to determine the psychological state of its members and what psychological appeals might be most motivating to them. It should be recognized that "emotions are simply more motivating than facts,"[4] so you can gain and keep your listeners' involvement in your persuasive speech through the use of psychological appeals. We would urge, however, that you combine the psychological appeals with solid arguments and evidence (as we detail in the next section).

In selecting supporting materials, choose those that contain the desired elements of the appeals within them. There are a variety of psychological appeals from which you can choose:

Adventure: appealing to the listener's interest in trying something new and different. The travel industry, for example, appeals to the public's need for adventure to sell tourism.

Companionship: appealing to a sense of participation or group identification. The need to belong to a group is highly motivating. Advertisers seldom depict a product in an ad with just one person, as it might connote loneliness. Managers frequently appeal to companionship to get workers to "join the team" and produce more.

Creativity: appealing to the urge to design, invent, or create. The do-it-yourself and arts-and-crafts crazes in the United States reflect the need for the creative use of leisure time. In an effort to encourage greater creativity at work, some organizations even sponsor seminars on creativity to stimulate this side of human nature. Work that can appeal to a creative sense can motivate workers to be more productive on the job.

Enjoyment: appealing to a sense of pleasure. Americans are motivated by a need to derive pleasure from life. Thus, advertisers place products in pleasurable settings. Automobiles, for instance, are set in front of beautiful buildings with beautiful people who are enjoying life. Enjoyable experiences at work can be energizing to people in an organization.

Fear: appealing through threats of varying degrees from mild punishment to impending doom and disaster. If people fear for their health or for their lives, they may respond. A speaker, however, should be careful with this appeal. Research indicates that though people can be motivated through fear, overdoing the appeal can make the listener respond with "There is no hope, so why bother?" or "Yes, but it can't happen to me."[5] Moderate fear appeals tend to be more successful than excessive ones.

Guilt: appealing to insecurities and feelings of inadequacy. Some advertising today is aimed at the guilt of the working mother: "'I'm a single parent and I have to work,' Barbara said. 'But I feel terrible guilt. I just can't believe the research doesn't show that kids are more insecure, more unhappy, when their mothers work.'"[6] Thus, parents are urged to provide elaborate food and clothing and possessions for their "neglected" children. The appeal to guilt is quite pervasive.

Independence: appealing to a sense of doing "your own thing" or being "your own person." Our American heritage springs from an independent nation, so we place a premium on this value. The efforts to help senior citizens maintain their independence in the United States reflects this important motivator. This is also part of the need to make workers feel that their contributions are unique in the organization.

Loyalty: appealing to dedication or commitment. Patriotic appeals stem from our loyalty to the nation. People can be motivated to a sense of loyalty to an organization, corporation, or business; the stronger the sense of loyalty, the greater the commitment may be to doing the job well.

Pity: appealing to sympathy or to a need to express sorrow. Appeals to give to charitable organizations frequently use destitute children or even sad-looking animals in order to generate pity and thus elicit contributions.

Praise: appealing through compliments, flattery, positive reinforcement. People appreciate sincere compliments for good work and may work all the harder if rewarded for good efforts.[7] Sadly, praise is not enough a part of the verbal behaviors of most managers and workers in organizations.

Pride: appealing to a sense of satisfaction in doing something well. Some managers find results in appealing to a worker's sense of pride in a job well done, while others feel that such an appeal is not particularly compelling. It seems, however, that people do take some measure of satisfaction in getting the job done well and appreciate such recognition.

Reverence: appealing to a sense of deference to a higher authority. Product endorsements by sports heroes and movie stars represent an effort to appeal to a need for reverence or hero-worship. Religious and patriotic appeals reflect forms of this motivator. Research suggests that as people "are turning to religion in increasing numbers,"[8] this appeal could become increasingly pervasive and effective.

Revulsion: appealing to a sense of disgust, even intolerance. Environmental appeals that demonstrate the revolting effects of pollution, for instance, are aimed at the listener's sense of disgust and can be quite dramatic in illustrating the point.

Savings: appealing to the need to acquire material possession. This appeal can take two forms. One sparks the need to accumulate or collect things. The other appeals to the need to save time or money. Food store chains running special sales on meat and grocery products tap the need for Americans to save money, find a bargain. Financial institutions also use this appeal as the basis for much of their business.

Sexual attraction: appealing through the physical attractiveness of the opposite sex. Much advertising is based directly or indirectly on sex appeal.[9,10] Beautiful women draped over the hood of a car and the rugged Marlboro men are examples of this appeal. Again; in using this appeal, care must be exerted so that the effect is the desired one. After complaints from feminist groups that only bikini-clad young women appeared in their ads, the Florida Tourist Bureau included young men in ads promoting Florida tourism.

Resistance to Change

☐ Clearly, the speaker has any of a variety of motivational appeals from which to select to make the persuasive message more compelling. No matter what the appeals, you should be aware that some basic tensions might cause individuals to resist the appeals and be unwilling to change. The research on resistance to change suggest that people will not be motivated if:[11]

1. They have extreme attitudes on the matter being considered. For example, if a person lives in an area which a company has polluted, trying to change that person's mind to accept the good intentions of the organization will be more difficult than trying to influence those who do not live in the affected area.

2. The source is held in low esteem. You must establish yourself or the organization you represent as being credible and interested in aiding the person to satisfy a need in a forthright way.
3. The suggestion or idea is contrary to their own experience. No matter how logical it is to you, if it doesn't fit into the audience members' experience, you will have to find some way to show them that they may not have all the information necessary to make a decision.
4. It opposes their reference group. We identify with specific religious groups, political movements, or organizations. If the persuader goes against those groups, he or she will have a difficult time changing the strong affiliations and loyalties.
5. It requires altering habits developed in early life. If you have believed all your life in a specific idea or way of doing something, it will be quite difficult to alter that belief.
6. They have gone on public record as favoring or opposing an idea, movement, or process. To change one's mind is often perceived as a sign of weakness. Once a person has signed a petition, declared support for a candidate or a party, or taken some public action, it is difficult to convince that person to alter that stand.

Psychological appeals can provide a very compelling basis for gaining and keeping the attention of your listeners. It is important to recognize, however, that it is important to use these motivators as reinforcements of the solid argument that you present so that the audience has a substantial foundation for decision-making. One campaign expert has distinguished messages based strictly on emotion and messages with solid arguments as "persuasion that seduces or persuasion that saves . . . The former option takes what emotions the audience brings to the message and uses those feelings to your advantage without consideration as to whether there is any reasonable connection between the emotions and the topic, or whether the feelings are harmful, appropriate, or beneficial to the audience. The latter option says you argue your audience into the feelings justified by the evidence of your case . . . Its rule of thumb is that the emotions be appropriate to the evidence."[12]

Building the Arguments

☐   After determining the ways in which to develop speaker credibility and the selection of psychological appeals, structure the arguments in a way that accomplishes your objective.

Deductive Arguments

If you determine that your listeners already agree with your point of view, you may be able to build your speech deductively—arguing from general to specific points. The **deductive argument,** which is historically the traditional and formal method of viewing persuasion, typically follows a syllogism form:

Major premise: All speakers who prepare achieve their speaking goals.
Minor premise: You are a speaker who prepares.
Conclusion: Therefore, you achieve your speaking goals.

In most speaking we do, however, it is not necessary to spell out the entire deductive argument. Listeners will share common assumptions with you, so you do not need to talk in syllogisms. Instead, you may use what is known as the **enthymeme**—a deductive argument in which a shared premise is not stated.[13] Be careful, however, to ascertain that your listeners will indeed share the common premise on which you build your case.

We might argue, for example, that you will achieve speaking goals if you prepare carefully, without going back and stating the major premise in the speech. If we already agree on the premise, it is not necessary to reiterate it, but in some cases the audience has to be convinced of the initial premise. Speakers dealing with the need for Americans to conserve energy, for instance, sometimes mistakenly build arguments on the assumption that Americans believe in and care deeply about energy conservation. Opinion polls in the late 1970s, during the height of the oil crisis, suggested that the majority of Americans did not believe there was an energy crisis, so they needed to be convinced of this as a first step in the development of the persuasive argument. Indeed, this is an important step that many feel former President Jimmy Carter did not take with the American public when he attempted to sell his administration's energy program. Thus, the American public was not very responsive to his persuasive efforts.

Inductive Arguments

Should your analysis suggest that your audience opposes your point of view, it might be wise to structure your ideas as **inductive arguments**—taking listeners from specific examples they can accept to a general conclusion with which they may agree. For example, if you question whether or not you can be an effective speaker, we might inductively argue:

You are bright and articulate.
You have something to say.
You have been trained in speaking skills.
Therefore, you can be an effective speaker.

Careful presentation of the appeals that are most suitable to your particular audience, coupled with your credibility and clearly-developed arguments, will strengthen the impact of your persuasive message and hopefully lead your listeners to respond to your persuasive objective.

Persuasive Structure

In constructing a persuasive argument, it is helpful to spell out to your listeners what you want them to believe and then use statistics, examples, illustrations, testimony, and appeals to develop the arguments. If, for example, a speaker attempts to persuade a group of company executives to purchase personal computers for the organization, the outline for the speech might be:

I. Introduction
    A. Last year, our personnel department estimated that the average letter typed by this organization cost $3.12.
    B. Our department has just completed a study indicating that this organization could actually save money by spending money.

II. Central Idea
    A. Based on our research, it is clear that personal computers could save us money.

III. Body
    A. The present cost is a problem, resulting in unnecessary expenses.
        1. Necessity of typing each letter individually.
        2. Inability to make corrections quickly.
        3. Lack of special features slows down the process.
            a. No automatic centering.
            b. No automatic search and find.
            c. No automatic inserts and deletes.
            d. No automatic storage.
    B. Personal computers are cost effective.
        1. Cost comparisons of prices on typewriters in contrast to personal computers
        2. Internal corrections on a letter and automatic storage could save as much as $2.98 per letter.
        3. Cost savings can also be found in address files in storage.

IV. Conclusion
    A. The comparative data makes it clear that purchasing personal computers could result in tremendous cost saving.
    B. Organizations today cannot afford to lose money because of antiquated word processing systems.

TYPES OF PERSUASIVE SPEECHES
■

The Sales Talk

□

One of the important persuasive tasks of most businesses is the sales of products or services. The American Marketing Association defines the **sales talk** as "the personal or impersonal process of persuading a prospective customer to buy a commodity or service, or to act favorably upon an idea that has commercial significance to the seller."[14]

The selling may be accomplished in person or not. Personal selling involves a direct verbal contact between the salesperson and the prospective customer or group of customers. This may be done by actually meeting the customer or by talking to the person

The sales approach should gain attention, establish empathy, and provide a smooth transition to the actual presentation. (© Laima Druskis/Taurus Photos)

on the telephone. Some sales are made in an impersonal way, in which there is no face-to-face contact. The most common types of impersonal sales are conducted through advertising and display.[15]

In any sales attempt, customers are different. You must go after some customers while others seek you out. Presentations will, therefore, differ according to the customer. It is almost always necessary to use a benefit-centered sales presentation plan[16] in which you custom-tailor the presentation to meet each prospect's unique requirements, explaining how the product or service is going to work for that customer. Do this in specific terms, focusing on the customer's expressed needs or needs that you have discovered through asking questions.

The opening of a sale is known as the **sales approach.** "The salesperson tries to gain the customer's attention and ensure his or her willingness to hear more about the product or service being sold. To do this, the salesperson must accomplish three objectives: (1) gain favorable attention and stimulate interest in the product or service; (2) establish empathy with the customer; and (3) provide for a smooth transition into the actual presentation."[17] One of the most important devices of the approach is **probing**—asking questions to discover whether or not individuals or firms are potential customers and their specific needs.

Four steps generally form a sales presentation:[18]

1. Establish a confident and friendly atmosphere. You can accomplish this with a warm greeting, a friendly smile, and a sincere attitude. Select words that will gain attention and stimulate interest. By introducing yourself to the cus-

tomer and making the customer feel that you are there to be of service, you may create buyer conditioning, which develops a positive relationship with the potential customer.

2. Focus attention on the prospect's problem or need. By asking questions that allow you to find out what problem your product can solve, you ascertain what need will be satisfied, and you can focus on the specific ways your service or product will be used. The prospect's problems are the real reason for the sales presentation. With good value analysis, discussing the needs of the prospect and not the product, per se, you are more likely to make a sale. Note the differences between the effective and the ineffective methods of these sales-people:[19]

PROSPECT: "I noticed your ad in the paper. I would like to look at the television sets that are on sale."

INEFFECTIVE SALESPERSON: "Yes sir. Step right over here. The console has just been reduced from $385 to $295. It is a wonderful buy at that price. You can't go wrong on this one."

EFFECTIVE SALESPERSON: "I'll be very happy to show you some of the sets. We do have some excellent buys during our sale. What kind of a set did you have in mind? . . . And how large is the room in which you plan to have the set?"

In the ineffective method, the salesperson is not finding out anything about the buyer and is narrowing the choice immediately to a single unit. In the preferred method, the salesperson is probing to find out the needs of the potential buyer and then will use these expressed needs to make a recommendation if the customer seems open to suggestions. Note how this requires the salesperson to be an effective listener and speaker. The old "tell and sell" method of sales tends not to be effective in today's communication climate.

3. Solve the problem or need by linking product features to customer benefits. The prospect's thinking must be guided to see the salesperson's product as the solution to a problem or need. "The skilled salesperson maintains a 'you-and-your problem' attitude throughout the sales story. Every product has certain key points which make it stand out in comparison to competing products. These salient points should be highlighted in the presentation, and they should be explained in terms of potential benefits to the customer."[20]

4. Make the purchase easy. "The decision to buy should be a gradual one. Most people have a natural tendency to postpone making decisions, particularly if they are of major importance. It is wise, therefore, for the salesperson to encourage the customer to make many minor decisions throughout the sales process. Color, model, special features should be agreed upon when they are discussed. The final decision thus becomes a natural conclusion to a series of small decisions or agreements."[21]

These general principles are useful when putting together any sort of sales presentation:

Avoid very technical information unless your analysis indicates that this is the type of customer who must know the specific details.

Demonstrate the product if it will help the potential customer to understand it better.

Stay in tune with the prospect. Ask questions that will allow you to know if he or she understands. Notice the person's nonverbal feedback for understanding, agreement, or boredom.

Don't overlook the value of audio-visual aids that can help sell the product. Organizations spend millions of dollars annually to prepare video cassettes, transparencies, films, charts, graphs, multi-media presentations, brochures, catalogs, and all sorts of sales kits.

Let the product speak for itself by permitting the customer to try it out, if possible.

Use a survey approach, if feasible. Find out about the potential buyer's company, personal habits, and what competition you may have.

Fill in the knowledge gap. Your knowledge of the product or service and the customer's usually are not the same. Fill in the details that you feel are necessary for the prospect to know without overloading on ideas and technical information. Consider offering general information about compact disc equipment, for instance, before detailing the advantages of your particular compact disc system.

Remember that people are motivated by both rational and emotional appeals. Fit the appeal to the customer's needs. As the customer's needs change, so should the sales appeal.

Be aware, when selling to businesses, that different organizations operate with different cultures and communication patterns. Find out who the true decision-makers and buyers really are and spend your time dealing with them. While it takes time and money to research the company, it will be time and money well spent.

Work on the presentation techniques so that you present yourself and your product persuasively.

Be aware that there is something in each of us that takes comfort in securing the very best product, system, or plan on the market. It is necessary, thus, to convince your prospect that you are offering the very best.

Find the triggering device that makes the customer want the service or product. Catch phrases such as "expensive equals good," or "reduced from . . ."[22] can be such signals.

Use the contrast principle. If we are presented with two points, one right after the other, and the second item is somewhat different from the first, we tend to perceive it as more different than it actually is. Thus, the real estate agent who shows a client two different styles of house may reinforce a customer's desire for one of the particular styles under consideration.[23]

The Motivational Speech

A popular form of persuasive speaking that is prevalent in business and industry today is the **motivational speech**—a speech presented to the staff to encourage greater productivity and happiness in their work and in their personal lives. "Every year, millions of Americans attending meetings and trade shows are exhorted to sell more, live better, enrich their lives, create, enjoy, prosper, and have it all."[24] The motivational speech is especially popular at annual meetings of the staff, particularly if a well-known figure is booked as the speaker.

To have maximum impact, a good motivational speech should be carefully adapted to the needs and interests of the listeners. The speech, designed to inspire or stimulate the meeting attendees, usually develops from the personal experience of the speaker. Often, the speakers will use their experience in rising through the corporate ranks or achieving their life goals as the example for how "you, too, can make it in today's competitive society." The famous motivational speakers may offer books or cassette tapes which reinforce the "be all you can be" message so that those in attendance can carry the theme with them beyond the meeting.

Motivational speaking has become a million dollar business. Speakers agencies and private bookings have propelled such speakers as Debbi Fields (of Mrs. Fields Cookies), Tom Peters, George Plimpton, Patricia Fripp, George Will, and many politicians into popular "draws" for corporate meetings and dinner presentations. As one observer puts it, "The once humdrum world of stodgy lecturers who went from college to college or from Rotary Club to town hall has undergone a revolution, with speakers from the worlds of politics, business, the media and sports making phenomenal amounts of money speaking to corporations and associations, which seem to have insatiable desires to have the latest hot speaker."[25]

Testimony

Yet another special form of persuasive speaking that many business people consider to be important is the presentation of testimony. The term *testimony* in speech communication has a variety of denotations: *testimony* as in quotations from expert sources; *testimonial* as in presentation to honor an individual; and (our use of the term—a persuasive speech) **testimony** before a legislative or judicial body to attempt to influence the outcome of the deliberations.

Expert testimony requires the development of a careful persuasive argument which addresses thoroughly the issues at hand. Individuals who are called upon to present testimony to a legislative body often will write out a complete statement which spells out in some detail the persuasive arguments concerning the legislative analysis of the policy under consideration. The statement should be compelling and targeted to the particular legislative body and their concerns. Recognize that the legislators will undoubtedly hear a great deal of testimony on the issue, so it is important to prepare the presentation carefully. The most effective presentation strategy is to reinforce the written statement with an extemporaneous oral presentation. Rather than reading the paper (which will have been distributed to all members of the legislative body), it is more compelling to speak to the issues so that the members will sit up, take notice, and listen attentively to what you have to say about the issue.

During deliberations on the reorganization of higher education in the state of Maryland, for example, a campus undergraduate student in biochemistry appeared before the legislative committee reviewing the proposed merger of the Maryland campuses. He presented a very dramatic, eloquent speech in a short time frame, explaining that the students were very concerned about the effect of the merger on the market value of their degrees from the institution. Following his effectively-delivered speech, legislators applauded him, and his impact on the legislation was considerable.

It is necessary to be a persuasive speaker who will make a difference in any sort of testimony. As a witness to the legislative hearings or to a courtroom trial, you should target your arguments and appeals to the intended listeners, rehearse carefully so that you will exhibit eloquent force and stay within a short time frame. Remember that your listeners will be facing any number of long hours of testimony from other experts, so you need to be timely and forceful in order to be persuasive.

PERSUASIVE SPEECH FORMAT

■

Here is a sample of a persuasive speech. Note the clear structure, the way in which the arguments are developed, and the use of examples and statistics to clarify and back-up the ideas presented.

Purpose statement: to persuade the audience that mutual funds offer attractive investments for small investors by demonstrating the advantages over other investments, how they are managed, the ease of entry and exit into the funds, and the types of funds.

 I. Introduction
  A. Do you presently have a small amount of money you'd like to invest? In the future, where will you put your savings?
  B. Many people are wondering where best to place small amounts of money.
   1. Mutual funds are organizations through which a person can invest an amount of money in one source and receive investments in many companies.
   2. Mutual funds are gaining popularity as places to invest an amount of money.
   3. There are over 850 mutual funds in the United States.
   4. $288.5 billion dollars were accumulated by these funds as of 1983.
 II. Statement of Central Idea
  A. Mutual funds are an attractive investment opportunity for any investor, but they are most attractive to the small investor.
  B. Today, I am going to encourage you to consider mutual funds as a present or future investment opportunity.
 III. Body
  A. Advantages of mutual funds.
   1. Variety of funds to choose from.

2. Offer professional management.
   a. Information available.
   b. Expert analysis.
3. Diversification of investments.
   a. Money is in many organizations, so if one does not do well, the others can carry that loss.
   b. One or two bad investments will not have a large impact on any single investor's investment.
4. Easy entry and exit from the funds.
   a. Broker may be used to handle investing, redeeming, and switching funds.
   b. Transactions may be made directly with the mutual fund organization by phone or mail.

B. Types of mutual funds.
   1. Very risky funds.
      a. Growth Funds.
         (1) Concentration of purchase on growth stocks.
         (2) Can be risky, so they should show a rate of at least 8 to 12 percent profit over a five-year period.
         (3) According to the Capital Research and Management Company, a $10,000 investment in a typical Growth Fund in 1974 would have been worth $59,879 in 1983.
      b. Growth Income Funds.
         (1) Principal goal is income to be achieved by investment in high-yielding stocks and bonds.
         (2) Capital-gains are an incidental objective.
         (3) Funds tend to be more conservative than growth stocks.
         (4) Because of this conservatism, their popularity swings up and down, depending on shifting investor interest.
         (5) According to the Franklin Custodian Funds' annual report, an investment in their Growth Income series of $10,000 in 1948 would have been worth $51,695 in 1982.
   2. Risky funds.
      a. Bond Funds.
         (1) Have been around for many years.
         (2) Became popular in the sixties when stock market investments were being reappraised.
         (3) Invest most of their funds in debt-type securities such as corporate bonds and debentures.
         (4) Take the role of lender in the market.
         (5) Value usually fluctuates with the country's going interest rate.
         (6) In a special study published by *Forbes* magazine in 1984, bond funds' changes in net asset values ranged from a

profit of 5 percent to a profit of 11.7 percent, with the average over 11 percent.

   b. Balanced Funds.

      (1) Invest approximately 60 percent of funds in high-quality bonds.

      (2) Invest remainder in high-quality, income-producing, "blue chip" stocks.

      (3) Do well in period of market decline, if that decline has not been caused by extraordinarily high interest rates.

      (4) The *Forbes'* Special Report also shows that Balanced Funds averaged around 11 percent profit for 1984.

   c. Index Funds.

      (1) Duplicate the Standard & Poor's 500 Stock Index.

      (2) In effect the investor is buying a prorated interest in all stocks that make up the S&P Index of Stocks listed on the New York Exchange.

      (3) Can be expected to match closely the performance of the stock market.

      (4) The January 1985 edition of *Forbes* magazine indicates that one of these funds charted a six month's return of 29.6 percent.

 3. Safe Funds.

   a. Money Market Funds.

      (1) Money is invested in short-term instruments.

      (2) Can be purchased in very small amounts and thus gets the same advantages of the relatively high rates that big investors get when they buy large blocks of stock on the open market.

      (3) Not meant to be long-term investments.

      (4) A safe place to keep money at work that is temporarily out of the stock markets or that you must keep in the most liquid form.

   b. Municipal Bond Funds

      (1) Funds which are exempt from federal taxes.

      (2) Earn enough to maintain a regular investment program.

      (3) Avoid undue risks by investing in only quality funds.

      (4) Municipal Bond Funds, as reported in *Forbes'* Special Report, indicated a range of .8 percent to 10.7 percent, with the average percent of positive change set at 7 percent. It must be remembered that this amount was tax free.

IV. Conclusion

  A. Because of the advantages over the other types of investments, the wide variety of choices, the style of management, and the ease of entrance and exit into the market, mutual funds are a wise investment for the small investor.

    B. I invested $1000 in a growth mutual fund ten years ago; it is now worth $7150. In that period of time, I increased my money over seven times. You, too, should be able to make that kind of profit if you invest now in mutual funds.

SUMMARY

In this chapter, we have discussed principles of persuasive speaking. The major points were:

A persuasive speech is intended to influence the opinion or the behavior of an audience.

Though good reasons are the basis for developing persuasive arguments, people tend to attach the label *good* to those reasons that are good for them. Therefore, it is virtually impossible for all members of an audience to be persuaded by the same appeal.

Decision-making analysis may be accomplished by using field-related standards, group standards, or individual standards of judgment.

Attitude change is difficult to achieve, since there are patterns of resistance to attitude change.

Persuasive messages can be developed by enhancing the speaker's credibility and through careful use of psychological appeals.

Psychological appeals include appeals to adventure, companionship, creativity, enjoyment, fear, independence, loyalty, pity, praise, pride, reverence, revulsion, savings, and sexuality.

The sales talk is designed to sell a product to a customer.

The motivational speech is designed to inspire or stimulate workers to excel.

To be persuasive, expert testimony must be targeted to the intended legislative or judicial body and presented in a forceful and timely manner.

THINGS TO DO

1. Cut out three advertisements from newspapers or magazines. Analyze the appeal the advertiser is using to persuade the reader to buy the product. What are the appeals?

2. Listen to three different television or radio commercials. What kinds of appeals are the advertisers using to persuade the audience to buy the product?

3. Select a topic about some action or change of procedure you feel should be taken. Explain the present situation and then describe the changes you feel should be made. Support your assertions with specific reasons for the proposed change.

4. Select a business-related subject about which you have a strong feeling, or a business-oriented problem for which you have a solution. Present a speech to the class in which you state the problem, the possible solutions or sides to the controversy, your stand on solution, and the reasons for your stand or solution. The speech should be followed by a question-and-answer session in which the class will challenge your points.

5. You or a group of students in the class will select a mission that necessitates persuasive action (getting a college policy changed; convincing a local company to change an operation; persuading a store to remove an unsuitable product). You should attempt to accomplish the perceived goal. As a result of the action, a report will be written stating what you did and what results were accomplished. In addition, present an oral report to the class describing what was attempted, the procedures used, and the results.

6. A videotape production of *Subliminal Persuasion* vividly portrays how we are influenced by sexual appeals in advertising and communication. After viewing the videotape, the class should discuss the effect of subliminal motivation and the ethical nature of such manipulative approaches.[26]

NOTES

1. For an expanded discussion of these concepts, see Stephen Toulmin, *The Uses of Argument* (Cambridge: Cambridge University Press, 1969). Also see Richard Crable, *Argumentation* (Columbus, OH: Charles E. Merrill, 1976), 200–201, 209–214.

2. Winston Brembeck and William S. Howell, *Persuasion: A Means of Social Influence* 2nd ed. (Englewood Cliffs: Prentice-Hall, 1976), 151–152.

3. James C. McCroskey and Thomas J. Young, "Ethos and Credibility: The Construct and Its Measurement After Three Decades," *Central States Speech Journal* 32 (Spring 1981):24–34, provides an excellent discussion of the dimensions of credibility.

4. Chuck Cilo, "Emotion A Powerful Tool for Advertisers," *Advertising Age,* 18 (July 1983):28.

5. See Franklin J. Boster and Paul Mongeau, "Fear-Arousing Persuasive Messages," in Robert Bostrom, ed. *Communication Yearbook,* 8 (Beverly Hills: Sage, 1984):330–375.

6. Ellen Galinsky and Judy David, "Say Goodbye to Guilt," *Family Circle* (September 1988):106.

7. The effective manager should know how to use motivators to motivate and to reinforce his or her workers. An interesting summary of the research on the entire subject of motivation at work may be found in Harold Rush, "The Behavioral Sciences in Training and Development," in *Training and Development Handbook,* Robert I. Craig, ed., 3rd ed. (New York: McGraw-Hill, 1987). See also Sharon Nelton, "Motivating for Success," *Nation's Business* 76 (March 1988):18–26.

8. Howard Means, "God Is Back," *The Washingtonian,* 22 (December, 1986):151.

9. See the works by Wilson Bryan Key such as his book *Subliminal Seduction* (New York: Signet Books, 1973)

10. Mark McKinley, *Subliminal Persuasion* (Elyria, OH: Lorain County Community College, 1978), Videotape.

11. Winston L. Brembeck, "Source of Resistance to Attitude Change" (unpublished paper).

12. Celia Kuperszmid Lehrman, "Compelling Reason," *Public Relations Journal* (January 1986):18.

13. Thomas M. Conley, "The Enthymeme in Perspective," *Quarterly Journal of Speech,* 70 (May 1984):168–187.

14. George Shinn, *Introduction to Professional Selling* (New York: McGraw-Hill, 1982), 3.

15. Ibid.

16. Richard Cummings, *Contemporary Selling* (Chicago: Rand McNally College Publishing Company, 1979), 113.

17. Shinn, *Introduction to Professional Selling,* 167.
18. These four steps are a compilation of the concepts expressed in Shinn, *Introduction to Professional Selling;* Cummings, *Contemporary Selling;* and Carlton Pederson and Milburn Wright, *Selling: Principles and Methods,* 6th ed. (Homewood: Richard D. Irwin, 1976).
19. Pederson and Wright, *Selling: Principles and Methods,* 266.
20. Ibid.
21. Ibid., 268.
22. Robert Cialdini, "The Triggers of Influence," *Psychology Today* (February 1984): 42–45.
23. Ibid.
24. Michael Adams, "Motivational Speaking: Is It Just A Quick Fix?" *Successful Meetings* (June 1987):40.
25. Sharon Warren Walsh, "The Lucrative Business of Speaking," "Washington Business," *The Washington Post* 14 March, 1988:34.
26. The videotape of *Subliminal Persuasion* may be obtained by writing to Dr. Mark McKinley, Lorain County Community College, 1005 North Abbe Road, Elyria, Ohio 44035.

18

Special
Occasion
Speaking

☐

OVERVIEW	Special occasion speeches include speeches of introduction, welcome, presentation, acceptance speeches, and after-dinner speeches. Business speakers should also be prepared to participate in questions-and-answer sessions and media presentations.

KEY WORDS

question-and-answer session
speech of introduction
speech of welcome
speech of presentation
speech of acceptance
after-dinner speech

interviewee
interviewer
on-line camera
floor manager
teleprompter
idiot cards

QUESTION-AND-ANSWER SESSIONS

■

Following a speech, the speaker is often asked to respond to inquiries in a **question-and-answer session.** When preparing for a speech, assume that part of your time will be spent away from your carefully prepared message. It is therefore necessary to be ready to go beyond what you said in the formal presentation. This requires that you have as much back-up information and material as possible. If the area about which you have spoken is familiar to you, you may not have to do any additional preparation. If, on the other hand, you have spoken about something that required a great deal of research on your part, you would be wise to gather more information than that which is to be included in the speech itself. Try to anticipate questions and be prepared with the necessary facts, examples, and illustrations to help you to develop your answers.

Speakers have employed some useful techniques in handling question-and-answer sessions. These techniques include:

1. Make sure you understand the question. In order to check it, paraphrase it for the inquirer. For example: "You would like me to state my opinion on whether or not I believe that gasoline prices will rise, and why I believe as I do."
2. If you don't understand the question, ask for clarification.
3. Repeat the question for the benefit of the other members of the audience. They may not be able to hear the questioner.
4. Don't let the questions take you off the topic. If the speaker asks for information that is beyond the scope of the speech topic or purpose, note that, "I'm sorry, but that goes beyond what I was speaking about this evening," or, "That's an interesting question, but I'm not sure that it is relevant to today's discussion."
5. Answer directly. Indicate what you know, why you believe it, or what you believe. If you have no answer, either say so or volunteer to find out the information and send it to the questioner or provide it at the next session.
6. Before answering you might want to compose yourself and think through the answer. Some speakers jot a quick outline or write down some key words.
7. Look at the person as you answer his or her question.

8. If the questioner starts to give a speech, politely interrupt and ask for his or her question. Use a statement such as, "The points you're making are interesting, but do you have a specific question you'd like me to answer?"
9. After answering, check with the questioner to ascertain whether you answered the question to his or her satisfaction.

SPECIAL OCCASION SPEECHES

■

As a representative of a business, you may find yourself presenting speeches on special occasions. Though there are a great variety, those in which you are most likely to participate as a member of the business world are the speech of introduction, speech of welcome, speech of presentation, speech of acceptance, and the after-dinner speech.

In giving any special occasion presentation, the speaker should be well prepared. The audience and the occasion should be carefully analyzed, for not only does each type of special occasion speech fulfill a very specific need, but each presentation requires unique adaptation.

Speech of Introduction

□

A **speech of introduction** is one in which a chairperson, friend, colleague, or specially selected individual introduces a speaker to the audience. This type of speech should let the audience know who the speaker is, the subject, the speaker's qualifications to speak about that subject, and other interesting ideas about the speaker or the subject. It is imperative that the introducer make arrangements to obtain the necessary factual material in advance of the presentation so that a well-structured and factual speech can be prepared. A letter requesting a résumé (a summary of the speaker's educational background, experiences, special awards, and other vital statistics), a telephone call, or a personal interview are all possible ways to secure the information. The speech should be brief (from one to a maximum of five minutes), draw attention to the speaker and not to the introducer, and not embarrass the speaker (unless for some special reason this is appropriate). Make sure you can correctly pronounce the speaker's name. If possible, repeat the speaker's name several times during the speech of introduction so that the audience becomes familiar with it.

Be sincere,[1] avoid trite phrases like "I'd now like to turn the floor over to" (it's meaningless); "I'm sure you will all enjoy this presentation" (it sets a very difficult task for the speaker); and "It is an honor, privilege, and pleasure to present to you . . ." (it has been so overused it has lost its impact).

Take your place at the podium, wait for the room to grow quiet, address the audience in an extemporaneous style, use natural gestures, create eye contact with the audience, and indicate when the speaker should come forward by stating so ("I'd like to present _____ who will speak to us tonight about _____ "), and turning to the speaker. Make sure that when you face the speaker, you do not turn away from the microphone too soon or the person's name or topic may be lost.

The following outline develops a speech of introduction by the chairperson of the Hillcrest Manufacturing Company's Famous American Lecturers Series.

PURPOSE: to welcome Senator X to the corporation's Famous American Lecturers Series

I. Introduction
   A. Congratulations to the corporation for donating the funds that have made the Famous American Lecturers Series possible
   B. Purpose of the series
      1. Allow workers to gain an outlook on national views
      2. Encourage outsiders to come onto the corporate grounds to gain an insight into the organization as more than a producer of products
II. Statement of Central Idea
   A. Welcome to Senator X
   B. Thank Senator for participating in the series
III. Body
   A. Senator has done excellent work in the Senate
      1. Membership on Foreign Relations Committee
      2. Appointment to membership on Special Investigative Committee
      3. Perfect attendance record
   B. Senator has been an ardent supporter of the business sectors responsibility to maintain the environment
      1. Sponsored legislation to require industries to repay all costs of restoring damage caused by any company
      2. Has worked for consumer action in aiding communication action groups
   C. Long a strong representative of his constituents
      1. Brought business to the area through personal hard work
      2. Office staff deals with numerous constituents' personal problems
         a. Immigration problems
         b. Passport
         c. Consumer information and follow-up
IV. Conclusion
   A. Thanks Senator
      1. Good work in Senate
      2. Ardent supporter of the business responsibility to maintain the environment
      3. Long a strong representative of his constituents
      4. Agreeing to be part of the series
   B. Topic: The government, the consumer, and the corporation. Are they working together or competing with each other?

Speech of Welcome

☐   The purpose of the **speech of welcome** is to extend a sincere greeting to a person or to a group. In the business context, this is a common courtesy when a person or a group visits a company or special guests are being honored at a special event. It is usually a short, well-planned, and cordial presentation. The speaker indicates the identity of the group that is being welcomed and the person or the organization offering the welcome. Honest complimentary remarks are made about those being greeted. The reason for the visit or the honor is mentioned as well as the desire for a mutually pleasant experience.

Since it is important that the welcome sound sincere, use the extemporaneous mode of presentation. A statement that is simply read from a manuscript lacks sincerity. Create eye contact with the members of the group and speak directly to them.

This is an outline for a speech of welcome by a company vice president greeting executives from a Japanese sister company who are visiting the United States.

   I. Introduction
      A. "Sayonara"—"Welcome"
      B. Cultures are different, yet the purposes of the companies are the same
  II. Statement of Central Idea
      A. Welcome on the part of the leadership and employees of the local company
      B. Purpose of visit is an exchange of business ideas as well as cultural exchange
 III. Body
      A. As a businessperson . . .
         1. Enthusiasm of how business has improved since the companies have merged
         2. Company has strengths and weaknesses
            A. Need for mutual troubleshooting
            B. Need to examine both Japanese and American business procedures
               1. Theory X
               2. Theory Y
               3. Theory Z
      B. As people
         1. Warmth that can come from understanding people from various cultures
         2. Understanding of cultural differences can lead to personal rewards
         3. Can share
            a. Proximity laws
            b. Territoriality
            c. Perceptions of time
            d. Social patterns

IV. Conclusion
   A. Repeat welcome
   B. Invite visitors to sample the city, the people, and the culture of the United States.

Speech of Presentation

☐ Many organizations utilize public observances to present awards, gifts, and memorials. The speech usually culminates in the giving of a tangible token, such as a medal, ribbon, plaque, scholarship, or check. The **speech of presentation** includes mentioning the award, the persons receiving it, the donor, why the presentation is being made, and the qualifications of the winner. A decision has to be made as to when the winner's name will be announced and when the recipient is to come forward. In some instances, in order to build suspense, the recipient's name is withheld until the last line of the presentation. In other cases, the name is announced immediately, the winner's credentials are given, and then the actual presentation of the award is made. The mood of the presentation should be sincere, and it is recommended that the extemporaneous mode be used.

This is an outline of a speech given by an employer to present a twenty-five year award to the organization's executive secretary. Note the speaker's use of personal experiences, humor, and human touches.

I. Introduction
   A. I'm Mr. Reed, and I'm the boss. There's only one person in the firm who's more important than I am.
   B. This is my executive secretary, Miss Martin, the real boss in this firm.

A speech of presentation is most effective when it is sincere and extemporaneous. (H. Armstrong Roberts)

II. Statement of Central Idea
   A. Gathered here for two purposes.
      1. Thank Miss Martin.
      2. Wish her the best of luck in Florida.
III. Body
   A. The legacy Miss Martin leaves.
      1. I first met Miss Martin many years ago.
         a. Both had golden hair.
         b. Neither wore glasses.
         c. Both scared to death.
      2. Miss Martin has been here longer than has any other employee.
      3. She knows the firm and its operations better than anyone.
      4. Has seen the firm go through many changes.
      5. She has been an integral part of our growth.
   B. What she does for the business.
      1. Keeps it running smooth.
      2. Works whenever she is needed—weekends, overtime.
   C. What she does for people.
      1. Keeps the corporation human.
      2. Always has time for people.
         a. Helps new people learn the ropes.
         b. Lovingly known as the corporation's Dear Abby and Ann Landers rolled into one.
      3. Organizes social activities.
         a. Employee picnic.
         b. Showers, birthday parties, going-away parties.
            (1) Jumped out of a cake at a stag party.
            (2) Played right field when the regular player was injured.
IV. Conclusion
   A. For her endless dedication to the company.
      1. Present gold pendant watch.
      2. Picture will be hung in executive office suite.
   B. Wish good luck.
      1. Company will not be the same.
      2. Happy retirement in Florida.

Speech of Acceptance

☐   When a person receives an honor, an award, or a gift in a public presentation, the recipient is expected to express an appropriate appreciation in **a speech of acceptance.** In some instances, a simple "thank you" is in order, while sometimes recipients feel a need to further express appreciation, pay tribute to the donor, or share the honor with others by referring to their contributions. Many speeches of acceptance, as witnessed on such occasions as the televised Oscar and Tony Awards, are too long, mention too many people, and lack sincerity. If appropriate, humor sometimes breaks the tension and is a welcome addition to the proceedings. The acceptance should be presented in a "real you" manner, and it is inappropriate to read your message. Few, if any, notes should be used, and the speaker should speak directly to the presenter, donor, and the audience. Do not apologize or belittle yourself for receiving the honor. Since you received the recognition, the individuals who selected you felt you were worthy of the award. By telling them you are not worthy, in an attempt to feign humility, you are really questioning their judgment.

This outline of a speech given by the recipient of an award at an employee-of-the-year presentation demonstrates how to develop an acceptance speech.

    I. Introduction
        A. The words "thank you" are so overused that they often seem to be meaningless. In this case the appreciation is real!
        B. I sympathize with the difficulty of the decision.
            1. Can personally vouch for the integrity, tireless efforts, and enthusiasm of my coworkers.
            2. Am proud to be a coworker of these people.
    II. Statement of Central Idea
        A. An employee is only as good as the firm for which he or she works.
        B. This company is responsible for much of what I am today.
    III. Body
        A. The business I work for . . .
            1. Has had other jobs previously.
                a. Quit others because of a lack of corporate integrity.
                b. This company has high ideals and aids workers to help reach those ideals.
            2. This company is a company that challenges me.
                a. No threats.
                b. Supportive atmosphere to be creative.
                c. Encourages and accepts employee input.
            3. Has made me a better person by challenging me to strive for high goals.
            4. The company's goal of "people profit" over "monetary profit" is inspiring.
        B. The people I work for . . .
            1. People make this company, not a hollow entity.
            2. Proud to know people who are proud of what they are doing.
                a. Spend one-third of our lives working.
                b. Spend one-half of my life at this firm.
                c. Too selfish to have spent it with people I don't like.
    IV. Conclusion
        A. Thanks for the award, the corporate policies, and the people who work here.
        B. The financial award that comes with this honor will be given to the American Cancer Society for research.

After-Dinner Speech

The primary purpose of most **after-dinner speeches** is to entertain. Entertainment is normally considered to be humor, but it is not always necessary to inspire laughter in order to entertain. A speaker who is interesting or gets an audience to relax can also be called entertaining.

Humor is very difficult for some people to communicate. Professional comics hire teams of writers in order to be funny, and even they sometimes fail. There are some clues, however, to aid in developing the after-dinner speech, which center on how to organize the speech, devices that arouse humor, and some do's and don'ts.

The usual components of an after-dinner speech are: (1) a series of anecdotes that are loosely developed about a central theme: (2) a chronological narrative built on the speaker's own experiences or the experiences of the person or organization being honored; or (3) a series of stories built around a theme.

Devices that arouse humor are exaggeration and understatement: depicting some concept or thing in inappropriate terms until it becomes ridiculous; satire, which consists of making fun of some type of custom, mannerism, or behavior of someone or some group; anecdotes, which dramatize an event in such a way that the audience believes that something will happen and at the last moment an unexpected turn of thought or language produces the laughter; and puns, which rely on double meanings of words, or using one word in place of another that is close in pronunciation but obviously is misused.

Some *do's* for presentation of after-dinner speeches include making sure the topic selected fits the purpose of the occasion, adapting the material to the audience, and being clear and brief.

On the other hand, do not preface stories by telling the audience how funny they are. Do not attempt to be a comedian unless you feel comfortable with the role. You cannot fool the audience; your discomfort will be obvious. Some people should decline the after-dinner speaker role if they feel it is impossible for them to fulfill the responsibility.

Most libraries have books specifically prepared for after-dinner speakers. H. V. Prochnow is the author of a series of books that can be of aid: *The Public Speaker's Treasure Chest; Speaker's Handbook of Epigrams and Witticisms; A Dictionary of Wit, Wisdom and Satire;* and *The Speaker's Treasury of Stories For All Occasions.* Other sources are Edward Friedman's *Toastmaster's Treasury,* Louis Untermeyer's *A Treasury of Laughter,* and Jacob Braude's two-volume *Lifetime Speaker's Encyclopedia.* Robert Orben, a comedy writer who headed the speechwriting office for President Ford, publishes a comedy newsletter for speakers and writers.

At a dinner for the dedication of a new wing of a local historical society, a businessperson who had been responsible for aiding in the fund raising presented an after dinner speech:

    I. Introduction
        A. I don't know about you, but right about now I'm feeling like that blue whale up there on the wall: STUFFED!

B. Important day in the community and in the lives of the people in this room: we set a goal and reached it.
II. Statement of Central Idea
   A. After years of fund raising and building, it's a thrill to be at this dinner.
   B. Personal satisfaction.
   C. Relieved that it's over.
   D. All should be excited and proud.
III. Body
   A. The Fund Raising.
      1. Seems that when I started the fund raising for this project, the dinosaurs still ruled the earth.
      2. Struggle for support through various stages of the economy and administrations.
         a. Pie-in-the-face booth at the county fair.
         b. Increased building costs and decreasing value of money.
   B. The Building of the Wing.
      1. You know, if God could create the world in six days, I'll be damned if I can understand why it took us five years to stuff a few dead animals and put them in a museum.
      2. Every stone has a history all its own.
         a. Wrong marble delivered.
         b. Sculpture piece mounted upside down.
   C. The Future.
      1. When I told Bill the dedication would have to be postponed another six months, he looked just about like the Tyrannosaurus Rex you see on that wall behind you.
      2. Thousands of people will walk through these halls.
         a. People who never would have had such an experience.
         b. Will always be indebted to the people at this dinner.
         c. Remember the work of the past and the glory of the future.
IV. Conclusion
   A. (Gazes at the prehistoric display behind him) It's tragic really—that the dinosaurs had no consciousness of their own mortality. And, in many ways, neither do we. Fortunately, we will leave a living memory behind us: this building.
   B. (Laughingly)
      We start raising money for the new wing next week!

APPEARING ON TELEVISION

■

It is common for business people to appear on the media. Executives, managers and workers may be asked to represent the organization through an interview, making a public statement, or participating in a discussion. In some instances, businesspeople may be asked to appear in the company's commercials.

It is becoming the responsibility for firms to clarify and defend their actions on shows such as "60 Minutes" and "20/20." Videotapes of lectures concerning new products have increasingly showcased corporate staff rather than using paid professional actors. Chrysler's Lee Iaacoca and other corporation's employees have taken on the role of telling the public about the products of their companies.

The trend is clear: knowing how to prepare for and participate in a media event is a valuable asset for present or future businesspeople.

Television Interviews

☐

It is usually the purpose of a television interview to discover information or attitudes of the participants concerning a specific subject. For example, if your company has recently moved to a new area, the local population may be interested in finding out about the company's products, services, and the nature of the workforce. Or, a representative may be responsible for explaining some aspect of his or her area of expertise.

Some basic principles will help you be an effective **interviewee**—the person being interviewed. These principles include learning all you can about the interview process, knowing what you want to say, and knowing your rights and exercising them. It is also important for you to be aware of the need to interact and be in control of yourself and the interview.

Learning About the Television Interview

It is often necessary to gain information about an interview. Information needed includes the interview's purpose, why you are appearing, the identification of the interviewer, the technical and physical setting, the presence of an audience, and the questions to be asked.

Interviews are Purposeful It is important that you find why the interview is being held and its goal. This knowledge will help in preparing for the questions the **interviewer**—the person asking the questions—will pose.

It is also important to determine if you will be the sole guest or part of a group. In a one-to-one interview, you will be the center of attention and will only have to deal with the questions asked. In a multi-participant interview, you may be forced to not only answer the questions but also respond as the other panelists questions and answers. You may have to counter their answers if you disagree, or defend or clarify if they probe your answers. A multi-person interview also forces you to give short answers so the other participants get a chance.

Clarify Why You Are Appearing Are you representing the company or your own views? Are you there to be a spokesperson or as the subject of the interview? These are important questions. As a company representative, if the organization has a stance, your duty is to present their view (which may or may not be yours). On the other hand, if you are speaking for yourself, you are responsible only to yourself.

The Interviewer   It often helps to know who will conduct the interview. Knowing the style and types of questions that person asks can help you prepare. Is the person a surface-level interviewer, who will accept your answers and move on, or is that person a digger, someone who will challenge your answers and expect you to defend your ideas? Or, is the interviewer the "star" of the show, so that your role is actually quite secondary?

Technical and Physical Setting   Knowing the technical and physical setting and expectations of the interview is imperative. Know the interview's location and time. Knowledge of any special dress requirements is helpful. Showing up wearing a suit when you are going to be asked to demonstrate some physical task would be impractical. If it is an on-the-job presentation, are you expected to wear your working clothing? Is special make-up required?

Audience Presence   It is sometimes important to know if an audience will be present. Being interviewed in a studio with no audience is different than having a group of people present who will react to you. This is especially true if you are speaking about a controversial topic or taking an unpopular stand.

The Questions   How do you find out the answers to the questions you have concerning the interview process? Simple—ask. Ask questions that will get the information you need. Because media people do so many interviews they often forget that the interviewee may not be knowledgeable about the process. They assume you are ready and informed unless you ask questions.

Know What You Want to Say

Though interviews are best when spontaneous, you should still have a clear idea of what you want to say. "In a typical interview, the respondent talks approximately 70 percent of the time."[2] This is the time to get your ideas across. If you have a general idea of what you want to say you will be less apt to ramble, will have the facts, stories and examples you need to defend or develop your ideas, and will be much less likely to make a fool of yourself.

In some instances, you will be asked to submit questions in advance. Other times, the interviewer will prepare the questions and allow you to see them before you go on the air. Sometimes there will be a pre-interview in which you will be told the general nature of the material to be covered.

When you are engaged to do the interview, ask which questioning method will be used. If there is flexibility in the process, suggest the one with which you will be most comfortable.

Know and Exercise Your Rights

Many people are intimidated by a television appearance. Don't be intimidated; don't be servile. Ask for the information you need.

Questions you might want answered include:[3]

1. Will I meet the interviewer before air time?
2. May I have an idea of the type of questions that will be asked?
3. Will I be able to use notes? If not, why?
4. Will I be able to use visual aids? If not, why?
5. Will I be furnished with a written or video transcript of the interview?
6. Will I be informed of the basic ground rules—time, location, right to edit the material?

Recognize that during the interview you don't have to answer any question you would prefer not to answer. Don't allow yourself to be badgered or intimidated into responding if you feel it is not in your best interest or your company's.

Interact

Interacting involves listening and speaking. Unless you do both effectively, the interview will not accomplish your goal.

The basic rule of listening is simple: if you don't hear the question, you can't supply the answer. To be an effective listener:[4]

- Start listening from the outset
- Don't fake attention
- Be aware that you can think faster than the interviewer can talk
- Whenever necessary, take notes
- Try to identify the main point of the question
- If you don't understand a question, ask the interviewer to repeat it.

As for speaking, recognize that you are appearing because you are knowledgeable on the subject or are representing a point of view espoused by your organization; you are the expert. Answer as well as you can. Don't answer questions that you are uncomfortable answering. If you don't know the answer to a question or have no opinion, say so.

These are general suggestions for effective speaking:

- State your main point and clarify it with statistics, stories, examples or whatever is needed to ensure clarity.
- Be brief.
- Be accurate.
- Don't be evasive.
- Stay calm—even during difficult times.
- Use clear language.
- Establish your credibility by commenting on your experience and education in the area.

Maintain Control

One of the difficulties of participating in a media interview is the possibility of losing control of the interview. This happens because the interviewee perceives he or she is at the mercy of the interviewer. Though the interviewer asks the questions and is responsible for the format of the program, it is difficult to ensure that the interviewee will be able to respond in the desired way. There are, however, some actions that the interviewee may take in order to ensure that the message gets across:[5]

- Come to the interview well informed.
- Ask questions whenever you feel they are appropriate.
- Don't allow the interviewer to interrupt if what you are saying is relevant. Assert your rights as the guest.
- Don't be misinterpreted. Refute misconceptions as they occur.
- Try to have the last word so that the interviewer does not have the opportunity to alter your ideas.

EFFECTIVE PUBLIC COMMUNICATION MEDIA PRESENTATIONS

■ Making a public statement on television is basically the same as giving a speech, however, there are some differences. In any type of speaking experience, it is important that the speaker have a purpose, structure a clear message, and develop ideas in a sequential pattern. The statement will be interesting, clear, and indicate a reasoned approach if the speaker uses appropriate statistics, quotations, examples, stories and analogies. Differences include the presence of cameras, time limits, teleprompters, studio personnel, cameras, mikes, and the use of visual aids.

There are some helpful physical and speaking presentation techniques that make media performances effective. Knowing about television cameras, time limits, teleprompters, studio personnel, the microphones, visual aids, and physical techniques assist a media speaker.

Television Cameras

☐ Audience focus is obtained by looking into the camera that is on-line. The **on-line camera** is the one which is broadcasting the picture. If you are speaking in a setting when there is only one camera, then the problem is slight. Your responsibility is to look directly into the camera. If there is more than one camera, you will be able to identify the camera in one of two ways. The **floor manager**, the link between the director and the production people, is responsible for the activities on the studio floor. As the speaker, you are part of that production team. During the show, the floor manager will give you signals by pointing to the camera which is on-line. When cameras are about to change, the floor manager will hold up an open hand, palm facing you, with all fingers extended. When a camera goes on, the pointing finger will indicate the active camera. If there is no floor manager, the camera people will usually have a procedure to indicate the active camera. Another way to know which camera is on-line is to watch the cameras. The one on-line camera will have a glowing red light on top of the camera.

If you have any questions about the process, ask. Asking questions prevents confusion, builds your confidence, relaxes you, and insures that your message is directed to the on-line camera.

Time Limits

☐ Time limits are extremely important in media. In daily life, a few seconds here or there are usually unimportant. In the media, however, exact time is essential. If you talk too long, you will be cut off. If you talk too short, there will be blank air time. To assure exact timing, media speakers commonly use a manuscripted form.

Teleprompters

☐ **Teleprompters** are devices placed in front of the lens of a camera to allow the presenter to read words while looking at the camera. If you are to use a teleprompter, ask for some practice time to get used to the device.

If you are not using a teleprompter, make sure that you are familiar enough with your script to ensure that you can look up to give the impression of speaking rather than reading.

In some instances **idiot cards**—pieces of posterboard with the script written on them—are used in the place of teleprompters. This is common when the production is done outside the studio. Idiot card preparation may be done by the production staff or the speaker. If you need notes in addition to your script, be sure to check who is responsible for idiot card preparation.

Studio Personnel

☐ Studio personnel can be very distracting. Normally, while you are presenting a media message, camerapeople, the floor manager, and other technical aids will be moving around adjusting cameras, lights, and props. These activities cause distractions not present when speaking to an audience. It is important that you concentrate on your presentation and leave the work of production to the technicians.

Speaking to the Camera

☐ Speaking to a camera is not the same as speaking to a live audience. If you are used to looking into peoples' eyes, watching for verbal and nonverbal reactions, speaking to a camera can be frustrating. Cameras don't respond.

Effective media speakers learn that they should address the lens of a camera just as they address the eyes of a person. Look directly into it, imagine that the mechanical device is a real entity, and speak with enthusiasm and directness.

Microphones

☐ As a media speaker, you must be aware of the role of microphones. Microphones are capable of picking up your voice with clarity. It is unnecessary to raise your volume. You do not have to lean into a microphone to be heard. Once the microphone levels are set, you don't have to worry about the volume. As you raise and lower your voice, the audio person compensates for these changes.

If you are asked to "give a level," the audio person is requesting you to speak so the level of your voice can be evaluated and the proper settings made on the audio board. Start talking normally. You can count or read your speech. Do not blow into the mike; it's bad for the equipment and doesn't help set the level.

Moving around will be impossible when using a stationary microphone, such as one attached to a stand or placed in a holder on a desk, or a lavaliere mike, a small mike clipped to your clothing. Stand and desk mikes can't move, and if you get too far from them, you will not be heard. Lavaliere mikes are very sensitive and pick up noise if you walk around. These mikes will restrict your actions.

Other mikes, such as cordless, hand-held mikes or mikes mounted on apparatus capable of following a moving performer, will accommodate movement.

Check with the technicians to ascertain the limitations of the mikes that will be used. If you know you need to go to visual aids or want to move around, then inform the media people of your needs.

Visual Aids

☐ Though they are often needed in both media and audience presentations, the use of visual aids in these settings is quite different than when used before a line audience. If you need charts or pictures or must display objects, let the media people know. They will advise you if you have to prepare the aids in a different format because of the requirements of the television process.

There are mechanical ways of producing materials to aid media speakers that are not available to public speakers. For example, if you wish to display a small object, the camera can take a close shot to reveal the details.

Charts on posterboard, a common tool of public speakers, are often difficult for cameras to reproduce. Using an overhead projector, a device common in business speaking, is not an effective tool for television. It is possible, however, to use mechanical devices to reproduce the charts for media usage.

As with any media-centered problem, tell the production team your requirements and ask for advice on how best to use the media process to enhance your presentation.

Physical Presentation Techniques

☐ Normally, the entire body of a public speaker is seen. On television, the body as a whole, or any part of it, may be on screen. It is not unusual for the camera to show only a waist-up shot, or the face, or a tight shot of the mouth, or even a single finger drumming.

Being aware of some presentation techniques can help a prospective media speaker. These techniques include being natural, using gestures and movements, and controlling idiosyncratic mannerisms.

In general, be as natural as you can. The eye of the camera is critical and will detect fake smiling, unnatural movements, and forced gestures. Former President Jimmy Carter was noted for what appeared to be a forced and unnatural smile when he was uncomfortable. Richard Nixon, during camera appearances, displayed a steely stare when being confronted. The 1988 Democratic Presidential candidate Michael Dukakis may have lost the election because of his discomfort with the intimacy of television. He never quite mastered looking comfortable on camera, giving some the illusion that he was covering up true feelings.

Although you must be natural, you must also realize that due to the size of the television screen, there are limitations on movement. Sweeping and rapid gestures are often difficult for the camera to follow. Gesturing toward the camera creates distortion. Crossed legs can be distracting, especially those of a female in a short skirt or if the person swings a leg.

It is wise to keep gestures close to the body. If not, the viewer may see an arm and wrist without a hand when the camera shows a close shot.

Stance can be important for a natural look. Some media speakers complain about a dry mouth or shaking hands or legs. Often this is the result of standing with locked knees. Locked knees cause the body to tighten-up and results in shaking. Distribute your weight by placing your feet about six inches apart with one foot slightly in front of the other. Place your weight on the back foot. This posture should relax your body, relieve tightness, and stop the shaking.

Try to keep your gestures and facial expression appropriate for the topic. Facial reactions will be picked up by camera close-ups. A smile, for example, would be inappropriate if you are discussing a serious topic. Try to avoid such things as drumming your fingers on the lectern or fiddling with your glasses.

A television presenter may not be able to control all of the factors in any given presentation; however, being aware of the television process and preparing for the experience will go a long way toward assuring a purposeful experience. Television is an important outlet for business and industry and those prepared to work with it can do a lot to ensure their place in an organization.

SUMMARY

In this chapter, we have identified types of special occasion speeches and the theory and methods of effective question-and-answer sessions and media appearances. The major points were:

A question-and-answer session follows many types of public speaking situations.
Special occasion speeches include speeches of introduction, welcome, presentation, acceptance, and after-dinner.
It is common for business people to appear on radio and television.
Knowing how to prepare for and participate in a media event is a valuable asset for businesspeople.

THINGS TO DO

1. Research the life of a businessperson or business author such as Lee Iaccoco, Sylvia Porter, Donald Trump, Liz Claiborne, or Tom Peters. Assume that the person was going to speak before your class. Prepare a speech of introduction for a presentation entitled, "My life, its successes and failures in the world of business."
2. When your class presents its informative or persuasive speeches as part of its activities, each person will be introduced by a member of the class. Your in-

structor will indicate who you are going to introduce. Plan and present the introduction speech.

3. Select an occasion. Prepare an appropriate special occasion speech and then present it to the class.

4. Watch an interview program. Write a critique of the interviewer and interviewee. Specifically identify the strengths and weaknesses of each as a television presenter.

5. Following one of your informative or persuasive class presentations, you will participate in a question-and-answer session. The class will be encouraged to ask you a minimum of four questions.

NOTES

1. Though most introductions tend to be serious, a good humorous presentation is also acceptable. Gary Lyle's book, *I Am Happy to Present,* contains some excellent introduction examples.
2. Evan Blythin and Larry Samovar, *Communicating Effectively on Television* (Belmong, CA: Wadsworth Publishing Company, 1985), 181.
3. Ibid., 183.
4. Ibid., 186–188.
5. Ibid., 198.

INDEX

A

Acceptance speech, 367–368
Accommodation, 118
Accountability, ethical, 186–187
Acquired-needs Theory, 163
Action
  bias for, 149
  chain, 88
Action question-statement, 304
Actuation, 342
Adaptation, 13
Ad lib, 317
Adventure, appeal to, 345–346
Aesthetics, 85–87
Affect displays, 75
After-dinner speech, 369–370
Agenda, 258–259, 265. *See also* Hidden
  agenda
Aging population, 158–159
Alarm, 28
Alternative solutions, 201
  assessment of, 202–203
American Statistics Index, 279
American time, 90
Analogies, 296–297
Anecdotes, 369
Animation, 327
Anxiety. *See* Communication anxiety
Appearance, 83–85
Appreciative listening level, 41–42
Arguments
  building of, 348–350
  deductive, 348, 349
  inductive, 349
  persuasive structure of, 349–350
Artifacts, 83–85
Assertive messages, 122–123
Assertiveness, 121–122, 124
  messages of, 122–123
  principles of, 122
Assertiveness training, 19
Association, 46–47
Assumptions, 57, 66

Attending, 6, 38
Attention-getters, 287
  type of, 287–290
Attention span, 38
Attitudes, 344
  changing, 358
Audience, 273, 283. *See also* Listeners
  adaptation to, 332, 342
  attitudes of, 344, 358
  interests of, 273–274
  level of interest of, 333
  in TV interview, 372
Audio aids, 303, 311
Audio teleconferencing, 249
Audio-visual aids, 303, 311
  in informative speech, 334
Auditory stimuli, 38
Authoritarian leaders, 255
Autonomy, 150
Avoidance, 118

B

Baksheesh, 185–186
Behavioral Kinesiology, 85
Bibliography, 281, 283
  sample, 282
Biological stress response, 26
Blackboards, guidelines for use of,
  302–303
Black English, 55
Bodily self, 18
Body language. *See also* Nonverbal
  communication
  learning of, 72
Book of Facts, 279
Bottom-up process, 169–173
  implementation of, 173
Brainstorming, 197
  sessions for, 244
Bureaucratese, 102
Burn-out, 27
Business. *See also* Organizations
  appropriate clothing for, 84

changing role of interpersonal
    communication in, 124
communication difficulties in, 134, 151
communication in, 130–151
competition in, 132
corporate communication in, 138–142
creating listening environment in, 37
decision-making in, 193–205
ethics and, 180–190
external communication in, 132, 135
grapevine in, 136–138
group communication in, 240–265
informal communication in, 136
interdepartmental communication in,
    135
internal communication in, 132,
    134–135
interpersonal communication in,
    98–124
interpersonal skills in, 107–116
interviewing in, 211–235
intradepartmental communication in,
    134–135
obstacles to effective corporate
    communication in, 147–150
organizational structure, climate, and
    culture in, 142–144
proprietary and confidential
    communication of, 136
research information sources for, 280
spatial arrangements in, 81–83
stress and, 26–27
time spent communicating in,
    132–133
Business ethics, 181
  definition of, 184–185
Buzz sessions, 244–246
Buzz words, 43

C

Call-in show, 230
Camera, TV, 374
  speaking to, 375

Capitalism
  defense of, 183
  ethics and, 185
Categorizing, 7
Causal arrangement, 293
Change
  conflict and, 117
  inability to, 148
  nature of in corporations, 149
  resistance to, 347–348
Charts, 300
  in media presentations, 376
Chronemics, 87–88
Chronological order, 291
Citations, 281
Civil Rights Act (1964), 215
Clarifiers, 296
Clarity, 57–58, 66
Clinchers, 304–305
Clothing, 83, 86
  image and, 85
  importance of, 92
Clusters, 74, 93
Cognitive modification, 21, 30
Cohesion (group), 243
Color, 86–87
  symbolic meaning of, 87
Communication. See also Communication
  skills; Language; Nonverbal
  communication; Speaking;
  Speech
  as activity function, 145–147
  assertive, 121
  in business organization, 130–151
  confidential, 136
  definition of, 5
  downward, 143, 151
  effective, 5
  as employee function, 174–175
  external, 135
  female-male, 62–66
  group, 240–265
  indefiniteness of, 7
  informal channels of, 136
  interdepartmental, 135
  interpersonal, 98–124
  intradepartmental, 134–135
  intrapersonal, 16–30
  as management function, 168–174
  models of, 9–12, 13
  multichanneled, 99, 124
  nonverbal, 8–9, 70–93
  organizational styles of, 176
  problems in, 57–60
  process of, 5–9, 13

proprietary, 136
  in small groups, 241–243. See also
    Group communication
  on telephone, 107–109
  upward, 143, 151
  verbal, 52–66, 71
Communication anxiety, 19, 30. See also
    Speech, anxiety over
  effects of, 19–20
  overcoming, 20–21
  work-related, 21
Communication audit, 214
Communication barriers, 194
Communication departments, 140–142
Communication networks
  in groups, 263, 264
  ineffective, 148
Communication policy, lack of, 147–148
Communication skills
  in corporate communication, 140
  needed in employees, 174–175
  process of developing, 325
  training in, 145
Communication training, 21, 30, 145
  insufficient, 149
Communicators, 156
  ethical, 189
Companionship appeal, 346
Comparative advantage reasoning system,
    294–295
Comparison-contrast arrangement, 293
Competition, 119
Complementing relationships, 73
Comprehensive listening level, 40
Compromise, 119
Computerconferencing, 249
Computer-generated graphics, guidelines
    for use of, 302–303
Conclusions, process of reaching, 21–22,
    30
  distortion and, 22–23
  experience in, 25
  perception in, 23–25
  stereotypes in, 25
Concreteness, 58–59, 66
Conferences, 252–253
Confidential communication, 136
Conflict
  definition of, 116
  defusion of, 120
  resolution of. See Conflict resolution
  in work environment, 116–117
  working through, 120–121
Conflicting relationships, 74
Conflict resolution, 117–119, 175

assertiveness and, 121–123
  definition of, 117
  options for, 117–118, 124
  steps in, 120–121
  styles of, 118–119, 124
Confrontation, 120
Confronting response, 122–123
Congruency, 74, 93
Connotation, 59
Consensus, 260
Consequentialism, 184, 189
Consumer advocates, 185
Consumer groups, 183
Contemporary motivation theories,
    163–165
Conversation, cultural differences in,
    89–91
Conviction, 342
Coordinators, 256
Coping
  indirect, 112
  reactive, 113
Corporate communication, 151
  issues management by, 139
  obstacles to, 147–150
  organizational commitment and, 142
  role of, 138–142
  speaking activities of, 139
Corporate communication department,
    140–142
Corporate image, 84
Corporate responsibility, 185–187, 190
Cosmetics, 84–85
Counseling interview, 226–227, 235
Craft, Christine, case of, 84–85
Creativity appeal, 346
Credibility, 344–345, 358
Crisis decision-making, 204–205
Crisis decisions, 194
Critical incident analysis, 147
Critical listening level, 41
Critical reasoning structure, 294
Criticizing, 110–111
Culture
  effects on communication, 88–91
  interference with communication by,
    104–105
Customer relations, 149–150
Cutaways, 300
Cybernetics, 72

D
Decision
  definition of, 195
  good, 195, 205

Decision-making, 175, 193
    analysis of, 343, 358
    crisis, 204–205
    guidelines in, 194–195
    importance of, 194–195
    inductive process of, 196–198, 205
    nominal group technique of, 244–246
    1-3-6 technique of, 245–246, 265
    practical process of, 198–204, 205
    procedure in, 199–204
    process of, 195–196
    situations of, 196, 198–199
    techniques of, 196–204
Deductive argument, building of, 348–349
Democratic leaders, 255
Denotation, 59
Description, 332
DESC Scripting, 123
Desensitization, systematic, 20, 30, 325
Diagrams, 300
Dialects, 54, 66
    nonstandard, 55–56
    Standard American English, 55
Didactic method, 298
Differentiation/integration theory, 143
Difficult personalities, dealing with, 112–113
Directing, 113–114
Direct intervention, 112
Direction giving, 114–115, 332
Directive therapeutic listening, 41
Disciplinary communication, 227
Discriminative listening level, 40
Discussion
    facilitator, 261
    private, 243–251, 265
    public, 251–252, 265
Disinformation, 181
Dissatisfiers, 162
Distortion, 22–23
Distractions, control of, 45
Dramatic devices, 289, 305
Dressing for success, 84

E

Effective communication. See
    Communication, effective;
    Interpersonal communication,
    effective
Egospeak, 45
Emblem classifications, 75–76, 93
Emblems, 75
Emotional climate, 276–277
Emotional pollution, 195

Emotions
    display of, 75
    in facial expressions, 76–77
    hiding of, 79
    interference in communication by, 104
Empathic statement/response, 122–123
Employee
    communication skills training of, 140, 145
    surveys of, 139
Employer
    researching, 219
    screening prospective, 221
Employment interview, 215
    participating in, 220–221
    preparing for, 217–220
    regulations governing, 215–217
    role of interviewer in, 221–222
    unlawful questions in, 216
Enjoyment, appeal to, 346
Entrepreneurship, 150
Environmental interference, 100
Equity Theory, 164
ERG theory, 163
Ethical analysis, 188
Ethics
    business, 180–190
    in business communications, 189–190
    capitalism and, 185
    changes in, 184
    codes of, 187–188, 190
    corporate responsibility and, 185–187
    definition of, 181, 183–184
    dilemma of, 181–182
    use of, 187–188
Evaluation, 174
Exhaustion, 28
Existence needs, 163
Expectancy Theory, 164
    simplified, 165
Expectations, 6–7
Experience, in reaching conclusions, 25
Expert, 297
Exposition, 290
Extemporaneous presentation, 318, 326
External communication, 135
Extrinsic factors, 162
Eye behavior, 76
Eye contact, 76
    cultural differences in, 89
    interference in communication by, 105
    maintaining, 91

F

Facial expression, 75–77

Facilitators, 256
Fact, 59, 66
    versus inference, 59–60
Facts on File, 279
Factual statement, 59
Fear, 116
    appeal to, 346
Feedback
    decoding of, 12
    definition of, 13
    importance of, 10
    by listener, 39–40
    nonverbal, 11
    in organizational structure, 143
    receiver, 43
    sender, 43
Female language styles, 65
Fight-or-flight response, 28
Films, 303
Fitch Corporation Manuals, 219
Flip charts, guidelines for use of, 302–303
Floor manager, 374
Flowchart, 300
Focus group, 251
Followership, 262
Forum, 252
Functional organization, 142
Funnel schedule, 232
    inverted, 232–233
Furniture, arrangement of, 81–83

G

Gap-filler, 257
Gestalt therapy concept, 324
Gestures, 75
    cultural differences in, 90
    practicing, 325
    in speech, 319–320
Global economy, 157
Goal-setting Theory, 165
Good intentions, 343
Government publications, 280
Grammar, 53
Grapevine, 136–138, 151
Greetings, cultural differences in, 89
Grievances, handling of, 111–112
Group communication
    in business setting, 240–265
    conferences in, 252–253
    in group maintenance and task
        functions, 253–265
    nature of, 241–243
    private discussions in, 243–251
    public discussions in, 251–252
    setting purpose in, 241–242

Group polarization phenomenon, 263
Groups, 240. *See also* Group
    communication; Small group
    communication networks in, 263
    criteria of, 261
    leaders and leadership in, 254–257
    maintenance and task functions of,
        253–265
    participants in, 261–263, 265
    private discussions in, 243–251
    procedures in, 258–261
    purposes of, 265
    rules of operation in, 259–260, 265
    starting, 253
    structure of, 243
    time and place of meetings of,
        263–264
    voting procedures in, 260
Groupthink, 263
Growth needs, 163
Guilt, appeal to, 346

H

Hair style, 84
Hesitations, 79
Heterophily, 106
Hidden agenda, 116–117, 259, 265
Hierarchy of needs Theory, 161
Hiring, 145
Homophily, 106
Human relations model, 160, 175
Humorous devices, 369
Humorous stories, 288, 304
Hygiene factors, 163
Hyperkinetic, 87
Hypokinetic, 87

I

Illustrations, 288, 295
    as clincher, 304
    type of, 296–303
Illustrators, 75
Image, 83
    clothing and, 83–84
Image consultants, 18–19
Immaturity-maturity theory, 160
Implication, method of, 298–299
Impromptu presentation, 317–318, 326
Inanimate objects, 92
Inciting words, 43
Independence, appeal to, 346
Indexes, 280
Inductive argument, building of, 349
Inductive decision making, 205

Inference, 59, 66
    versus fact, 59–60
Inferential message, 43, 59
Informal communication channels, 136,
    151
Informal discussion group, 243
Information, 5
    categorization of, 7
    expanding base of, 157, 158
    feedback of, 39–40
    gathering of, 200–201
    interpretation of, 24–25
    major sources of in organizations, 138t
    organization of, 24
    primary, 200
    receiving, 38
    responding to, 7
    secondary, 200
    selection of, 23–24
    sending and receiving of, 5–7
    sources of, 279–283
    storage of, 39
Information explosion, 157, 158
Information interview, 235
Information speech, 334, 338
Informative briefing, 334–335, 338
Informative interview, 212
    outline for, 213
Informative speaking, 330–338
    audio-visual materials in, 334
    characteristics of, 332–334
    format for, 336–338
    purposes of, 331–332
    structure of, 333
    types of, 334–336, 338
Innovation, lack of, 149
Innovative organizations,
    characteristics of, 149–150
Integration, 119
Interactional communication model,
    11–12
Interactions, cultural differences in, 89–90
Interdepartmental communication, 135
Interest
    level of, 333
    listening and, 39
Interference, 100, 124
    environmental, 100
    organizational, 103
    physiological, 101
    psychological, 104
    semantic, 101–102
    social, 104–105
    syntactic, 102–103

International Listening Association, 253
Interpersonal communication
    in business, 98–124
    changing role of in business, 124
    conflict and resolution of in, 116–123
    definition of, 99
    effective, 99
    interference in, 100–105
    in organization, 106
    self-disclosure in, 105–106
    skills of in business environment,
        107–116
Interpersonal relationships, in business
    organization, 106
Interpersonal skills, in business
    environment, 107–116
Interpersonal space, cultural differences
    in, 89–90
Interpreting, 6, 24–25
Interrogation interview. *See* Stress
    interview
Interview
    body of, 232–233
    closing, 233
    communication responsibilities in,
        233–235
    definition of, 211, 212
    format of, 232–233
    interviewee responsibilities in, 234,
        235
    interviewer responsibilities in, 234–235
    opening of, 230–231
    procedure for, 220–221
    purpose statement in, 231
    questions in, 232
    in researching, 281
    structure of, 230–233, 235
    on television, 371–374
    types of, 212–230, 235. *See also*
        specific types
Interviewee, 212
    in performance appraisals, 224
    in press conference, 229–230
    responsibilities of, 234, 235
Interviewer, 212
    responsibilities of, 234–235
    role of in employment interview,
        221–222
    in TV interview, 371, 372
Interviewing, 174
    as business function, 211–235
Intimate zone, 80
Intradepartmental communication,
    134–135

Intra-dialect alienation, 56
Intrapersonal communication, 16–30
    definition of, 17, 30
Intrinsic factors, 162
Introduction speech, 363–364
Inverted funnel format, 232–233
Iran-gate, 185
Issue arrangements
    causal, 293
    chronological order, 291
    comparison, contrast, and comparison-
        contrast, 293
    problem-solution, 294–295
    spacial order, 292
    topical order, 292
Issues management, 139, 151

J

Japanese management style, 169, 171
    quality circles and, 247
Jargon, 43, 102
Jewish dialect, 55
Job maintenance, 146
Job performance, 146–147
Job satisfaction, factors in, 162
Job training, 115–116
Judgment
    field-related standards of, 343
    group standards of, 343
    individual standards of, 343

K

Kinesics, 74–79
    definition of, 74
    reading, 78–79

L

Laissez-faire leaders, 255
Language. *See also* Communication;
        Speech
    clarity of, 57–58
    concreteness of, 58–59
    definition of, 63–54
    female-male, 62–66
    learning of, 54
    male and female usage of, 63–65
    negative connotations in, 102
    principles of meaning in, 56
    prosocial, 65
    sexism in, 62–63, 66
    system of, 8
    verbal, 52–66
    written and spoken, 60–62
Laughter, 79

Leaders, 254
    roles of, 256–257
    styles of, 167, 255
Leadership, 174, 265
    role of, 257
    skills of, 150
    styles of, 167, 255
Libraries, 280, 283
Lighting, 86
Linear communication model, 9–10
Linguistic racism, 55, 66
Linking-pin concept, 143–144
Listeners. *See also* Audience; Receivers
    attitudes of, 344
    characteristics of good, 45–47
    feedback of, 39–40
    interests of, 273–274
    meaning within, 43
    motivation of, 38
    role of, 10
    of speech, 283
Listening, 35–47, 175
    areas of, 36
    biology of, 42
    effective, 36, 45–47
    ignorance of principles of, 44
    improving, 45–47
    levels of, 40–42
    poor conditioning for, 44
    problems with, 42–44
    process of, 38–40
    proficiency in, 42
    role of, 36
    skills of, 45, 46–47
Listening environment, 37
Listening training, 37
    poor, 44
Lose-lose approach, 117–118
Low degree of empathy pattern, 112
Loyalty, appeal to, 346

M

MACH, 163
MacRae's Bluebook, 219
Male language styles, 64
Management
    authoritarian attitude of, 148
    bottom-up process of, 169–173
    communication in, 168–174
    evaluation function of, 174
    leadership role of, 174
    organizing function of, 173
    too many levels of, 149
    top-down process of, 169

Management by Objectives (MBO), 147
Management-employee relationships,
        109–110
    criticizing in, 110–111
    difficult personalities in, 112–113
    directing in, 113–114
    giving directions in, 114–115
    handling grievances in, 111–112
    in job training, 115–116
Manager behavior, 176
    analysis of, 167
    theories of, 165–167
    types of, 165
Managerial Grid, 167, *168*
Managers
    creating listening environment, 37
    roles of, 165, 166–167*t*
    styles of, 167, *168*
Manuscript presentation, 318–319,
        326
Material self, 18
Meaning(s), 66
    differences in, 101–102
    principles of, 56
Mechanical devices, use of, 303
Media appearances, 322–323
Media presentations
    effective, 374–377
    time limits of, 375
Meetings
    cultural differences in, 91
    location of, 264
    seating arrangements in, 91, 264
    of small groups, 263–264
Memorized presentation, 319, 326
Message
    assertive, 122–123
    attending to, 38–39
    inferential, 43
    interest in, 39
    internal, 17
    interpreting, 39
    monitoring of, 46
    paraphrasing of, 46
    receiver of, 5
    receiving, 38
    responding to, 39–40
    source of, 5
Microphones, 375–376
Mintzberg's managerial roles, 165,
        166–167*t*
Mock-ups, 301
Monitor role, 257
Monotone, 322

Monthly Catalog of U.S. Government Publication, 280
Moody's Manuals, 219
Moral responsibility, 188
Motions, 260
Motivated sequence, 294
Motivation, 175
    of listener, 38
Motivational speech, 354, 358
Motivation-Hygiene Theory, 162–163
Motivation theories
    contemporary, 163–165, 176
    early, 160–163, 176
Motivator factors, 163
Movement, 75
Music, 85–86

N
Need-satisfaction, 106
Negative cognitive appraisal, 326
Negative self-concept, 42–43
Neurolinguistic programming, 72
New York Times Index, 280
Non-accountability pattern, 112
Nonassertiveness, 121, 124
Non-directive therapeutic listening, 40–41
Nonverbal channels, 74–88, 93
Nonverbal communication, 8–9, 70–72, 92–93
    aesthetics in, 85–87
    clusters and congruency in, 74–88
    cultural effects on, 88–91
    definition of, 71
    importance of, 72–73
    improvement of, 91–92
    physical characteristics in, 83
    relationship of with verbal communication, 73–74
    sources of, 72
Note-taking, 46, 283
    in research, 281–282
Nounery, 61

O
Objectives
    restatement of, 200
    statement of, 199–200
Observer, 256, 257
One-Minute Manager theory, 110, 124
On-line camera, 374
On time, meaning of, 88
Oral footnotes, 281, 283, 299
Orator's pitch, 310
Order giving, 113–114

Organizational interference, 103
Organizational structure, 116, 142–144
    communication flow in, 143
    theories of, 143
Organizations. *See also* Business
    changes in, 157–159
    climate of, 144
    communication in, 130–151
    communicators in, 156–177
    culture of, 144
Organizing, 173
Overhead projectors, 303

P
Panel discussion, 251–252
Paralanguage, 79
Paraphrasing, 46, 281
Parliamentary procedure, 259–260, 265
Part-of-the-whole voting method, 260
Passive voice, 61
Pause, 79, 321, 327
Perception(s), 6
    categorization of, 7
    definition of, 23
    expectations and, 6–7
    interpretation stage of, 24–25
    listening and, 39
    organization stage of, 24
    in reaching conclusions, 23–25
    selection stage of, 23–24
    self-concept and, 19
Perceptual filter, 39
Performance appraisal, 147, 222, 235
    effective, 223–225
    methods used in, 222–223
    outline for, 225–226
Personal experience, 287
Personalities
    differences in, 116
    difficult, 112–113
Personal references, 304
Personal space, 80–81
    respect for, 92
    zones of, 80, 93
Persuasion, 175
    achievement of, 342–344
Persuasive interview, 214–215, 235
Persuasive message, development of, 358
Persuasive speaking, 341
    achievement of, 342–344
    format for, 355–358
    goals of, 342, 358
    strategies in, 344–350
    types of, 350–355

Persuasive strategies, 344–350
Philosophy, 183
Phony fancies, 60–61
Photographs, 300
Physical characteristics, 83
Physical presentation, 319
    suggestions to help, 320–321
    techniques for in media presentations, 376–377
Physiological interference, 101
Picture, 300
Pitch, 321, 322, 327
Pity, appeal to, 346
Planning, 168
    meetings for, 244
Plurality, 260
Posterboards
    guidelines for use of, 302–303
    in media presentations, 376
Posture, 92
Power role, 116
Praise, appeal of, 347
Presentation. *See also* Speech
    modes of, 316–319, 326
    speech, 366–367
Press conference, 229–230, 235
Pride, appeal to, 347
Privacy Act, 136
Privacy space, 81
Private discussions, 243, 265
    informal, 243
    types of, 244–251
Probing, 351
Problem
    definition of, 195–196, 199
    identification of, 197, 205
Problem-solution format, 294–295
Problem-solving, 175, 193
    inductive process of, 196–198, 205
Problem-solving appraisal method, 223
Problem-solving interview, 214, 235
Productivity, 150
    decline of in U.S., 157
Professional paper, 336
Proprietary communication, 136
Prosocial language, 65
Proxemics, 80–83
Psychological appeals, 345–347, 358
Psychological interference, 104
Public discussions, 251–252, 265
Public relations, 135, 175
Public Speaker's Treasure Chest, The, 288
Public speech. *See* Speech

Public zone, 80–81
Punctuation, 53
  in speech, 53–54
Purpose statement, in speech, 278

Q

Quality circles, 171–173, 176, 246–247,
    265
  operation of, 171, *172*
  process of, 248
Question-and-answer session, 11, 252,
    362–363, 377
Questioning techniques, 175
Questions
  in speech, 289
  types of, 232
Quotation, 281
  as clincher, 305
  in speeches, 289–290

R

Radio talk show, 230
Rationalization, 25
Reader's Guide to Periodical Literature,
    279–280
Reality, distortion of, 22–23
Real objects, 300
Real Security, The, 25
Receiver, 5. *See also* Listeners
  feedback of, 43
Receiving, 5
Recruiting, 145
Regulating relationships, 73
Regulators, 75–76
Regulatory agencies, 183
Reinforcement Theory, 165
Relatedness needs, 163
Relationships, 99
  building of, 175
Relaxation techniques, 29–30, 324–325
Remembering, methods of, 46–47
Reprimanding interview, 227, 235
  format in, 232
Research information, 279, 283
  interview sources of, 281
  printed and recorded sources of,
    279–280
Resistance, 28
Responding, 7
Resumes, 216
  preparation of, 218–219
  sample, *218*
Reverence, appeal to, 347
Revulsion, appeal to, 347

Rhetorical questions, 289
  answers to, 304
Risky shift concept, 263
Robert's Rules of Order, 259, 260, 265
Round table discussions, 244

S

Sales approach, 351
Sales talk, 350–353, 358
  principles of, 352–353
  steps in, 351–352
Satisfiers, *162*
Savings, appeal to, 347
Scientific management model, 160,
    175
Seating positions
  cultural differences in, 91
  in meetings, 264
Self
  changing image of, 18–19
  components of, 18, 30
Self-actualization, 106
Self-concept, 17–19, 30
  negative, 42–43
Self-disclosure, 105–106, 124
Self-esteem, 106
Self-fulfilling prophecy, 17–18
Self-help, 21, 30
Self-knowledge, 279
Self-managing work teams, 248
Self-talk, 26
Semantic interference, 101–102
Semantics, 8, 53, 66
Sender, 5
  feedback of, 43
Sender-receiver clarity, 57–58
Sender-receiver relationship, 43
Sending, 5
Sensory channels, 5
Sentence, 53
Sexism, 62–63, 66
Sexual attraction appeal, 347
Sexual harassment, 183
Shyness. *See also* Communication anxiety
  overcoming, 19
Simple assertive statement, 122–123
Skill deficit, 325
Skills training, 21, 30. *See also*
    Communication skills, training in
Small group, 241. *See also* Groups
  cohesion in, 243
  communication in, 241–243
  facilitation of, 174
  purposes of, 265

setting purpose of, 241–242
  structure of, 243
Small-group communication. *See* Group
    communication
Smile, 76
Smoothing-over, 118–119
Social interference, 104–105
Social Psychology of Organizations, The,
    307
Social self, 18
Social zone, 80
Society, ethics in, 181–182
Solutions
  selection of, 197
  testing of, 197
Source, 5
Spanglish, 55
Spatial arrangements, 81–83
Spatial order, 292
Speak Easy: How to Talk Your Way to
    the Top, 281
"Speak Easy" training, 140
Speaker, 273
  credibility of, 344–345, 358
  techniques of in handling question-
    and-answer sessions, 362–363
Speaker's Treasury of Stories for All
    Occasions, The, 288
Speaking
  competence in, 175
  informative, 330–338
  parameters of, 272–278
  persuasive, 341–358
  special occasion, 362–377
Speaking development training, 140
Special occasion speech, 362
  in public communication media
    presentations, 374–377
  on television, 370–374
  types of, 363–370, 377
Specific instances, 296
Speech. *See also* Communication;
    Speaking
  anxiety over, 323–326, 327
  attention-getters in, 287–290
  body of, 291–303
  clincher in, 304–305
  conclusion of, 303–305, 311–312
  emotional climate of, 276–277
  exposition in, 290
  forms of support in, 295
  function of, 278
  illustrations in, 295–303
  impromptu, 317–318

informative, 330–338
introduction of, 287–290, 311
issue arrangements in, 291–295
in media appearances, 322–323
modes of, 316–319, 326
participants in, 272–273
parts of, 311
persuasive, 341–358
physical elements of, 319–321,
    326–327
place of, 275
planning of, 271–283
practicing, 324–325
preparation of, 285–312
preparing notes for, 310–311, 312
presentation of, 316–327
punctuation in, 53–54
purpose and purpose statement in,
    278, 311
putting together, 305–310
rate of, 321, 322, 327
references to occasion or setting in,
    289
setting of, 275–277, 283
sources of information for, 279–283
special occasion, 362–377
speech-planner model of, 308
statement of central idea in, 290
structure of, 278
summary of, 303
supplementary aids for, 299–303, 311
on telephone, 107–109
time of, 276
transitions in, 295
units of, 53–54
vocal delivery in, 321–322
wording of manuscript, 308–310, 312
working outline for, 306–308, 312
versus written language, 60
Speech notes, 310–311, 312
Speechophobia, 323–324, 327
    overcoming, 324–326
Speech-planner model, 308
Spiritual self, 18
Stammering, 79
Standard American English, 55
    sexism in, 62–63
*Standard and Poor's Corporation
    Records,* 219
Statistics, 296
Stereo equipment, 303
Stereotypes, 25
Stimulus, 38
Stories for Speakers, 288

Stress
    business and, 26–27
    causes of, 26
    controlling, 29–30
    dealing with, 28–29
    decision-making under, 194
    definition of, 26
    positive aspects of, 26
    reacting to, 28
    stages of, 28
Stress interview, 228–229, 235
Studio personnel, 375
Study circle, 246–247
Substituting relationships, 74
Summary, methods of, 304
Supplementary aids, 299–303, 311
Support, 295
    details, 333
    forms of, 311
    incorporation of into speech, 297–299
    tests for forms of, 297
Symbols
    dehumanization through, 102
    of English language, 53–54
    language as, 8
    meanings in, 66
Symposium, 252
Syntactic interference, 102–103
Syntax, 53, 66
Systematic desensitization, 20, 30,
    325
Systematic process, 194
Systems management, 167

T
Talk show interview, 230
Tape recording, 303
Tape-slide presentation, 303
Team-oriented leader, 167
Technical report, 335–336, 338
Technological changes, 157, 175
Teleconferencing, 248–249, 265
    participation in, 250–251
    problems in, 250
    types of, 249
    uses of, 250
Telephone use, 107–109, 124
    techniques for placing calls, 109
    techniques for receiving messages,
        108–109
Teleprompters, 375
Television appearance, 370–374
    preparation for, 377
Television cameras, 374

Television interview, 371–374
    interaction in, 373
    knowing rights in, 372–373
    knowing what to say in, 372
    learning about, 371–372
    maintaining control of, 373–374
Television talk shows, 230
Tell and listen interview method, 223
Tell and sell interview method, 222–223
Testimony, 297–299, 354–355, 358
Theory G, 174
Theory X, 161, 176
Theory Y, 161
Theory Z, 170
Therapeutic listening level, 40–41
*Thomas' Register of American
    Manufacturers,* 219
Time
    cultural differences in, 90 standards
        of, 87–88
Top-down process, 169
Topical order, 292
Touch, 78
Trainer, 256
Training programs, 145. *See also*
    Communications skills, training in
Trait analysis, 147
Transactional communication model, 12
Transitions, 295
Truthfulness, importance of, 189

U
Utilitarianism, 184–185, 189

V
Verbal communication, 52–66
    definition of, 71
Verbal-nonverbal relationships, 73–74,
    92
Victimization pattern, 112, 121
Videotapes, 303
Video teleconferencing, 249, 251
Virgules, 322
Visual aids, 300–301, 311
    in media presentations, 376
    preparation of, 302–303
    use of, 301–302
Visualization technique, 324
Visual stimuli, 38
Vocal cues, 79
Vocal delivery, 321
    hints regarding, 322
Vocal elements, 321, 327
Voice, passive, 61

Volume, 321, 327
Voting procedures, 260

W
Walk, 92
Wasted words, 62
Watergate scandal, 185
Welcome speech, 365–366
Whistle-blowing, 187
Who's Who, 279
Win-lose approach, 117

Win-win approach, 118
Women
    language styles of, 65
    nonverbal communication of in
        business, 91
    in work force, 158
Words, wasted, 62
Worker motivation theories, 159–165,
    175–176
Work force
    changes in, 157–159

    women in, 158
Working environment
    quality of, 171–173
    stress in, 26–27
Work performance
    color and, 87
    communication anxiety and, 21
    lighting and, 86
    music and, 85–86
Work schedules, flexibility of, 158
Written language, 60